SALVATION
AND THE
PERFECT SOCIETY

The Eternal Quest

Alfred Braunthal

The University of Massachusetts Press
Amherst, 1979

Copyright © 1979 by
The University of Massachusetts Press
All rights reserved
Library of Congress Catalog Card Number 79-4705
ISBN 0-87023-273-8
Printed in the United States of America
Library of Congress Cataloging in Publication Data
appear on the last printed page of this book.

To my family

Contents

Preface

The plan to write a treatise tracing the history of both the quest for salvation and for a perfect society resulted from the convergence of two sources of thought. While I have always regarded my activities—first among European and then among American and international labor organizations—as a modest contribution to the great secular movements aimed at progressing toward a more perfect society, I have also increasingly felt the need to understand the sources from which the major world religions have been deriving their faith in the ultimate salvation of man.

My experiences and studies have resulted in the conviction that the two approaches—the religious and the secular—neither exclude each other, as is frequently maintained, nor merge, but tend to supplement each other. Mankind has the capacity to open many avenues through which human beings may hope and strive to overcome their sufferings. In an age such as ours, so replete with sufferings, doubts, and dangers, it is a consoling thought that longing, striving, and struggling, be it for salvation or for a more perfect society, are very much alive.

I wish to express my gratitude to my wife Hilde, who helped me clarify the principal concepts; to Sir Karl Popper, who made a number of valuable suggestions; to my son Gerard and his wife Sabina, who helped me through painstaking labor to adapt my writing to English style; and to Dr. Otto F. Ehrentheil, who smoothed out a number of uneven passages.

Introduction

While man's quest for salvation has always had a religious meaning, the quest for the perfect society has usually been given a secular meaning. In fact, however, ties have always existed between them. It is the main purpose of this survey to trace the history of both quests, the relations between them, and the various changes this relationship has undergone.

The longing for protection by transcendental forces—first spirits, then gods—against all evils which threaten man, and the yearning for transcendental assistance in man's undertakings, is as old as mankind itself. Since the beginnings of civilization in the Paleolithic era, man has conjured divine powers for protection and assistance, and has moved this longing into the sphere of the sacred: he began to understand divine protection as salvation. With the evolution of societal structures, the ordering of society was likewise made an object of divine protection and therefore also acquired a sacral character. The concept of the perfect society arose, merging religious and secular ideas.

With the rise of the major religions, the longing for salvation deepened. Man yearned to be saved not only from evils threatening him from without, but also from evil forces within himself, and he sought salvation through deliverance from those evils. This holds true not only for the eschatological religions (Zoroastrianism, Judaism, Christianity, and Islam), which regard evils residing in man as sins and seek deliverance from them by divine, redemptive acts. It is also true of the Eastern religions (Hinduism and Buddhism), which regard evils chiefly as intellectual failings and seek to overcome them by man's efforts alone or with divine assistance.

As the major religions arose in highly developed societies, the quest for salvation assumed increasingly societal features. At the same time as the longing for salvation was directed toward redemption from sins or from life's burdens, it was also aiming for a world of peace, harmony, and justice. Judaism, Christianity, and Islam are most characteristic of this blend of a quest for salvation and for societal perfection. Just as the late-Jewish prophets predicted that once the people were purified from their sins, the kingdom of God would dawn—a perfect society of peace, justice and well-being—so did Jesus conjure the people to purify themselves in order to make themselves worthy of being admitted into the kingdom of God. Christianity and Islam promise that at the end of time, the kingdom of God will descend to a purified people.

In modern times, however, a process of differentiation set in between the concepts of salvation and societal perfection. It was heralded by the humanism of the Renaissance and consistently carried out in the Age of Enlightenment. The men of the Enlightenment concentrated on the quest for the perfection of society. They emphasized the rights of man and proclaimed their trust in human progress, which they believed would produce a gradual perfection of society. But because the Age of Enlightenment was also characterized by a trust in divine Providence, the quest for societal perfection still contained a religious element: divine Providence would ensure progress toward this goal. Marxism, too, inherited the humanism of the Enlightenment, and revealed its eschatological roots by prophesying the ultimate triumph of a classless and stateless society of freedom, harmony, and prosperity. But in spite of these religious elements, the basis of the humanist quest for the perfection of society has remained a secular one.

On the other hand, with the growth of social movements and social conscience, currents arose in the religious world which showed a concern for societal perfection similar to that of secular humanism. Many adherents of religious humanism are, no less than their secular counterparts, convinced of the need for thorough societal change and consider it a prerequisite for the perfection of society.

This book investigates the major changes that the quest for salvation has undergone in various societies, beginning with the evolution of the ancient societies. It examines how this quest, originally confined to the longing for divine protection against material evils and for assistance in man's undertakings, became a driving force in the development of the major religions; how the conceptions of salvation and the institutions based on them varied during the history of these religions; how societal ideals became enmeshed with the religious quest for salvation; how in the Jewish-Christian-Islamic religions the faith in the coming of the kingdom of God arose; how in the modern age, beginning with the Enlightenment, a secular humanism evolved, through which the quest for the perfect society gradually acquired a meaning more or less independent of religion; how the striving for societal perfection gave rise to powerful social and political movements; how the quests for salvation and for societal perfection, although sometimes antagonistic toward or sharply separated from each other, often converge; how, particularly among religious thinkers, insistence on societal change has frequently become an element of the quest for salvation; and how modern humanism endeavors to find answers to the complex societal problems of our time.

Religious man seeks ultimate salvation not in the confines of history, but outside history, at the end of time. His quest for salvation is eternal. The humanist quest for the perfection of society can harbor the same determination, fervor, and passion as the yearning for religious salvation, but it has lost that trust in the certainty of its fulfillment which characterized the Age of Enlightenment and which later was sparked by the triumphs of biological evolutionism. Yet humanism has not resigned itself to accept as inevitable the existing political, economic, social, and human conditions. It is convinced that they can and should be substantially improved, that many of the wounds life inflicts on man can be healed, and that many frailties and failings afflicting man and his society can be overcome. In other words, modern humanism trusts that the world can be made a better place in which to live, a place with less misery and oppression, strife and warfare, one with more welfare, justice, and harmony. Yet it realizes that while all men and women of good will should strive for these goals, no future point can be set for their fulfillment. The quest for the perfect society is no less eternal than the quest for ultimate salvation.

CHAPTER I

Salvation on Earth

1. MATERIAL SALVATION

If the longing for deliverance from evils that threaten man, his family, and his tribe can be regarded as a yearning for salvation, this feeling was certainly present in the earliest history of mankind. During that time, all of nature—plants, animals, and man himself—was believed to be moved by friendly or hostile spiritual forces, which had to be conjured and pacified by magic devices. Even when man could fight back the hostile forces with his own strength, he would still call on spiritual powers to deliver him from evils, whether they be brought about by adverse weather, disease, or men, living *or* dead—particularly personal, tribal, or national enemies.

This material meaning of salvation was not confined to the animist stages of human evolution. It remained a fundamental meaning when the forces to which man was subjected were first spiritualized as gods, then as a paramount god above other national gods in rank, and finally as a universal God. Even then salvation still meant deliverance from or protection against material evils, and success in the pursuit of material strivings, such as material welfare, fertility of man, his cattle or crops, victory over his enemies, and conquest of new lands.

The fifth book of the Old Testament, the Book of Deuteronomy, persuasively described material salvation in the blessings that obedience to Yahweh, Israel's national God, would bring upon Israel: "A blessing on the fruit of your body, the fruit of your land and of your cattle. . . . May the Lord grant you a blessing in your granaries and in all your labours. May the Lord open the heavens for you, to give rain upon your land at the proper time and bless everything to which you turn your hands" (Deut. 28:4–12).[1] All of these material blessings were promised to Israel in a late stage of social, economic, and religious development, long after Yahweh had emerged as the sole national God.[2] Such divine blessings were in substance no different from those which, in the Homeric era—a period of Greek history comparable to that portrayed in the Book of Deuteronomy—a country expected under a "blameless king [who] fears the gods and upholds right judgment; then the dark earth yields wheat and barley, and the trees are laden with fruit; the young of his flocks are strong and the sea gives abundance of fish."[3] So important was fertility in most early religions that even Zarathustra prayed to God to add to his wealth in cattle.

In Christianity and Islam the material aspects of salvation also have their place. The Gospels of Matthew and Luke include "our daily bread" in the Lord's Prayer, and both assure the Christians that God knows of their need for food and clothing (Matt. 6:31–32; Luke 12:29–30). The Koran assures the believers that God will give them all things necessary for their bodily sustenance (Sura 15:20).

Thus the human, animal, or cereal sacrifices that early man offered to the gods, the prayers he addressed to them, the sacrifices he made with his own body, whether by self-mutilation, mortification, or cult prostitution, were all designed to propitiate the divine powers. Originally these offerings were aimed exclusively at material salvation, but even in the later religions they continued in part to have a material meaning. Even today rain processions and prayers for or against rain are widely conducted by Catholic communities in certain countries. As long as the heavens of all peoples were populated by numerous gods and goddesses who personified a range of natural powers, different deities were invoked to deliver men from any number of evils or dangers and to grant them different blessings. In later religions these protective powers were frequently delegated to saints.

Many important gods to whom men prayed or sacrificed, and who emerged as paramount or sole national gods, were connected with aspects of material salvation, mostly as meteorological or war gods. Like the Hindu storm god Indra, storm gods were venerated in the Middle East: Enlil, the wind god, and his son Ningirsu, the rain god, in Mesopotamia; El, the Ugarit rain god, and Dagon, the Ugarit storm god; Teshub, the storm god of the Hittites and Hurrians; Hadad, the Syrian storm god, who in the Gilgamesh epic already appeared in this capacity; and Yahweh, the storm god of the Hebrews.[4] Farther west, Zeus was the thunderer, and Odin was the storm god of the Germanic tribes.

The weather god on whom the fertility and prosperity of the people depended might also lead them to warfare and assure their victory. Thus Indra, Hadad, and Yahweh were not only storm gods but also war gods. The Song of Deborah, one of the oldest if not the oldest preserved Old Testament document, described how the earth trembled and the mountains shook when Yahweh marched from Edom to help Israel in its fight against the kings of Canaan (Judg. 5). Even much later, at the end of the first millennium B.C., when David fought the Philistines, Yahweh intervened personally, directed David's military tactics, and "went out before him to defeat the Philistine army" (2 Sam. 5:23–24).

Just as Yahweh granted victory to Israel, Chemosh, the paramount god of the Moabites, granted victory to his people in their rebellion against Israel (Northern Kingdom) in the ninth century B.C., as the famous Moabite stele in the Louvre indicates. Divine assistance in warfare assured the unprecedented triumphs of the Muslim armies from the seventh to the seventeenth century A.D. In the wars between Christian nations, in which both sides invoked the help of the same God, the weapons of their armies were consecrated with the same cross.[5] Thus the quest for divine assistance in the material spheres of life was an essential element of man's religious past and has remained crucial to present-day religious practices.

2. THE SOCIETAL ASPECTS OF SALVATION

With the rise of agrarian societies and their urban centers organized in class-structured states, the material aspects of salvation were gradually supplemented by societal aspects. The gods were conjured not only to save the people from starvation and enemies but also from anarchy and social oppression. The laws that evolved as the framework within which society organized itself were placed under the protection of the gods. Laws were thus regarded as divine instruments for the salvation of the people. Even where laws were not considered as having been decreed by gods, they were believed to be divinely sanctioned.

When monarchic forms of rulership evolved, it was the king's duty as the earthly representative of the gods to establish and maintain justice in his realm through divine guidance. Thus in Egypt in the era of the New Kingdom, the king ruled under the obligation to maintain Maat, the goddess of truth and justice.[6] Where the king was replaced by republican regimes, as in the Greek city-states, the gods charged the republican rulers with meting out justice, as demonstrated by the creation of the Athenian jury: as Aeschylus related in the *Eumenides*, Apollo and Pallas Athena commanded the citizens of Athens to act as a jury to judge Orestes who had fled to Athens after having killed his mother Clytemnestra.

This notion of the divine origin of law and justice has remained intact in modern times, as reflected in the two most fundamental documents of the Age of Enlightenment, the American Declaration of Independence and the French Declaration of Human Rights. Both documents refer to the deistic God of the Age of Enlightenment as ruler over human rights: in the Declaration of Independence, the Creator endowed all men with certain inalienable rights; in the Declaration of Human Rights, the French National Assembly declared the human rights "in the presence and under the auspices of the Supreme Being."

A significant divinization of law and justice documented in ancient times took place in Mesopotamia and then in Phoenician and Jewish lands. In the third millennium B.C. (c. 2370), a Sumerian king concluded an "agreement" with the god Ningirsu; the king presented an edict freeing the working folk from servitude under officials and priests, and proclaimed it as the word of Ningirsu.[7] Guided by the same religious concepts, one of the most famous divine-human law codes was established by Hammurabi (who reigned from c. 1792 to 1750 B.C.), the powerful Babylonian king who united the Sumerian-Akkadian city-states into a large empire. In the preamble to his code "establishing justice in Sumer and Akkad," Hammurabi stated that "Anu and Bel [Babylonian deities] called me, Hammurabi, the exalted prince, who fears the Gods, to make righteousness prevail in the land, to destroy the wicked and the evil, and to prevent the strong from oppressing the weak."[8]

In the same spirit of divine sanction of human laws in which Hammurabi created his law code—and which found successors in other parts of the Mesopotamian-Phoenician world—the best-documented law codes of the ancient world were established by the Jewish people in the centuries following the conquest of Canaan. Modern Bible research has established the fact that the laws pronounced in the Pentateuch date from several periods. The most detailed and advanced law code formed chapters 12 to 26 of the Book of Deuteronomy. In all likelihood, this code was a collection of legal and cultic provisions from various periods, some ancient, some more recent, finalized in Deuteronomy, the "Book of the Law" which was "found" under the reformer king Josiah (who reigned from 641 to 610 B.C.). According to that law code, Yahweh himself was the lawgiver. In the preamble to the code Yahweh enjoined the people: "You shall be careful to observe all the statutes and laws which I set before you this day" (Deut. 11:32). In the same spirit, one of the Psalmists implored Yahweh: "O God, endow the king with thy own justice and give thy righteousness to a king's son" (Ps. 72). The social meaning of divine justice was indicated in the following verses: "[The king] may judge thy people rightly and deal out justice to the poor and suffering . . . and help those of the people who are needy; he shall crush the oppressor."

The law, by thus acquiring a numinous character, promised deliverance from all the terrors that lawlessness entailed. Yet in spite of assertions in the law codes and other sources that the king, by observing the law, would ban poverty and social oppression, the fact remained that distinctive economic and social differences developed everywhere between upper and lower classes, frequently in such crass forms as slavery. What divinely sanctioned law *could* accomplish, however, was to set limits to exploitation and oppression, limits that at least were more humane and of a higher degree of social justice than was the arbitrary use of social and political power.

The specific Jewish institution that constituted a foundation for the edifice of material and societal salvation was the Covenant between Yahweh and the Jewish people. They have always been regarded as "the people of the Covenant." While it has been generally believed that a people's welfare and warfare enjoy divine protection, there is hardly another people who has systematized and institutionalized its relationship with divinity to such an extent as has the Jewish people through the instrument of the Covenant.

A covenant implies some kind of relationship between two parties. It was a rather common belief among ancient peoples that the salvational relationship between a people and its gods was a mutual one: the gods protect the people, but in turn need veneration and sacrifices. Thus in Sumerian-Babylonian myths the gods created man in order to be worshipped.[9] Even more materialistic was the widespread belief that the gods must be fed by men and therefore needed sacrifices for their "daily bread." This held true for Vedic India no less than for Zoroastrianism and the Middle Eastern religions, including the beginnings of the Jewish religion. The Vedic gods were hungry and needed offerings. They had to be fed to retain their strength.[10] Even in the Bhagavad Gita man is admonished: "Nourish the Gods with this; may those Gods nourish you; mutually nourishing, may ye both attain well-being."[11] Zarathustra stated that sacrifices renewed the strength of Ahura Mazda and ensured His immortality (Yasna 34). In the Middle East, God was widely viewed as the owner of the land who had to receive offerings for his daily sustenance.[12] In the first stages of the Jewish religion, the nature of the sacrifices as food for Yahweh is cited in numerous passages of the Pentateuch. Yahweh received all fat "as food offered to the Lord." The priests shall be holy to their God, for it is they who "present the food-offerings of the Lord, the food of their God" (Lev. 21:6).

While this kind of mutual relationship between a people and its gods was common to many peoples, its sanctification through the instrument of a covenant, that is, a solemn treaty consecrated by religious rites, was unique to Israel. Covenants were not uncommon in the ancient Middle East, but outside of Israel they were confined to relations between kings and their peoples, or between tribes and families.[13] The Jewish people extended the institution of the covenant to its relationship with God. Its Covenant was a treaty of protection and loyalty between a people and its divine overlord.

There is no way to ascertain when in Jewish history the concept of the Covenant arose. In the Pentateuch, divine covenants were attributed to Noah (Gen. 9:9), Abraham (Gen. 15:18−21) and, most important of all, Moses (Exod. 20−24). None of these covenants can be historically verified, but references to them in early Old Testament passages suggest that the belief in a universal Covenant between Yahweh and the Jewish people must have arisen early in its religious and societal evolution, projecting back into the presettlement period, before the end of the thirteenth century B.C.

In any event, the conception of a universal Covenant between Yahweh and "His" people could not have originated before Yahweh was recognized by the Jewish people as their paramount divinity, at the end of a process merging the tribal gods, which the Old Testament attributed to Moses. Indeed, the Old Testament linked the two events—the emergence of Yahweh as the paramount God of the Jewish people, and the conclusion of the Covenant between them as revealed to Moses. Whether this attribution is historically justified matters less than the logical link that actually exists between the two events. It can be argued that the victory of Yahweh over all the other divinities worshipped by the Hebrew tribes led to the unique event of a covenanted relationship between a people and its God.

The Covenant appeared in the Pentateuch as a code of religious, social, and economic laws which God revealed to Moses. It was based, as was the First Commandment, on the identification of Yahweh and on his claim to have delivered the Jewish people from Egyptian slavery ("I am the Lord your God who brought you out of Egypt, out of the land of slavery"), as well as on the injunction to abandon the worship of any other deities: "You shall have no other god to set against me" (Exod. 20:3).[14]

The monopoly of worship implied the monopoly of sacrifices. The sole God of the people was also the sole Lord of the land, to whom tribute had to be paid, as was customary in the entire Middle Eastern world. Sacrifices had to be offered to Yahweh not only in the form of "the choicest first fruits of your soil," but in a more terrifying way: "You shall give me your first-born sons" (Exod. 23:19 and 22:30). That men had to sacrifice to their gods their first-born sons makes modern man shudder; but human sacrifices were common in many ancient religions, especially those of the Middle East, including Carthage. In Israel, however, the offering of the first-born sons was abolished at an early stage of religious evolution and was replaced by a "redemption" tax.[15]

The most important feature of a covenanted relationship is its reciprocity. The Jewish people understood their relationship to Yahweh as a reciprocal one. Hence the heavy obligations to Yahweh which the Covenant imposed upon the Jewish people were balanced by obligations imposed upon Him. If Israel were obligated to worship Yahweh alone and to offer sacrifices to Him alone, His obligation to Israel was a particular way of protecting the Jewish people. Since He was regarded as the owner of the Jewish people, He had to protect His possession against any damage inflicted upon it. Thus when the Covenant was concluded, Yahweh declared to the Jewish people: "If only you will now listen to me and keep my covenant, then out of all peoples you shall become my special possession" (Exod. 19:5). Surrounded by countries in which the belief in paramount national gods prevailed, it was natural for the Jewish people to believe that, since each nation's paramount god had chosen his nation from among all nations, the Jews were Yahweh's chosen people. They maintained this conviction even after they had elevated Yahweh to the rank of the sole God of the universe. The belief in being God's chosen people, with all the glory but also with all the obligations this honor implies, has survived all the tragic trials to which Jews have been subjected.

The fact that the Pentateuch identified the Covenant with the law code of the Jewish people offers a striking example of the societal aspects that—in a certain stage of social, economic, and political development —the relationship of a people to their god or gods assumed: God is the creator of the order of society. If man observes God's societal laws, he will be protected by God. Salvation is obtained by observing the laws God has imposed upon His people.

3. THE ETHICAL ASPECTS OF SALVATION

The myth of the Covenant concluded between the Jewish people and their God is an example of the emergence of the societal aspects of salvation, and also marks the ethical stage of religious evolution. The same law code that imposed upon the Jewish people the obligation to sacrifice to Yahweh their first-born sons also enjoined them not to pervert justice entitled to their poor and not to oppress those aliens who dwelled in their midst. They were also commanded to give rest on the Sabbath day to their oxen, asses, and slaves, not to ill-treat widows and orphans, and not to exact interest in advance from the poor. In return for observing these injunctions, Yahweh promised that He would take away sickness from them, that their wives would be fertile, and that He would make an end of their enemies (Exod. 22:21–25; 23:9–24). Thus the Jewish God was still the god of fertility and of victory in warfare; His relationship to the people was still that of a material give and take. But at the same time, He was a god who imposed social and ethical principles. The conception of salvation, prevailingly material at first, gradually acquired an ethical content.

The same evolution can be observed in many other ancient civilizations. The gods became the protectors of justice and righteousness and imposed on the rulers and the people the obligations that derived from these concepts. However powerful Hammurabi might have been, the paramount God Marduk imposed justice upon him; Hammurabi's law code reflected God's justice. Confucius, in spite of his pronounced agnosticism, taught that "the ordinance of God is . . . the law of our being. To fulfill the law of our being is . . . the moral law." [16] While Buddha, even more agnostic than Confucius, did not derive moral laws from divine commandments, his Eightfold Path imposed powerful religious obligations of a moral order on the people.[17]

Fundamental to the process of ethicizing man's relationship to the deities was the belief in divine retribution. The gods reward good conduct and punish bad conduct. They save the righteous and damn the wicked. This trust in just retribution remained for most early civilizations on a this-worldly basis. Divine retribution must be meted out here on earth and must consist in well-being for the righteous and misery for the wicked. This concept of divine retribution on earth can be found in all ancient this-worldly religions. Confucius said, "Heaven bestows its will on the virtuous, but . . . condemns and punishes the guilty." [18] In Greece, Hesiod's poem, *Works and Days*, was devoted to the theme of divine justice and retribution: Zeus bestows prosperity on the man who speaks just sentences, but the immortals mark all those who oppress one another; there are even "on earth thrice ten thousand ministers of Zeus, immortal watchers of mortal men; they keep watch over deeds of justice and unkindness." [19] The same trust in divine retribution can be found in the works of the Greek tragedians. Sophocles exclaimed in *Antigone*, "Blest is their portion whose life has not tasted of evil"; while Euripides said in *Ion*, "When a man has an evil nature, the gods punish him." [20]

Man's cry to God for salvation from evils, ills, and enemies—the *Miserere mei Deus* ("Have mercy upon me, O God," Ps. 51:1)—has been raised throughout the millennia. But the ethicizing of man's relationship to the deity meant that man could expect a divine response to his cry for salvation only if he could hope that God's justice would work in his favor, that is, if justice were on his side. When Hecuba in her cruel affliction cried to Zeus for deliverance, she was convinced that justice was on her side, for she exclaimed: "Zeus, on Thee I call, for along the noiseless path Thou treadest, all mortal things are guided in the way of justice" (Euripides, *The Trojan Women*).[21]

However, man cannot always expect justice to be on his side, for he is not a perfect being. Even where the concept of original sin did not arise, no human being could believe that he was always sinless and guiltless. He could not expect divine retribution to be always in his favor; he would have to recognize that the inequities and sins he had committed might block his salvation. Thus he could not expect deliverance from the divinity unless he repented for the inequities and sins that he had committed. Where this stage of ethicizing man's relationship to his gods was reached, prayers for deliverance became frequently penitential prayers. Such prayers could be found in highly developed civilizations, particularly in Mesopotamia. Confessions of guilt were combined with the willingness to expiate "the offence which I know and the offence which I do not know." [22]

Even kings would humble themselves before the gods in the awareness of the inequities they or their peoples had committed. From the Neo-Babylonian period (625–538 B.C.), inscriptions have been found that called the kings "the meek and humble ones." [23] The Hittite king Mursilis II (who reigned at the end of the fourteenth century B.C.) besought the gods to reveal the sins that had caused pestilence to ravage his country so that he might atone and expiate—although he claimed to be sinless himself.[24]

Repentance—the awareness of having neglected or violated divine laws—can be felt with respect to ritual or moral laws. Many religions insist that repentance prove its genuineness not only by thoughts and deeds, but also by an outward expression of formal confession. In Vedic India, confessing sins was regarded as a way of attenuating guilt.[25] In the rites of the Buddhist monks, confessions were institutionalized and had to be made regularly and publicly within the community of monks. An analogous institutionalization took place in the Christian Church, and is to this day an indispensable requirement for divine forgiveness in the Catholic Church.

With the ethicizing of man's relations to God, the feelings of guilt and repentance moved from the ritual to the moral sphere. In Jewish history this evolution was clearly delineated. The early stage was characterized by a strict ritual of confession and guilt-offerings for the violation of both ritual and moral divine laws.[26] Later, a more profound ethical relationship of man to his God evolved, particularly in response to the classical prophets' attacks on social and moral evils and on the frequently hypocritical ritualism of the Jewish society of their day.

The scriptures of the prophets and many of the psalms emphasized the need for genuine repentance in deep humility for the exculpation of sins, rather than the need for ritual penitence. Who can remain unmoved in face of the humility of the *cor contritum et humiliatum*,[27] with which the psalmist approached God, the awareness of his sins, the recognition that God is right in His charge and just in passing sentence; and finally his prayer to God to create in him a pure heart (Ps. 51). The notion of repentance acquired in fact a new meaning with the deepening of the ethical relationship between man and God. It was no longer a confession of and penitence for this or that transgression, but a complete change of "heart," a turning away from an old way of life to a new frame of mind, a renewal for which the New Testament found the adequate Greek term, *metanoia* (see below, chapter IV, section 7).

Ethicizing the concepts of salvation and damnation brought about a downgrading of the cultic, ritual character of religious observance. Homer marked this transition from ritual to ethical retribution. He assured a blameless king that while the reward for his piety and justice would be the fertility of the country, his gods could still be bribed by sacrificial rites: "The very immortals can be moved. . . . With sacrifices and offerings for endearment, with libations and with savour men turn back even the immortals in supplication when any man does wrong and transgresses." [28] Yet if originally sacrifices were offered to propitiate the gods, the ethical conception of man's relationship to God meant that righteousness, love, and good deeds were exalted above sacrifices and other rituals. "Loyalty is my desire, not sacrifice; not whole-offerings but the knowledge of God," declared the Jewish prophet Hosea (6:6), as early as the eighth century B.C. "Spare me the sound of songs . . . let justice roll on like a river and righteousness like an ever-flowing stream," exclaimed a contemporary of Hosea, the prophet Amos (5:23–24). Similar views were expressed by most Jewish prophets of the classical era.

Parallel "Protestant" tendencies can be observed in many other religions. Even in ancient Egypt, with its strict ritual traditions of several thousand years, voices were heard which placed good conduct above sacrifices. An important aspect of Buddhism was its opposition to the ritualism of the Brahmin caste. Plato too downgraded rituals. Divine justice, he stated in the *Laws*, cannot be bribed by rituals, such as flattering addresses to the deity and magical prayers. [29] This downgrading of the sacrificial rites that followed from the rise of the belief in just divine retribution did not necessarily imply a rejection of propitiatory sacrifices. The ancient religions generally retained their sacrificial systems. Although with the fall of Jerusalem in A.D. 70 the sacrificial rites ceased in Israel—they had been centralized in Jerusalem—Orthodox Judaism has to the present time maintained the hope that these rites will eventually be restored. [30]

The early Christians likewise were not opposed to the sacrificial system. Jesus' parents, according to Gospel tradition, were described as observant Jews who, after the birth of their son, journeyed to Jerusalem in the ritually prescribed time in order to offer the required sacrifice of "turtle doves or young pigeons" (Luke 2:22–24). Jesus himself did not express any opposition to sacrifices, although his preaching breathed the same opposition to ritualism as that of the classical prophets. Moreover, according to the Acts of the Apostles, the original Christian community of Jerusalem was loyal to the Temple, which obviously included the observance of the sacrificial laws. For those Jews in the Diaspora who were converted to Christianity, the problem of continuing the observance of the sacrificial laws hardly arose, since the sacrificial rites were confined to Jerusalem. But when Paul came to Jerusalem, he observed the sacrificial rites like any Jew who lived in or near Jerusalem (Acts 21.26). It was only with the emigration of the Christian community from Jerusalem, in connection with the Jewish War (A.D. 66–70) and with the spreading of Christianity to all parts of the Roman Empire, that the sacrificial system disappeared from the Christian communities. Formal abolition of the sacrificial laws, however, was not attested before the Letter to the Hebrews (A.D. 80–96).[31] From the viewpoint of Christianity, the Letter to the Hebrews used a convincing argument against the observance of the sacrificial rites. While it showed a deep understanding for the vicarious nature of the Jewish sacrifices by claiming that "without the shedding of blood there is no forgiveness," it also argued that with the vicarious shedding of Christ's blood, the sacrifice of "goats and calves" had become obsolete (Heb. 9:22 and 12).

In the history of Christianity, rebellions against ritualism—born of a similar spirit as those of the Jewish prophets—arose from time to time, such as the iconoclasm of the Eastern Church in the eighth and ninth centuries and the iconoclastic Protestantism of the sixteenth century in the Western Church. Thus while in the course of societal development religions were generally undergoing a process of ethicization, tensions arose time and again between their rituals and their ethical foundations.

4. COLLECTIVE AND INDIVIDUAL RETRIBUTION

The conception of divine retribution for man's good and evil deeds and thoughts arose in an era when, to a much greater degree than in later stages of human evolution, man was and felt himself to be a member of a collectivity rather than an independent individual. Tribal ties were still so strong that the responsibility of the individual was merged with that of the collectivity. If the collectivity were headed by a chief or king, it was he who bore the responsibility for the whole. His good or evil deeds were subject to a divine retribution which determined the fate of the community.

Thus, when Agamemnon killed a deer in a place sacred to Artemis, the goddess punished the whole Greek army and fleet by blocking their departure from Aulis. When the Pharaoh refused to let the Jewish people go, Yahweh sent plague after plague upon the Egyptian people. When pestilence ravaged the land of the Hittites, its king, Mursilis II, was ready to make atonement. When the Hivite Shechem defiled Dinah, a daughter of Jacob, two of Dinah's brothers killed all the males in Shechem's town; their father Jacob, in turn, on the eve of his death foresaw that God would punish his sons' progeny by scattering their tribes within Israel (Gen. 34 and 49:5–7).

Further evidence of this kind of divine retribution—affecting not only the individual but also the collective—is found in the conclusion of the Mosaic Covenant. There Yahweh proclaimed He would punish "sons and grandsons to the third and fourth generation for the iniquity of their fathers" (Exod. 34:7). This was a logical expression of the belief in divine retribution for a society in which the collective represented an individual entity.

In Jewish society this belief lingered long after the principle of individual responsibility and retribution had been defined. Even the prophets Jeremiah and Ezekiel, in whose books later editors established the principle of individual responsibility, actually believed in collective responsibility and retribution. Jeremiah held the apostate king Manasseh responsible for the national disaster that the Babylonian power brought upon Israel (Jer. 15:4). Ezekiel, after having castigated Israel for its apostasy and its rebellion against God, told the people that God had ruled that "your righteous and your wicked equally" would be cut off from Israel (Ezek. 21:3−4). Similarly writers of the second and first centuries B.C. still believed in collective divine retribution.[32]

It was in this spirit of divine collective retribution that prophetism arose in Israel as the great movement of social and spiritual protest— protest against the injustices and social oppression brought about by the militarization, bureaucratization, and social inequities that characterized the Jewish society in the period of the monarchy. The prophets' most powerful weapon against the corruption of their time was the stern warning of divine retribution; in the spirit of their era, they conjured collective retribution. Divine collective retribution could mean salvation or damnation for a whole people. At the time of Amos, one of the first classical prophets, a popular belief seems to have been rife that a "Day of the Lord" would dawn which would bring everlasting prosperity to Israel. Amos, conscious of the iniquities committed in Israel, the oppression of the poor, the crushing of the destitute, turned the popular belief around: "The day of the Lord . . . will be darkness, not light . . . a day of gloom with no dawn" (Amos 4:1 and 5:18−20).

Thus the Day of the Lord, as it was conceived by Amos and then by other Jewish prophets, was a day of doom, of just divine retribution for the sins of the people as a collectivity. It was the belief in a tragic fate of a people who had once been chosen by their God, but had betrayed their divine mission. Amos expressed the tragic tension between election and downfall, glorious beginning and ignominious ending, with the portentous verse: "For you alone had I cared among all the nations of the world; therefore will I punish you for all your iniquities" (Amos 3:2). The people will be punished for the sins of their rulers.

The time came, however, for Israel no less than for other peoples, when the individual emerged fully from the collective. The great prophets of Israel themselves were products of this evolution. They were strong individuals who dared to rebel against their own community. With this evolution, the concept of individual responsibility separated itself from that of collective responsibility. The emphasis on individual personality, conscience, and responsibility led to a rebellion against the concept of divine collective responsibility. It made itself felt even in very ancient societies, for instance in the Gilgamesh epic in connection with the myth of the Flood. Although in both the Sumerian-Babylonian and the Old Testament versions of that myth collective retribution was meted out for the sinfulness of mankind, in each instance the sole righteous man (Utnapisht in Babylon, Noah in the Old Testament) was saved.[33] Moreover, in the Old Testament version, God expressly committed Himself never again to "curse the ground because of man" (Gen. 8:21). In effect, God Himself set limits to the principle of divine collective retribution.

In many ancient civilizations the urge for divine individual retribution may have been one reason for the rise of the belief in a continuation of one's earthly life in another realm, since retribution during a man's lifetime could not always be expected. In the ancient Jewish civilization, on the other hand, which remained earthbound, it took a long time to turn away from the belief in divine collective retribution; indeed, it never disappeared entirely. The time came, nevertheless, when even in Israel people began to wonder whether the collective should suffer for the sins of their rulers and whether sons should suffer for the sins of their fathers. The beginnings of a doubt in the justice of divine collective retribution can be found in the narrative of the census that David took, an action regarded as a grave sin which God punished by a pestilence. The author of the chapter attributed to David the words: "It is I who have done wrong, the sin is mine; but these poor sheep, what have they done? Let Thy hand fall upon me and my family" (2 Sam. 24:17).

As this last sentence shows, the protest against the principle of collective retribution did not yet extend to the family. The primordial institution of the family or the clan as the acting and responsible unit was still recognized. Rebellion even against that institution appeared in the plaint raised in Lamentations, that heart-rending elegy about the fate of Israel after the fall of the Jewish Kingdom: "Our fathers have sinned and are no more; and we bear the burden of their guilt" (Lam. 5:7).

In the same spirit of rebellion against the heavy burden of collective retribution, editors of the Books of Jeremiah and Ezekiel enunciated a new principle of divine retribution.[34] "Every man shall die for his own wrongdoing," proclaimed the editor of Jeremiah (31:30). And in the

Book of Ezekiel, God Himself abrogated the principle of collective retribution by declaring that "the soul that sins shall die," that the righteous man "shall live," that the wicked son of a righteous man shall die, and that "a son shall not share a father's guilt" (Ezek. 18:4 and 20). There can be no doubt that the deepening belief in the sole responsibility of the individual for his thoughts and deeds, and in divine retribution as an act that affects the individual rather than the collective—a belief that began to spread in the Jewish nation—was a link in the evolution that led to the emergence of Christianity, with its strong emphasis on individual responsibility and retribution.

5. THE PROBLEM OF THEODICY

Once the belief in divine collective retribution was more or less abandoned, the vexing problem of theodicy arose: the problem of whether divine justice is really meted out and whether trust in it is well warranted. For all religions that visualize divine retribution as an act of God that occurs on earth, the problem of theodicy arose from the moment divine retribution was regarded in light of individual responsibility. Collectives have generally a long life, during which periods of victorious warfare, peaceful or military expansion, and material prosperity may alternate with periods of decline, national disaster, and misery. Because it can never be determined which types of people prevail in a community, ascending periods may always be attributed to a prevalence of righteous men, and declining periods, to that of the wicked. In other words, as long as the belief in divine collective retribution on earth prevails, the ascent and decline of a community may always be attributed to divine retribution, with the consequence that the problem of theodicy is not a serious one.

Modern man is inclined to attribute the decline and fall of the two Jewish kingdoms to the vast military superiority of the Assyrian and Neo-Babylonian "superpowers" over the tiny Syrian-Phoenician-Jewish states. But in the eyes of the Jewish prophets—and probably also of the vast majority of the victims—the disasters were due to the impiety, apostasy, and social injustice that prevailed in the Jewish community. Compared to collectives, however, individuals have short lives. It is therefore much easier to determine than in the case of communities whether, according to religious standards of the society in which men live, individuals are righteous or wicked. Unfortunately the chances are slight that divine retribution will ensure a better lot for the righteous than for the wicked. In all societies, but particularly in periods of crass social injustice and grave political or social oppression, it happens all too frequently that the righteous and pious suffer while the wicked and ungodly triumph.

Thus arose the problem of theodicy which has plagued all this-worldly religions, but which is also known to other religions. The problem was posed time and again, particularly in civilizations of an entirely this-worldly character, such as Babylon, other Middle Eastern regions, including Israel, and Greece outside of the Orphic-Platonic circles.[35]

A famous literary product of the rebellion against the deficiencies of divine retribution was the *Babylonian Poem of the Righteous Sufferer*, commonly known as "The Babylonian Job." It was named after a man who, although righteous and pious, lost his wealth and was afflicted by severe diseases.[36] In despair he laments: "I have cried to God, but he did not show his face." He concludes that divine will is incomprehensible to man.[37] While "The Babylonian Job," similar to the Book of Job, ended with a deus-ex-machina salvation of the sufferer, this happy ending cannot detract from the poem's basic idea: that although there is a divine purpose, it is inscrutable and in any event not geared toward an equitable retribution for the thoughts and deeds of man, as human beings understand it. In other words, man cannot hope for salvation by being righteous and pious.

Voices critical of the effectiveness of divine retribution were also heard in Greece. In his *Elegies*, the poet Theognis, writing in the late sixth and early fifth centuries B.C., "wondered" about Zeus and asked him how "Your spirit can endure to keep the sinner and the righteous man in the same state."[38] Sophocles likewise—in contrast to the trust in divine retribution expressed in *Antigone*—exclaimed in *Aietes* (if the fragment is authentic): "Strange that impious men . . . should prosper while good men should be unfortunate." And he squarely blamed the gods for this injustice: "It is not right that heaven deal so with men."[39] Indeed, Greek tragedy generally presented man as helpless in the face of the overwhelming power of destiny (*ananke*). Greek tragedy did not hope for divinely ordained salvation for the righteous.

In Israel the problem of theodicy also stirred up religious thinkers, particularly when the communal ties began to weaken in connection with the decline and fall of the Northern and then of the Southern Kingdom. Jeremiah above all—who personally had to suffer so much from a society in which the wicked ruled and prospered—exposed the contradiction between God who was believed to be a just judge and a world in which the wicked prospered. The prophet, in utter despair, posed the problem of theodicy: "O Lord, I will dispute with Thee, for Thou are just; yes,

I will plead my case before Thee: Why do the wicked prosper and traitors live at ease?" (Jer. 12:1).

In the ancient world, the problem of theodicy found its most profound expression in the Book of Job. That great poem expressed in the most moving, haunting words the despair over the lack of a moral order in the world and the awareness that man cannot hope for just divine retribution; that in the human community the righteous often are poor and oppressed, and perish while the wicked prosper and triumph. The Book of Job posed the problem dramatically, by introducing to Job's tragedy witnesses who still represented the old concept of just divine retribution. Job refuted, one after the other, all the arguments of the representatives of the old school and in the harshest terms accused God of injustice. "When a sudden flood brings death, [God] mocks the plight of the innocent. The land is given over to the power of the wicked; and the eyes of its judges are blindfold" (Job 9:23−24).

This passage breathes purest cosmic monism. There is no devil, no Satan on whom to lay partial or full responsibility for the evils of the world.[40] Furthermore, there is no original sin which would make every human being potentially liable for damnation. Job claims expressly that he is right and blameless; but even if he were not blameless, "and wash myself with soap . . . Thou [God] wilt thrust me into the mud" (Job 9:20 and 30−31). Repentance is useless, for God is not always a just judge.

Never before or afterward has God been accused of and condemned for injustice in such bitter terms. In spite of that, the Book of Job closes with a kind of theodicy. God reveals himself as *Rex tremendae majestatis* (King of awe-inspiring majesty), the omnipotent creator and ruler of the universe, the heavens, weather, sea and land, light and darkness, life and death, and the stars with their celestial music. Can man contend with his all-powerful creator? Job asks, "Is it for a man who disputes with the Almighty to be stubborn? Should he that argues with God answer back?" As God is infinitely more powerful than man, man's purposes cannot prevail over God's. "No purpose is beyond Thee [God]" (Job 40:2 and 42:2).

In other words, Job believed that it is not blind, purposeless destiny that rules the world, but God's purpose and design, which are different from those of man. God's design is not that moral design which man has always attempted to establish on earth, however unsuccessfully or with whatever limited success. God's design remains a mystery. The humbled Job confesses: "I have spoken of great things which I have not understood, things too wonderful for me to know" (Job 42:3). Thus the epic of Job ends in effect with a counsel of resignation. There is no certainty for man's salvation on earth, even if he is the most righteous and pious man. The God who rules the universe and man's destiny has established rules that mortal man cannot understand, but which in any event do not include equitable divine retribution.

In the Book of Job, the Jewish people's trust in God's justice was shattered, but it was replaced by another religious concept based on the belief in a God whose majesty lies beyond the human sense of justice, salvation, and damnation. That belief did not expect divine rewards in this life or in an after-life, but was founded on faith in an unknown God beyond human values and expectations.

Job's view that the inscrutability of God makes the quest for salvation illusory did not remain isolated in post-classic Israel, the period in which the Book of Job was written.[41] Voices could be heard time and again in Old Testament scriptures, composed at the same or at a later period, which expressed similar pessimistic views about divine retribution. Many psalms deplored the unjust fate that had befallen the righteous. The problem of a just retribution on earth continued to haunt the Jewish people as long as their religion remained this-worldly. In a later period, about 250 to 200 B.C., a writer who in the Scriptures was called Koheleth, the Teacher or Preacher (and Ecclesiastes in the usual Greek form) based a poem on this theme: "I saw the tears of the oppressed and I saw that there was no one to comfort them. Strength was on the side of the oppressors, and there was no one to avenge them" (Eccles. 4:1). What does God do in the face of this gross social injustice? Koheleth's answer was in effect the same as Job's: God's will is inscrutable, which means incompatible with man's search for salvation through equitable divine retribution (Eccles. 8:16–17).

These pessimistic views about the failings of divine retribution notwithstanding, the belief in just divine retribution on earth did not vanish in Israel; it merely ceased to be so naive as in earlier periods. But the Jewish people began to place their hope in a process of moral renewal that would render their nation worthy of being saved by God.

6. NATIONAL SALVATION THROUGH PURIFICATION

When after the return of the Jewish elite from the Babylonian exile (around 450 B.C.), the Prophet Malachi raised the fateful question of theodicy, "Where is the God of justice?", he gave the triumphant answer, "God will send his messenger, refining and purifying." After this process of purification which the Jewish people will undergo, God will reassure them that "all nations shall count you happy, for yours shall be a favoured land" (Mal. 2:17, 3:2 and 12).

This hope for national salvation through purification found its earliest expression in the belief in the survival of a "remnant." It meant that whereas the nation as nation was doomed, those individuals who had remained righteous and faithful would be spared and would form the nucleus of a renewed, purified nation. This belief constituted, in effect, a bridge between the notions of collective and individual retribution. It was first expressed by Isaiah, who described in glowing colors how God's flame would devour sinful Israel; but he added that a remnant of Jacob would turn again to God (Isa. 10:21).

The mainstream of Jewish thoughts, however, evolved neither along the lines of a search for individual salvation, which showed its futility in the Book of Job and in the writings of Koheleth, nor along the lines of the concept of a remnant. Instead it returned to the notion of a collective destiny for the Jewish people, which can be summarized as follows: We, the Jewish nation, have transgressed. We have turned away from the paths of righteousness and piety which our God had taught us to tread. God has, therefore, turned away from us and has subjected us to national humiliation and misery. There can be no salvation for anyone of us unless salvation be granted to the nation as such; but we cannot expect salvation unless we as a nation turn back to God, away from our sinful ways of injustice and oppression. In other words, only a profound change of heart and in our way of life can save us.

According to the classical prophets, return to God implied a revolutionary change from a social order replete with social, economic, and political injustice to one of righteousness and social justice. "Hate evil and love good; enthrone justice in the courts," as an editor of Amos admonished sinful Israel (Amos 5:15). Salvation for the nation meant not only a religious but also a societal renewal of the nation. The first inkling of this revolutionary salvational concept seems to have appeared in the writings of Hosea, a contemporary of Amos. Whereas Amos saw no salvation for Israel, and conceived the Day of the Lord as a day of reckoning and doom for the sinful nation, Hosea—while no less harsh than Amos in his judgment of the Jewish society of his time—held out the hope that God would succeed in alluring Israel back into the austere purity of its "wilderness" days. Then God "will restore her vineyards, turning the Vale of Trouble into the Gate of Hope" (Hos. 2:14 and 15).

The severe accusations and sharp warnings issued by the prophets of the eighth and early seventh centuries B.C.—Amos and Hosea, Isaiah and Micah—combined with the approach of national disaster near the end of the seventh century B.C., must have made a profound impression on the Jewish people and must have strengthened the currents aimed at renewing their spirit and institutions. The people, or at least their spiritual leaders, began to realize that their only hope for national salvation lay in *metanoia*, a genuine change of heart and mind and in the ways of life, which also meant a reform of the social and moral institutions. The Book of Deuteronomy used the metaphor of circumcision in order to circumscribe the need for reform. It is not enough to circumcise the foreskin: "Now you must circumcise the foreskin of your hearts" (Deut. 10:16).

The meaning of circumcision of the heart was made clear in the new legislation King Josiah decreed, which was contained in the Book of Deuteronomy. The purpose of the new legislation was to legalize the social and economic reforms demanded by the classical prophets. The first goal was to make the royal, judiciary, and social institutions of the country the guardians and servants of a just society. The king was enjoined not to acquire many horses and wives for himself, not to become prouder than his fellow countrymen, and to keep all the words of the law (Deut. 17:16–17, 20, and 19). The judges and officers were enjoined to dispense true justice to the people, not to pervert the course of justice, not to show favor, and not to accept bribes (16:18–19). The rich people were enjoined to lend liberally to the poor and not to oppress their hired servants (15:7–8 and 24:14). Moreover, a Sabbath year was instituted with the decree to release all debtors from their debts and to liberate all native slaves at the end of every seventh year (15:1–2 and 12–14).

Some of these injunctions were repetitions or liberalizations of older legal provisions which must have partly fallen into disuse, as the protests of the prophets implied. Moreover, the question arises whether and to what extent the Deuteronomist law code was enforced. Jeremiah's denunciations of the Jewish society of his time would indicate that conditions had not really changed much since the days preceding Josiah's reforms. Of importance, however, was the revolutionary spirit that animated both the prophets and the Book of Deuteronomy.

The prophecies of Jeremiah, which followed the reforms of Josiah, were imbued with the spirit of urgency. Jeremiah was no less pitiless in his denunciations of the Jewish society than were his great predecessors, understandably so as he was a victim of the national catastrophe. Using the same metaphor of circumcision as in the Book of Deuteronomy, he exclaimed: "The days are coming, says the Lord, when I will punish all the circumcised . . . [for] all alike . . . are uncircumcised in heart" (Jer. 9:25–26). Again, as in the Book of Deuteronomy, Jeremiah appealed to faithful Israel to return to God: "Come back to Me, apostate Israel, says the Lord" (3:12). He left no doubt that by the renewal of the heart he meant not only religious faithfulness, but also social justice. As a reward he held out to the Jewish people the promise of salvation: "Mend your ways and your doings, deal fairly with one another, do not oppress the alien, the orphan and the widow, shed no innocent blood. . . . Then will I [God] let you live in the land which I gave long ago to your fore-fathers" (7:5–7). For these valiant words and for the prophecy of doom which he added if his admonitions were not heeded, Jeremiah was immediately arrested by the priestly party (26:8). But the renewal of the heart which he preached became the core of the striving for salvation in the following generations.

Thus what the great Jewish prophets meant was not "repentance" in the usual, often purely ritualistic sense, but a complete change in the direction of life as the only means of attaining salvation. Their views coincided with those of the great prophets of other religions—Buddha, Zarathustra, Jesus, Paul, Mohammed, and Luther. The "Repent" was pronounced not only by the Jewish classical prophets, but also by the late-Jewish prophet, John the Baptist, and by Jesus (Matt. 3:2 and 4:17).

The prophecies of the great classical prophets should not, however, be regarded as eschatological, if by eschatology we mean the end of the world as we know it and the dawning of a new world.[42] While they did prophesy disaster for their nation unless the people turned away from their evil ways, the end of the nation would not have meant the end of the world. Nor did the classical prophets prophesy that if Israel were to turn back to God, a new world would be created for the Jewish people, fundamentally different from that in which they had lived "when Israel was still a boy," beloved by God, called by Him out of Egypt (Hos. 11:1), and marching under Yahweh's wings from victory to victory. The kingdom of God for which the classical prophets yearned was an earthly kingdom to be granted by God. But it could come into existence only through a process of religious and moral purification. That was the hope of the Jewish people, or at least of its spiritual leaders. This hope was the beginning of the belief in a kingdom of God in which justice, purity, and love would reign.

7. ESCHATOLOGICAL SALVATION

The Birth of the Universal God. A time came when a new concept of Yahweh and salvation arose. This occurred obviously in connection with the trauma inflicted on the Jewish people by Nebuchadnezzar's conquest of Israel (586 B.C.), and with the deportation of the Jewish elite into the Babylonian Empire. Yahweh was elevated from the rank of national God to that of the universal, sole God, and the salvation of the Jewish people was envisioned as an eschatological act of God.

The turning point from the vision of Israel's salvation through purification to that of an eschatological salvation through a universal God stems from the prophecies of the great religious creator, Deutero-Isaiah. Although this prophet has remained anonymous, his writings are well known and sharply delimited. Old Testament scholars agree that chapters 40 to 55 of the Book of Isaiah were composed by an unknown prophet, generally known as Deutero-Isaiah or Second Isaiah, who lived in the sixth century B.C., in the era of the Babylonian exile.[43]

In these chapters, in a language unexcelled in poetic beauty and power, Deutero-Isaiah voiced his belief in a universal, sole God and announced the good tidings of eschatological salvation not only of the Jewish people but of the whole world. His beliefs in the universal God and in an eschatological salvation were organically connected: only a universal God could bring about the eschatological salvation of the world at the end of time.

The belief in a sole, universal God was indeed a new religious concept, revealed for the first time in Jewish history. The prophet sang a hymn to the only, all-powerful God, the Alpha and Omega of the universe: "I am the first and I am the last, and there is no God but me."[44] Similarly in another verse: "I am the Lord who made all things, by myself I stretched out the floor of the earth" (Isa. 44:6 and 24). True, Deutero-Isaiah was not the first thinker in Israel to attribute the creation of the world to Yahweh. The Book of Genesis did so long before him; and the attribution of the Creation to Yahweh was in the spirit of similar myths, particularly of Middle Eastern peoples, based on the belief that their paramount god had created the world. However, whereas the Mosaic religious revolution elevated Yahweh to the rank of the sole God of the Jewish people, the gods of the foreign peoples were, from the age of the Judges down to Jeremiah, recognized as the divine rulers of their respective nations.[45]

The belief in the coexistence of national gods merged eventually with a belief in the superiority of Yahweh over the other gods. There is even a cryptic passage in the so-called "Song of Moses" (Deut. 31:30–32:47) —which in the prevailing opinion of Old Testament scholars was composed in the late seventh or early sixth century B.C.—that attributed to Yahweh a kind of lordship over the gods of the other peoples: "When the Most High parcelled out the nations when He dispersed all mankind, He laid down the boundaries of every people according to the number of the sons of God; but the Lord's share was His people, Jacob was His allotted portion" (Deut. 32:8–9). Beliefs of this kind were obviously rife in Israel and may have been the forerunner of monotheistic beliefs.

It must, however, have been the spiritual impact of the triumphal march through the Middle East by Cyrus—the creator of the Persian empire, who reigned from 559 to 530 B.C.—that created the conditions for the monotheistic turn that Deutero-Isaiah gave to the Jewish religion. In glowing colors, Deutero-Isaiah portrayed the rise of Cyrus to world power (Isa. 47). Cyrus, the liberator, who was about to break the power that had oppressed and imprisoned the Jewish people, must have been placed upon the earth not by a national god but by a sole, universal, all-powerful ruler of the world. For a Jewish prophet, this could be no one but Yahweh, the God whom the Jewish people already worshipped and whom they regarded as superior to other gods. It must have been Yahweh as universal God who anointed Cyrus (45:1)—a unique case in Jewish Scriptures of the anointing of a foreign king. Deutero-Isaiah linked the triumphs of Cyrus closely with his belief in the universality of God: "I will strengthen you though you have not known Me," said God to Cyrus, according to the prophet, "so that men from the rising and the setting sun may know that there is none but I" (45:6).

Deutero-Isaiah viewed God's anointment of Cyrus as a step toward the liberation of the Jewish people from their Babylonian yoke. He ascribed to God these words to Cyrus: "You shall be My shepherd to carry out all My purpose so that Jerusalem may be rebuilt" (Isa. 44:28).[46] In a grandiose cosmic vision, however, the prophet widened his horizon from a belief in the universality of God to an eschatological future of the world in which the God of the universe, who had previously designated Israel as the chosen people, now entrusted the Jewish people with a universal eschatological mission: "It is too slight a task for you, as My servant, to restore the tribes of Jacob, to bring back the descendants of Israel: I [God] will make you a light to the nations, to be My salvation to earth's farthest bounds" (49:6). Thus it appears that Deutero-Isaiah was the first Jewish prophet to enter the realm of eschatology, by entrusting to Israel the mission of enlightening the whole world about the Lord of the universe. As the servant of God, a purified and renewed Israel would bring salvation to the nations: a truly eschatological mission, to be carried out by Israel as the chosen instrument of God.

Deutero-Isaiah still based his belief in a universal God and in His eschatological purpose on a narrow national concept, which was derived from Yahweh as the national God of Israel and was to color the later history of the Jewish religion. Moreover, the prophet's vision was not quite free from apocalyptic features, which some centuries later would play a dominant role in Israel. God's power would be involved in Israel's carrying out her God-given mission: "I [God] support you with My victorious right hand." Furthermore, not only shall aggressors against Israel be vanquished, but "all who take up arms against you shall be as nothing" (Isa. 41:10 and 12). These assurances of divine intervention in power contests between Israel and other nations notwithstanding, the primary weapon Israel would wield was the teaching mission she would carry to the nations of the world: "Never faltering, never breaking down, he [God's servant Israel] will plant justice on earth, while coasts and islands wait for his teaching" (Isa. 42:4).

Deutero-Isaiah understood Israel's mission not only intellectually, as that of a teacher of nations; he also visualized Israel as the suffering servant of God, whose sufferings would help him accomplish his salvational mission.[47] The suffering servant is the vicarious victim who "was pierced for our transgressions, tortured for our iniquities. . . . The Lord laid upon him the guilt of us all." Yet his sufferings help also all others: "The chastisement he bore is health for us and by his scourging we are healed" (Isa. 53:5−6).

The myth of the vicarious victim who suffers for the sins of others or of the community was deeply rooted in ancient religions, including the Jewish religion, as shown by the ritual of the scapegoat on the Day of Atonement (Lev. 16:20−22). Some scholars have drawn attention to the analogy between the vicarious suffering of Deutero-Isaiah's servant of God and the Babylonian New Year's rites in which the king was castigated and humiliated as an atonement for the sins of the people.[48]

Thus Deutero-Isaiah probably derived the vision of the vicarious sufferings of the servant of God from ancient myths and rites, with which his vision shared its salvational character. But he blended these myths with his belief that Israel was given by God a mission to become a teacher and beacon to the nations. The nature of these teachings follows directly from his belief in Yahweh's being the sole God of the universe. "Look to Me and be saved, you peoples from all corners of the earth," exclaimed God through the mouth of His prophet. "To Me every knee shall bend, by Me every tongue shall swear" (Isa. 45 : 22–23).

Deutero-Isaiah's vision of God as savior of the universe was truly eschatological—salvation coming at the end of the ages—as the following verse indicates: "The heavens grow murky as smoke; the earth wears into tatters like a garment . . . but My delivery is everlasting and My saving power shall never wane" (Isa. 51 : 6). The everlasting salvation of the world would be in the form of an everlasting kingdom of God on earth. When Deutero-Isaiah exclaimed, "Your God is King" and "My [God's] arm shall rule the nations" (52:7 and 51:5), he envisioned a world in which all men know that the universe is ruled by one God to whom every knee will bend, and that God, through the ministry of His servant Israel, will establish justice on earth. That is the redemption and salvation of which Deutero-Isaiah did not tire to speak; that was the "good news" which he announced (52:7). There will be justice on earth (42:1 4), as well as general well-being and prosperity: "[God] will tend His flock like a shepherd. . . . He will carry the lamb in his bosom" (40:11)—divine words which, if possible, were made even more immortal by Handel's *Messiah*. In another immortal verse the prophet exclaimed: "Come, all who are thirsty, come, fetch water, come, you who have no food, buy corn and eat; come and buy, not for money, not for a price" (55 : 1).

Thus Deutero-Isaiah, the first preacher of the universal God, was also the first Jewish prophet to preoccupy himself with the perfect society, for which all the great prophets yearned. And he was the first among them to preach as the ultimate destiny of mankind the good tidings of the approaching kingdom of God, a society from which social, economic, and political injustice, oppression, and poverty would be banned. In Deutero-Isaiah's kingdom of God there would also be merciful love. In the concluding verses of the poem of the suffering servant, the prophet said that the servant would "vindicate many himself, bearing the penalty of their guilt" and would intercede for their transgressions (Isa. 53 : 11–12). The belief that the righteous could intercede for the sinners was not uncommon in Jewish tradition.[49] What was unique in the ethical thoughts of Deutero-Isaiah was that the martyred servant, who suffered for the sins of the others, interceded for them.

Deutero-Isaiah's religious concept of Yahweh—as the sole God of the universe, who will at the end of our ages bring about a reign of peace, well-being, and love on earth—was accepted by the Jewish people for the next three and a half centuries and contributed essential elements to the Judaic and Christian religions. This can be shown by analyzing the canonical Scriptures of that period, both those of the post-exilic prophets (Joel, Obadiah, Zechariah, and the anonymous author of the Book of Malachi), and the eschatological insertions in the Scriptures of nearly all pre-exilic prophets (Amos, Hosea, Isaiah, Micah, Jeremiah, Ezekiel, and Zephania). All of these Scriptures breathe the spirit of Deutero-Isaiah.

The fact that the religion of post-exilic Israel differed in important respects from that of the pre-exilic era remained no less hidden for two thousand years than did the foundation of these new religious concepts by Deutero-Isaiah. Because the identity of many authors of post-exilic Scriptures was concealed by the insertion of their writings in those of pre-exilic prophets, later generations of Jews and Christians were led to believe that the earlier prophets themselves had adhered to the new beliefs. It took painstaking research by Old Testament scholars of the last hundred years to uncover the real facts.

Not all elements of Deutero-Isaiah's teachings remained unchanged in the post-exilic era. What did remain unchanged was his monotheism. Post-exilic Israel indeed believed in one universal God. What also remained unchanged was the eschatological nature of this belief, that is, the hope that there would be a final stage of history in which the universal God, as well as Israel which proclaimed the belief in Him, would triumph. There were, however, different visions of the circumstances of this triumph. Deutero-Isaiah had already wavered between different views. He believed that God would support Israel with His "victorious right hand" and that those who would defy Israel would vanish (Isa. 41:10-11). But he also believed that Israel would be "a light to all peoples to open eyes that are blind" (42:6-7).

In the post-exilic era both of these views were widespread. There was, on the one hand, the prophecy inserted in identical terms in both the Book of Isaiah (2:2-4) and the Book of Micah (4:1-3), that all the nations would stream to Zion, where the mountain of the Lord would be set, that the word of the Lord would come out of Jerusalem, and that many peoples would be ready to be taught in God's ways and to walk in His paths.[50]

There were, on the other hand, a number of prophecies based on the vision of an eschatological stage brought about by a cataclysmic war between Israel and the other nations, from which Israel would emerge victorious and the enemy nations would be destroyed. The most redoubtable visions of this kind were those of the war against Gog in the land of Magog, inserted in the Book of Ezekiel (chapters 38 and 39), and the slaughter reserved for all nations in the post-exilic chapter 34 of the Book of Isaiah. It was the spirit of a humiliated, defeated, scattered, martyred people that created such horrible visions, not the spirit of Deutero-Isaiah's suffering servant of God, who interceded for the transgressors.

The victorious wars against the hostile nations and the final triumph over them were frequently envisioned not simply as military actions but as the outcome of a divine judgment over "all the nations" (Joel 3:1 and 12). But in the end God's judgment over the nations will be followed by universal peace, as the prophecy inserted in the Books of Isaiah (2:4) and Micah (4:3) envisioned, and "all humble men on the earth" will be delivered, as Psalm 76:9 prophesied.

The Kingdom of God. What the spiritual leaders of the post-exilic era of Israel really had in mind was the eschatological belief in the ultimate erection of the kingdom of God. The ancient belief that God is the real king of the land was akin to that of other Middle Eastern peoples in the kingship of God, the earthly king being but God's governor on earth.[51] What post-exilic Israel understood by the kingdom of God was, however, different from the concept of God's kingship through the person of the earthly king. Post-exilic Israel's was an eschatological belief that the day will come when God will inaugurate a reign of righteousness, peace, and well-being on earth; it was, in short, the vision of Deutero-Isaiah. Thus Deutero-Zechariah proclaimed that "the Lord shall become king over all the earth," and "on that day there shall be neither heat nor cold nor frost. It shall be all one day" (Zech. 14:9 and 6–7).[52]

What some of the prophets of the post-exilic era dreamed of was the dawn of a new world, entirely different from the existing world. According to Trito-Isaiah, God proclaimed: "I create new heavens and a new earth," an earth, where "never again shall your sun set nor your moon withdraw her light" (Isa. 65:17 and 60:19–20).[53] Yet in the imagery of these eschatological prophets the revolution on earth would be even more important than the cosmic revolution. The kingdom of God will be an earth where everlasting peace will be established, where injustice, oppression, and misery will be abolished, where "the Lord God will wipe away the tears from every face" (Isa. 25:8).

This then is the kingdom of God as the spiritual leaders of post-exilic Israel envisioned it as the ultimate destiny of mankind: a realm where all nations "shall beat their swords into mattocks and their spears into pruning-knives, [where] nation shall not lift sword against nation nor ever again be trained for war" (according to the prophecies inserted in Isa. 2:4 and Mic. 4:3). Peace on earth may even extend, symbolically or really, to the animal kingdom, where "the wolf shall live with the sheep and the leopard lie down with the kid." [54]

The very foundation of the kingdom of God envisioned by these prophets would be justice and righteousness, which the Middle Eastern peoples had always viewed as the ideal of the good society. It was the lack of justice and righteousness in Jewish society that aroused the wrath of the classical prophets and induced them to prophesy the doom of Israel. Hence for the citizens of the kingdom of God, "the sun of righteousness shall rise, with healings in its wings" (Mal. 4:2).

The "Messianism" of post-exilic Israel should be understood in this context. If by a Messiah a human or superhuman savior is meant, post-exilic Israel prior to the Book of Daniel (c. 165 B.C.) was not Messianic. She fervently believed in a savior, but the savior was God, not a human being. The pre-exilic kings had been Messiahs so-to-speak ex officio, for Messiah is the Hebrew word for anointed, and in accordance with the Samuelic tradition every Jewish king was anointed. Being God's anointed governors on earth, the kings were regarded as sacred, but not as saviors, however exalted the epithets may have been with which they were sometimes addressed. [55]

The house of David collapsed with Nebuchadrezzar's conquest of Israel, and a sovereign kingdom was not established again until Danielic times. But the post-exilic, eschatological hope for the erection of a true kingdom of God was frequently blended with the vision that Israel would be ruled again by kings, not by the historical Davidic kings with all their weaknesses and injustices, but by the righteous kings of whom the Psalms spoke and of whom Isaiah dreamed. As God promised (in an insertion in the Book of Jeremiah): "There will I give you shepherds after my own heart, and they shall lead you with knowledge and understanding" (Jer. 3:15).

In this verse and in other similar prophecies of the post-exilic period there was no indication who these shepherds should be and how they should be chosen. In the four hundred or more years that elapsed from the election of David as king (c. 1012 B.C.) to Nebuchadrezzar's conquest of the Southern kingdom, the Jewish people were never governed by any kings other than those from the house of David. Thus, the identification of kingship with the house of David remained so strong in Jewish tradition that it also slipped into many eschatological prophecies: the future king shall come forth from Bethlehem, the birthplace of David (Mic. 5:2); or God will restore David's fallen house and rebuild it as it had been long ago (Amos 9:11).

However, what post-exilic Israel dreamed of was never the literal restoration of the harsh and unjust regimes of the historical kings of the house of David, but the coming of an ideal king, just and wise. Two identical insertions in the Book of Jeremiah expressed this longing: "The days are now coming, says the Lord, when I will make a righteous branch spring from David's line, a king who shall rule wisely, maintaining law and justice in the land" (Jer. 23 : 5 and 33 : 15). The future king was not seen as the savior of his people, but as being "raised" by God after He would have saved Israel. Thus in the Book of Jeremiah: "I [God] will bring them ['the remnant of my sheep'] back to their homes, and they shall be fruitful and increase. I will appoint shepherds to them" (Jer. 23 : 3–4).

In all post-exilic canonical writings preceding the Book of Daniel, there is only one prophecy that might lend itself to a Messianic interpretation: Deutero-Zechariah's famous prophecy of the king who will come to Zion, triumphant and victorious, humble and mounted on an ass, but speaking peaceably to every nation, and with a dominion from sea to sea, from the River (Euphrates) to the ends of the earth (Zech. 9 : 9–10). Yet even that prophecy heaped upon the king only courtly flatteries similar to those found in many psalms.

This analysis of canonical eschatological writings in the period from Deutero-Isaiah to the Book of Daniel—which is in effect the period that elapsed from Cyrus's decree allowing the exiles' return to Israel (538 B.C.) until the victorious rebellion against foreign rule under the Maccabees (165 B.C.)—indicates the impact of Deutero-Isaiah's teachings on his people during this span of Jewish history. In effect all the prophecies of that period, collected and accepted in the canonical Scriptures, breathed the spirit of that great prophet.

A new element, however, may have bridged the pre-Danielic prophecies, which planted the kingdom of God on earth, and the otherworldly beliefs of the Danielic and post-Danielic era: the revival of the belief in individual, as distinguished from collective, responsibility and retribution. While most of the post-exilic prophecies envisioned the dawning of an eschatological age for the Jewish people or ultimately for all nations, the earlier belief in just retribution which God bestows on the righteous and on the wicked appeared in a new, eschatological form: the day of the Lord on which His chosen people will be saved and the enemy nations punished or converted to the belief in Him as the sole, universal God will also be a day on which His internal enemies, who dwell in the midst of the Jewish community, will be punished. In other words, God will mete out punishment on the basis both of collective retribution for whole nations and individual retribution for the sinners among the Jews.

It had become a widespread conviction in the post-exilic era of the Jewish people that in the world in which we live, just divine retribution for the righteous and the wicked could not be expected during their lifetime or upon their death, but could be hoped for only in eschatological terms: on the day of the Lord, which would become a day of reckoning, a day of judgment. Thus Malachi, in his vision of the messenger who would clear a path before God, announced to Israel: "I [God] will appear before you in court." For just judgment God would use a "written record in which the names of those who feared Him were written" (Mal. 3 : 5 and 16).[56] On that day God would distinguish between the righteous and the sinners. He would punish the sinners among the Jewish people, the apostates, the idolaters, and the godless, affirmed Trito-Isaiah (Isa. 65 : 11 and 66 : 17). Nor would He spare those who had committed social sins. Malachi, in drafting a catalogue of punishable sins, particularly laid emphasis on those social sins which had been the object of wrath among the critics of Jewish society. He even added, in a modern spirit, sinners "who wrong the hired labourer" (Mal. 3 : 5).

According to the pre-Danielic eschatological Scriptures, neither salvation nor damnation could be meted out in a realm beyond our earthly world, as this world still remained the only theater of human and divine actions. Hence salvation could mean only a life enveloped in security and peace. Typical of the eschatological dream of the post-exilic writers was the assertion that the righteous "shall dwell on the heights, his refuge a fastness in the cliffs, his bread secure and his water never failing" (Isa. 33 : 16). For the sinners, on the other hand, the day of judgment would bring the ultimate perdition. Not only on the hostile nations but also on "all the sinners of My people," as an editor of the Book of Amos and Trito-Isaiah asserted, God pronounces the death sentence: "They shall die by the sword, all the sinners of My people" (Amos 9 : 10 and Isa. 65 : 12).

The pre-Danielic era also witnessed for the first time in Jewish history a foretaste of hell. In the Book of Malachi, "all the arrogant and the evildoers shall be chaff, and that day when it comes shall set them ablaze" (Mal. 4 : 1). The same vision of the burning of the evildoers appeared in the addition to Isaiah: "Rebels and sinners shall be broken together . . . and the two shall burst into flames together, with no one to quench them" (Isa. 1 : 28 and 31). Moreover, a belief in everlasting hellfire as punishment for the sinners was foreshadowed in the prophecy inserted in the Book of Isaiah: In Zion sinners quake with terror, the godless are seized with trembling and ask, Can any of us live with a devouring fire? Can any live in endless burning?" Moreover, the righteous men who would inhabit the new earth would "see the dead bodies of those who have rebelled against Me [God]; their worm shall not die nor their fire be quenched" (Isa. 33:14 and 66:24).

This conception of hell may have grown out of ancient Jewish traditions, deeply rooted in primeval beliefs, that stressed the crucial importance of burials, and the curse attached to the failure to bury the dead or to the refusal to permit their burial. It was therefore considered the gravest punishment for the corpse of an evildoer to remain unburied. In the Book of Jeremiah (8:1−2), God decreed that the bones of the apostate kings and of other leaders of Judah and of the inhabitants of Jerusalem should be brought out of their tombs, spread out and become "dung on the ground." [57]

The evolution of the Jewish religion—from the worship of tribal gods to a national god and finally to a universal God—can be understood as an indigenous development. The same is also true of the evolution of the Jewish people's belief in their salvation. In the tribal and early national stages, the concept of salvation was still on a material plane; in these periods Yahweh was expected to ensure the material welfare of the people and victories over their enemies. But in the era of the classical prophets, salvation for the Jewish people, envisioned as the dawn of an age of security and welfare, was conditioned on their readiness to establish a regime of righteousness and social justice. The further step from a belief in a realm of righteousness to the belief in an eschatological kingdom of God at the end of time—a kingdom in which Israel would enjoy the privileged position as the people of the Covenant, but which would also be open to the converted nations—was probably also the fruit of an indigenous evolution. However, the strange belief in a fire that would subject the corpses of the evildoers to everlasting pain may have been derived from the late Zoroastrian belief in a hellfire into which the evildoers would be thrown after death. [58] The fact that Israel was subject to Persian rule for two hundred years (from 538 to 332 B.C.) may have contributed to Zoroastrian influences on the Jewish religion.

The Historical Religion. The unique Jewish eschatology of the post-exilic period cannot be understood on any other basis but that of the unique historical character of the Jewish religion from the moment of its birth, and of the historical nature of Yahweh as He emerged as Israel's paramount deity. Other religions also had a vision of a beginning and an ending of the world, but both periods were viewed as lying outside and beyond human history. They were cosmic events, occurring either once or in recurrent cycles. Zoroastrians believed in the unique cosmic events of the creation of the universe and of its transformation at the end of time. All religions that derived from the Vedas and from much of Greek thinking had in common a cyclical conception of the universe in the form of a never-ceasing recurrence of its birth and death.

The Jewish religion also visualized a cosmic beginning. Its holy Scriptures commenced with the words, "In the beginning" (Gen. 1:1). But this cosmological beginning, as well as the myths of Eden and the Flood, were common Middle Eastern myths which, only after Yahweh's elevation to the rank of Israel's national God, were conceived as referring to Him. The real history of Israel began with the loose coalescing of traditionally twelve tribes into a nation and the recognition of a national God. It may be assumed that this historical event was preceded by the emigration of the Hebrew tribes from Egypt (the Exodus) and their nomadic existence, and was followed by the conquest of, and the settlement in, Canaan.

This history, with all its mythological and legendary elements, constituted the most important formative element of the Jewish religion. Whereas the Exodus in all likelihood preceded the emergence of Yahweh as the national God, in the conscience of the Jewish people both events were indissolubly interwoven. Yahweh was projected back into the Exodus story as the God who saved Israel from servitude. From His beginnings He emerged as a Savior God. The Ten Commandments begin with the words, "I am the Lord who brought you out of Egypt, out of the land of slavery" (Exod. 20:2). What the Jews considered as a historical fact was thus cited as the reason for Yahweh's claim to exclusive worship.

This close connection between the formation of the Jewish nation in the wake of the exodus from Egypt and the emergence of Yahweh as the national God has remained in the conscience of the Jewish people as the determining factor in their history. One of the most important Jewish holy days, Passover, still celebrates as a saving act of God the exodus from Egypt, a historical event that happened more than three thousand years ago. The Jewish people have also viewed as a historical event and as a saving act of God the myth of the conclusion of a Covenant between them and God which elevated them to the rank of God's chosen people.

This beginning also determines the end. As the beginning was a divine act of salvation, so will be the end. As the belief in divine salvation at the beginning of Jewish history coincided with the elevation of Yahweh to the rank of Israel's sole God, so arose in the conscience of the Jewish people the belief in the eschatological act of salvation at the end of history. Thus Israel's religion conceives both the beginning and the end simultaneously as historical and cosmic events. The God who was believed to have saved Israel from Egyptian slavery became the creator of the universe. The expected salvation of Israel through a divine act is thought of as an eschatological end of the world as it exists today, through the creation of "new heavens and a new earth" (Isa. 65:17), that is, of the kingdom of God.

In other words, human history, as seen by the Jewish eschatological prophets, has a beginning and an end. The beginning was the creation of the world and of man. The end will be the erection of the kingdom of God on earth. For while this event was visualized as occurring within history, once the kingdom of God is ushered in, once all mankind has acquired a new heart, once all swords have been turned into ploughshares, once social justice has been established, once injustice, oppression, and misery have been banned from the earth and all tears have been wiped away, history as we know it will end. There is no history in paradise even if it is dreamed of as a this-worldly abode.

In Judaism and Christianity the historical character of the Jewish religion was profoundly modified as its eschatology turned other-worldly. Nevertheless, the Christian Alpha and Omega has been the continuation of the Jewish Alpha and Omega: "I am the first and I am the last" (Isa. 44:6). God is the beginning, the creation of the world and of man, and is the end, the ultimate salvation. In between there is human history. Undoubtedly the Jewish religion, as well as Christianity and Islam—which have maintained the belief in the eschatological direction of human history by accepting the Old Testament and adding their own sacred history—have drawn much of their strength from this belief in the eschatological process of human history, which obviously responds to a profound urge in human beings.

CHAPTER II

Salvation from Suffering and from Rebirth

Ancient civilizations east of the Indus River nurtured religions that originated in India and spread through the vast expanse of land from the Indus southeastward and northeastward, and finally to Indochina, China, Korea, and Japan. In many areas they succumbed to Western religions (Christianity and Islam), as was the case in Pakistan and Bangladesh, Indonesia and the Philippines. But where they met indigenous religions (Confucianism, Taoism, and Shintoism) they tended to prevail, partly by way of symbiosis. The remarkable vitality of the Indian-born religions seems to have been due to their extraordinary ability to meet the religious needs of the people and to satisfy the longing for ultimate salvation, to a large extent by transforming themselves into religions more responsive to these needs than were the original Upanishadic and Buddhist doctrines. This chapter traces the evolution of Eastern religions, along with the original Chinese contribution to it, Confucianism, and Taoism.

1. VEDAS AND UPANISHADS

The conception of life and salvation that evolved in India and spread to the Far East differed in essential features from the concept that prevailed in countries west of the Indus. Whereas in the ancient Middle Eastern and Western world men yearned for salvation from the troubles of life, in the East life itself was considered a suffering, and rebirth was dreaded. Release (*moksha*) from the "wheel of existence" (*samsara*), which comprised life and rebirth, came to be the center of religious striving.[1]

After the Aryans settled in India, apparently in the sixteenth century B.C., this concept of salvation took many centuries to pervade the life of the East. The early Vedas[2] reflected the same desire that characterized other early civilizations: the desire for a full, happy, and joyous life on earth among the self-conscious young people who had arrived on the Indian subcontinent. A full life meant a life long enough to beget children and to acquire wealth and friends. After such a life, death was not feared but welcomed, provided it occurred in old age. The Rig-Veda[3] defined salvation in material terms in a prayer to the sun: "May we not suffer want. . . . May we live happily and reach old age. Every day with fine spirits and clear eyes, rich in offspring, free from sickness, free from sin, may we live long."[4] The desirable life span was one hundred years. In one of the Vedas a prayer for a child reads: "Let Father Heaven and Mother Earth in concord give thee death in old age that you mayest live . . . a hundred years."[5] By implication, death at or after that age was not something to be dreaded.

Since ancient times the Indian people believed in life after death, in heaven or in hell, as well as in rebirth or reincarnation. The Rig-Veda affirmed that after death the souls of the righteous go to the land of the Fathers, the land of Yama (the god of death), where paradisiac pleasures await them, while the souls of the wicked go down to a dark land. A delightful passage speaks of "that deathless undecaying world wherein the light of heaven is set . . . where joys and felicities combine and longing wishes are fulfilled."[6]

The belief in rebirth after death seems to go back to an early stage of the Vedic religion, but remains alive to the present time in Hinduism and in the other religions that evolved from the Vedic and Upanishadic stages of Indian religion (Jainism and Buddhism). Rebirth, however, was dreaded rather than desired because it meant a second death; repeated rebirths meant repeated deaths. Moreover, rebirth could mean birth into a lower existence, as a worm, insect, or dog, as a man of a lower caste, or even as an outcast. Only the small number of the virtuous and righteous could be reborn into a higher caste.[7] Thus death came to be feared, particularly premature death, which was very common due to the hardships, misery, and unsanitary environment which was, and unfortunately still is, the lot of many people in that part of the world.

Consequently the cycle of life, death, and rebirth—the wheel of existence—came to be viewed as an evil from which release was sought. In the later Vedic period this release was seen as a heavenly existence after death which would liberate the soul from a second death, which means, from rebirth. Heaven was conceived of as a realm in which there was no hunger, thirst, sorrow, fear, or death.[8] Those who during their lives had performed good works—which meant in the first place the proper rites— were assured of a heavenly existence after death: "They who know this or they who do this holy work come to life again when they have died, and coming to life, they come to a life free from death," reads a Brahmana text.[9] The others, however, the "fools" who had no knowledge and had not performed the proper rites and deeds, "come to life again when they die, and they become the food of death, time after time."[10]

The Upanishads[11] marked a turning point in the history of Indian civilizations, because with their appearance an originally primitive religion was converted into a metaphysical system without losing its character as a religion. Being collections of the teachings of a great number of gurus, they did not constitute a homogeneous, coherent system. Nevertheless, the various Upanishads enjoyed so high a degree of agreement on the essential elements that they can be considered a distinct religious system.

The Upanishads maintained the Vedic belief in rebirth. Thus one of the most important Upanishads, the Chandogya Upanishads, declares: "Those whose conduct has been good will quickly attain a good birth, the birth of a Brahmin, the birth of a Kshatrya, or the birth of a Vaisya; but those whose conduct has been evil quickly attain an evil birth, the birth of a dog or the birth of a hog."[12]

In both the Upanishad and Vedic religions, salvation and damnation depended on *karma*, literally, the law of "sowing and reaping." This law meant that a man's deeds and thoughts throughout his life determine his destiny thereafter: as you sow in the present life, you will reap in the next one. However, the Upanishadic belief in rebirth differed from that of the Vedas in one fundamental respect: whereas in the Vedas the law of karma could be bent by ritualistic devices, the Upanishadic doctrine of karma was no longer based on divine retribution. Sacrifices to the gods would not alter the destiny that awaits man after his death; they could not bring about release from suffering and from recurring death, for retribution was independent of the existence or nonexistence of gods. It was not meted out by deities. There was no book of judgment. There were no scales held by gods or archangels. There was no bridge over which the soul of the dead must tread. Karma, in the Upanishads and in the religions derived from them (Jainism and Theravada Buddhism), was an impersonal power which could not be swayed by any considerations of mercy or grace, nor by imprecations, intercessions, prayers for the dead, Books of the Dead, or indulgences.

With their concept of karma the Upanishads paved the way for Buddhism, but they were based on metaphysical doctrines that Buddhism does not share. They believed in a higher reality than that which appears to our senses, a supreme reality, a world soul, called the Brahman. The concept of Brahman (lit., "growth") was in effect pantheistic. Brahman, uncreated, all-creator, eternal, without attributes, immutable, and impersonal, embraced as the supreme reality the whole world. According to an Upanishadic text, "That which is above the heaven, that which is beneath the earth, that which is between these two, heaven and earth, that which the people call the past, the present and the future, across space is that woven, like warp and woof." Another text defines Brahman as "that whence all beings come into existence, wherein they reside, and where unto they return at the end." [13]

The concept of the Brahman was paralleled in Upanishadic literature by the Atman, man's soul. Although the Atman was believed to be attached to individual man, it is eternal and after rebirths, it fuses with and becomes ultimately identical with Brahman: "This soul of mine within the heart, this is Brahman." [14]

In that Brahman world, according to an Upanishadic text, there is salvation, deliverance from day and night, from old age and death, sorrow and all works, good and evil. [15] Such salvation does not mean that every human soul after death immediately returns to, or is merged with, Brahman. If the fusion of the Atman with Brahman is the ultimate salvation, this path is blocked for all those whose karma forces them into rebirths on earth. Salvation can be found only by those who have acquired knowledge of the Atman-Brahman, the ultimate salvational reality. They will be able to merge with Brahman after death. But this fusion means abandoning the earthly individuality. "As the flowing river disappears in the ocean, quitting name and form, so the knower, delivered from name and form, goes to the heavenly man, higher than the high," says an Upanishadic text. [16]

Who, however, is the knower? This term should not be interpreted in a modern Western sense to mean a philosopher, a theologian, or a scientist who has thoroughly studied the elements that constitute the universe and has formed conclusions about its nature. Rather, the term "knower" should be understood in its ancient Indian setting, as a man who after having lived an active life in family and society, has withdrawn into solitude and devoted himself to a Yoga life of spiritual concentration, meditation, austerity, and withdrawal from all the trappings of life.[17] Understood in this way, the knower is the only one who during his lifetime can hope for deliverance from the fetters of desires. His knowledge, based on an austere, hermitic life, constitutes salvation, if not yet ultimate salvation. Whatever he did during his earlier life, including the evil deeds he performed, does not generate new karma although it continues as his karma. He may not yet attain Brahman immediately after his death; he may have to expiate, through rebirth, deeds which he committed before his enlightenment. But eventually he will be delivered from rebirth and will fuse with Brahman. "When all the desires that dwell in the heart are cast away, then does the mortal become immortal, then he attains Brahman here."[18]

2. JAINISM AND THERAVADA BUDDHISM

While the Upanishads left an indelible imprint on Eastern thinking, a religious revolution of important consequence for southeast and northeast Asia occurred with the birth of Jainism and Buddhism in the sixth century B.C. The rise of Jainism at about the same time as Buddhism was remarkable since it marked the same rebellion as Buddhism—inspired by the Upanishads—against ritualism and sacrificialism and against the domination of India by the Brahmin caste, whose power was derived from a widespread belief in its divine nature.[19] Both new religions shared the Upanishadic belief that salvation was dependent on an individual's decision about his way of life. What is needed for release is the right direction of karma by means of right conduct. There is, however, a strong ascetic note in the ethical rules of Jainism, whereas Buddhism does not consider asceticism itself as a means of release.

The founder of Jainism was Vardhamana Inatriputra Mahavira—Mahavira means literally, "great hero"—who, according to Jain tradition, lived from 599 to 527 B.C. Like Buddha, Mahavira attained enlightenment only after years of struggle and asceticism.[20] The Jains believe that he was preceded by twenty-four legendary Jainas (lit., "conquerors") who had attained release. However, the Jains do not implore the Jainas to help them in the quest for salvation. The Jainas can be invoked only as models of good conduct. Even the Jain meaning of salvation is not very different from that taught by Buddha: salvation is a state of tranquillity beyond human sufferings and pleasures.

Jain ethics are based on the principle of nonviolence (*ahinsa*), not only among human beings but also toward animals, including the smallest insects. The ahinsa principle is the heritage that Jainism left to India. It has remained in the conscience, if not always in the practice, of her people. Her greatest son, Mahatma Gandhi, made it one of his leading maxims.[21] It was, however, not Jainism which became the great religion of salvation in Asia and the Far East but the more profound humanist rebellion against Brahmanism initiated by Buddha.

Like the lives of Zarathustra and Jesus, and to a certain extent even of Mohammed, the life of Buddha is clouded in a mist of legends and myths. There is general agreement among scholars that Buddha (lit., "The Enlightened") lived in the last half of the sixth century B.C. His name seems to have been Siddharta from the Sakya clan; but claims that he was the son of a king, that he abandoned his wife and child in order to seek release as a hermit before he found enlightenment under the Bo tree, are not very reliable. However, there can be no doubt that after a long spiritual struggle, he at last attained enlightenment and became one of the greatest teachers of mankind. He laid claim to a growing retinue of disciples, and since he lived in their midst and wandered with them, his disciples acquired a nucleus of his teachings which they transmitted to the Buddhist community from generation to generation.

Whereas a definite version of Mohammed's Koran was established only twenty years after his death; whereas the oldest parts of the Avesta (the Zoroastrian scriptures) were written during Zoroaster's lifetime or shortly after his death; and whereas the synoptic Gospels were written only one to two generations after the death of Jesus, the teachings of Buddha were confided to oral transmission through several centuries, and were written down some four hundred years after his death. The Theravada Canon, the oldest complete collection of Buddhist scriptures, was not written down before the second half of the first century B.C.

Nevertheless, the nucleus of Buddha's teachings can be isolated from later additions with more or less certainty, and appears to have contained the following elements: Buddha retained from the Upanishadic teachings the belief in karma and samsara (the wheel of existence through rebirths), beliefs that had become so deeply ingrained in the structure of Indian thinking that they were not even felt to be lacking in evidence; there is not a single source in Buddhist writings that would indicate any doubt in the reality of karma and rebirth. Buddha also shared with the

Upanishads a skepticism in the existence of gods and in their power to intervene in man's destiny. He consequently shared with the Upanishads the opposition to the Brahminic sacrificial system, which has remained very strong in India as a bulwark of the power of the Brahmin caste. Yet while Buddha retained the Upanishadic belief that man's karma is determined solely by his conduct in life, he did not adopt the doctrines of Atman and Brahman. Rather, he seems to have believed that the individual soul is not an enduring entity—let alone an entity that has a changeless core, the Atman—but a bundle of sensations, desires, and activities subject to continuous change; the soul is held together during a person's lifetime and is reborn in future lives unless moving into the stillness of Nirvana.

The decisive aspect of Buddha's teachings is the doctrine of the Four Noble Truths, which includes the famous Eightfold Path. The first truth is that the most essential facts of life—birth and death, sickness and old age, painful sensations, and separation from or inability to engage in desired sensations—are marked by suffering. The second truth is that suffering is caused by the desires themselves, the craving for lustful sensations. The third truth is that suffering ceases if the desires cease. And the fourth truth is the Eightfold Path which leads to the cessation of suffering.

The Eightfold Path is a blend of the following intellectual and moral commandments: (1) right understanding—the intellectual understanding of Buddha's Dharma,[22] that is, in substance, the understanding of the Four Noble Truths; (2) right thought—a thought that avoids involvement in desires; (3) right speech—truthfulness, sincerity, and righteousness in everything one says; (4) right conduct—leading a virtuous life that avoids vices and crimes; (5) right livelihood—earning the means of livelihood in righteous ways and avoiding unrightful gains; (6) right endeavor—abstaining from evil and lustful thoughts; (7) right attention—living a conscious life of attention that should be extended to each state of body and mind; (8) right concentration, through meditation, on the understanding of the Dharma.

Concentration, meditation, retreat from a sensuous life are, however, only paths toward salvation. Ultimate salvation itself can be attained only in Nirvana (lit., "waning away"), a state of being in which there are no more desires. Consequently all the sources of suffering are stilled and a state of perfect tranquillity is achieved. In such a state karma and samsara cease to operate. Nirvana cannot be attained simply by an act of will or knowledge, but only by leading a life which treads all the arduous avenues of the Eightfold Path. For those unable to observe strictly all the rules of the Eightfold Path, the wheel of existence cannot be stopped, that is, rebirth cannot cease. But even they can hope that some future life will bring them closer to the attainment of Nirvana. The man who through his ability to follow the Eightfold Path has at last achieved Nirvana becomes an *arahat* (lit., "the deserving one"). He will not be reborn again; he has found everlasting peace.

This brief analysis of the Four Noble Truths and the Eightfold Path should underscore the fundamental differences between the Judaic-Christian-Islamic and the Buddhist concepts of salvation. In Buddhism there is no divine being to grant us everlasting peace. Instead of *pacem eternam dona eis* ("grant them eternal peace") for which the Christian prays, the Buddhist must struggle through life on a thorny path with no assistance from beyond or above, until he or the man into whom he has been reborn attains everlasting peace through his own efforts. Thus, while there can be salvation for man, it occurs without the intervention of a divine being and without the acting or suffering of a savior; for Buddha, like Mohammed, never claimed to be a savior.

The question remains whether Nirvana transcends life as we know it. If rebirth has been stopped for the arahat, does Nirvana which he has attained reach beyond his life? It appears that Buddha, in accordance with his agnostic attitude toward anything that transcends the world of experience (such as gods or the all-soul), refrained from answering the question. "Have I said to you," queried Buddha in one of the discourses attributed to him, "come and be my disciple, and I will teach you whether the world is eternal or not, infinite or not, whether the soul is identical with the body or separate, whether the saint exists after death or not?"[23]

In any case Buddha, or the disciples who interpreted his teachings, obviously considered ultimate salvation in Nirvana to be a state of body and mind that can be achieved at the end of the Eightfold Path, but he was indifferent to the possibility of a beatitude outside and beyond human life. In the teachings of Buddha, there is neither a merging of the arahat with the all-soul nor a beatific vision of God. In short, Buddhism, as it was originally taught by Buddha and his disciples and adopted by Theravada Buddhism (Buddhism's split into the Theravada and Mahayana schools is discussed in section 4, below) is essentially a this-worldly religion. This position is reflected in a description of the arahat-hood common in Theravada usage: "Destroyed is rebirth, lived is the higher life, done is what had to be done, after this present life there is no beyond."[24]

It is obvious that Buddha's philosophy of life derived from that prevailing in the era of the Upanishads and in the Indian world generally.

His philosophy was based on the conviction that life, seen as a whole, means suffering. Salvation, therefore, can mean only release from suffering. But this release cannot be attained by an active life or earthly successes and triumphs, because the thirst for pleasure and success leads only to graver suffering. The conditions for release can be created only by denying the pleasures of life or by physically withdrawing from society. While Buddhism prefers monasticism to a hermitic life, the basic philosophy holds true for both ways of release.

It is difficult to determine which factors prompted Indian society— once animated in the era of early Vedism by the same life-affirming spirit as other societies in the same stage of cultural evolution—to create in the latter era of the Upanishads, Jainism, and Buddhism the ideal of the hermit or of the monk who withdraws from society. Nor can it be determined what led to the doctrine of the Four Noble Truths, which considers life as suffering and preaches abstention from sensations as a way of release. Life may have been hard in India for the ordinary man, oppressed as he was by the Brahminic sacrificial system and by petty sovereigns and nobility. But there is no reason to assume that he was worse off than his contemporaries in Western civilizations, who did not arrive at life-denying conclusions. Life-denying attitudes of this kind arose in Western civilizations only much later when the beliefs in salvation shifted from one on earth to one at the end of time or in heaven.

With the rise of Bhakti Hinduism in India and Mahayana Buddhism in many Buddhist countries (see below, sections 3 and 4), life-affirming attitudes again gained ascendancy. But it would be erroneous to infer from the Buddhist doctrine of suffering that Buddhism was indifferent toward life in general. After all, some branches of the Eightfold Path imply a positive attitude toward life in society: the commandments of right speech, right conduct, right livelihood, and right endeavor are concerned with man's conduct in society and reveal ideals worthy of any society.

Moreover, Buddha himself, as can be inferred from his conduct as a teacher, was compassionate rather than aloof toward life. He has remained an object of adoration for Buddhists not only as the Enlightened One, but also as the Compassionate One. One of the many legends that surround his life tells of the temptation to which he was subjected in the wake of his enlightenment. Mara, the Tempter, in order to prevent Buddha's salvational message from being spread among mankind, tried to persuade him to reap the rewards of his enlightenment by withdrawing immediately into Nirvana. But Buddha, moved by compassion for suffering mankind, resisted the temptation. He decided to delay attainment of

Nirvana in order to communicate his message so that release from suffering might ultimately be attained by all men.

The resemblance of this legend to that of the temptation of Jesus is striking. In both cases the Tempter approached the future teacher of salvation immediately after his enlightenment, tried to prevent the spread of the salvational message, and made similar promises of individual gratification. In both cases the teacher resisted and carried the message of salvation to mankind. It is not difficult to account for this resemblance. The legends reflect the troubles and tribulations that every religious creator must undergo before he is ready and able to follow the commands of his conscience and of his compassion: to communicate his enlightenment by spreading the gospel of salvation to all mankind, rather than being saved alone.

Buddha's compassion, difficult perhaps to reconcile with the doctrine of cessation of suffering through withdrawal, induced him to become the first great missionary in the history of religions. By postponing his own salvation until the end of his life (for forty years if tradition can be trusted), by leading the stern life of a teacher-monk, by assembling disciples and teaching them the Dharma intellectually and through his conduct, he succeeded in spreading his message of salvation through India and the Far East. He was rivaled in the success of his mission only by those who spread the messages of Christianity and Islam through the world.

3. BHAKTI HINDUISM

Both Upanishadic Vedism and Buddhism had a profound impact on the religious life of Asia because both religions underwent essential transformations. The element that was chiefly responsible for this impact was also a determining factor in the evolution of Western religions: the introduction of savior figures as essential to the process of salvation.

In Upanishadic Vedism, Jainism, and Theravada Buddhism, salvation was solely based on self-effort. There was no god, no savior who could save man. There were only teachers to show him the way: the sages who composed the Upanishads; the twenty-four conquerors of Jainism; Buddha and the monks who transmitted his Dharma. But the thorny path toward salvation must be trod by each human being individually.

The great turn in the history of the Eastern religions came about when this belief was replaced by the conviction that, in addition to self-effort, there must also be some help "from above." In Hinduism the belief in help from above coincided with the rise of late-Vedic or post-Vedic gods, of whom two have evolved as the principal founts of salvation: Shiva and Vishnu, in particular Krishna, one of Vishnu's *avatars* ("reincarnations").[25] Indians, however, usually recognize and worship only one or the other as the paramount deity, as the sole God. To this, his God, the believer owes *bhakti* ("devotion") and the love of his whole heart and soul.

The decisive turning point from Upanishadic Hinduism to Bhakti Hinduism was marked by the Bhagavad Gita. Literally, "Song of the Holy One," the Bhagavad Gita was incorporated into the great epic Mahabharata, which may have been completed at the end of the second century A.D. It is a unique literary and religious possession of the Indian people, perhaps its most precious one, both because of its poetic beauty and its profound religious content.

Although derived from the Upanishads, the Bhagavad Gita is the gospel of a new religion whose core is the belief in a savior God, Krishna, in whom the Upanishadic world-soul is personified. The all-soul, Brahman, appears in the Bhagavad Gita in its purest Upanishadic majesty: "Brahman is the imperishable, the supreme; its being is called essential self."[26] At the same time Krishna is identified with Brahman, indeed is Brahman himself. "Those who turn to Me [Krishna] . . . know that Brahman. . . . Those who know in Me essential being, essential deity and essential sacrifice . . . know Me truly" (Bhagavad Gita 7:29–30).

This personification of the supreme reality allows man's relationship to the "essential deity" to become a personal one, the essential feature of which is devotion (bhakti). The Bhagavad Gita did not forget or neglect the Upanishadic ideals. It recognized the Yoga way of meditation, the way of the ascetic, and of the man of spiritual knowledge, as the legitimate paths toward salvation. But it subordinated all these ways to the royal path of devotion. "Neither by the Vedas," Krishna assured Arjuna, one of the Mahabharata heroes to whom He revealed Himself, "nor by austerity, nor by alms, nor yet by sacrifice, can I be seen in such a form as thou hast seen. But by devotion undivided, Arjuna, in such form can I be known and truly seen and entered" (11:53–54).

Devotion to be effective must pervade all human activities: "Whatever work thou doest, whatever thou doest eat, whatever thou dost sacrifice or give, whatever be thy austere practices, do all as an offering to Me." As in Christianity, it is by the grace of God that devotion to Him will win salvation: "In [Krishna] alone seek refuge with all thy being; by His grace shalt thou win peace supreme, the eternal resting place" (9:27 and 18:62).

Another essential element of the Bhagavad Gita's concept of salvation was that in addition to adhering to the ethics of austerity, meditation, and withdrawal as paths toward salvation, one must also emphasize the positive values of humaneness, action, the duties of work, and devotion to the all-pervading reality of God. This synthesis of the ancient roots of Indian ethics with the new societal ideals of Bhakti Hinduism was beautifully expressed in the verse, "He who hates not any being, he who is friendly and compassionate, without a thought of mine and I, regarding pain and pleasure all one, long-suffering, ever content, ascetic, self-restrained, of firm conviction, with mind and reason dedicated to Me [Krishna]—that man is dear to Me, My worshipper devout" (12: 13–14).

The dramatic setting of the Bhagavad Gita also illustrates the work ethics of Bhakti Hinduism. In the critical moment of a battle in which Arjuna is to fight against contenders belonging to his own clan, he is vexed by doubts about the rightfulness of killing men in battle. Just then Arjuna's charioteer reveals himself as Krishna and enjoins Arjuna to take up the fight: "Do the work thou art obliged to do for the sake of work, not of reward: For if without attachment . . . a man works, he gains the highest" (3:8, 19).

Yet the work ethics of the Bhagavad Gita were still linked with the caste system. Krishna even asserted that the order of the four castes had been created by Him (4:13). About the God-given duties of the castes, the Bhagavad Gita stated: "Of Brahmins, Kshatryas, Vaisyas, and Sudras the duties are distributed according to the strands which are in the nature of each" (18:41). Arjuna, born and raised as a Kshatrya, must fight because fighting is the chief duty of that caste. On the other hand, the spirit of the Bhagavad Gita is far from aristocratic arrogance. Salvation is open to everyone, regardless of caste and sex. "Even those who are born of the womb of sin—women, Vaisyas and Sudras too—, if they resort to [Krishna], go on the highest way" (9:32).

The caste spirit of the Bhagavad Gita has remained the spirit of India, just as the religion of devotion which this Mahabharata-born work inspired has remained the religion of India. India still stands in the middle of the crusade initiated by her loftiest spirits, her Gandhis and Nehrus, to overcome the caste spirit of the Bhagavad Gita without shaking its devotional basis or that of the life-enhancing ethics it introduced.[27]

Because the Indian people has never completely abandoned the belief in many divinities, the Krishna cult has not remained unchallenged. Among the Hindu gods, the Trimurti (Triad) of Brahma, Vishnu, and Shiva acquired a privileged position in connection with the belief, originating in Upanishadic Vedism, in an ever-recurring cosmic cycle (*kalpa*). This cycle consists in the creation of the universe, its evolution, and its descent into nothingness, followed by ever-new cycles of creation, evolution, and destruction. The Trimurti symbolizes the cosmic cycle: Brahma cyclically creates the world, Vishnu preserves it, and Shiva destroys it. Whereas Vishnu-Krishna became the beloved savior in the Bhagavad Gita, Shiva, the dancing destroyer God of the Trimurti, competes with him as the sole object of veneration and devotion and as the sole savior. Shaivanism, the cult of Shiva, thus contends with Vaishnavism, the cult of Vishnu-Krishna.

The transformation from the pantheistic religion of the Upanishads into the savior religion of Bhakti Hinduism can also be traced in the history of Indian philosophy. The outstanding figures of Indian philosophy in the period following the disappearance of Buddhism from India were Shankara and Ramanuja. Shankara's Upanishadic pantheism and Ramanuja's Bhakti Hinduism constituted in effect the two poles of Indian thinking. Shankara (A.D. c. 700–c. 750) was the great philosopher of the Vedanta (lit., "end of the Veda"), philosophically the most consistent version of the Upanishads. The Vedanta reduced the world of experience nearly to an illusion (*maya*). Shankara has been credited with originating the concept of *advaita* (nondualism or monism), Brahman being the absolute reality. Only in Brahman can there be salvation: "That which is real in the absolute sense, immutable, eternal, all-penetrating . . . all-satisfying, undivided . . . in which neither good nor evil, nor past nor present has any place, this incorporeal is called liberation."[28] Shankara's monistic philosophy sharply contrasted with the dualism of Sankhya (lit., "enumerating"), a philosophy that played a major role in the late-Upanishadic period and found its classical form in the *Sankhykarikas* (third century A.D.). It shared with the Upanishads the opposition to Brahmanism, and with Buddhism the agnostic or atheistic position. Its dualism was between universal matter and the self (the soul).

While Shankara viewed salvation as open to those who have acquired the true knowledge of the Vedantic pantheistic philosophy and have adjusted their conduct in accordance with it, Ramanuja (d. A.D. 1137), being a Vaishnavi, identified Vishnu with the Supreme Deity. Yet in Ramanuja's view the human soul has an individuality different from the All-Soul and will not be merged with it after death, but will retain its identity. In further contrast to Shankara's philosophy, Ramanuja taught that it is not knowledge but Bhakti, loving knowledge of the Godhead, that leads to salvation if assisted by God's grace.

Because the supreme reality is personified in God, questions arose in Hinduism, similar to those raised in Christianity, about the nature of the relations between man and God. Does the saving act originate in God or in man? Does God's grace grip man and enable him to tread the way toward salvation, or does the initiative lie with man, while God, through His grace, only helps in the process of salvation? Different Hindu schools have found different answers to these questions, which were symbolized in the metaphor, typical of the Eastern poetic spirit, of the "cat way" and the "monkey way." As the mother cat grabs her baby to save it from danger, God may draw man's soul to Himself and thus save it. Contrariwise, as the monkey baby clings to its mother, the soul may actively ascend to God, with the same salvational result. In whatever way the relationship between man and God is visualized in the various schools of Hinduism, ultimate salvation cannot be attained before man has fulfilled the law of karma. Even all the grace of God cannot release man from the wheel of existence (recurrent rebirths) until he fully deserves ultimate salvation. Only then will he be allowed to see God's eternal light in heaven.

Bhakti Hinduism has had an overwhelming impact on the Indian people. In the nearly two thousand years that have elapsed since the Bhagavad Gita was composed, this religion has not lost its appeal. When one asks why Buddhism more than a thousand years after its inception completely vanished from India, it does not seem adequate to answer that in the end the Brahmin caste proved stronger than the Buddhist monks. The answer may rather lie in the popular appeal of a religion of a savior god and of devotion to him as a way toward salvation.

Nevertheless, the Upanishadic spirit has not entirely disappeared from India. The two great currents of Indian philosophy, the Vedanta philosophy of Shankara and the Bhakti philosophy of Ramanuja, still represent Indian thought. Among the adherents of Bhakti Hinduism were great religious figures such as Sri Ramakrishna Paramahansa (1836–1902) and Mahatma Gandhi, who was a deeply religious Hindu in the spirit of the Bhagavad Gita.[29] Yet the Vedanta philosophy has also produced prominent representatives, such as Sri Ghose Aurobindo (1872–1950) who, like Vivekananda (1862–1902), another prominent adherent of the Vedanta philosophy, founded an important school in India and the West.

These and other schools are, however, not the only channels through which Eastern thought has pervaded the Western world. Indeed, the spiritual traffic between East and West does not use a one-way street. The Vedanta and Bhakti-Hindu philosophies are no less elements of the spiritual evolution of modern man than are the new currents in Western religions and in the secular schools of thought.[30] Conversely, if nationalism can be regarded as a movement that originated in the Western world, it penetrated deeply into the religious thought of India. Thus Gandhi was both the great leader of the nationalist liberation movement and a profoundly religious man in the spirit of Bhakti Hinduism. Vivekananda's Ramakrishna Mission likewise called for building the Indian nation in the spirit of Hinduism; and the Vedanta philosopher Aurobindo was a leading, and even a fanatic, Indian nationalist.[31]

In any case, India, the birthplace of the profound thoughts of the Upanishads and Vedanta, of Jainism and Buddhism, as well as of Bhakti Hinduism, has remained faithful to her heritage. She is far advanced on the way to becoming a modern nation, vying with the West in intellectual pursuits, but she has not abandoned the religious and philosophical ideas that evolved on her soil.

4. MAHAYANA BUDDHISM

Upanishadic Vedism receded in favor of a successor religion which personalized the concept of salvation by replacing the Upanishadic belief in salvation through self-effort alone with a belief in self-effort aided by a savior god. Likewise, a powerful movement arose in the ranks of Buddhism, intent on bringing about a parallel transformation of the Buddhist Dharma. This movement triumphed in a large part of the Buddhist world at the price of a fundamental split between Theravada and Mahayana Buddhism—strikingly parallel to the secession of Protestantism from the Catholic Church and to the split between Sunnites and Shiites within Islam. The split within Buddhism ran along geographical lines even more strictly than did the Christian and Islamic schisms. A large part of southeast Asia, comprising Sri Lanka (Ceylon), Burma, Thailand, Cambodia, and Laos, has remained faithful to Theravada Buddhism, whereas in Tibet, Vietnam, China, Korea, and Japan, Buddhism has spread in its Mahayana version.

Soon after the death of Buddha various traditions were collated in oral canons. One canon, transmitted in Pali (a language related to Sanskrit), was completely preserved. It was brought to Sri Lanka in the third century B.C. and was written down in the second half of the first century B.C. The School of Elders (in Pali, Theravada) claims that this canon is the only authentic one. It is in any event the only one recognized by Theravada Buddhism. Aside from certain legendary embellishments and mythological accretions, this canon—commonly called the Pali Canon or Tripitaka—contains rules for the life of the monks, as well as the teachings of Buddha and his early disciples in the form of sermons, discourses, and poems. By confining canonical acceptance to the Tripitaka, Theravada Buddhism has retained the faith substantially in the form in which Buddha and his early disciples seem to have taught it.

The Mahayana school of Buddhism apparently split off from the orthodox Buddhist doctrines, which survived in the Theravada school. This split occurred during the early period of Buddhism, long before the Pali Canon was written down. In striking resemblance to the early Christian controversies about the nature of Jesus, a controversy about the nature of Buddha—whether he should be considered human or divine—paved the way for Mahayana Buddhism.

In later stages of the Theravada scriptures, however, a transcendental element was added to Buddha's original teachings, bringing Theravada Buddhism closer to Mahayana doctrines. This was a belief in a cycle of Buddhas corresponding to the cosmic cycle (*kalpa*) which Buddhism had adopted from Upanishadic Vedism. From the belief in a cosmic cycle, later Theravada scriptures deduced that a Buddha existed in every cosmic cycle and that, consequently, there also will be a Buddha in the cosmic cycle that will follow our era. At the end of the present cycle, physical and moral decay will set in and Maitreya, the name given to the future Buddha, will spread the Dharma again. Present-day Theravada Buddhism shares with Mahayana Buddhism this belief in the coming of Maitreya.[32]

Mahayana Buddhism was born from the same needs and longings which transformed Upanishadic Vedism into Bhakti Hinduism, and the original Jewish religion into late-Judaism and Christianity. The transformation sprang from the feeling that life is a heavy burden, and that striving for salvation adds to this burden if salvation can be achieved only by self-effort. The Eightfold Path, prescribed by Buddha as the only path to salvation, is a thorny one. Mankind has been accustomed from its earliest childhood to cry for help from the gods, to conjure and propitiate them. Buddha, the severe teacher, barred this path toward salvation. The rise of Mahayana Buddhism indicated that the longing for salvation through the intervention of savior figures proved stronger than Buddha's austere approach.

While Buddha, the compassionate teacher, renounced release for himself for the duration of his life, Mahayana Buddhism created a world of Buddhas and saints, the Bodhisattvas (lit., "being enlightened"), who renounced release for themselves for the sole purpose of helping others attain release. In contrast to the Christian and Islamic saints who were to a large extent historical figures, these Buddhas and Bodhisattvas are sheer products of Mahayana fantasy and perform their compassionate savior role beyond our own world. The beyond of the Mahayana Buddhas and Bodhisattvas resembles the Christian heaven, and the help they extend to mortals is based on virtually the same doctrine as that of the treasure of merits adopted by the Catholic Church.[33] To be sure, the belief of Mahayana Buddhism in man's salvation through the treasure of merits remains Buddhist: If a man follows the Eightfold Path, he accumulates merits which eventually will lead to salvation. But a saint, rather than attaining Buddhahood and entering Nirvana, may choose for compassionate reasons, such as pity for suffering mankind, to use his merits to help other men achieve salvation. He thus becomes a Bodhisattva.

The renunciation of Buddhahood by the Bodhisattvas is different from the concepts of sainthood in Christianity and Islam, in that the Christian and Muslim saints and martyrs already have attained salvation for themselves, but their merits may also help others achieve salvation. The Bodhisattva approach is in fact a social conception of holiness in contrast to the concept of individual salvation prevailing in other religions. Mahayana Buddhism has always been conscious of this difference. It appears in the distinction between the classical Buddhist figures, the arahat and the Bodhisattva. The arahat is the saint who through extreme self-effort and pursuit of the Eightfold Path ultimately attains salvation. He is the ideal figure of Theravada Buddhism. The Bodhisattva, in spite of the same self-efforts and of treading the same Eightfold Path, renounces Nirvana in order to save mankind. That is why the Mahayana Buddhists have called Theravada Buddhism the narrow route (Hinayana) and Mahayana the wide route toward salvation.

However, the savior role played by the Buddhas and Bodhisattvas in Mahayana Buddhism can be successful only if their feelings of pity, grace, and devotion toward suffering man are reciprocated. To be capable of being saved, man must respond to the efforts of the Buddhas and Bodhisattvas by being devoted to them and loving them. In Hinduism, the religious evolution led from Brahman as the impersonal all-soul of the Upanishads to the personal savior god, from the ideal of the knowledge of the Upanishadic truth to Bhakti love and devotion to the savior. Likewise, reliance on self-effort alone in early and Theravada Buddhism was replaced in Mahayana Buddhism by grace and compassion on the part of the Buddhas and Bodhisattvas, and by love for and devotion to the saviors on the part of the believers.

Like Theravada Buddhism, Mahayana Buddhism adopted the Hindu belief in a cosmic cycle. But it also incorporated those variations required for the belief in the savior role of the Bodhisattvas. In each of the cosmic cycles, there was and there will be not only one Buddha but an array of Buddhas and Bodhisattvas. Moreover, several Mahayana schools, such as the Lotus Sutra, believe in a supermundane, eternal nature of the Buddhas. According to these schools, even the historical Buddha was a god whose image only appeared on earth as the historical Buddha.[34] All Buddhas of the now-existing aeon and of all earlier aeons participate in the work of the salvation of mankind.

In contrast to Theravada Buddhism, Mahayana Buddhism has from its beginnings abounded in sacred literature, philosophic doctrines, and schools and sects. In the sacred literature certain sutras have exerted the greatest influence on Mahayana beliefs, particularly the Lotus Sutra, the Infinite Purity Sutra, and the group of the Perfection of Wisdom Sutras.[35]

The Lotus Sutra and the Infinite Purity Sutra are based on the belief that all human beings possess a "Buddha-nature" and are consequently capable of attaining enlightenment which will eventually lead to salvation. In the Lotus Sutra many Buddhas preceded the historical Buddha, who is eternal like his predecessors. He thrones in heaven with a great number of arahats and Bodhisattvas, the greatest of whom is Avalokitesvara (who in China became Kuan-Yin and in Japan, Kwannon, and who in both countries has become a much-worshipped goddess of mercy, resembling the Virgin in Catholic belief). The Lotus Sutra teaches that anyone who insists upon listening to the teachings of Mahayana Buddhism and adores Buddha can attain enlightenment and ultimately salvation. In this endeavor he will find the support of the Bodhisattvas.

The Infinite Purity Sutra centers upon the figure of Amitabha (in Japan, "Amida"), literally, "immeasurable light." This Sutra asserts that Amitabha, a monk on the way toward Buddhahood, made a vow to renounce enlightenment and Nirvana unless all men who sincerely desire to be saved and adore him would be saved. He became a Buddha and Lord of the Western Paradise, the Pure Land of eternal bliss. By his merits and grace he enables the believer who invokes his help and adores him to dwell with him in the Western Paradise. As in all other Eastern creeds, understanding of the doctrine implies a conduct worthy of ultimate salvation, a life of love and charity.

The third group of Sutras, the Perfection of Wisdom Sutras, were treatises which played a great role in Mahayana philosophy. Some of them may have been composed as early as the first century B.C. Derived, it seems, from the doctrine of the impertinence of the human soul attributed to Buddha, they teach a doctrine of the void and emptiness of the phenomenal world. Thus nothing is real; the thought of the enlightened is nonthought; there is neither existence nor nonexistence; there is only the void that is immeasurable and imperishable. This doctrine was the basis of a philosophical system propounded by the Indian Mahayana philosopher Nagarjuna, who lived in the second century A.D. According to him, the void is the foundation of salvation: "He who looks upon all things as utterly void has practiced the way." [36]

Once implanted in China and then in Japan, Mahayana Buddhism split into a number of sects, some of which are still of great importance, especially in Japan. The attention of the West has been particularly caught by the Zen school, founded in China as the Chan school (*chan*, derived from the Sanskrit word *dhyana*, lit., "meditation"), according to tradition by Bodhidharma, an Indian sage who supposedly arrived in China in A.D. 520. In Japan, the Zen school has flourished since the twelfth century.

The Zen school was derived from the Perfection of Wisdom Sutras, with which it shares the doctrine of the void. But Zen rejects the belief in a Mahayana Paradise and insists that Buddha was a historical rather than a divine figure. The outstanding feature of Zen is its particular concept of the Buddha-nature, which seems to have been influenced by Taoism. Like Tao in Taoist philosophy, the Buddha-nature is everywhere, indescribable, and inconceivable.[37] Yet it can be awakened in the Zen disciple by inspiration and spontaneous intuition. Prepared by austere conduct and meditation, the enlightenment, brought about with lightninglike inspiration, will lead the disciple to salvation on earth.

The Chan school in China and the Zen school in Japan may have been important and influential during the feudal era, since Zen philosophy and ethics were congenial with the spirit of both the military aristocracy and the warrior class, the Samurais. In present-day Japan, however, Zen has less adherents than those sects that were derived from the Lotus Sutra and the Infinite Purity Sutra, both of which promise salvation through savior figures.

The oldest of the Japanese Buddhist sects is the Tendai school, founded by Saicho (A.D. 767–822) but of Chinese origin. It is based on the Lotus Sutra. In the following centuries, additions were made to the Tendai doctrines until Nichiren (1222–1282) founded a "pure" Lotus school (Nichiren Shoshu), based on the belief and faith in the eternal Buddha rather than in Amitabha (Amida). The path that leads to salvation, according to Nichiren, is opened by true faith in Buddha and by striving for the growth of one's Buddha-nature. The sect gained importance in modern Japan when in 1937 Tsunesaburo Makiguchi (1871–1944) founded the Soka Gakkai (lit., "Value Creating Society"), which in turn in 1964 organized a political party, Komeito (lit., "Clean Government Party").[38] The growth and appeal of Komeito quickly moved it into the first ranks of the political parties. While Komeito in 1970 formally severed its ties to Soka Gakkai, Nichiren Buddhism remains one of the strongest Mahayana Buddhist sects in contemporary Japan.

It seems, nevertheless, that the Pure Land sects still prevail in present-day Japan. They go back to the twelfth century when Japan was torn by internecine warfare among feudal lords, and the people had a deep longing for peace and a divine savior. During a grave national crisis, Honen-Shonin (1133–1212) founded Jodo, the Pure Land sect, based on veneration for, devotion to, and invocation of Amida, the Lord of the Western Paradise.[39] By invoking Amida's grace, the believer would be reborn into Amida's Pure Land. Honen's chief disciple, Shinran Shonin (1173–1262), founded the Jod Shin-Shu sect (lit., "True Pure Land"), which ties salvation to Amida's grace even more closely than had the original Pure Land school.[40]

After the Communist revolution in China left Buddhism in the state of an outlaw religion, Japan became by far the world's largest Buddhist country. Buddhism not only has a huge following in Japan, but it is still a living and dynamic force in that country, reflecting a deep longing of the Japanese people for ultimate salvation. Nevertheless, as in the other religions, tendencies toward the pursuit of national or social secular goals have been growing in Theravada and Mahayana Buddhism. Only one example is the rise of Komeito in Japan as a political party emphasizing political, economic, and social reforms. In Theravada countries subject to foreign rule, such as Burma and Sri Lanka, the nationalist fight for liberation from foreign domination found strong support among Buddhist monks.

The most significant evolution of Buddhism as a secular force occurred in Sri Lanka. In 1956, immediately preceding the elections which brought the nationalist-socialist coalition of S. W. R. D. Baranaike to power, the All-Ceylon Buddhist Congress published a report which insisted not only on religious reforms, but also on radical economic and social reforms designed to raise the living standards of the people. This action was preceded by the publication of a book which held that Buddha's message is this-worldly and that it advocates an active life, particularly one in the service of society. Since then the monks of Sri Lanka have played an active role in the political life of their country.[41]

5. THE WAY OF CHINA

Several events occurred in the religious world of Asia at about the same time that India was shaken by Buddhism's rebellion against the oppressive role of the Brahmins: Asia west of the Indus River was stirred by the thrust of Zoroastrianism; the Jewish people were roused by the monotheistic and eschatological doctrines of the late-classical prophets; and China was swept by two revolutionary spiritual movements, Confucianism and Taoism, directed against the oppressive and chaotic rule that prevailed in the contending petty states which constituted China in the fifth and fourth centuries B.C. Confucianism and Taoism searched for release from this burden of rule along paths different from but complementing one another. Although in the next two thousand years both movements underwent substantial changes, their fundamental ideas are still alive in China, in spite of the vigorous disclaimers in the Mao era. Moreover, if Buddhism is rightly regarded as a third essential element in Chinese civilization, then the Zen school, the most creative Buddhist school born in China, was decisively influenced by classical Taoism.

Asserting that Confucianism, Taoism, and Zen Buddhism have been the most constructive spiritual forces in China is tantamount to stating that spiritual China, from the inception of her classical philosophical and religious systems, was and has remained a country devoid of any conception of a personal god. Both Confucianism and Taoism sought salvation, but not through the grace of a god or gods. And Confucius's path toward salvation was an outright secular one; he wanted to erect a perfect society on purely secular foundations. Even the term "salvation" is meaningful in classical Confucianism only if understood as a synonym for "perfect society."

Classical Taoism, on the other hand, was not secular, but found reality and salvation in a universe which has no divine foundation. It was only later, when religious Taoism arose—which borrowed much from popular beliefs—and when Mahayana Buddhism penetrated China, that the Chinese people's quest for salvation began to show religious features similar to most other countries.

The Teachings of Confucius. Confucius (a Latinized version of his name, K'ung Fu-Tzu, lit., "Master Kung," 551–477 B.C.) is a figure almost free from legendary embellishment. He was born in one of the several Chinese states that existed before the unification of China. After unsuccessful attempts to graft his societal ideas on his own government, he travelled from state to state in a vain search for rulers who would accept and implement his ideas of political and social reform. Success, however, lay in a different direction. Like Buddha and Jesus, he attracted disciples who preserved and spread his teachings ultimately through all China.

Confucius's disciples spread his teachings first from mouth to mouth; but the translation from the oral to the written form took much less time than in the case of Buddha's teachings. Scholars agree that a large part of the *Analects* (in Chinese, Lun Hu, lit., "Conversations"), which contain a collection of his teachings, was written down in the middle of the fourth century B.C. The *Analects* can be considered authentic in the sense that the substance of the teachings as presented in certain parts of the collection is likely to have come down from the Master and to have been more or less faithfully preserved.[42]

Although Confucius was a thoroughly secular thinker, he was not an agnostic or an atheist. He believed in Heaven as the supreme deity, the common belief in China since the twelfth century B.C. He insisted that the laws of Heaven must be respected: "He who has put himself in the wrong with Heaven has no means of expiation left" (*Analects* 3 : 13). Yet he never invoked Heaven as a divine power that would reward good conduct and punish bad conduct. Rather he held that man alone is responsible for his deeds and cannot expect help from any divine powers in his striving for salvation, or, to Confucius's way of thinking, in his striving for a good society.

Confucius lived in a period of near anarchy when China was split into several states warring among themselves, when kings and ministers ruled autocratically and arbitrarily, when bribery, injustice, and oppression of the lower classes were rampant. Confucius searched for a way to transform the rotten society of his era into a good society. The way he chose was neither one of divine command nor of withdrawal from communal life, but one of social man. To initiate the reign of social man required the establishment of rules of conduct for the individual and for the government. To produce the good society, Confucius undertook to establish such rules. He started with a simple categorical imperative, similar to those preached by other ethical teachers, ancient and modern: "Do not to others what you would not like yourself." He based this rule on a more fundamental one: to love men. "The good [ruler] . . . loves men" (12 : 2 and 22).

The social rules that Confucius established resemble those of the Jewish prophets: to be humane, to be true, to do justice. In Confucius's words: "In dealing with the aged, to be of comfort to them; in dealing with friends, to be of good faith to them; in dealing with the young, to cherish them" (5:25). Further, "A gentleman takes as much trouble to discover what is right as lesser men take to discover what will pay" (4:16). Above all, Confucius called for social justice: a good society must be established in a way that will help the distressed rather than enrich the wealthy: "A gentleman helps out the necessitous; he does not make the rich richer still" (6:3).

Confucius realized that a good society cannot be erected on the foundations of a corrupt societal system. He had full confidence in man, provided he were to live in a society that fosters goodness. Such a society, however, can be established only by a virtuous government: "Govern [the people] by moral force . . . and they will keep their self-respect and come to you of their own accord" (2:3). In other words, good government fosters goodness of the governed. Two Confucian rules testify to this maxim: "If only you were free from desire, they would not steal even if you paid them to" and, "If you lead along a straight way, who will dare go by a crooked one?" (12:18, 17).

Although Confucius was convinced of the innate goodness of man, provided society were organized in such a way as to stimulate goodness, he was not a utopian, but a rationalist thinker. He knew that his society was ruled by hereditary kings through an administration of ministers chosen mainly from the aristocracy. If, instead, ministers and other officials were selected on the basis of their civic virtues, their ability, and their education in the art of governing according to the rules for good government, there was hope that the state would become a real commonweal. Confucius not only established such rules but spent his whole life teaching people to become good and efficient servants of the commonweal. In this practical endeavor he seems to have succeeded in several instances: some of his disciples became high officials and proved themselves in their office.

In a highly developed society, as was Chinese society when Confucius lived, good government presupposes an administration manned by good public servants. That goal can be achieved only by educating them in the spirit of high moral principles. China adopted Confucius's principle of selecting public servants on the basis of an appropriate education rather than on nobility or wealth. Yet Confucius was not so naive as to believe that education alone makes a good public servant. He stated: "A man may be able to recite the three hundred Songs; but if, when given a post in the government, he cannot turn his merits to account . . . , however extensive his knowledge may be, of what use is it to him?" (13:15).

This sound warning was more often than not neglected by Chinese governments. Selecting public servants by examinations, which were to prove one's aptitude for absorbing the appropriate education and for carrying out office duties efficiently, did remain the rule until the end of the Chinese empire. But this system certainly did not turn out to be a foolproof guarantee for good and wise government. It was, moreover, often petrified by formalistic education and falsified by limiting the selection of high officers to elitist cliques. In addition, as literacy was confined to narrow strata of the population, class rule by birth or wealth appeared as class rule by higher education. Thus the democratic spirit of Confucius's teachings was slowly lost. Yet what did remain throughout China's history was the emphasis on learning and thorough education, however formalistic it may have become, for those who were called to govern and administer the country.

Confucius's moral principles made a deep impression on Chinese society and thought, although it was only during the first few centuries after his death that they were followed faithfully by his disciples. Among the outstanding Confucian thinkers, only one, Mencius, contributed greatly to the elaboration of the teachings in a truly Confucian spirit.

Mencius (a Latinized version of his name, Meng-tzu, lit., "Master Meng") lived in the fourth century B.C. His teachings were founded on those of Confucius, but constituted a valuable addition in three respects. First, he elaborated on the Confucian doctrine of the aptitude of men to respond to good government by becoming good themselves. Mencius became a precursor of the philosophers of the Enlightenment by maintaining that man is by nature good; yet, he did not neglect Confucius's view that a good education and healthy environment are necessary to foster goodness. Mencius stated: "If rightly tended, no creature but thrives; if left untended, no creature but pines away." [43] Second, he introduced a concept of humanity that has remained central in Confucian thought: being innately good means being humane, righteous, genteel, and wise.[44] Third, he again anticipated the philosophy of the Enlightenment by establishing two of its fundamental doctrines about government: that governments derive their just powers from the consent of the governed; and that the people have not only the right but the duty to rebel against and overthrow rulers unable or unwilling to provide for their welfare.[45]

In the ups and downs of the formation of the Chinese empire in the succeeding centuries, the spiritual authority of Confucianism grew until the Han dynasty (202 B.C.–A.D. 220) ensured to Confucianism a firm foothold within the country's political structure. During the consolidation of the Han empire, Confucianism became the official political doctrine, and an educational system claiming descent from Confucianism was adopted as the basis for admission to public service. The more authoritarian the governing system became, however, the more Confucianism was identified with autocratic government, and the more the humanist teachings of Confucius and Mencius were neglected in practice.

Another modification of Confucianism occurred with the rise of philosophical schools in the Sung period (A.D. 960–1279). These schools transformed the rationalist, secular foundation of Confucianism into a metaphysical system based on the belief in a "Great Ultimate of existence, absolute, eternal, the form according to which all things have their being, and the source and totality of goodness and truth." [46]

The revolutionary movements which led to the downfall of the Manchu dynasty (1911–1912) strongly opposed the petrified, oligarchic Confucianism of the imperial regimes. But whereas both liberals and Communists have opposed traditional Confucianism, the truly Confucian conceptions of good government and humanity have not disappeared from the China that emerged in the wake of the collapse of the empire and the internecine wars that followed.

Classical Taoism. The mystical quietism of classical Taoism was the second element of Chinese thought that grew out of an impassionate rebellion against the oppressive conditions of society in the period preceding the unification of China. It is difficult to trace the origins of Taoism. Even the figure of Lao-Tzu has turned out to be of doubtful historicity. He was venerated in China for thousands of years as the founder of Taoism. And under his name one of the chief works of classical Taoism was written, first called *Lao Tzu*, later known as *Tao-te-Ching* (lit., "Classic of the Way and Virtue"). It is certain, however, that the systematization of Taoism as a great philosophical-ethic system was due to Chuang-Tzu, who lived in the fourth century B.C. He appears to have been the chief author of *Chuang-Tzu*, the fundamental work of classical Taoism.

Whereas Confucianism taught a secular way toward salvation, Taoism searched for a mystical response to the misery and the iniquities of Chinese society, a way which, however, did not imply a withdrawal from society. In its view the universe, which Taoism identified with the "path" (*Tao*), is an all-embracing but at the same time mystical entity. "The Tao cannot be heard. . . . The Tao cannot be seen. . . . The Tao cannot be talked about." [47] On the other hand, the Tao is "everywhere, in this ant. . . . In this grass. . . . It is in tiles. . . . It is ordure and urine" (p. 31). Man need not strive for unity with Tao, for he is part of it: "Heaven and earth were born together with me, and all things with me are one" (p. 14).

In the view of Taoism, salvation does not mean release from life or death. Alive or dead, we are part of Tao: "The universe carries in our bodies, toils us through our life, gives us repose with our old age and rests us in our death" (p. 32). Salvation is rather the knowledge of man's identity with the universe and of the consequences he should rationally draw from it, namely, tranquillity and peace with the world: "The universe is the unity of all things. If one recognizes his identity with this unity, then . . . death and life, end and beginning disturb his tranquillity no more than the succession of day and night" (p. 42). In other words, salvation grows out of enlightenment, as it did for the Upanishads and Buddha. Taoist enlightenment, however, does not result in withdrawal, as taught by the Upanishads and Buddha, but in acceptance of the earthly things. For Taoism, the ideal is not the Hindu hermit or the Buddhist monk, but the wise man who lives in harmony with the universe and with the world of man.

Thus Taoism, unlike Confucianism, did not adopt concrete rules for the establishment of the good society. It simply applied to society its rules for natural living. Its precept of living in tranquillity and in harmony with nature, of taking "no action" (*wu-wei*) that was not in conformity with nature, is valid for government as well as for the individual.

In the first century A.D., Taoism was transformed by a religious movement that drew its strength from magical beliefs and practices, deeply rooted in the Chinese people. According to that religion, salvation can be achieved by rites and charms which would ensure immortality. This religious Taoism has no more in common with philosophical Taoism than the name. Although religious Taoism gained great popularity in China, classical Taoism retains its hold on Chinese civilization. The ideals of tranquillity, harmony, and serenity have not been abandoned. While China has turned Communist and has placed communal activism into the center of its "way," the personal and cultural life of the people still seems to a certain extent colored by the classical Taoist outlook on life. It might indeed be helpful for the understanding of contemporary Communist China to consider the impact that pristine Confucianism and classical Taoism have made upon the Chinese people in the twenty-five centuries since the initiation of these two doctrinal systems.

CHAPTER III

Ultimate Salvation:
Life after Death

In the Mesopotamian, Jewish, and Greek
netherworlds into which the souls of man
descended after death there was no salvation.
Salvation, be it an individual, national, or
universal kind, could be hoped for, if at all,
solely on earth. The Indian Upanishads
taught that the union of the knower with the
all-soul meant salvation, but at the price of
the loss of individuality. The Nirvana of
Theravada Buddhism was attainable only by
the most perfected men, and could not be
perceived as part of the world of the living.
In the Eastern world, only Mahayana Buddhism introduced the belief in a Western
Paradise.

Aside from Mahayana Buddhism, however, there were prior to Judaic and Christian beliefs in an after-life only two ancient
religions which believed in ultimate individual salvation after death: those religions indigenous to Egypt and Persia. This belief and
its counterpart—belief in ultimate damnation—spread to the Middle East directly and
through the intermediary of Greek and Hellenistic doctrines. In its Judaic and then
Christian and Islamic forms, this belief in an
after-life has become the dominant salvational creed in the Western world for two
thousand years.

I. SALVATION IN ANCIENT EGYPT

Man's belief in salvation, through divine intervention, from specific ills and sufferings during his lifetime was as common in ancient Egypt as it was in most ancient civilizations. There were a great number of gods and goddesses in ancient Egypt, each with highly developed protective functions. And the people knew which deities, frequently distinct by regions, had to be invoked through sacrifices, prayers, spells, incantations, and amulets in order to obtain relief, protection, and salvation.[1]

What distinguished Egypt from other ancient civilizations, however, was a belief in the continuation of life after death in a realm other than that of the living. Its origin may have been the belief in the divinity of the king. The belief that the king was the earthly representative of God was common to many civilizations. But the Egyptian king was believed to be not merely a representative of God, but a son of the sun-god Re.[2] It was, therefore, logical that after his death, the king was believed to have become a god. Since the first Egyptian dynasties, dead kings were identified with gods. A dead king was believed to travel with the sun-god by day and to stay in Osiris's netherworld by night. Thus in a pyramid text dating from the second half of the third millennium B.C., the dead king was identified with Osiris: "Thou hast not departed as a dead one, but as a living one. Sit down on Osiris' throne so that you mayest reign as a living one. O Re, this is Thy son Osiris."[3]

While other mortals could not secure life after death as easily as the king did, eventually it could be secured for many of them. The belief in life after death seems to have been derived from the myth of the resurrection of the king-god Osiris. His death and resurrection were at the origin of a fertility cult that was gradually embellished by a colorful mythology: Osiris was killed by his enemy, the god Set; Osiris's sister-wife Isis sought and found his corpse; Set hewed it in pieces, but Isis recomposed it and brought Osiris back to eternal life as king of the netherworld. Osiris appeared already in the Old Kingdom (c. 2686– c. 2160 B.C.) as the lord of the netherworld, the realm of the souls of those worthy of being granted life after death.

Admission into this realm required a blend of religion, mythology, and magic. First, the body of the deceased had to be preserved in the grave as if it were still alive. Hence the rite of mummification, which can be traced to the second dynasty (2890–c. 2686 B.C.). Man also possessed a spiritual nature. The Egyptians distinguished between man's *ba* ("soul"), which was born with his body, and a spiritual entity of *ka* ("divine nature"), which gives him life, good fortune, and health.

Man's ka was believed to exist imperishable in the beyond. When he died, his ba would strive to be united with ka in the beyond.[4]

Thus the ancient Egyptians did not believe in bodily resurrection at some eschatological date. Rather, with the body preserved in the grave, they believed in the ascent of the soul into a blessed beyond, provided all conditions for the immortality of the soul were met. This belief was clearly expressed in Egyptian texts, as in this pyramid inscription from the sixth dynasty (2345–c. 2160 B.C.): "Thine essence is in heaven, thy body is in the earth."

While the belief that man's soul can continue its life in a heavenly realm runs through the history of ancient Egypt, ideas varied about the way this goal could be achieved and about the nature of the beyond. In the later stages of Egyptian history, and particularly from the New Kingdom (1570–1085 B.C.) on, the ascent of the soul into the beyond was thought to depend on a divine judgment and on a blend of rituals, all difficult to observe. The rituals consisted of mummifying the body of the deceased, giving it a dignified funeral, burying it in a dignified tomb, offering libations, and placing into the grave food and objects useful for a life after death, such as figures of servants and slaves who were supposed to do the work which the deceased would otherwise have to perform himself. The conditions under which the deceased could hope to attain immortality of the soul were customarily spelled out in the Book of the Dead, which was placed in the burial chamber or grave.

The Book of the Dead was a collection of all the rites that the deceased was supposed to perform in order to achieve immortality. It also set forth the dangers he had to overcome, the judgment awaiting him, and the life he could expect in Osiris's realm which he hoped to enter. This book, the product of a religious evolution lasting several thousand years, varied considerably through the ages. The inscriptions in the burial chambers of the first pyramids and in the tombs of the dignitaries of that early period represented the first versions of the Book of the Dead in an extremely concise form. Gradually the book became more complicated. From the eighteenth dynasty (1570–1320 B.C.) on, it was written down on papyri. The numerous papyri found in burial chambers and graves testify to the existence of a number of versions of the Book of the Dead.[5]

The main features of the Book of the Dead, however, remained rather constant. They consisted chiefly of a collection of spells which the deceased was supposed to perform in order to retain or restore the life of his soul, to overcome all the dangers which threatened him, particularly from mythical serpents and insects, and to prepare him for the divine judgment. The ritual of the judgment seems to have been rather uniform. It was carried out in Osiris's judgment hall. In the presence of Osiris as judge and forty-two divine assistant judges, the god Anubis, the Lord of the Scales, held a balance. The heart of the deceased was laid on one scale and a feather symbolizing Maat, the Goddess of Truth, was laid on the other. If the good deeds of the deceased prevailed, he was declared justified and could rise into Osiris's realm. Otherwise his heart was devoured by the monster Amemei, the Eater of the Dead, and his soul was annihilated. As this ritual suggests, the ancient Egyptians did not believe in hell as an abode for evildoers. It was only in a late period of Egyptian history that beliefs in a post-mortem torture of the wicked began to intrude from other religions.

The scales of the balance symbolized the concepts of righteousness and wickedness. The ancient Egyptians regarded both concepts as relative: man can never be totally sinless and righteous, but he can be admitted into the divine realm after death, provided he has been so virtuous that his good qualities and deeds surpass his bad ones. Yet in view of the remaining sinfulness purification was still needed, and even those deceased who had been found justified would pray to God to remove sin, wickedness, and transgressions from them.[6]

The concepts of righteousness and wickedness were spelled out in the so-called "negative confessions," one of which has been preserved in the Theban Recension of the Book of the Dead from the eighteenth dynasty (see note 6, above). In that confession the deceased asserted that he had not committed any of forty-two sins. He addressed himself to any one of the forty-two assistant judges who were competent to decide if one of these misdeeds had been committed.[7] It was thus assumed that while the deceased claimed he had not committed a specific sin, it was up to the judges to verify that assertion.

Significantly, the deceased claimed not to have committed a number of social sins, such as: "I have made no man to suffer hunger. I have not carried away the milk from the mouths of children. I have not defrauded the oppressed one of his property. I have not ill-treated servants. I have not made . . . excessive labour to be performed for me."[8] As this text shows, the moral conceptions of righteousness and social justice, rather lofty ones for a society based on slavery, were sanctioned by religious commandments comparable to those in the Middle East, including Israel.

The negative confessions were part and parcel of the magical spells through which man hoped to attain immortality. By the same token, the funeral rites testified to the conduct of each individual during his lifetime which had a bearing on his destiny after death. The deceased appeared in the role of a defendant who pleads his case by attempting to prove his innocence, but the judges made the final decision on the basis of the facts revealed to them. The *nil inultum remanebit* ("nothing will remain unrevenged") of the Catholic Requiem Mass dominated the procedure of the divine judgment in ancient Egypt.

The belief that spells, prayers, and sacrifices could not sway the gods if a man's conduct did not make him acceptable was indeed of long standing in Egyptian religion. Thus the instructions for King Merikere of the fourth dynasty (end of the third millennium B.C.) stated that "the good conduct of the righteous man is more acceptable than the [sacrificial] ox of the evildoer." [9]

If all dangers to which the deceased was subjected were overcome, and if the divine judgment were in his favor, his soul ascended into the realm of everlasting happiness. The bliss conferred there on the souls of the justified deceased was originally conceived of as a continuation of the positive aspects of earthly life, such as eating and drinking, loving and feasting, and leaving chores to those servants whose likenesses had been brought into the tomb. With the later theological refinement of Egyptian religion, the soul of the deceased merged with the deity, without, however, losing its personality. Thus in the Book of the Dead the soul exclaimed: "While remaining entirely myself, I am fused with God." [10] Ultimate salvation in ancient Egypt, then, was not a mystic union with the all-soul, but resembled the visions of Christian and Islamic mystics.

In Egypt, while ultimate salvation in a beyond was originally a privilege of the aristocracy, it slowly became more or less democratized. Admission into Osiris's realm seems to have gradually filtered down, first to the king's highest servants—as attested by their numerous preserved tombs—and then to the secular and priestly aristocracy. It is not certain whether the democratization of heaven ever reached the lower strata of the population, which could not afford to comply with the intricate and extremely costly requirements of the funeral rituals. If a poor man could not afford to have the rites performed by his family, how could he hope that his soul would ascend into Osiris's realm? Poor man, indeed. Poor in life and in death! Perhaps his remote ancestors, who had been killed upon the death of their master in order to serve him in the after-life, had been better off than he; they at least could hope for an after-life, if only as their master's servants.

In a later era of Egyptian history, however, a popular belief seems to have arisen which brought hope for ultimate salvation after death even to the poor man. This is evidenced by a fable preserved in a demotic papyrus of the first century A.D. The fable dealt with a poor man and a rich man who were buried at the same time. A passer-by who visited the netherworld saw the poor man clothed in the garments of the rich man and occupying a place of honor, and the rich man suffering torments for his evil deeds.[11] The story probably reveals religious influences from outside Egypt which slowly modified the rigid aristocratic beliefs of earlier times.

Even with all these limitations—the magical spells designed to influence divine justice and the plutocratic obstructions to eternal beatitude for the lower classes—the fact remains that for the first time in history the Egyptian people believed in ultimate salvation, the immortality of the soul of the righteous, divine justice and retribution, and a divine judgment designed to reward the virtuous and to punish the evildoers after death. Egypt maintained these beliefs during her Christian and Islamic periods. Can it be a coincidence that the symbol of divine justice, retribution, and judgment—the balance on which the Lord of the Scales weighed the deeds and thoughts of the deceased—is also a Christian symbol which can be found on the tympanums of the most beautiful Gothic cathedrals?

Another feature of Egyptian religion which reappeared in Christian doctrine was the hope, in spite of the belief in equitable divine justice, to be able to influence divine justice and to achieve salvation by the intercession of a third party. The family of the deceased would pray for his salvation, and those who were believed to have entered the divine realm earlier were implored to intercede for the dead soul. Tombstones have even been found on which a passer-by was implored to intercede for the person buried beneath. Who does not think of the elaborate apparatus of intercession for the dead in the Catholic Church? And of the inscription on some Christian tombstones beseeching the passer-by: *Ora pro me* ("Pray for me")?

The analogies between the ancient Egyptian and Christian beliefs, however, do not imply that they shared the same conception of ultimate salvation. The ancient Egyptian hoped for a life after death because he loved life as it was, because he yearned to continue it after his death. For the Christian, in contrast, salvation still means a higher, purified, spiritual life, be it resurrected on earth or moved into heaven.

In a late stage in the evolution of the Egyptian religion, under the influence of priestly theologians, the concepts of life after death were spiritualized. And in an even later stage, when Middle Eastern and Greek mystery religions penetrated Egypt and other countries of the ancient world, salvational beliefs of the Hellenic-Christian type took root in Egypt. But by that late period the spirit of ancient Egypt had already died.

2. ZOROASTRIANISM

For the long period from 1525 to 1085 B.C., Egypt held sway over her neighboring Mediterranean countries. Even during the period of her political decline, she maintained close relations with them. Yet in spite of her power, Egypt's highly developed religious system and particularly her belief in salvation after death did not exert any considerable influence on her neighbors. By the time they adopted this belief, another salvational system had been conceived on the eastern rim of the Western world which influenced the religions of the Mediterranean civilizations more immediately and directly than Egypt did. This system was Zoroastrianism, a religion which, like Buddhism, Christianity, and Islam, owed its origin exclusively to one great, charismatic personality.

Zoroastrianism arose in an area far west of the borders of the Indus, that great divide between Eastern and Western civilizations and religions. To the Eastern world, as noted in the preceding chapter, life generally meant suffering, and release from suffering required withdrawal from active life in society. Conversely, Zoroastrianism—according to its founder Zarathustra (in Greek, Zoroaster) and the traditions which derived from him—always accepted life and remained rooted in the life of society. It called upon men to fight actively within society for good and against evil. Zoroastrianism was thus from its inception an activist religion, inspired by the same fighting spirit that characterized Judaism, Christianity, and Islam.

While many details of Zarathustra's life are legendary, and while many religious beliefs ascribed to him belong to later periods, enough information is authenticated to ensure his renown as a profound religious creator. What can be more or less regarded as authentic about his life is that he lived from c. 628 to c. 551 B.C., in the northern region of present-day Iran; that he taught a monotheistic religion, in contrast to the then-popular Persian religion related to that of the early Vedas; and that after long years of unsuccessfully preaching and teaching his new religion and meeting strong resistance, he found a protector and sponsor in the person of Vishtespa (in Greek, Hystaspes), ruler of one of many countries that Cyrus conquered soon after. The fact that soon after the death of Zarathustra the country in which his teachings had been diffused became part of the Persian empire, opened the doors to the spread of Zoroastrianism throughout the territories of the new world power.

Zarathustra's teachings have been preserved in a more authentic version than those of the other founders of great religions, with the exception of Mohammed. The holy Scriptures of Zoroastrianism, the Avesta, consisted of a number of writings of which a few have been preserved. The first of its extant parts, the Yasna (lit., "sacrifice," meaning liturgy in general), contains a group of Gathas ("hymns") which, according to scholars of Zoroastrianism, were written either by Zarathustra himself or by his contemporary disciples.[12] The Gathas thus constitute the authentic teachings of Zarathustra.

Zarathustra's unique role in the history of mankind was that this one creative person gave birth to a multitude of religious thoughts which in other parts of the world took many centuries of gestation: the monotheistic concept; the supremacy of the purely ethical aspects of the deity; the call to all men to follow good and to fight evil; salvation through self-effort; divine retribution after death; and the eschatological belief in an end of the world as it exists today and in a new world to come. A further religious concept of Zarathustra's, which had a particularly important impact on the religious beliefs of late Judaism and Christianity, was a dualistic concept of the cosmic forces.

Although Deutero-Isaiah can be credited with having elevated the national God Yahweh to the rank of the sole God of the universe at about the same time that Zarathustra elevated Ahura Mazda (lit., "Wise Lord") to the same rank, the revolution initiated by Zarathustra was even more profound than that produced by Deutero-Isaiah. For while Yahweh had been virtually the sole God of the Jewish people for centuries, Ahura Mazda had been only one among many gods in the Persian pantheon. Thus, Zarathustra's change from polytheism to monotheism was an abrupt one, and as a consequence, it had to overcome strong opposition.

Although Ahura Mazda was believed to be the sole creator of the world, even from nothingness,[13] and the sole ruler of the universe, he was surrounded by his "attributes," the Amesha Spentas (lit., "Bounteous Immortals"). (After the death of Zarathustra, the Amesha Spentas evolved into personal divine figures which may have given rise to the late-Judaic and Christian archangels.) And in spite of his monotheism, Zarathustra became the originator not only of ethical, but also of cosmic dualism. Actually Zarathustra derived his dualism from his monotheistic doctrine. He taught that Ahura Mazda, in the beginnings of time, had created two spirits, Spenta Mainyu (lit., "Holy Spirit"), the supreme Amesha Spenta, and his twin, Angra Mainyu. Angra Mainyu was in a perpetual state of war with Ahura Mazda. This cosmic battle is reflected on earth as a battle being waged in men's hearts. Every man must make a choice: whether to follow the "truth," fathered by Ahura Mazda, or the "lie," fathered by Angra Mainyu. Thus, like the karma doctrine of the Eastern religions, Zarathustra proclaimed the full responsibility of man for his deeds, which implied the rejection of any predestinarian doctrine of election by God. Neither God nor the Devil chooses his followers; man chooses to follow either God or the Devil. Salvation can thus be attained only through personal effort. While Zarathustra prayed to Ahura Mazda for the knowledge that would enable him to fight for the good, he was aware that he must wage the fight himself.

Zarathustra's belief in the full responsibility of man for his deeds is even reflected in the supermundane beings who populated his universe. Angra Mainyu was not created as an evil spirit but became evil by choice. Thus the myth of the fallen angels arose, which later became an important Christian doctrine. Even the myths of Eden and original sin find their analogy in Zoroastrian mythology. Zarathustra's universe, like that of the Old Testament, began with a sinless world into which Angra Mainyu was able to intrude when Yima, the mythological Primeval Man, swore a false oath in order to please man (Yasnas 32 and 45). This was followed by the present, post-paradisiac world which contains a mixture of light and darkness, truth and lie. At the end of time it will be supplanted by a third world in which Angra Mainyu will be defeated and evil will again have disappeared.

Zarathustra's way of dealing with the thorny problem of theodicy constituted a stroke of genius: There is a sole God, but He creates two spirits. One of them, by his own volition, turns evil and tempts men to follow him. Those men who succumb do so of their own volition. Man has no predestined fate; he has the choice between good and evil. While the argument has its flaws—why did Angra Mainyu turn evil and why do men follow him?—at least it was a serious attempt to deal with evil without impairing the dignity of an almighty God and of man's will-power.

Zarathustra not only created the concept of the Devil but also concepts of heaven and hell, divine judgment, and resurrection which doubtless had an impact on the late-Judaic and Christian religions. These concepts can be summarized as follows: Immediately after death the souls of the dead must cross the Bridge of the Requiter on which Ahura Mazda executes the judgment. The souls of the righteous are received in the House of the Good Mind (the Good Mind being one of the Amesha Spentas), where they have the beatific vision of Ahura Mazda and of the Spentas, Good Mind and Truth. The followers of the lie, on the other hand, are condemned for all eternity to dwell in the House of the Lie (Yasna 46), an abode of darkness, foul food, cries, and woe (Yasna 31). Yet the souls of the righteous do not remain disembodied forever. At the end of time there will be a divine judgment, in effect a second judgment, following those made on the Bridge of the Requiter. That ultimate judgment will be an ordeal of fire and molten metal (Yasna 51), from which the righteous will triumphantly emerge and enter upon a second existence when all things will be re-created in perfection (Yasna 45).

While Zarathustra envisioned the end of the existing world as the beginning of a new one, he did not describe this "kingdom of God." Obviously wickedness would disappear from the world after the defeat of Angra Mainyu. Although Zarathustra did not elaborate beyond that, it can be inferred from the names of the Amesha Spentas how he envisioned the world to come: in addition to Spenta Mainyu (Holy Spirit), there would be Vohu Mana (Good Mind), Asha Vahista (Truth or Righteousness), Kshathra Vairya (Divine Kingdom), Spenta Amaiti (Rightmindedness or Devotion), Haurvatat (Salvation), and Ameretat (Immortality). The world to come would thus be a kingdom of God in which all men would be of highest righteousness, have a good mind, and devote themselves to truth. As a reward they would be granted immortality.

Thus Zarathustra created a system of divine retribution and ultimate salvation and damnation which deeply influenced the late-Judaic, Christian, and Islamic religions. This system became a living creed for the next twenty-five centuries, obviously because it was based on the conviction that salvation and damnation in the form of equitable divine reward and punishment cannot be ensured in our earthly existence.

Zarathustra's religion was considerably modified during the thousand years in which Zoroastrianism was the national religion of Persia. It appears that immediately after the death of Zarathustra, new Gathas were composed which assigned to the Boundless Immortals a role as precursors of a polytheistic regression of Zoroastrianism.[14] These new Gathas taught the doctrine of the eternal preexistence of the Fravashis ("souls of the righteous"), who as guardian spirits were to help man attain salvation. The Fravashis appear to have continued to play this role in late-Judaic and Christian popular beliefs.

The regression of Zoroastrianism into polytheistic beliefs dates to the Achaemenid period (539–330 B.C.) and especially to Artaxerxes II, who reigned from 404 to 359 B.C. Under this king the worship of the pre-Zarathustrian goddess Anahita and the ancient Persian god Mithra was restored. (Centuries later Mithra emerged as one of the great mystery deities.) Yet even in that period fundamental elements of the original Zoroastrianism seem to have remained intact. The Greek historian Theopompus (born c. 380 B.C.) related that the doctrine of resurrection, which was essential to Zarathustra's belief in divine retribution and ultimate salvation, had long been in existence in Persia.[15]

How Zoroastrianism fared in the Seleucid and Arsacid periods (305 B.C.–A.D. 224) is virtually unknown. The Sassanid era (A.D. 224–651), however, definitely marked a radical reform of Zoroastrianism. The polytheistic intrusions were purged from the original Zoroastrian religion, and its eschatological elements were strengthened. Sassanid eschatology also strengthened the dualistic elements of Zoroastrianism by adding the following mythology: There is an eternal battle being waged between Ahura Mazda, renamed Ormuzd, and Angra Mainyu, renamed Ahriman. In an earlier cosmological period, Ormuzd had created the Fravashis as his auxiliary troops. In the present cosmological period, Ormuzd is being aided by the souls of the righteous and by their Fravashis. In the final battle Saoshyans, a savior figure, will arise and will raise the bodies of all the dead and unite them with their souls. An ordeal of molten metal will purify all men, even the wicked, and a renewed world will dawn, a true kingdom of God, liberated from old age, illness, and death.

It cannot be ascertained whether the apocalyptic fantasies of Sassanid Zoroastrianism and particularly the figure of the savior Saoshyans were based on earlier Zoroastrian traditions or on late-Judaic and Christian apocalypses. But there can be no doubt that the fundamental elements of pre-Sassanid Zoroastrianism exerted a powerful influence on late Judaism and Christianity. The dualistic figure of the Devil, the belief in divine judgment, salvation and damnation after death, bodily resurrection of the righteous at the end of time, and the erection of an eschatological kingdom of God—elements which had been foreign to the Jewish religion prior to the Persian rule over Israel and which slowly intruded into late Judaism—were to a large extent assimilated into the Jewish and Christian religions.

3. GREEK SALVATIONAL BELIEFS

Most medieval, Renaissance, and modern literature describes ancient Greece as the classical pagan country, with a multitude of gods, goddesses, half-gods and demons who eventually had to cede their place to the Christian Trinity. Religious history, however, portrays Greece as a country of mystery cults and doctrines about the immortality of the soul, beliefs which were a major contribution to the shape of the Christian religion.

The part that Greece played in the history of religion was due to the gradual intrusion into her ancient polytheism of new religious concepts based on a dualism substantially different from that of Zoroastrianism.

Whereas Zoroastrian dualism was one between righteous and wicked divinities and men, Greek dualism was one between body and soul. The soul was believed to be immortal. During one's lifetime it was imprisoned in a weak or wicked body, but after death it could be released and ascend into a heavenly world.

The original Greek beliefs about the destiny of the soul after death were similar to those of other ancient peoples. The Greek Hades, like the Mesopotamian and Jewish netherworlds, was a dreary place where every human being landed after death, regardless of merit or demerit. But unlike Sheol, the Jewish netherworld, which was considered to be cut off from God, Hades was an intrinsic part of the universe ruled by the Olympian gods. Hades was not only the netherworld, but was also the name of the god who ruled it.

Early in Greek history, popular fantasy created an Isle of the Blessed (Elysium or the Elysian Fields), a land of perfect bliss where heroes favored by gods were brought without dying. It also created a hell, Tartarus, where the souls of those who had perpetrated particularly heinous crimes were subjected to torments. One should not, however, infer from these myths that the popular Greek religion stood for divine retribution after death as a way to correct injustices which occurred on earth. Both Elysium and Tartarus were reserved for extremely rare cases.[16] The bulk of mankind had to be content with a dreary shadow life in Hades.

Orphism and Pythagoreanism. The belief in the immortality of the soul and its abode after the death of the body in a beyond, according to merit, arose in Orphic and Pythagorean circles outside the popular Greek religion. Orphism originated in Thrace, at the periphery of the Greek world, probably as early as the seventh century B.C. From the outset it seems to have been an orgiastic cult, the germ of a mystery cult, with many followers in the Hellenic world. Although it derived its name from the legendary Orpheus, it was apparently based on the cult of Dionysus. Orphism was never a sharply defined religion; its ideas were not clearly outlined in sacred scriptures and it had no religious organization. Yet references in Greek literature suggest that two doctrines seminal to the evolution of Greek thought should be regarded as a heritage of Orphism. First, the doctrine that man's soul and body are of different origin, the soul being of divine essence, the body being a prison, or a tomb, of the soul.[17] Second, by inference from Plato's account in *Cratylus*, Orphism viewed salvation as the liberation of the soul from its imprisonment in the body, and its ascent after death into a divine realm for those who deserved salvation based on their conduct during life.

Greek literature spoke of an "Orphic life" of virtues as a path toward salvation.

A further element of Orphism, which was important in ancient Greece but did not survive in Christianity, was the belief in rebirth after death. Like Hinduism and Buddhism, Orphism viewed rebirth as an instrument of retribution after death: only through a virtuous life could rebirths into higher forms of life and ultimate salvation be attained. In one of his odes, *Olympian* II, the poet Pindar (c. 520–c. 438 B.C.) depicted the Orphic heaven and hell: the life of the righteous, provided they have gone through three lives without wrongdoing, in the Isles of the Blessed will be free of tears and toil, while the evildoers after death will endure pain "that no eye can look upon." [18] The Orphic belief in rebirth displayed the same kind of pessimistic view about man's destiny on earth as did the Upanishadic and Buddhist doctrines: the path of life is painful, and rebirth is a punishment; only the virtuous can escape rebirth and attain salvation.

The sway that Orphism held over poets and over philosophers of repute can be judged from the writings of Empedocles (c. 490–430 B.C.). As a philosopher, physicist, and biologist he was a rationalist, yet his religious beliefs constituted a fantastic version of the Orphic belief in rebirth. In a poem, fragments of which have survived, Empedocles asserted that whoever has committed wicked acts shall wander "thrice ten thousand seasons, far from the blessed, being born from time to time in all manners of mortal shapes, passing from one to another of the painful paths of life," while the souls of the wise men become gods, "free from man's woes, from destiny and from all harm." [19]

Pythagoreanism may have arisen at the same time as Orphism. Pythagoras (c. 580–c. 500 B.C.) seems to have founded a political-religious society in south Italy, but it is virtually impossible to ascertain which of the philosophical-religious teachings that bear his name can be ascribed to him and which to his school. A contradiction can be seen between the central Pythagorean doctrine of the universe as an orderly, harmonious cosmos, and the dualism of the Pythagorean religion, which was closely related to Orphism. Like Orphics, the Pythagoreans believed in the immortality of the soul as a part of the world-soul, its imprisonment in the body, and its ultimate return to the world-soul. They also believed in rebirth after death in subhuman and human forms until ultimate salvation could be attained. Unlike Orphics, however, the Pythagoreans regarded not only a virtuous life but also the understanding of the cosmos and its forces as paths leading to ultimate salvation in an after-life.

The Orphic-Pythagorean dualism between soul and body gained acceptance in Western civilization in the succeeding centuries. But its triumph was due not to the Orphic and Pythagorean sects themselves, which were lacking in a systematic exposition of their doctrines, but to the spread of idealistic philosophies in Greece since the fourth century B.C. Above all, the victory of the dualism between body and soul was secured when Plato, the greatest philosophical genius of the ancient Western world, adopted the Orphic and Pythagorean doctrines as the basis of an imposing philosophical system.

Plato. Plato's views about man's soul and body and their interrelationship were no less fantastic than those of the Orphic and Pythagorean thinkers. But Plato succeeded in spiritualizing the dualistic concept of soul and body by adapting it to his metaphysical dualism between the eternal, immutable forms and their phenomenal, sensuous, temporal images. His views about the dualism between soul and body and the destinies of man arising from this dualism can be summarized as follows: The human soul is one of the eternal forms, unbegotten and immortal.[20] It existed before it entered a mortal body, and continues to exist after the death of the body: "The soul is in the very likeness of the divine, and immortal, and rational, and uniform, and indissoluble, and unchangeable."[21] However, the soul suffers a fall when it enters a human body. In *Phaedrus*, Plato explained how this fall comes about: Even in its pre-existent form the soul is animated by two forces, one which wants to drive it upward, the other downward to earth.[22] Finally, the downward drive prevails and the soul settles on earth, acquires a body, and becomes man. In Orphic-Pythagorean fashion, Plato regarded the fusion of a soul with a body as a fall, an imprisonment of the soul, an enshrinement in a living tomb, a corruption of a pure form, an infection with the pollution of the flesh.[23]

Plato's contempt for the body was destined to become the model of the Gnostic and Pauline views of the body, which in turn became dominant in Christianity. According to Plato, the body is the evil associate of the soul: "While we are in the body, and while the soul is mixed with the evils of the body, our desire will not be satisfied, and our desire is of the truth."[24] Salvation meant, for Plato, release of the soul from the "foolishness of the body." During our lifetime we can speak of salvation only to the extent that "we have the least possible intercourse or communion with the body and do not suffer the contagion of the bodily nature, but keep ourselves pure until the hour when God Himself is pleased to release us."[25] To attain release from the imprisonment of the soul in the living tomb, man must above all arrive at an understanding of the true realities, the true essence of the soul. The soul, which in its preexistent state had participated in the divine world of forms, must learn again to perceive the higher reality of the divine world. The Platonic doctrine of learning as recollection should be understood in this connection. Plato perceived learning as the recollection (*anamnesia*) of something the soul had known before it entered the body, as "recollection of those things which our soul once saw while following God." [26]

The learning process leading to salvation was not, however, in Plato's view merely an intellectual process. True, he held up the ideal of the "philosopher" not only for the life of the community (as he did in the *Republic*), but also for man's personal life. But by philosopher, Plato meant a man who, having acquired the knowledge of the supreme reality of the absolute good, would be able to dissolve to the highest degree possible for mortal man the attachment of the soul to the body. This could be done by voluntarily avoiding connection with the body as much as possible, by abstaining from sensual pleasures: "The true votaries of philosophy abstain from all fleshly lusts." That, then, is the path toward salvation in our earthly existence: "Philosophy offers them purification and release from evil." [27] Hence the relationship of the philosopher with the supreme reality—which is identical with the absolute good and the absolute beautiful—is not only on an intellectual but also on an emotional plane. It is in effect the relationship of the lover with the beloved object. The philosopher desires the contemplation of the supreme reality. "All desire of the good and of happiness is only the great and subtle power of love." [28]

In spite of his contempt for fleshly lust, Plato did not reject love that desires the earthly good and beautiful. On the contrary, in the *Symposium*, that delightful hymn on love, he showed a deep understanding for the earthly forms of love, between men and women, parents and children: "The union of man and woman is a divine thing, for conception and generation are an immortal principle in the mortal creature." [29] Earthly love, according to Plato, is not ultimate salvation, but salvation it is. What he called the "true love," which the philosopher experiences when he perceives "a nature of wondrous beauty . . . , a nature everlasting . . . beauty absolute," [30] is not something fundamentally different from earthly love, but of a higher rank.

However, in Plato's view, the path to God and to immortality is not solely one of love and rapture, but also of righteousness. He expressed this view in *Theaetetus*, where he defined as the proper means of "flying away" from the earthly ills, as the proper means of salvation, "to become like God as far as this is possible, and to become like Him means to become holy, just and wise . . . and he of us who is the most righteous is of all things most like Him."[31]

Plato knew very well that holiness, righteousness, and wisdom are not always properly rewarded on earth and that wickedness is not always properly punished. The great tragedy of his youth, the trial and execution of his beloved teacher Socrates, must have appeared to him as cruel testimony to the fact that there is no divine retribution on earth. Nonetheless, he firmly believed in the righteousness of God,[32] and his theodicy required divine retribution after death.

Plato's conviction about the righteousness of God and the certainty of divine retribution was primarily due to his faith in the perfect order and harmony of the universe, which he shared with the Pythagoreans and which was rather common in Greece. He tied the doctrine of the perfect order of the universe to the act of creation. "God made the world one whole," he stated in *Timaeus*, "having every part entire, and being therefore perfect."[33] It is this perfect order in Plato's universe that calls for divine retribution. Since divine retribution cannot always materialize in our this-worldly lives, the cosmic order would be disturbed if there were no after-life in which divine retribution could be meted out. For the same reason, Plato held that the existing world is the best of all thinkable worlds. He came to regard the obvious evils in human society as part of the divine scheme. He derived this philosophy of resignation directly from the doctrine of the perfect order of the universe. In a famous passage in the *Laws* he stated: "The ruler of the universe has ordered all things with a view of the excellence and preservation of the whole. . . . This or every other creation is for the sake of the whole, and in order that the life of the whole may be blessed, . . . you are created for the sake of the whole, . . . what is best for you in the universal scheme is also best for you singly."[34]

Plato wrote the *Laws* late in his long life, but he wrote *Phaedo*, his classical dialogue on the immortality of the soul, when he was young and when the execution of Socrates still raged in his mind and cried for revenge. True philosopher that he was, he found revenge in the most unique apotheosis of his martyred teacher. In *Phaedo* he blended his own metaphysical doctrine of the immortality of the soul with an immortal memorial to the death of Socrates. By relating how Socrates faced death, Plato wanted to prove that the true philosopher, even if doomed or unjustly sentenced to death, has no reason to be distressed about his fate, for he knows that a celestial beatitude awaits him. Thus while the doctrines of the immutable, eternal forms and the perfect order of the universe were the metaphysical roots of Plato's belief in the immortality of the soul, his urge for perfect divine justice was its emotional root.

While Plato never wavered in his faith in divine retribution after death and in the divine bliss that awaits the wise and virtuous philosopher, he frequently changed his ideas about the destiny of the soul after the death of the body to which it was attached. In *Phaedo*, Plato expounded no less than three visions of the destiny of the soul after death. He was aware that none of these visions could stand any of the tests he usually applied to his doctrines. He admitted that "a man of sense ought not to assert that the description which I have given of the soul and her mansions is exactly true." [37] Yet his deep emotional urge to speculate about man's destiny after death was obviously stronger than his urge for what he considered scientific truth.

In his first vision of man's after-life, Plato saw the soul of the true philosopher sever its tie with the body and depart "to the invisible world, to the divine and immortal and rational," where it "forever dwells in company with the gods." But those souls which had been polluted and had been "servants of the body," roam around as ghosts between tombs "in payment of the penalty of their former evil way of life . . . until they are imprisoned finally in another body." Plato enumerated a whole range of animals in which the damned souls would be reborn. Only the souls of those who had practiced social virtues, such as temperance and justice, would be reborn as worthy men.[36]

In the same dialogue, however, Plato's vision changed and he expressed a belief in heaven, hell, and purgatory, which much later was to become widely accepted in Christianity. According to that version, the average citizens of the world, "those who have lived neither well nor ill," would dwell in the Acherusian lake, a mythological lake underneath the earth. They would be purified of their evil deeds and, having suffered the penalty of the wrongs they had done to others, would be "absolved and receive the rewards of their good deeds." This then is purgatory. The truly wicked would have to expiate their sins in Tartarus. Plato distinguished two categories of evildoers. There were those who appeared incurable due to the severity of their crimes: "Such are hurled into Tartarus . . . and they never come out." This then is hell. "Those whose crimes were not irremediable were plunged into Tartarus for a year only and afterwards may receive mercy." This then is purgatory again. Heaven, Plato believed, awaits those who have been exemplary in the holiness of their lives. They "go to their pure home which is above . . . and of these, such as have duly purified themselves with philosophy, live henceforth altogether without the body, in mansions fairer still." [37]

In later years, Plato's fantasies about life after death changed again. In *Phaedrus* the souls of all men, save those of the philosophers, were due for correction for ten thousand years until they could return to the place whence they came; the philosophers' souls would find rest at the end of three thousand years.[38] Later still, Plato again changed his views on the destiny of man after death. In *Timaeus* he derived them from the strange cosmology of that dialogue: The stars which God had created as divine and eternal were the dwelling places of the preexistent souls. After the soul had been incorporated in human bodies on earth and had died, that of the man who had lived righteously "is to return and dwell in his native star," while the man who lived ill, "at the second birth he would pass into a woman"(!) and if "he did not desist from evil, he would continually be changed into some brute . . . until by the victory of reason over the irrational [he] returned to the form of his first and better state."[39]

In a last, simplified version of man's destiny after death, Plato distinguished in the *Laws* only between two categories of men: the criminals and the divinely virtuous. He described their lot as follows: "Those who have . . . become . . . criminal sink into Hades and other places in the world below. . . . And whenever the soul has communion with divine virtue and becomes divine, she is carried into another and better place, which is perfect in holiness."[40]

Notwithstanding the lively and variegated fantasies with which Plato embellished his belief in man's destiny after death, one outstanding feature remained memorable to the following generations: the doctrine in which the soul of the "guileless and true philosopher" returned to the beatific existence of its prenatal life. The philosopher, having remembered his former life in the realm of the eternal forms, having recognized the true nature of the universe, having withdrawn from the earthly desires and pleasures, would behold again the absolute good, the absolute beautiful, the supreme reality. Plato thus anticipated the Christian hope for the beatific vision of God after death. The supreme reality which the soul had beheld in its prenatal state would be beheld again by the blessed souls of the pure, virtuous men after their release from the fetters of their bodily existence. In their prenatal existence their souls had already "beheld the beatific vision and were initiated into a mystery which may be truly called most blessed."[41] After their death they will be graced again with the beatific vision of the absolute good, which is God. Then they will find the ultimate salvation.

The vertiginous sweep of Plato's metaphysical and religious imagination, blended with the genius of his intellect and the mystical ideas he inherited from Orphism and the Pythagoreans, never ceased to fascinate the following generations. Its impact can be traced in the evolution of the Hellenistic mystery religions, Gnosticism, late Judaism, and Christianity. Yet Plato never reconciled his concept of the preexisting souls as dwellers in the realm of pure forms with the reality of the imperfect souls in their earthly prisons. The parable of the charioteer with his two horses of different breeds was very poetic, but left this problem of theodicy up in the air. Is not God responsible for the horse of ignoble breed which cannot be controlled by the charioteer and which drives the poor soul into the prison of bodily existence, from which only the few flawless souls can extricate themselves?

Plato must have realized the weakness of his theodicy, at least at the time he wrote the *Timaeus*. For in that late dialogue, he attempted to absolve God of the responsibility for the evil deeds and thoughts of the human race by introducing the myth of the creation of the human soul by different divinities: God did not create the entire universe, but left the creation of the imperfect parts of the human soul to His divine children, that is, to the other gods. For if He had created the entire soul of man, "[the human race] would be on equality with the Gods." In other words, like the gods of ancient Sumeria and Babylon and like Yahweh (Gen. 3:22), the Platonic God wanted man to remain in a state inferior to that of the gods. He therefore undertook only one part of the creation of man, "the part of them worthy of the name immortal, which is called divine and is the guiding principle of those who are willing to follow justice." To the inferior gods He left the work of interweaving the mortal with the immortal, of fashioning men's mortal bodies and furnishing what was still lacking to the human soul, the task of ruling over them, piloting them in the best and wisest manner of which they were able, and averting from them all but self-inflicted evils.[42]

This strange division of labor in the act of creation was an attempt to solve the problem of theodicy by removing from God the responsibility for the existence of evil. For Plato stated that God made all these arrangements in order "that He might be guiltless of future evil in any of them."[43] This device may have given to theodicy a more logical foundation than did the Zoroastrian myth of Ahura Mazda's creation of the spirit Angra Mainyu who turned evil on his own volition, and the late-Judaic, Christian myth of Lucifer as the head of a rebellion of angels. According to Plato, it was not a rebellion of inferior deities that was responsible for the evils of the world, but the conscious decision of the supreme deity to delegate this responsibility to inferior deities. Whether Plato's foundation of theodicy, while more logical, was also more plausible than that of the other myths is yet another question. The fact is that it had a certain appeal: Gnosticism took over Plato's myth of the double creation, although on a different basis than had Plato himself.[44]

The double creation of the human soul did not change the fact that Plato's concept of ultimate salvation could never still the thirst for salvation of "the many." Whether he gave a time limit of one thousand, three thousand, or ten thousand years for their potential ascent to a blessed existence in heaven, the only candidate for ultimate salvation who really counted was the guileless and true philosopher, able to understand the complicated metaphysical structure that Plato had erected and to live a life worthy of this perception. The aristocracy of the spirit which Plato preached as a political goal, as the prerequisite for the perfect state, he also taught as the prerequisite for salvation: Heaven is only for the philosopher.

To still the thirst for salvation, man, in Plato's view, needs both wisdom and love. Both elements played their part in the post-Platonic, Hellenic world, as well as in late Judaism and Christianity. The rationalist wisdom school of salvation was represented by Stoicism, while mystical love and devotion found expression in the mystery religions.

Stoicism. Plato's idealism, dualism, contempt for the body, and his eschatology strengthened the mystical elements of the Greek religion. His concepts also contributed to the growth of the mystery religions and, both directly and through the intermediary of these religions, were important formative elements in the transformation from early to late Judaism and Christianity. Stoicism strengthened the rationalist elements in Hellenic and Roman thinking and became a powerful spiritual and ethical force in the Hellenic and Roman worlds. It eventually helped to shape Christian doctrines.

Stoicism arose in the period when, in the wake of the victories of Alexander the Great, the Hellenic civilization began to spread through the Western world. Although founded by three Greek philosophers— Zeno of Citium (c. 335–c. 263 B.C.), Cleanthes (c. 330–c. 232 B.C.), and Chrysippus (c. 280–c. 206 B.C.)—it became a major spiritual force in the Roman civilization as well, with such prominent representatives as Seneca (c. 4 B.C.–A.D. 65) and the Emperor Marcus Aurelius (A.D. 121–180).

Because Aristotle's philosophy already marked a distinct retreat from Plato's idealism of form and matter, soul and body, it paved the way for Stoicism. In his mature period Aristotle rejected the Platonic doctrine of the transcendental existence of the forms and replaced it with the concept of the substance, which constitutes the individual concrete thing.[45] Stoicism went a step further by establishing a monistic philosophy based on a pantheistic concept of God or the world soul as being reason and matter simultaneously: "Zeus is the reason [*logos*] which pervades the universe, the soul of the world, and . . . all things have life by participating in Him, even stones," stated Chrysippus.[46]

However, Platonism and Stoicism shared an essential concept that, through the influence of Stoicism, became a dominant feature of Western civilization: the doctrine of the perfect order of the universe, of the universe as a cosmos. This Platonic doctrine lay at the core of the Stoics' metaphysical, religious, and ethical doctrines. Cleanthes, in his beautiful *Hymn to Zeus*, invoked Zeus as "Omnipotence, who by Thy just decree controllest all . . . and all things rulest righteously."[47]

Thus law and justice rule the universe and, just as Plato postulated, even the evil in the world does not disturb, but is part of, the prestabilized order and harmony of the universe. The Platonic theodicy also reappeared in the Stoic doctrines. Cleanthes in his *Hymn to Zeus* expressly absolved God from the responsibility for the evil in the world: God's "purpose brings to birth whate'er on land or in the sea is wrought, . . . save what the sinner works infatuate." Yet whatever wicked men in their folly do, although not brought to birth by God, remains within God's world scheme and within His eternal law. Said Cleanthes, "Thou knowest to make crooked straight: Chaos to Thee is order. . . . Then didst harmonise things evil with things good, that there should be one world through all things everlastingly."

This doctrine did not imply, though, that evildoers would escape divine retribution. "Evil things," asserted Chrysippus, "are apportioned according to God's world scheme either for punishment or as part of a dispensation related in some way to the universe as a whole."[48] Divine retribution requires the survival of the soul after death, but the Stoics blended this belief with that in a cosmic cycle, similar to the belief of the Eastern civilizations: The cosmos will be destroyed by fire at the end of the cycle (*ekpyrosis*) and will be rebuilt to run through the next cycle. The rational part of man's soul will survive his death, but the less reason a man possessed, the less will survive until the end of the cosmic cycle. Divine retribution thus means the degree and duration of the survival of the individual soul. Chrysippus thought that only the souls of the wise would survive until the end of the cosmic cycle.

Yet the wise man (*sophos*), according to the Stoics, will find salvation already in his earthly life. By understanding the harmonious order of the universe and by living in conformity with it—which means, by living a rational, virtuous life—the wise man can find salvation. The ideal of the good (*to agathon*) appears to him worthy of striving for. He is indifferent (*adiaphoros*) to everything else, to all earthly treasures and pleasures, even to their extinction and that of life itself.

This then was the Stoic virtue that made such a deep impression on the ancient Western world that it became proverbial: the ideal is to live a life of spiritual peace (*euthymia*) and tranquillity (*ataraxia*). This ideal, however, does not require withdrawal from society but asks man to strive for the highest good that can be found on earth, a good that makes a man independent, free both from struggling for earthly goods and from the affliction of suffering. Thus wisdom meant striving for the highest good. But whereas for Plato the highest good for which the wise man labored was the contemplation of the supreme reality, for Stoicism it meant living in accordance with the law of nature. Stoicism placed into its center the concept of natural law and derived from it the ethical imperative of living in accordance with nature.

The Stoic law of nature had a strong impact on late Judaism and Christianity. But the *logos*, the reason which, according to the Stoics, rules nature, was there interwoven with the traditional concepts of divinity and salvation. The Stoic logos appeared first as "Wisdom" in late-Judaic literature. Wisdom was interpreted as an eternal attribute of God in the Book of Proverbs: "The Lord created [Wisdom] at the beginning of His works . . . long before the earth itself." [49] In effect, in a large part of the Proverbs it was Wisdom-Reason rather than God directly which brought salvation to the wise: "[Wisdom] is a staff of life to all who grasp her, and those who hold her fast are safe" (3:18).

Of those products of the Judaic wisdom literature composed in the Hellenistic era, the apocryphal writings Ecclesiasticus (or the Wisdom of Jesus, Son of Sirach) and the Wisdom of Solomon constituted a synthesis of Stoic philosophy and Judaism. In Ecclesiasticus, as in Proverbs, Wisdom appeared as an attribute of God: "Before time began, [God] created me [Wisdom] and I shall remain forever" (Eccles. 24:9). According to Ecclesiasticus and Proverbs, salvation can be attained by the wise: "The man who attains her [Wisdom] will win recognition; the Lord's blessing rests upon every place she [Wisdom] enters. . . . The Lord loves those who love her" (Eccles. 4:13–14).

Whereas in the Proverbs and Ecclesiasticus, Wisdom was still an attribute of God, in the Wisdom of Solomon, it had become "a pure effluence from the glory of the Almighty" which "can do everything" and "makes all things new" (Wisd. of Sol. 7:25–27). According to that scripture, immortality is ensured in Stoic fashion for those who abide by the laws of nature: "The love of [Wisdom] means the beginning of her laws; to keep her laws is a warrant of immortality, and immortality brings a man near to God." Wisdom ushers in the kingdom of God: "If, therefore, you value your thrones and sceptres, you rulers of the nations, you must honour Wisdom, so that you may reign forever" (Wisd. of Sol. 6:18–19 and 21).

While Wisdom (*Sophia*) became an emanation from God in the Wisdom of Solomon, the Logos became another emanation from God in the philosophy of Philo of Alexandria.[50] Finally, Logos became God's pre-existent Son in the Gospel of John. Wisdom-Logos gradually attained a savior role in Judaic-Christian thought.

4. THE MYSTERY RELIGIONS

No one religion prevailed in the Hellenic world, which blended with Roman civilization after Alexander conquered the vast area from the borders of the Parthian kingdom to those of Rome and Carthage. The old popular Greek religion had not completely died out; in Greece and Ionia proper the sanctuaries of Apollo, Artemis, and Asclepius remained centers of worship. The intellectual strata of society, on the other hand, found their spiritual home in the teachings of the philosophical schools. But gradually mystery religions, originating in Greece and in countries which belonged to the Hellenistic orbit, became popular in the Mediterranean world.

The mystery religions were derived from ancient secret fertility rites which were believed to ensure some kind of salvation to those initiated into them, particularly from cults that believed in dying and resurrected divinities. The deaths of Tammuz, Osiris, and other deities and semi-gods were mourned, and their resurrection was celebrated with jubilation.

The first mystery cults were devoted to Dionysus and Demeter-Persephone. Dionysus was originally a vegetation god of Phrygian-Thracian descent. The rites dedicated to him were initially orgiastic, and survived from ancient to late Roman times (the Bacchanalia in Rome). In those rites Dionysus was probably represented as having been killed and brought back to life.[51] It is difficult to ascertain the salvational substance of the Dionysian rites beyond the belief in the life-renewing symbol of the dying and resurrected deity. One of the myths about Dionysus, however, formed a bridge to the belief in ultimate salvation. According to that myth, Dionysus brought his mother Semele (who had been killed by Zeus's thunder after having given birth to their son, Dionysus) back from the netherworld to Olympus. He also granted this kind of salvation to the faithful initiates of his cult.

The salvational substance of the Demeter-Persephone cult is better known than that of the Dionysus cult. One of the *Homeric Hymns*,[52] the "Hymn to Demeter," relates the myth of Hades's abduction of Demeter's daughter Persephone; of Demeter's search for her daughter; of the drought which Demeter, as goddess of vegetation, imposed upon the earth; and of the final solution of the drama—Persephone was to stay in Hades's netherworld one-third of each year and with Demeter for the rest of the year. Demeter taught her ritual service and mysteries to the kings who administered justice. One passage reads: "Happy the man who . . . has beheld [the mysteries]. The uninitiate . . . never gets any portion of similar benefits, blessings, whatever, once he has perished and passed away under the vaporous darkness." The "Hymn to Demeter" thus implied that the Eleusinian rites, through which the Demeter-Persephone mysteries were celebrated, ensured to the initiates benefits and blessings both during their lifetime and after their death. The initiates would relive the resurrection of Persephone after she had been abducted by Hades into his realm of "vaporous darkness." Although the Eleusinian rites were observed through many centuries and were officially celebrated by the Athenians (including the famous annual procession from Athens to Eleusis immortalized in the Parthenon frieze), they were kept so secretive that to the present time, little is known about them except that they included purifications, initiation rituals, and a state of blessedness.

With the background of Orphism, Pythagoreanism, and Platonic philosophy, mystery religions rapidly spread in the Hellenistic-Roman world, a result of the decline of national life and national-cultural ideals and of the widespread longing for salvation during and after life which could not be fulfilled by the official religions. Aside from the Dionysian and Eleusinian mystery cults, the most popular mysteries centered on the deities Attis-Cybele, Adonis, Isis-Osiris, and Mithra. In these cults it was always the seasonal cycle of vegetation that symbolized the death and resurrection of a deity or a semi-divine figure and on which the initiates based their hope for a blessed life after death.

The cult of Attis, originally a vegetation deity worshipped in Phrygia and other parts of Asia Minor, was closely connected with that of the Great Mother of the gods (Cybele in Greece and Rome). Although the myths about Attis varied, in all of them he castrated himself or was castrated, died, was mourned by the Great Mother of the gods (who in some myths was his lover), and was resurrected. The Attis-Great Mother rites were still observed in Imperial Rome. They often included self-laceration or self-castration and ranged from mourning to jubilation. The Adonis cult, celebrated in Syria and Greece, had a similar origin as the Attis cult. Adonis appears to have originally been a Syrian vegetation deity. In the Greek version Adonis, a beautiful youth loved by Aphrodite and Persephone, was killed by a boar and resurrected.

The Mithra cult was not known prior to the first century B.C., although Mithra was originally a pre-Zoroastrian Indian-Iranian god who acquired prominence in the late-Zoroastrian period. It spread through the Roman Empire in the first century A.D. The nucleus of the cult was Mithra's slaying of a bull, followed by his ascent to heaven in the chariot of the sun god; the bull, obviously a fertility deity, created life on earth through his death, while Mithra's ascent to heaven symbolized a celestial after-life for the initiates.

Significant to all these mystery cults were not only the death-resurrection myths from which the mystery rites were derived, but also the ceremonies connected with them. Although these rites were shrouded in mystery, enough is known to suggest that the nucleus of many rites was a mystic transformation of the initiates. The transformation symbolized an act of salvation through resurrection.

This shroud of mystery was once lifted when the Roman philosopher Lucius Apuleius (A.D. c. 124–c. 170) related his own initiation into the mystery religion of Isis.[53] As both the savior deity who had found and resurrected the mutilated body of Osiris,[54] and as the mother of the god Horus, Isis had become the object of veneration and worship in Egypt and in other regions of the Roman Empire. As described by Apuleius, the Isis rites constituted in effect a savior religion. The initiation was open only to those chosen by the goddess. No one was allowed "to partake of the mysteries, without direct orders from the Goddess herself." The initiate had to commit himself to dedicate his life to the service of the goddess, to obey carefully the ordinances of her religion, and to live a life of perfect chastity. The rites of initiation may have been similar to those in other mystery religions. The novice was washed and sprinkled with holy water, and had to fast for ten days; on the day of initiation he was clothed in a new garment and underwent a mystical experience, which Apuleius described as follows: "I approached the very gates of death . . . yet was permitted to return, rapt through all the elements. . . . I entered the presence of the Gods of the underworld and . . . of the upperworld . . . and worshipped them." When the initiate emerged from the sanctuary, he was wearing twelve different garments, dressed like the sun. The ceremony closed with a sacred breakfast and a banquet.

The new garments symbolized the initiate's belief in the death and resurrection of the deity and of himself. "By [Isis's] grace, [the initiates] are in a sense born again and restored to a new and healthy life," explained the High Priest to Apuleius. In a dream, Isis promised Apuleius not only a life of happiness and fame under her protection, but also a prolongation of his life beyond the limits appointed by destiny, and after the end of life, the ascent to the Elysian fields and the beatific vision of Isis as queen of the netherworld.

It cannot be ascertained whether the initiation rites of the Isis cult and of the other mystery cults were always as strict as those Apuleius related, or whether they demanded from the initiate similar devotion and high moral conduct. Common to all mystery rites, however, was their symbolic nature as the entrance into a blessed existence after death.[55]

The mystery religions exerted a tremendous appeal in the Hellenistic-Roman civilization. They offered personal deities who had suffered and died like human beings and were then resurrected, who seemed close to the common, suffering man and thus could be approached by him with love and devotion. The mystery of death and resurrection—which man experienced in the phenomenon of the seasons and which in ancient civilizations had engendered fertility religions—found in the mystery religions a new, sublime form. Resurrection could be understood by the initiates in two ways: as a new, purified life, a kind of sacred existence, and as a resurrection after life. Thus, salvation could be attained during the initiate's lifetime and, after death, ultimate salvation could be hoped for. The deity of the mystery religion was the savior to whom the initiate owed his salvation.

Can Christianity then, with its belief in Jesus Christ as the Savior, in his death and resurrection, with its initiation rites of baptism, and the consecration of bread and wine, also be regarded as a mystery religion? Indeed, to the average citizen of the Hellenistic-Roman world who lived in the era of Apuleius and Plutarch, Christianity may have appeared as a Judaic mystery religion. Yet closer scrutiny reveals some fundamental differences between Christianity and the mystery religions.

One of the most obvious differences was the exclusive nature of the mystery religions in contrast to the universal character of Christianity. The mystery religions never ceased to be esoteric, and therefore were inaccessible to the common man. His thirst for salvation could not be sated by esoteric mystery religions whose portals of paradise were closed to him.

Some social differences may also have existed among the mystery religions themselves. The Isis cult seems to have been particularly esoteric, accessible only to those whom Isis personally selected (obviously through her priests). In contrast to this aristocratic cult, the Mithra cult appealed to lower social strata, particularly to the Roman soldiers. In many border regions of the Roman Empire, where the Roman legions planted their eagles, Mithra sanctuaries could be found. Uprooted from their homes, often strangers within the empire, facing death any minute, many Roman soldiers saw in Mithra a warrior god who promised them salvation if they were to die in battle. But the Mithra cult, which otherwise came closest of all mystery religions to competing with Christianity, banned women. And because the cult was organized in a strict hierarchy and prescribed severe ordeals for the novices, even the initiation into Mithraism remained beyond the reach of the common man and his yearning for salvation.

Christianity, on the other hand, from its beginnings was a missionary religion. It made the greatest efforts to reveal its mysteries to the ordinary men and women of the Jewish people and, soon after, to the entire Hellenistic-Roman world. Even if Christianity had delivered a message no more profound and appealing to the masses than that of the mystery religions, it might still have triumphed over them. It is, in any case, probable that the resemblance between the spirit of the mystery religions and that of Christianity contributed to the rapid acceptance of Christianity within the confines of the Hellenistic-Roman world.

5. GNOSTICISM

Gnosticism was the last and most fantastic product of Hellenistic religious thought, blended with Persian and Middle Eastern elements. The origin of Gnosticism is approximately contemporaneous with that of Christianity, from which it received powerful impulses. Certain Gnostic systems even claimed to represent Christianity better than the official Christian creed. As a consequence, the Christian Church had to fight Gnostic heresies for many centuries.[56] The influences were, however, mutual: Gnostic thinking was one of the elements that shaped Christian religion.

While the origins of Gnosticism are rather obscure, philosophical-religious ideas of a Gnostic type permeated various parts of the Mediterranean world in the first century A.D. From the second century on they formed the basis of several religious sects. The most important of these communities were the Marcionic and Valentinian sects, against which the Christian Church Fathers waged a spirited battle; the Mandaeans, who to the present time have maintained small communities in Iraq and Iran; and the Manichaeans, whose religion spread throughout virtually the whole ancient world and continued into the Middle Ages.

However variegated the Gnostic systems may have been, they shared certain fundamental concepts which can be traced to Orphism and Platonism on the one hand and to Zoroastrianism on the other. The outstanding Orphic element was the concept of the human body as the prison of the soul or of the soul's higher element, the spirit. The outstanding Platonic element was the division of the deity into both a superior, transmundane God and an inferior deity, the Demiurge. The outstanding Zoroastrian element was the dualism of two cosmic entities, good and evil. Christian Gnosticism, in addition, recognized Christ as a docetic, divine savior figure, instead of the human Jesus of the synoptic Gospels.[57]

The first literary traces of Gnosticism seem to have appeared in the writings of the Jewish philosopher Philo of Alexandria (c. 15 B.C.–A.D. c. 40). His thinking was too deeply rooted in the Jewish religion to counterpose God with a Demiurge responsible for the evil in the world, and to regard the sensible world as fundamentally evil. Yet Philo's God was no longer the personal God of the Old Testament, but was related to Plato's impersonal God who was remote from the sensible world. In effect, Philo's God was the unknown God of the Gnostics. "It is wholly impossible," wrote Philo, "that God according to His essence should be known to any creature."[58] Philo's unknown God acted indirectly on the world, through His mediator *Logos*, the "first-born," "the elder brother of the world." Even the angels of the Old Testament became Logoi, the sun, the moon, and the stars among them. On the other hand, the Gnostic belief in a cosmic evil was foreign to Philo's thinking: he asserted that the Logoi cannot disobey the divine will. Yet his concept of salvation forms a steppingstone to that of Gnosticism: the souls of the wise and virtuous strive to rise again to God, have a vision of God, and after death return to God.

Among the Jewish apocalypses, similar beliefs in the soul's return to God after death can be found. Thus in Enoch's apocalypse, which probably dates from the first half of the second century B.C., the returning soul traverses three heavens, and in the highest heaven the soul sees God's throne and splendor.[59] Some other late-Judaic apocalypses could also be regarded as sources of Gnosticism, such as those in which Satan with his various names played an important role as a dualistic figure. Parallel with apocalyptic beliefs, mystic currents arose in late Judaism that to a large extent centered upon God's throne (*Merkabah*), and thus came close to Gnostic concepts. However, in the mystic speculations of Jewish philosophers—which ran from Philo's Logoi ultimately to the Cabala with its fantastic construction of the *Sephirots* ("Powers," standing between God and the world)—the dualism of Christian and Manichaean Gnosticism was never fully embraced, nor was the monotheism of Deutero-Isaiah ever completely abandoned.[60]

Closer to Gnostic speculations than Judaic apocalypses and Philo's writings was the "Poimandres," the first treatise of the *Corpus Hermeticum*.[61] With its roots in Hellenistic-Egyptian soil, the "Poimandres" assembled some of those fantastic elements which characterized Christian Gnosticism. There was first the dualism between light and darkness: the Light was *Nous* ("Mind") or God the Father (who was called Poimandres in the treatise), whereas the appalling and hateful Darkness was borne downward. The divine Nous brought forth the Demiurge, who in turn fashioned the seven *Archons* ("Governors") of the sensible world, the world of Darkness. This belief in the dual creation of the world was probably derived from Plato's *Timaeus*. But while the Platonic God commissioned his divine "children" expressly to guide the world of man as well as they could, the world which the Gnostic Demiurge created was an abode of darkness and evil. The Nous first created Primal Man who, although he bore the likeness of God, saw in the lower nature the reflection of his own beauty (Narcissus motive) and was drawn downward into the region of the Demiurge. Man, having thus become a blend of mind and body, could find salvation only through *gnosis* ("knowledge"), which for the Gnostics meant a mystic-mythological vision of transmundane and transcendental entities. The knowing man, assisted by Nous, would after death ascend to God and enter the realm of Light through seven zones.

In spite of its similarities to the Gnosticism of the *Corpus Hermeticum*, Christian Gnosticism does not seem to have been directly derived from the Hellenic sources which had inspired "Poimandres," but from the Gnostic elements which appeared in the Letters of the Apostle Paul and in the Gospel of John, which in turn revealed Orphic-Platonic influences.[62] It is this early Christian heritage that the Christian Gnostics transformed into their bizarre dualistic systems.

The greatest Gnostic "heresiarchs" of early Christianity were Marcion and Valentinus. Both were originally Christians who came to Rome from their native provinces around A.D. 130, spread their gospels there, broke with the Church (Marcion was excommunicated), and were attacked in learned treatises by some Church Fathers, but survived these attacks. Marcionite and Valentinian sects continued to exist for centuries and may have ultimately merged with Manichaean Gnosticism and its Christian heirs.

The cosmic dualism of Marcion (A.D. c. 85–159) split the Jewish-Christian God into two deities: the Old Testament's God of justice, as the creator of the sensible world who imposed on man his law (the Torah), a just but loveless law; and the unknown God, the God of love. Salvation meant deliverance from the sensible world of the just but unloving God through the intervention of a savior figure, Christ, Son of the unknown God, sent down by Him to redeem the believers through His blood. Christ's blood, however, was for Marcion a docetic substance because his Christ was not a truly human figure.

The Gnostic constructions of Valentinus (who died after A.D. 160) and his disciples were even more bizarre than those of Marcion.[63] Valentinianism, known through the writings of its Christian adversaries, was based on the belief in two worlds: a heavenly, spiritual, transmundane world, called the *Pleroma* ("Fullness"), and our own sensible world. The Pleroma was filled by thirty Aeons, all of which emanated from each other but ultimately from a Father God.[64] The latest of the divine emanations, *Sophia* ("Wisdom"), however, suffered a fall. Her own progeny were expelled from the Pleroma and produced the Demiurge, who created the sensible world. Man is a blend of substances which he has received from the Demiurge, and of spiritual substances which seeped down from the Pleroma. Christ, an emanation from the Pleroma, came down to earth and entered into a docetic Jesus who died on the cross, but was lifted up by Christ. Spiritual men will be saved by Christ and their spirits will eventually pass into the Pleroma.[65]

Another Gnostic sect, of Jewish origin, the Mandaeans (lit., "Gnostics"), deserves attention for two reasons. First, they have kept aloof from any contacts with Christianity; they claim to have originated in the Jordan area in the first century A.D., and their spiritual mentor is indeed John the Baptist; like him, they recognize baptism as essential for salvation. Second, they have survived through nearly two thousand years as a small, tightly knit sect in Iran and Iraq. Their Gnosticism is based on the strictly dualist cosmology of a Supreme Being and an evil deity. They believe in several savior figures and in the ascent of the knowing, ethical soul to the world of light.

The Gnostic religion, however, that for one thousand years made the strongest impact upon the aging ancient civilizations and the medieval world was Manichaeism. With its roots in Zoroastrianism, it was a missionary and martyr's religion from its beginnings in the third century A.D. until its tragic end in the thirteenth century. Its founder Mani (A.D. 216–c. 276), after his enlightenment, began an intense missionary activity which in the following centuries spread Manichaeism through the Roman, central Asian, and Chinese civilizations. Persecuted by the Zoroastrian priests, Mani died a martyr's death. Indeed, persecutions were the lot of Manichaeans in many lands, culminating in the bloody Crusade against the Cathars in the beginning of the thirteenth century.

Mani must be counted among the religious creators gifted with a rich imagination. Born in Babylon and having spent virtually all his life in Sassanid Persia, he constructed a Gnostic system on the basis of Zoroastrian dualism. He brought dualism to its extreme form by making the Prince of Darkness (the Devil) coeternal and coequal with the Father of Light. He merged this hyper-Zoroastrian dualism with the Orphic-Platonic concept of the human soul as a blend of superior and inferior elements imprisoned in the body. The fight between the realms of Light and Darkness preceded the creation of the world. Primal Man (recalling a Hermetic figure) had been created by the Father of Light to fight against Darkness, but had been defeated and devoured by Darkness so that his soul became a blend of light and darkness. Although Primal Man was rescued by the Living Spirit (another emanation of the Father of Light) and was brought back to the realm of Light, the human souls remain divided between Light and Darkness.

Salvation consists in the liberation of the human soul from the elements of darkness that dwell in it, and it depends on the individual. If man acquires knowledge (in the Gnostic sense) and lives a liberating life of separation from the evil world, a life of asceticism and celibacy, he becomes an Elect. After his death the Just Justice (another emanation of the Father of Light) will grant to his soul the ascent to the Paradise of Light. All the other believers (the Auditors) will have to be reborn after death until they become Elect themselves, whereas the evildoers will land in the realm of Darkness. Ultimately, after the realm of Light has drawn the bulk of humanity into its sphere by way of transformation into the ranks of the Elect, the hour of the final consummation of the world through the holocaust of fire will dawn and the Prince of Darkness will be bound forever in his realm.[66]

Manichaeism survived in the East, particularly in central Asia, for about one thousand years. In the Christian West it appeared in the form of three heretic sects which were derived from each other: the Paulicians, the Bogomils, and the Cathars. In common with the original Christian

Gnostic sects (the Marcionites and the Valentinians), the three sects believed in the savior figure of a docetic Christ, but their dualistic features stemmed from Manichaeism.

Paulicianism originated in the seventh century in Manichaean territory —the Armenian borderland between Sassanid Persia and the Byzantine Empire.[67] The sect was Manichaean in its belief in two Gods: the good God who created man's soul, and the evil God who rules the material world. But it was Christian to the extent that it recognized parts of the New Testament. Its belief in Christ, on the other hand, was docetic. This Gnostic Manichaean-Christian syncretism entered Christian Europe first in Orthodox and then in Roman Catholic areas. The portal was Thracia, where a strong Paulician colony existed. Through contact with this community, a daughter sect, the Bogomils, sprang up in Bulgaria. Founded by the Orthodox priest Bogomil in the tenth century, the Bogomils adhered in the beginning to a moderate Paulicianism. They viewed Satan as a fallen angel who had been the creator and ruler of the human world. Their belief in Christ was docetic. Eventually many Bogomils turned to a radical Paulicianism and considered Satan as an original god of darkness rather than as a fallen angel.

The Bogomils inherited from their Manichaean origin contempt for the sensible world, which induced them to advocate asceticism and celibacy. A consequence of their teachings was the religious class distinction— which Manichaeism had introduced—between the ascetic and celibate "Perfect ones" and the "Faithful ones" who had to obey the Perfect ones. The Bogomils survived until the fifteen century, chiefly in Bosnia and Hercegovina, but they disappeared when the Turks overpowered these countries in the second half of the fifteenth century. Many Bogomils converted to Islam, which still has a strong foothold in the area (now a member state of Yugoslavia).

Through the intermediary of the Bogomils, Christian Manichaeism spread to Western Europe, particularly to two of its economically most advanced regions, northern Italy and southern France. There the new religion appeared as Catharism in the twelfth century and soon became the most powerful competitor to Roman Catholicism prior to Hussitism and the Reformation. But Catharism differed from these two reform movements by virtue of its Gnostic heritage. Like the Bogomils, the Cathars[68] were split into radical dualists for whom Satan was coeternal with God, and into moderate dualists for whom Satan was a fallen angel. Also like the Bogomils, they were Christians insofar as they generally recognized the New Testament—Jesus, however, was recognized only in a docetic form. Comparable to the Manichaeans and the Bogomils, the

Cathars recognized a religious class distinction between the Perfect ones and the simple believers. Cathars believed that salvation lay in cutting those ties that bind men to the sensible world. As the Perfect ones lived pure lives of asceticism and celibacy, they could be saved during their lifetime through a ritual of initiation. For the simple believers who did not follow the ascetic rules of Catharic ethics, salvation was open by initiation on the death bed.

The tragic battle between Catharism and the Catholic Church ended with the collapse of Catharism. During this time southern France was ravaged, the Inquisition was born, and a Crusade, called by Pope Innocent III in 1208, raged for twenty years. Nevertheless, the great Catholic mendicant orders, which were founded at the height of the fight between Catholicism and Catharism—the Franciscans in 1209 and the Dominicans in 1216—vied with the Cathars in their ideals of living, such as celibacy and austere conduct. This diminished the attraction of Catharism for those broad strata of the population who were repelled by the luxury and corruption rife within the Catholic hierarchy.

The impact of Manichaean Gnosticism, in its Paulician, Bogomil, and Cathar versions, was and has remained important.[69] Due to this influence, the Gnostic elements, which had already appeared in the doctrines of the Apostle Paul, were strengthened in Christianity. The Devil became a virtually independent deity, and man became a battlefield between God and Satan. This dualism has not completely disappeared from the Christian world. Manichaeism in various forms has remained a living force.

6. LATE JUDAISM IN THE AGE OF APOCALYPSE

For many centuries the Jewish people resisted the flood of other-worldliness that had poured into the ancient world. From the Indus to the Nile the belief in salvation and damnation after death through divine judgment had become prevalent. Moreover, at the time the Book of Daniel was composed, which marked the turning point from this-worldliness to other-worldliness, the Jews had first been under the domination of Zoroastrian Persia for two hundred years and subsequently under Hellenistic rule—with the influence of Orphism, Platonism, and mystery religions —for somewhat less than two hundred years. But in that long span of time the foundations of the Jewish religion did not substantially change. While Persian influence may be detected in the gradual development of the Jewish angelology, and Greek influence in the gradual evolution of the concepts of "Wisdom" and "Logos," these influences did not profoundly affect the nature of the Jewish religion. The Jewish God, who for the Jews was the sole God of the universe, still meted out rewards and punishment to the living. However, divine retribution gradually did acquire an eschatological character: the Jews increasingly believed that in the coming kingdom of God on earth, the righteous would be rewarded while the evildoers would be destroyed at the end of time.

Yet it was only after the era of the deepest humiliation of the Jewish people, during the reign of Antiochus IV Epiphanes (a Seleucid king who ruled from 175 to 163 B.C.), that a belief in salvation and damnation after death began to spread. By introducing the worship of Zeus into the Temple of Jerusalem (in 167 B.C.), Antiochus struck at the core of the Jewish religion. The Jewish response was twofold: politically, the Maccabean rebellion (in 163 B.C.); and religiously, the Book of Daniel, which introduced into Israel the belief in resurrection after death, an apocalyptic end of the existing world, and the dawn of a new world.

The Book of Daniel. The Book of Daniel, the last canonical Scripture of the Old Testament, opened a flood of apocalyptic literature. Written about 165 B.C., it characterized Jewish writing through three centuries, had a great impact on Christian doctrine, and culminated in an important Christian apocalypse, the Book of Revelation. The apocalypses grew out of the eschatological spirit that had dominated Jewish thought for centuries. As in the earlier eschatological Scriptures, the nucleus of all apocalypses was the prophecy of the day of the Lord, on which the world as it now exists would end and a new world would come into being. The new feature which the apocalypses introduced was their "historical" character: they all pretended to narrate ancient or recent history and to lead history to its finale, the day of the Lord.

The Book of Daniel set the tone. Under the disguise of allegories, it constructed a world of the past, present, and future. The past and present elements were more or less correct, whereas the predictions of the future constituted the apocalyptic character of the Scripture. The minute details, including even a timetable projected into the future, underlined the pseudo-historical character of this apocalyptic vision. Thus the Book of Daniel gave to the new religious visions the same historical perspective that had constituted the unique feature of the Jewish religion. By doing so, it broke the ground for the historical perspective of the late-Judaic and Christian doctrines.

The Book of Daniel was a determining factor in the evolution of these doctrines not only because of its apocalyptic spirit but also because it introduced three new elements into the late-Judaic religion which survived in Christianity: a highly developed angelology, a supernatural savior, and bodily resurrection. These three elements suggested a strong Zoroastrian influence.

As to angelology, the belief in protective guardian angels had appeared prior to the Book of Daniel.[70] What was new in that Scripture was the role angels played in the salvational scheme. The Book of Daniel introduced two angels by name, Gabriel (Dan. 8:15 ff. and 9:21) and Michael (chapters 10 and 12). Gabriel explained to Daniel his own visions. An angel (although unnamed, probably also Gabriel) helped Michael in his fight against the Persians (Dan. 10:13). Michael, referred to as "the great captain," was first involved in this fight and was then revealed as the guardian angel of the Jews "who stands guard over your fellow-country-men." He was obviously conceived of as the savior of the Jewish people in the last, eschatological struggle. He would appear in the critical hour, in "a time of distress, such as has never been since they became a nation till that moment. But at that moment your people will be delivered" (Dan. 12:1).

It was of great significance in the Danielic angelology, which was further developed in later apocalypses, that it removed God from direct contact with man and thus paved the way for Gnostic views of man's relations, or nonrelations, to God. From there it was only one step further to the apocalypse of Enoch, which introduced into Jewish-Christian-Islamic mythology the myth of the fallen angels, a fundamentally Gnostic element.

Michael's role in the eschatological deliverance of the Jewish people constituted the second new element that the Book of Daniel introduced into the Jewish religion: that of the celestial savior on the day of deliverance. The book divided the savior function. In addition to Michael, another supernatural savior emerged who would save or have dominion over all mankind, not only over the Jews. In what the book expressly called a vision, "one like a man"[71] comes with the clouds of heaven and receives from God "sovereignty and glory and kingly power ... so that all peoples and nations of every language should serve him." His will be "an everlasting sovereignty ... and his kingly power such as should never be impaired" (Dan. 7:13–14).[72]

The particular nationalist feature of this apocalypse, which can also be found in other eschatological Scriptures, was the occupation of the throne of the kingdom of God by the Jewish people. "The kingly power, sovereignty, and greatness of all the kingdoms under heaven shall be given to the people of the saints of the Most High. Their kingly power is an everlasting power and all sovereignties shall serve them and obey them" (Dan. 7:27). However, the Book of Daniel merged this traditional Jewish eschatological vision of the "new earth" (Isa. 65:17 and 66:22) under the dominion of a renewed Israel, with the Zoroastrian vision of resurrection after death, in the famous prophecy: "Many of those who sleep in the dust of the earth will wake, some to everlasting life and some to the reproach of eternal abhorrence" (Dan. 12:2). Thus, the third new element that the Book of Daniel introduced into the late-Judaic religion was the belief in resurrection after death. This belief did not yet appear as an article of faith, but as a vision. The book emphasized the esoteric and secret nature of this vision by expressly giving the instruction, "You Daniel, keep the words secret and seal the book till the time of the end" (Dan. 12:4).

Furthermore, resurrection was not supposed to be general, but confined to "many." It appears to have been preceded by a kind of divine judgment: only those will be "delivered" who are "written in the book." They will be resurrected "to everlasting life"; among them "the wise leaders shall shine like the bright vault of heaven, and those who have guided the people in the true path shall be like the stars for ever and ever" (Dan. 12:1 and 3). But while the Book of Daniel was fairly specific about the lot of the resurrected righteous, it was vague about the destiny of the resurrected evildoers. It failed to give any inkling of the nature of the earthly hell of "eternal abhorrence" that would await the evildoers. The fact remains that for the first time, a canonical Scripture of the Old Testament proclaimed the belief in bodily resurrection and an eternal life on earth.

Resurrection versus Immortality. The Book of Daniel apparently understood resurrection as a divine act of re-creation. Many of those who have returned to dust (Gen. 3:19) shall be awakened by the same act of God by which He had created the first man. By this divine act they will become living creatures again, with their bodies and the breath of life restored. In other words, the Book of Daniel did not express the thought that man's soul is immortal while his body sleeps forever in the dust of the earth, but rather set forth the belief that God by a divine act would restore some men to life, obviously at the end of time.

The fact that the Book of Daniel was admitted into the rank of canonical Scriptures suggests that the belief in resurrection must have acquired a high degree of popularity starting with the period of the Maccabees. Significantly one of the two writings which dealt with the Maccabean rebellion, the apocryphal Second Book of the Maccabees, took for granted the belief in resurrection. Furthermore, that book reflected the faith, obviously also popular at that time, in the effectiveness of inter-cessory prayers for the resurrection of the dead.

In the Second Book of the Maccabees, the story was narrated of fallen Jewish warriors who were found to have worn under their tunics amulets sacred to idols; and of Judas Maccabaeus who took up a collection for a sin offering for these men who had committed the sin of apostasy. The author of the book remarked that "if [Judas] had not been expecting the fallen to rise again, it would have been foolish and superfluous to pray for the dead. But since he had in view the wonderful reward reserved for those who die a godly death, his purpose was a holy and pious one. And this was why he offered an atoning sacrifice to free the dead from their sin" (2 Macc. 12:44–45). The spiritual climax of the book was the touching story of the seven brothers who died a martyr's death, each of them inhumanly tortured by King Antiochus Epiphanes IV, and each of them convinced of their eventual resurrection.

Despite the lapse of eighty to a hundred years that may lie between the Book of Daniel and the Second Book of the Maccabees, there was no indication in the latter of a belief in a general resurrection of all human beings after death. The men whose resurrection was expected were either warriors fighting for their liberation from a sacrilegious regime or they were martyrs. They hoped for a "wonderful reward" in their post-resur-rection life, whatever this reward might be. For the evildoers, on the other hand, there seems to have been no prospect either for life in any form, or for hell. This belief prompted one of the martyrs to say to Antio-chus: "There will be no resurrection to life for you" (7:14). If resurrec-tion with its wonderful reward is salvation, to which the martyrs could look forward, damnation is ultimate death, complete annihilation.

Along with the rise of the belief in resurrection based on a monistic conception of human life, came the influence of the Hellenistic civiliza-tion. This influence was reflected, in the Jewish literature, in the develop-ment of a dualistic concept of an antagonism between the good and evil principles in the universe and between body and soul, which culminated in the belief in the immortality of the deserving souls. The Wisdom of Solomon was an outstanding representative of this concept. It attested to the influence on Judaism of the Hellenistic and Persian civilizations. It ac-cepted the Zoroastrian dualism of God and the Devil, and the Platonic dualism of body and soul. Whereas in the Jewish religion God was con-ceived of as a monistic creator and ruler of the world, in the Wisdom of Solomon God was matched by the Devil. Its God was one of light, not darkness; of life, not death. It said expressly: "God did not make death." "It was the Devil's spite that brought death into the world" (Wisd. of

Sol. 1:13 and 2:24). By elevating the Devil to the rank of a cosmic principle, the Wisdom of Solomon transferred the Devil of the classical Jewish religion, who had been an agent of God, into a cosmic antagonist of God. This Zoroastrian-Gnostic belief was shared by the Wisdom of Solomon and a number of Jewish apocalypses.

Moreover, in Platonic fashion the Wisdom of Solomon believed that the soul is preexistent[73] and potentially immortal, whereas the body is perishable and is the prison of the soul. "A perishable body," the author lamented, "weighs down the soul and its frame of clay burdens the mind so full of thoughts" (Wisd. of Sol. 9:15). After death, "[the souls of the just] are at peace . . . they have a sure hope of immortality, and after a little chastisement [purgatory?], they will receive great blessings" (3:2–5). If the salvation of the just soul lies in its immortality, the Wisdom of Solomon does not clarify what will really happen to it after death. The author believed that the just souls "will kindle into flame . . . and will be judges and rulers over the nations of the world, and the Lord shall be their king for ever and ever" (3:7–8), but he did not reveal how that could be possible without bodily resurrection and rebirth. As to the godless men, the author thought that they "have asked death for his company . . . and have wasted away" (1:15–16).

The Wisdom of Solomon, written in Greek, was the literary product of an author who probably lived in Alexandria and was representative of a small Jewish elite. While he shared the Orphic-Platonic belief in the immortality of the soul, there is no reason to assume that that belief acquired much popularity in Israel (although in the history of Christianity it was destined to play an outstanding role). The influence of the Wisdom of Solomon, with its belief in the immortality of the deserving souls, could not match that of the Book of Daniel, with its belief in bodily resurrection.

The Post-Danielic Apocalypses. That the impact of the Book of Daniel on the Jewish people was strong can be inferred from the fact that the Jewish literature of the following centuries was chiefly of an apocalyptic nature. The more desperate the destiny of the Jewish people became in that period—surrounded as they were by the rising Roman Empire, struggling as a Roman colony to maintain their national and religious identity, and finally rising in open rebellion, for which they paid with ultimate defeat—the higher soared the apocalyptic flights. None of these post-Danielic apocalypses was recognized as a canonical Scripture in the Old Testament; only one of them, the Second Book of Ezdras, was accepted as one of the apocrypha. All other Jewish apocalypses have survived only as so-called pseudepigraphic literature.[74] Their influence, nevertheless, seems to have been very great. Not only were such sects as the Qumran community pervaded by apocalyptic visions; not only did that community highly value some pseudepigraphic writings; not only did a large part of the intellectual elite believe in resurrection after death and in the coming of a Messianic king; but it also can be inferred from the Gospels that Messianic hopes, however vague they may have been, were shared by a large segment of the Jewish people.

While the apocalypses differed from each other in essential features, their common feature was their outright eschatological character. They were all founded on the conviction that, mostly after terrible sufferings and conflagrations, there would be an end of the world as it exists today, that this end would be brought about by divine action through direct intervention of God or the intermediary of a human or divine Messiah, and that the triumph of the righteous would be ensured through the establishment of the kingdom of God either on earth or in heaven.

However, the concepts of man's destiny after death varied widely. A deep cleavage continued between the Greek belief in the immortality of the soul and the belief in bodily resurrection after death. Thus the *Book of Jubilees*, one of the first post-Danielic apocalypses (dating to the second century B.C.), expressly asserted that after the death of the righteous, "their bones will rest in the earth and their spirits will have much joy." [75] Regardless of the belief in life after death, however, the classical prophetic faith in the erection of a divine kingdom on earth appeared in some apocalypses, such as the Similitudes of Enoch, the Psalms of Solomon, and the Sibylline Oracles (dating from the second century B.C.).

The salvation dreams continued to contain strictly Jewish-nationalistic features. The Jews retained their belief in being God's chosen people. The Gentile nations might attack Israel, but in the final eschatological battle the Jewish people would be delivered, while the Gentiles would be subjugated (Psalms of Solomon) or simply end up in hell (Assumption of Moses). Yet the universalist spirit of Deutero-Isaiah did not completely vanish. The Similitudes of Enoch and the earliest sections of the Sibilline Oracles prophesied that those Gentiles who would escape destruction would be converted to a belief in God.

As the small Jewish kingdom in the era of the classical prophets was menaced and finally destroyed by hostile powers, the situation even in the era of Jewish independence under Hasmonean rule (142–63 B.C.) was likewise precarious. The Jewish community could not dream of bringing about the triumph of the kingdom of God by any human efforts. The classical prophets and apocalyptic writers were convinced that the founding of the kingdom of God could be expected only by supernatural intervention of an omnipotent God, be it directly or through a Messiah.

It was, however, generally believed that divine intervention would not follow a period of a gradual growth of the kingdom of God but would follow a catastrophe of cosmic dimensions. Apocalyptic literature portrayed the period of transition from the present world order to the world to come as a time of unspeakable woes and combats in which the powers of evil would attempt to prevail against the saving power of God. The Book of Daniel was the model; it abounded in terrifying visions of the anguish that would precede the salvation. Although the Book of Daniel introduced divine figures who would act as God's instruments in the process of salvation, some apocalypses envisioned a human Messiah. This concept seems to have been derived from the myth of the prophet Elijah's ascension to heaven. Elijah was the great pre-classic prophet of the ninth century B.C., who, according to Old Testament tradition, performed powerful miracles and was believed never to have died. Instead, in the midst of his life, he was carried up to heaven by chariots of fire (2 Kings 2:11).

When the belief in savior figures took hold among the Jewish people, the myth of Elijah's ascension to heaven was well suited to this concept. It made its first appearance even prior to the Book of Daniel, in the addition to the Book of Malachi, where God said: "I will send you the prophet Elijah before the great and terrible day of the Lord comes. He will reconcile fathers to sons and sons to fathers" (Mal. 4:5–6). The belief in Elijah's return to earth as a celestial messenger and savior seems to have remained with the Jewish people throughout the apocalyptic era.[76] Some apocalypses continued the concept of a human Messiah, but increased his tasks. Thus the earliest section of the Sibylline Oracles prophesied that a "king from the East" would destroy the attacking pagans and usher in the universal kingdom of peace and prosperity.

Another variant of Messianism appeared in the prophecies of the Qumran community, inhabitants of the Qumran valley in the Dead Sea area from c. 150 B.C. until its destruction in the Jewish War (A.D. 65–70). The Qumran community is today known in connection with the discovery and decipherment, since 1947, of the Dead Sea Scrolls; it seems to have been a branch of the Essenes, a puritanical Jewish sect which was well documented in contemporaneous literature. The Qumran community believed that a leader of their sect, whom they called the Teacher of Righteousness and who apparently had been persecuted by the Hasmonean priesthood, would return to earth and would be followed by two Messiahs, a priestly one and a royal one, who would divide their salvational work.

The Danielic vision of strictly divine savior figures also became the model for some post-Danielic writings. Thus in the Similitudes of Enoch, Daniel's "man coming with the clouds of heaven" reappeared as a preexistent king who played the part of the divine judge for the dead. In the Sibylline Oracles the Messiah, a holy prince, was obviously also conceived of as a supernatural being who would live forever in a kingdom of God on earth.

A conclusion that can be drawn from the variety of Messianic figures in the late-Judaic apocalypses is that, however widespread the Messianic longings might have been at the time Christianity adopted the Messianic belief, the Christian religion did not alter a firmly implanted image of the Messiah, but added a new one to the numerous Messiah figures conceived of in the apocalyptic literature.

It cannot be ascertained whether the Messiah of Jewish apocalypses was linked to the supernatural savior figure that arose in post-Zarathustrian Zoroastrianism. There is, on the other hand, little doubt that another supernatural figure that loomed large in the apocalyptic literature was the dualistic figure of Satan (or Belial or Beliar, as he was commonly called in the apocalypses). Satan broke into the late-Judaic community from the Zoroastrian world, since cosmic dualism had been foreign to Jewish thinking in the classical period. With all the tribulations the Jews had to endure, through all the wickedness that plagued their society, it never occurred to any prophet or poet to ascribe human or social evils, or oppression by foreign powers, to a supernatural cosmic adversary of God.

It was in effect the post-Danielic apocalyptic literature, accompanied by the Hellenizing Wisdom of Solomon, that introduced the Devil as a cosmic dualistic figure into the Judaic religion. His intrusion into Jewish monotheism was the most striking sign of the victory of Zoroastrian cosmic dualism over Deutero-Isaian monotheism in the apocalyptic era. Satan as a cosmic power, the antagonist of God, the creator of evil in the world, the eternal foe of God and the righteous, did not appear in Jewish literature before the last century B.C. It was in that period, probably due to the worsening political situation and the swelling flood of influences from foreign religions, that the Jewish religion began to exhibit outspoken dualistic features.

Of all apocalyptic currents none, it seems, showed a stronger Zoroastrian influence than the teachings of the Qumran community. In its literature, the *Fragments of a Zadokite Work* taught that throughout a period of wickedness Belial, prince of evil spirits, catches the Jews in his nets, and only a righteous remnant would subsist in that era. The *War of the Sons of Light against the Sons of Darkness* proclaimed the existence of two spirits, that of light and that of darkness. In accordance with Zoroastrian beliefs, the Qumran community distinguished two parties of men, the Sons of Light and the Sons of Darkness. In the eschatological war between the two parties, the Sons of Light will triumph and the Sons of Darkness will be destroyed. Significantly for the deeply ingrained nationalistic spirit that prevailed even in the puritan Qumran community, it envisioned that after the victory of the Sons of Light, the community would address God with the following words: "Blessed be the God of Israel who keeps the loyalty of the covenant and constantly evinces salvation to the people whom He redeemed." [77]

Many apocalypses enriched this dualistic theme. The First Book of Enoch introduced into the Jewish religion the myth of the fallen angels. The book traced it to an ancient myth, related in the Book of Genesis, of the "sons of the gods" who had intercourse with the daughters of men; these women bore children who "were the heroes of old, men of renown" (Gen. 6:1–4). The First Book of Enoch asserted that the Flood destroyed the children of these matings, but their spirits kept infecting the earth as the source of every kind of corruption. Beginning with the First Book of Enoch, the myth of the fallen angels has not ceased to enliven the Judaic, Christian, and Islamic demonologies. The ruler of these fallen angels is Satan (also called Belial, Mastema, Samael, or simply the Devil). In the eschatological battle he leads the forces hostile to God and to the righteous, and he will ultimately be destroyed.[78]

The apocalyptic literature reflected a profound evolution in the religious beliefs of the Jews. These new beliefs were destined to become a principal element in the birth of Christianity, but they also remained important to the Jewish religion. While the religious concepts which arose in the era of the apocalypses were still based on the biblical belief in the one, universal God, the literature surrounded Him with a host of angels who entered the human scene as salvational actors (guardian angels). And it contraposed God with the Devil and his host of fiendish spirits who act independently of God. Moreover, the belief in the coming of a Messiah—as liberator of the Jewish people and initiator of the renewal of the world, whose coming will usher in the kingdom of God —became increasingly popular.

Whereas Reform Judaism has replaced the belief in a personal Messiah with the more ancient prophetic hope in the coming of the kingdom of

God without the intervention of Messianic figures,[79] Orthodox Judaism still retains the faith in the coming of a Messiah. Above all, faith in a divine judgment at the end of time, and in ultimate salvation of the righteous and damnation of the evildoers, has remained a heritage of the apocalyptic age.

The Platonic belief in the immortality of the soul had been embraced by the Jews of the Diaspora. At various times it was either rejected in favor of the belief in bodily resurrection on the day of judgment or was blended with that belief, particularly under the influence of the great Jewish philosopher Moses Maimonides (1135–1204), who for centuries remained the leading authority in the interpretation of the Jewish religion. Modern Orthodox Judaism has retained this faith while Reform Judaism has abandoned it. Under the tutelage of the German-Jewish philosopher Moses Mendelssohn (1729–1786), Reform Judaism returned to the Platonic doctrine of the immortality of the soul. Thus the Pittsburgh Platform of Reform Judaism stated: "We reassert the doctrine of Judaism that the soul of man is immortal. . . . We reject as ideas not rooted in Judaism the beliefs both in bodily resurrection and in Gehanna and Eden [Hell and Paradise] as abodes of everlasting punishment or reward." The Guiding Principles of Reform Judaism (adopted in 1937) confirmed the doctrine of the immortality of the soul.

Post-biblical Judaism, with its blend of the original Jewish religion and elements that had filtered down from other Western civilizations, has remained a powerful force of cohesion among the Jewish people. Yet the religious conquest of the Western world was achieved by Christianity, which blended apocalyptic Judaism with the religious currents that had developed and grown within the broad confines of the Roman Empire.

CHAPTER IV

The Birth of Christianity

If in the first half of the first century A.D.,
there existed a great religious creator with
the spiritual power of Buddha or Zarathustra; if he had been intent on expressing the
longing for salvation that pervaded the
Western world through a new religion; and
if this religion was to fit as well as humanly
possible into the atmosphere of the age and
the great religious currents which swept it
from all sides, this creator could have fashioned nothing more adequate than Christianity. Yet history provided mankind with
several religious creators and thinkers whose
teachings merged to form the foundation of
the new religion: Jesus, the great Jewish
eschatological prophet, teacher, and missionary; the Apostle Paul, the keen Jewish-
Hellenic religious philosopher, teacher, and
missionary; and a number of prominent patristic thinkers. Thus Christianity is the creation of Jesus, Paul and the Church Fathers
of the pre-Nicene and post-Nicene periods.

The fact that Christianity was born as a
synthesis of several religious currents does
not diminish its claim to originality; Buddhism would have been unthinkable outside
the religious, philosophical, and ethical evolution through which India had passed before Buddha began his teachings. The spir-

itual world into which Jesus and Paul were born was the world of apocalyptic Judaism, Platonism, the mystery religions, and incipient Gnosticism. That world, subjected more and more to a military world power unable to satisfy from its own resources the spiritual needs of the people under its sway, cried out in anguish for deliverance and salvation. Mankind had no need for an entirely new path to salvation. The hope for salvation lay in synthesizing all those currents which had already flowed through Egypt, the Hellenistic world, Persia, and Israel. Through the new religion a union of the spiritual currents of the time was attained.

1. JESUS THE PROPHET

While Christianity constituted a synthesis of apocalyptic Judaism and other religious currents which characterized the Western world during the lifetime of Jesus, this union was not initiated by Jesus himself. It is even doubtful whether his beliefs were influenced by those of the apocalyptic writers. He certainly shared their belief in the coming of the kingdom of God, but this belief had preceded the age of apocalypse. What can be stated with certainty is that Jesus not only believed in the imminent coming of the kingdom of God, but taught, preached, lived—and died—for this faith; and that through his life and death, he opened a vast chapter in the history of human religions and civilizations.

Although Jesus lived about five centuries later than Buddha and Zarathustra, his life is shrouded in almost as much mystery as their lives. It is true that a literature about his life and teachings began to surface shortly after his death: the Apostle Paul, the oldest literary source, appears to have written his Letters fifteen to thirty years after the death of Jesus. But Paul was actually an outsider to the original Christian community in Jerusalem and to its beliefs; his Letters did not reveal much of Jesus' life and teachings. The Gospel of Mark, which dates from about A.D. 65, was already a product of the process of deifying Jesus, which the Christian community began to undergo immediately after his death. This process was further advanced in the last quarter of the first century when Matthew and Luke wrote their Gospels. They accepted not only the myth of the Virgin birth of Jesus, which had been unknown to Paul and Mark, but raised Jesus into a supernatural sphere to a higher degree than had the Gospel of Mark. It has therefore proved impossible to reconstruct the life and teachings of Jesus, in spite of the efforts of many New Testament scholars. What can only be done is to ascertain what the original Christian community in Jerusalem believed to be true of

Jesus' life and teachings before it was subjected to the influence of Paul's teachings. It is important to follow these leads because the beliefs of that community were one of the fundamental elements of Christianity.

There is good reason to assume that the Gospel of Mark came closer to reflecting the beliefs of the original Christian community than all other sources, with the exception of the Acts of the Apostles. The following account of Jesus' personality and teachings will therefore be based primarily on the Gospel of Mark, with brief references to the other synoptic Gospels.[1] This does not imply that the Gospel of Mark is a dependable source of the facts of Jesus' life and teachings; it is, however, a fairly reliable source of the original Christian community's beliefs about Jesus.

Mark did not pretend to know anything about the ancestry, birth, childhood, and adolescence of Jesus. He did not attempt, as the later synoptic Gospels did, to replace any knowledge of these facts with myths and legends. What he did offer was a clue to the origins of Jesus' religious ideas and to the development of his personality that deserves to be retraced—but with the understanding that these indications may reflect the way Jesus was regarded by the original Christian community, rather than the actual facts.

According to Mark's account, Jesus was baptized by John the Baptist and might even have been a disciple or follower of John (Mark 1:9). In any case, Jesus' meeting with John appeared so important to Mark that his Gospel begins with a brief account of John's personality and teachings. It appears indeed that the ministry of Jesus cannot be thoroughly understood without first grasping John's impact upon him and upon large segments of the Jewish people. Jesus openly acknowledged the debt he owed to John, his teachings, and his ministry. Jesus even seems to have regarded John as the greatest man who ever lived. This confession reflected the deep reverence Jesus must have felt for John (Matt. 11:11).

According to Mark, John was an ascetic who lived in the wilderness (Mark 1:6). He was not, however, a hermit who lived for himself, but a teacher and a missionary intent on helping the people attain salvation, by means of "proclaiming a baptism in token of repentance, for the forgiveness of sins" (Mark 1:4), repentance (*metanoia*) meaning, in the tradition of the great classical Jewish prophets, a thorough change in the direction of life. Moreover, Matthew (though not Mark or Luke) related that John preached the imminent coming of the kingdom of God (Matt. 3:2).

It can be assumed that John, as a Jewish prophet, called for repentance and promised the forgiveness of one's sins as a fruit of repentance in view of an imminent divine judgment. It is, furthermore, plausible to assume, in accordance with all synoptic Gospels, that John prophesied the coming of a Messiah. Matthew's assertion that John, exactly as Jesus after him, prophesied the dawn of the kingdom of God may therefore approach the truth, since a prophet of that era could envision forgiveness of sins as an eschatological event on the threshold of the kingdom of God.

John accompanied his preaching of repentance with the ritual of baptism. This was not surprising since water as a purificatory agent or symbol was a ritual element in many ancient civilizations, including Israel. Thus Isaiah, in his appeal to Israel as the "sinful nation . . . loaded with iniquity," used the ritual of washing as a symbol of repentance: "Wash yourselves and be clean. Put away the evil of your deeds. . . . Cease to do evil and learn to do right" (Isa. 1:4 and 16−17). In a similar vein the Book of Ezekiel's famous prophecy of the "new heart" that God would give to the Jewish people was preceded by an allegory of a kind of baptism: "I will sprinkle clean water over you, and you shall be cleansed from all that defiles you" (Ezek. 36:25). There was, however, a more contemporary source for the ritual of baptism as a purificatory act: the rites of the Qumran community. Every member of that community had to undergo baptism once a year after he had made repentance and had received the blessings of a priest.[2]

It is immaterial to speculate whether John had been a member of the Qumran community, broke with it, and then went his own way. More important is the fundamental difference between his way and that of the Qumran community. Whereas the community was a strictly esoteric group, living a saintly life outside the wider Jewish community for the sake of their own salvation, John was not intent upon saving himself but upon saving the people. Mark asserted that the whole Judaean countryside and the city of Jerusalem were baptized by John and confessed their sins (Mark 1:5). While this may have been an exaggeration, the impact of John's preaching on the Jewish people must have been very strong. Jewish historian Flavius Josephus (A.D. c. 37−c. 100) related that John's execution was due to the fear of King Herodes Antipas's (21 B.C.−A.D. 39) that John's great influence might lead the people to rebel. It was John's way of preaching and teaching, of seeking salvation for the people rather than for himself, that Jesus later followed.

Mark began the story of Jesus with the narration that "Jesus came from Nazareth in Galilee and was baptized in the Jordan by John" (Mark 1:9). There are good reasons to believe this story. When Mark wrote his

Gospel, Jesus' rank was already so elevated by the Christian community that he was considered to have been sinless, that is, not in need of purification by baptism. It is doubtful that Mark would have invented a story that diminished Jesus' rank. By relating the story of the baptism of Jesus, Mark recognized that prior to his baptism, Jesus was still a man needful of purification and of a decisive turn in the direction of his life in order to become worthy of preaching the coming of the kingdom of God.

Matthew, on the other hand, no longer admitted the full humanity of Jesus. He attempted to diminish the impact of Jesus' baptism by asserting that John first refused to baptize Jesus and consented only when the latter told him, "We do well to conform in this way with all that God requires" (Matt. 3:15). Twenty years or so later the Gospel of John omitted the baptism of Jesus entirely: a divine being is not in need of baptism.

Mark's story of John's baptism of Jesus plausibly explains the source from which Jesus drew his inspiration for his own ministry. For Mark related that when Jesus "came up out of the water . . . [he] saw the heavens torn open and the Spirit like a dove descending upon him" (Mark 1:10). The dove is a poetic embellishment, but in the Old Testament the spirit entering into a man was a common way to symbolize the inspiration that drove men to prophecy. Thus Ezekiel, at the beginning of his prophetic mission, saw the heavens opened and the spirit coming into him (Ezek. 1:1 and 2:2).

What Mark dramatically compressed into one great historic moment in the life of Jesus—the descending of the spirit upon him—may actually have been a long-drawn-out and painful process of learning and change. Mark himself symbolized and dramatized this process as a temptation by Satan lasting forty days, which Jesus, driven by the spirit, spent in the wilderness among the wild beasts (Mark 1:12–13). Hence, between baptism and ministry there was a period of "temptation," certainly a testimony of the genuine humanity of the founder of Christianity.[3]

There is a striking analogy among Jesus and other founders of religions with respect to temptation and the beginning of their missions. According to tradition, in the period between Buddha's enlightenment and the beginning of his ministry, he had to fight hard with Mara the Tempter. The difference, significant for the Indian spirit, in Buddha's temptation was that Mara tried to persuade Buddha that his immediate entry into Nirvana would be preferable to teaching, while according to Matthew, the late-Judaic Satan tried to seduce Jesus by promising him "all the kingdoms of the world in their glory" (Matt. 4:8). The symbolism of this story seems to be that Jesus rejected the temptation to become a Messiah of the late-Judaic type who would liberate the Jewish people and gain world dominion. Similarly, Mohammed seems to have been subject to periods of depression before taking up teaching, not to mention Martin Luther with his period of severe depressions, doubts, and despair before beginning his mission.

After having resisted the Tempter, Jesus, like the enlightened Buddha, went into the world, drew disciples to him, preached, and lived the life that his religious commandments required of him. Here the parallel ends. For Buddha, according to tradition, lived a long life, never interrupting his teaching, and was therefore able to found a large community of devoted disciples. But Jesus' ministry was extremely brief, cut short by his tragic death, so that the small community of his disciples underwent a painful struggle to survive the shock of his death.

Mark related that the first act of Jesus' ministry was a prophecy: "The kingdom of God is upon you." The belief in the imminent coming of the kingdom of God was indeed Jesus' fundamental doctrine, though it did not originate with John the Baptist or Jesus. It had been the dream and the vision of many Jewish prophets and apocalyptic writers and had gained an ever-firmer hold on the Jewish people, the more their fortune declined and the darker the fate of their nation appeared. Jesus' overwhelming impact on his disciples and followers sprang from his iron determination, untiring zeal and energy to spread the salvational gospel of the coming kingdom of God; from his ability to draw disciples to himself, to teach them and the people what they must do to enter the kingdom by the narrow gate "that leads to life," and how to avoid the wide gate "that leads to perdition" (Matt. 7:13).

The great classical prophets had essentially the same idea. They preached to the Jews that to enter the kingdom "by the narrow gate," a new and living heart was needed to replace their heart of stone. Thus, a number of Jesus' ethical teachings can be found not only in the writings of the prophets but also in those of later teachers who preceded Jesus. But what distinguished Jesus from the latter was the fact that his teachings formed a whole, an ethical universe so to speak, centered on the belief in the coming of the kingdom of God. Translated into secular terms, this would mean an ethically perfect society.

Jesus' concept of salvation was not an individualistic one, although he spoke in individualistic terms. While he defined under which conditions an individual may be saved or damned, what he really meant was not only the individual salvation, but the "kingdom." This concept distinguished Jesus from Buddha. Buddha was concerned with individual salvation, with escape of the individual from suffering. Buddha had no "kingdom." But Jesus, in accord with the other Jewish prophets and with certain apocalyptical writers, had the vision of a kingdom.

Jesus was both a great prophet and a great teacher. He was not, however, an academic teacher who would lecture on morals which should apply in the existing or in a future society. Instead, his teachings grew out of the conviction that to enter into the kingdom of God, a radical change in man's whole mental and moral structure was indispensable. He did not tire of pointing out that entrance into the kingdom of God requires repentance, an act which, in turn, would secure the forgiveness he considered prerequisite for admission. This concept of forgiveness had been common to Jewish religious thinkers and lawgivers, to Psalmists and prophets and, if Mark can be trusted, also to John the Baptist who was "proclaiming a baptism in token of repentance, for the forgiveness of sins" (Mark 1:4). But it was the thoroughness and consistency of Jesus' teachings that characterized his concept of forgiveness.

Indeed, the close connection between repentance and forgiveness was essential for Jesus. According to Mark, in the first stage of his ministry Jesus already was seated with "many bad characters—tax-gatherers and others," and he responded to scribes who objected to this violation of customary rules of conduct with the words, "I did not come to invite virtuous people, but sinners" (Mark 2:15–17). Luke enriched forever the folklore of world literature and of the graphic arts with his admirable parables of the lost sheep, the lost son, and the Pharisee and the tax-gatherer—the moral of which Jesus expressed in the words, "There will be greater joy in heaven over one sinner who repents than over ninety-nine righteous people who do not need to repent" (Luke 15:47 and 11–32; 18:9–14; 15:7). Joy in heaven about lost sons who return, and grief in heaven about sons who lose themselves, seem always to have been in Jesus' mind, and always with an eschatological view toward the kingdom of God.

However, Jesus was not a philosopher of the Enlightenment who might have thought in terms of stages of development from the existing society to the kingdom of God. With some violence done to modern semantics, Jesus could be called a social revolutionary rather than a social reformer. He did not preach a social gospel if by that term a doctrine of social and moral reform in preparation for a higher form of society is understood. The social gospel appears to be a fruitful modern idea, but it is not contained in Jesus' teachings.[41] His historical vision of the coming of God's kingdom was not that of a society that man would have to prepare and fight for, but that of an entirely new divine creation. In the same way as the world had been created by divine fiat, God will one day say, let my kingdom come, and it will come. That was indeed not only the belief but also the prayer of Jesus: "Thy kingdom come" (Matt. 6:10). Frail, sinful men can neither bring it about nor speed up its coming. Nor did Jesus make any pretense of bringing it about himself. Instead he was intent on preaching and teaching how men must conduct themselves to be able to enter the kingdom once it would come.

Consequently, the rules of conduct that Jesus established were rules for the kingdom, not for any society preceding the kingdom. True, many of his rules had been established by the Law, the various codes of the Pentateuch; and there were also rules that had been preached by prophets and psalmists, or that had appeared in the wisdom literature. But Jesus made it emphatically clear that he had not "come to abolish the Law and the prophets; I did not come to abolish but to complete" (Matt. 5:17). Completing these laws meant for Jesus fitting them into rules applicable to the kingdom of God. This gave Jesus the justification to modify some laws, such as the Sabbath laws, and other legislation, such as divorce.

Even so, many rules of Jesus' ethical code were based in Jewish history. They were above all preached by the classical prophets who fought against social injustice and the "heart of stone." Matthew, in two of the most wonderful passages of the New Testament, the Beatitudes of the Sermon on the Mount and the vision of the last judgment, attempted to sum up Jesus' ethical rules. In the Beatitudes, Jesus was said to have proclaimed that those who would inherit the earth are the sorrowful, those who hunger and thirst to see right prevail, who show mercy, whose hearts are pure, who are the peacemakers, and who have suffered persecution for the cause of right (Matt. 5:3–10). In the vision of the divine judgment, which Matthew ascribed to Jesus on the eve of his passion and death, Jesus said that at the last judgment those would be the sheep at the right hand of the King who gave him food when he was hungry, gave him drink when he was thirsty, took him into their house when he was a stranger, clothed him when he was naked, came to his help when he was ill, and visited him when he was in prison (Matt. 25:34–36).

True, many of Jesus' ethical rules can be found in substance in the teachings and preachings of religious and secular thinkers of other civilizations. Nevertheless, it is one of the saving features of world history that in their Christianized form, these rules have been preserved and preached to all those peoples who adopted Christianity; that numberless hosts of Christian priests, monks, nuns, missionaries, physicians, nurses, and social workers, the St. Martins, the Charles Borromeos, and the Albert Schweitzers, the Quakers and the Salvation Army, have found their inspiration in the rules of humaneness and mercy enunciated by the Gospels. On the other hand, the fact that Jesus' ethical rules were established as conditions for admission into the kingdom of God limits their applicability to only God's kingdom, the perfect society. No human society can claim to be so perfect as to meet all ethical requirements of the kingdom of God. Any ethical code which men may attempt to realize will have to be based on ethics that can fit into a human society, more perfect than the existing one, but still one of human rather than divine standards.

Even if there were societies that seriously attempted to come as close as humanly possible to the realization of Jesus' ethical rules, and could therefore be called "Christian," as human societies they would still differ from that perfect society understood by Jesus as the kingdom of God. In other words, societies founded on Christian ideals are, no less than all other societies, secular rather than eschatological. Since they have not attained perfection, they cannot adopt rules that were conceived for the imminent advent of the kingdom of God. Instead each society must adapt its ethical rules to the existing social, economic, political, and cultural conditions. Then they must attempt to "Christianize" these rules as much and as rapidly as societal conditions can be changed.

In fact, Christian societies were always subject to a process of adaptation. The moral standards and values of societies in which Christianity was the dominant faith have always differed from the ethical code established in the Gospels, and have differed from one another. The need to adapt to changing conditions those ethical rules and standards established in the early Jewish codes or preached by the prophets or Jesus has generally been recognized in practice. Yet resistance to such modifications on the ground that these rules are of a sacrosanct nature has been frequent and has repeatedly produced grave conflicts and misery. Examples of the consequences of such religious piety abound: the resistance of Orthodox Jewish groups to any relaxations in the Sabbath and dietary laws of the Old Testament or of later rabbinical rules; the slow and painful process of adapting Islamic law to modern societal conditions; the insistence of the Christian Church to strictly observe Jesus' views on the indissolubility of the marriage vows.

Steeped in the apocalyptic expectations that were rife among the Jewish people during Jesus' lifetime, and deeply convinced of the imminence of the advent of the kingdom of God, Jesus might have been expected to abound in apocalyptic prophecies. There is, indeed, a chapter in the Gospel of Mark (chapter 13, taken over by Matthew in chapter 24 and by Luke in chapter 21) that follows the pattern of many of the apocalyptic prophecies popular in that period. This prophecy has, however, been recognized by New Testament scholars as an alien element. There is also an intrinsic reason that militates against the authenticity of the Markian apocalypse. The spirit of Jesus' teachings and preachings, as attested by the synoptic Gospels, reveals that while Jesus was preaching the dawn of a perfect society brought about by an eschatological act of God, his thoughts were not of an apocalyptic type. He never—if the Markian apocalypse is recognized as spurious—prophesied the coming of a period of woes, let alone of gigantic fights between the divine and the satanic powers. On the contrary, he warned repeatedly that no one, not even he, could know on what day and in what hour the kingdom of God would appear. The core of Jesus' teachings was in fact to admonish the people to conduct their lives in such a manner as to be prepared at any minute for the advent of the kingdom of God, since no one could know when that would occur. In order to note clearly the distinction between Jesus' concept of the advent of the kingdom of God and that of many apocalyptic writers, Jesus emphasized that no signs would precede its coming: "You cannot tell by observation when the kingdom of God comes" (Luke 17:20).

Jesus appears to have taught that if there should be a period of transition from the present world order to the kingdom of God, it would not be an era of woes but a process of growing, like the seed which a man scatters on the ground, or like the "mustard-seed, which is smaller than any seed in the ground at its sowing. But once sown, it springs up and grows taller than any other plant" (Mark 4:26 and 31–32). Jesus may thus have thought in terms of a ripening process in the hearts of men. It would be logical to infer that he thought of his own ministry and that of his disciples as a part of this process. Yet it would have been alien to his way of thinking to expect that human actions such as his own, could speed up or retard the advent of the kingdom of God.

Seen in this light, Jesus' prophecies were closer to those of the classical prophets than to those of the apocalyptic writers. The same holds true of his vision of the nature of the kingdom of God. He envisioned it as an eschatological realm on earth, just as it had been envisioned by the classical prophets and in the Book of Daniel. Jesus never prophesied that the earth and all its inhabitants would be destroyed before the kingdom of God was established or that, parallel to human life on earth, a kingdom would be established in heaven where the saints would dwell after death. Jesus made it perfectly clear that he expected some of the people whom he addressed to see the kingdom of God come to power in their lifetimes (Mark 9:1). This prophecy was consistent with his fundamental belief that the kingdom of God is "upon us." Even if its advent were delayed for forty or fifty years, some of the younger people to whom Jesus preached would be alive when it arrived.

Moreover, Jesus' daily prayer, "Thy kingdom come," also seems to mean that it would come in the lifetime of the supplicant and would come on earth, as formulated in the Sermon on the Mount: "How blest are those of a gentle spirit; they shall have the earth for their possession." The supplication, "Thy will be done, on earth as in heaven," likewise suggests the interpretation that while the kingdom of God already exists in heaven, God would also establish it on earth (Matt. 5:5 and 6:10). Jesus' belief in the imminence of the advent of the kingdom of God on earth was compatible with a belief in the resurrection of the righteous when the kingdom arrives. The resurrected righteous could share the joys of the kingdom with those virtuous people who would still be alive on that day. After all, some of the apocalypses—beginning with the Book of Daniel, as well as the Pharisees—shared the belief in resurrection on earth as an eschatological event.

It is, however, questionable whether Jesus shared the popular belief in hell as the abode of the evildoers. The Gospels, to be sure, did believe in hell. The Gospel of Mark conjured the devouring worm and the unquenchable fire which would await the evildoers after death (Mark 9:45–48), just as Trito-Isaiah had done (Isa. 66:24). The Gospel of Matthew went even further. Matthew's eschatological king would throw the "goats" "into the eternal fire that is ready for the Devil and his angels" (Matt. 25:41). Luke, however, may have come closer to Jesus' thinking. He wrote about two disasters—the execution of some Galileans by Pilate, and the collapse of a tower that killed eighteen people in Jerusalem—and cited Jesus' remark that the death of these people was not due to their sins, but that "unless you repent, you will all of you come to the same end" (Luke 13:1–5). Jesus' response to the two disasters appears to mean that if a man has undergone repentance, he will be resurrected and enter the kingdom of God; but if he has not done so, his death will be "the end"; no after-life will follow.

It is also questionable whether Jesus envisioned both the admission of the righteous into the kingdom of God and the final death of the unrepenting as the outcome of a divine judgment, as Matthew did in his eschatological vision: of the day when the Son of Man would come in his glory and would separate the sheep from the goats, allowing the sheep to possess the kingdom and condemning the goats to lasting punishment in the eternal fire (Matt. 25:31–46). It may appear more compatible with Jesus' thoughts to regard the kingdom of God as a realm into which the righteous would enter, not so much as a reward for their virtue but because their way of life had prepared them for the kingdom; and that the evildoers must perish, not so much as a divine punishment, but because their way of life had not prepared them for the kingdom. Such thoughts would come close to the Eastern belief in the karma which determines the destiny of man after death without any divine judgment. The language Jesus used to describe the qualifications for entry into the kingdom of God, and the parables he created in this connection often reveal a spirit of karma, of an organic link between the conduct of a man and his capability or incapability to enter the kingdom. "The seed sprouts and grows—how, [the sower] does not know. The ground produces a crop by itself," said Jesus (Mark 4:27–28). Certain character traits, such as children possess, predispose a man to enter the kingdom: "Whoever does not accept the kingdom of God like a child, will never enter it" (Mark 10:15).

The forgiveness of sins could be understood in the same sense, not so much as a divine reward for, but as a consequence of repentance. If a man has changed his way of life, he will be able to enter the kingdom. This concept is entirely different from the Egyptian belief that the good and evil thoughts and deeds of the dead were weighed on a scale, and that a divine judgment was issued on the basis of the weighing procedure. For Jesus salvation was not a mathematical procedure. He was convinced that once a man had acquired the spirit of the kingdom of God, his sins would be forgiven. How different this concept is from the prayers for the dead, the treasure of merits, and the indulgences which have played a major role in Catholic doctrines and practices!

This analysis of Jesus' teachings and preachings would be an incomplete account of his personality and the impact on his disciples and followers unless it also considered the role that, according to the Gospels, his healings played. The Gospel accounts of Jesus' healing activities should be distinguished from the miracle stories, such as Jesus' walking on water and feeding the masses. The miracle stories fit into the concepts of the all-powerful nature of God which were common Jewish beliefs. The accounts of Jesus' healings, on the other hand, should be understood as an integral part of his ministry. Matthew specified some of the diseases Jesus cured: possession by devils, epilepsy, and paralysis (Matt. 4:24). This enumeration, as well as descriptions of various healings which can be found in the Gospels, leave no doubt that Jesus treated and was believed to have cured certain psychosomatic diseases. This kind of therapy was not unknown in Israel or elsewhere in ancient times, and was regarded less as evidence of Messianic powers than as a natural power of inspired men.[5] Because diseases were believed to be caused by evil spirits or the power of personal enemies, it was commonly held that they could be fought by using similar means, such as magic devices; magic exorcism was popular in many countries. There are stories of magic healing also in the Old Testament, but magic was always combined with prayers to God to restore the health of the sick person.[6]

Technically speaking, Jesus' healings were of the same nature as those narrated in the Old Testament. They were considered acts by the grace of God, but at the same time magic practices were used: the sick person touched him or touched his cloak (Mark 3:10; 5:27–29; 6:56); Jesus took hold of the hand of a thanatoid child or used other magic devices (Mark 5:41; 7:32–35; 8:21).

Yet in spite of the analogies, there was a fundamental difference between the healings related in the Old Testament and those accomplished by Jesus. His healings were an integral part of his ministry, not just chance events or success stories designed to establish his credentials as a prophet. Healing the sick was for him in the physical sphere what repentance was in the spiritual one. It was an essential aspect of salvation, brought about by a turning point in the life of a person. For this reason Jesus' healing acts were closely connected with faith in God. Significant in this respect is the story of the woman who had suffered from hemorrhages for twelve years, spent all her money on doctors in vain but was healed when she touched Jesus' cloak, and was told by him: "My daughter, your faith has cured you" (Mark 5:25–34). The symbolism of repentance in the case of healings was often that of exorcism. The resistance to repentance that had to be broken appeared in the form of evil spirits whom Jesus exorcised. In this respect Jesus remained a child of his time: his healing practice was not an anachronism—as exorcism is in our own time.

Thus Jesus' ministry was threefold: teaching, preaching, and healing, as the Gospel of Matthew affirmed (4:23). But everything Jesus did to accomplish his ministry was based on the same theme: You suffering men, suffering from your own sins, imperfections, and diseases, you can be saved if only you have faith in the good tidings, in the message of the coming of the kingdom of God, and if you live and act in accordance with this message. Then your diseases can be cured and your sins can be forgiven. Even though Jesus' disciples had fits of doubts in the efficacy of their master's message and anxiously asked him, "Then who can be saved?", Jesus answered, "For men it is impossible, but not for God; everything is possible for God" (Mark 10:26–27).

Jesus' unswerving trust that God would soon erect His kingdom—the perfect society—had also been expressed by the classical prophets and the apocalyptic writers. It has remained the trust of Christians at all times, as it has been and remained that of the Jews, Muslims, Zoroastrians and—as trust in the eventual perfection of society—the Marxists and other humanist faiths. What characterized Jesus' ministry was the unparalleled intensity and consistency with which he preached, taught, lived, and died for the gospel of the kingdom of God.

2. JESUS THE MESSIAH

However great and unprecedented the personality of Jesus was as the preacher, teacher, and healer of the kingdom of God, he was destined to live on in Christianity as infinitely more exalted: as savior of mankind. This transformation occurred in two stages: Jesus was first elevated to the rank of a Messiah (*Christos*, in Greek), and then to that of a divine being.

The process of the Messianization of Jesus appears to have commenced in Jerusalem very soon after his death, while that of divinization occurred somewhat later outside Jerusalem. Since all accounts of the life of Jesus were composed long after his death, that is, after the process of Messianization had been accomplished and that of divinization had set in, it cannot be ascertained whether anything in Jesus' teachings justifies the assumption—rather widespread among New Testament scholars—that he believed himself to be a Messiah. The answer may depend on a clarification of the term "Messiah." A difference must be noted among: first, the original, literal meaning of the Hebrew word "Messiah" (in English, "anointed"), which applies to all Jewish kings and to their successors in the post-exilic era, the high priests; second, the figurative meaning which grew out of the claims of the Jewish prophets to have received their mission from God; and third, the eschatological meaning it acquired in late-prophetic and apocalyptic writings.

Every Jewish prophet believed that he was inspired by God to bring a message to the people, and that God or God's spirit spoke through him to the people. The phrase, "These are the words of the Lord," as introduction to whatever the prophet himself had to say, was a commonplace since Amos uttered it in every chapter of his prophecies. The missionary visions of Isaiah and Ezekiel are particularly significant for the Messianic claim of the classical prophets. Jeremiah was no less conscious of his God-given mission. He believed that God had consecrated him as prophet to the nations even before he was born (Jer. 1:5).

Although prophets were not physically anointed, they considered themselves as having been figuratively anointed. Thus, God ordered Elijah to anoint Elisha as prophet in his place (1 Kings 19:16). The author of the famous poem, "The year of the Lord's favour," commenced his poem with the words, "The Spirit of the Lord God is upon me because the Lord has anointed me" (Isa. 61:1). Consequently, the prophet Jesus had a perfect right to consider himself figuratively "anointed," that means, to consider himself a Messiah. In that sense Jesus may indeed have made a Messianic claim. And from this point of view, the answer Jesus gave to the chief priests, lawyers, and elders when they asked him by what authority he intervened in the Temple order is the most plausible one: by the same authority by which John the Baptist was allowed to baptize men. That authority, in accordance with prophetic tradition, came from God (Mark 11:28–30).

However, the word "Messiah" had acquired an eschatological meaning long before Jesus. This metamorphosis had begun with the visions of classical prophets and apocalyptic writers about the sprout from the house of David who would be God's instrument for the eschatological liberation and triumph of Israel, or of the kingdom of God in a wider sense. Although some of the prophecies and apocalyptic visions did not always refer to Davidic kings as Messiahs, the Messianic role—whether performed by a man (king or otherwise) or by a supernatural being—was always that of an eschatological liberator of the oppressed people, mostly from a foreign yoke.

Some scholars, such as the German Marxist author Karl Kautsky and more recently S. G. F. Brandon, assumed that Jesus prepared himself to play the role of the eschatological Messiah, the liberator of the Jewish people from foreign domination.[7] Brandon asserted that Jesus' entry into Jerusalem and the cleansing of the Temple were political acts against the sacerdotal aristocracy, which was a tool of the Romans, and that these actions were designed to liberate the Jewish people from foreign rule.

However, the assumption that Jesus equated the kingdom of God with the liberation of the Jewish people from Roman domination implies a narrowing of his ideas about the kingdom of God that would contradict virtually everything the synoptic Gospels communicated about Jesus' teachings and preaching. Many of Jesus' contemporaries probably misunderstood his ministry in this sense. In the story of Jesus in Emmaus the two disciples told the stranger, who later was revealed as the resurrected Jesus, that "we had been hoping that [Jesus] was the man to liberate Israel" (Luke 24:19 and 21). Furthermore, according to the Acts of the Apostles, when the resurrected Jesus appeared to the disciples who reassembled in Jerusalem and admonished them to wait for the "promise made by my Father," they asked him, "Lord, is this the time when you are to establish again the sovereignty of Israel?" (Acts 1:4–6).

The belief in Jesus as a savior-king in the tradition of Jewish post-exilic scriptures was reflected above all in the tradition of his entry into Jerusalem. As Mark told this story, it was obviously modeled after Deutero-Zechariah's vision of the eschatological savior-king who will come to Jerusalem, "his cause won, his victory gained, humble and mounted on an ass" (Zech. 9:9). In Mark's version the crowd that received Jesus did indeed identify his prophecy of the coming kingdom of God with "the coming kingdom of our father David" (Mark 11:10), that is, with the eschatological Messianic Jewish kingdom.

As first narrated by Mark, the most plausible elements of the account of the trial and passion of Jesus point in the same direction: Jesus' message of the advent of the kingdom of God was interpreted as a message of the liberation of the Jewish people from the foreign yoke. According to Mark, Pilate based his verdict on the plainly false charge that Jesus pretended to be the king of the Jews, which to the people must have meant that he was their Messianic savior-king. This charge, according to Roman law and practice, involved the crime of sedition against Roman authority. The inscription of the charge was, in accordance with Roman custom, nailed to the cross on which Jesus was to die. It read: "The king of the Jews" (Mark 15:26).

If Mark's account of the trial and execution of Jesus is correct, and if Luke's assertion in his Gospel and in the Acts of the Apostles is correct that Jesus' own disciples interpreted his message as being the advent of the Davidic kingdom, the real tragedy of Jesus was that his message was not even understood by his own disciples to whom it was addressed. The tragedy of Jesus' life engendered that of his death. If Mark's account of the trial of Jesus can be trusted, the crowd, yearning for the savior-king who would liberate them from the foreign yoke, betrayed him by erroneously acclaiming him as the savior-king. And although Mark's curious story of Barabbas may not appear trustworthy, its symbolic meaning is clear: the crowd preferred the release of Barabbas to that of Jesus since, according to Mark, Barabbas was one of the rebels who had fought the Roman oppressors and committed murder during the uprising, whereas Jesus was regarded only as someone who had pretended to be a savior-king, but had failed (Mark 15:7–15).

The belief that Jesus was a savior-king who would deliver his people from foreign tyranny died with him on the cross. A savior-king who dies the death of a criminal, without having disturbed the foreign authorities that dominate his country, cannot be the Messianic savior of his people. Christianity could never have arisen had not an act of spiritual transformation occurred; an act by which the belief in the savior-king was replaced by the belief in the return of Jesus as God's instrument for the ultimate salvation of mankind—that is, the belief in an eschatological savior.

For this new belief a parallel existed in Jewish tradition: the return to earth of the prophet Elijah, prophesied in the Book of Malachi (4:5–6). The myth of Elijah rising to heaven and his expected return to earth as the messenger of the kingdom of God must have made a deep impression on the Messianic mind of the Jewish people at the time of Jesus. There may even have been a tendency among Jesus' followers to identify him with the risen Elijah (see Mark 8:27–28; 9:9; 9:11–14). Thus the vision of Elijah, who would be resurrected and would carry out the eschatological mission of preparing the kingdom of God, seems to have inhabited the consciousness of Jesus' disciples before and after his death. As Elijah was raised into heaven and would one day be resurrected to fulfill an eschatological mission, so Jesus would be raised into heaven after his death and would be resurrected to fulfill an eschatological mission.

Yet there was still a missing link. Elijah's ascent into heaven in the midst of his life was an ancient myth. The death of Jesus was a recent event. A bridge was necessary between the resurrection of Elijah and the hope for that of Jesus. What convinced Jesus' followers that he too was recalled to life although he had already suffered death were his appearances in Jerusalem (Acts 1:3–9).

There can be no doubt that Jesus' disciples and followers were convinced that he had appeared to them.[8] This fact was credibly attested to by the Apostle Paul. Although Paul told the story of the appearances about twenty years after the event, he stated that most of the more than five hundred brothers to whom Jesus had appeared were still alive at the time of his writing (1 Cor. 15:4–8). There is no reason to disbelieve Paul. He stated that the appearances occurred in three stages with a ripple effect. First Cephas (Peter) experienced the vision of his lost beloved master. He then revealed this to the other disciples. They were likewise gripped by the same vision and told the more than five hundred followers about it, with the same effect. Thus, what may have first appeared as a hallucination—that the master, whom they had already adored as the God-sent Messiah during his lifetime, appeared to his followers after his death—became in their eyes a certainty: God had raised the crucified Jesus up to His throne in heaven.

Hence, the true Easter miracle was what happened to Jesus' followers. Since during his life they had understood his message as that of a late-Judaic Messiah who would deliver his people from foreign domination, his death on the cross dashed this hope and threatened to nullify everything he had taught them about the kingdom of God and the life that must be lived to enter it. The appearances of Jesus convinced them that God had raised the crucified Jesus and thus preserved his role as a messenger of the kingdom of God, ready to return to earth when the eschatological time would arrive, as God's instrument for ushering in His kingdom.

Significantly, the conversion of Jesus' followers—from the belief in Jesus as savior-king to that in Jesus as the risen Messiah who would usher in the kingdom of God—was symbolized in the Acts of the Apostles similar to the way the beginning of Jesus' ministry was symbolized in the synoptic Gospels: by the outpouring of the spirit on his disciples, and by the baptism as a symbol of their repentance and the forgiveness of their sins (Pentecostal experience 2:1–4 and 38).

The original beliefs of the Christian community in Jerusalem about the nature of Jesus can be fairly well reconstructed by focusing on the first two speeches of the Apostle Peter (Acts 2:14–36 and 3:12–16) in which he asserted that Jesus was one of the true prophets whose coming Moses had foretold (3:22–24); and that he was a holy and righteous man, singled out by God through miracles, portents, and signs (2:22). In his first speech Peter also implied that Jesus was a direct descendant of David (2:30). Although the belief in the Davidic descent of Jesus was more fitted to the original belief in Jesus as a savior-king than to the new belief in Jesus as a messenger of God, it has continued to linger in Christian tradition. This is attested to by the Apostle Paul's Letters. In his Letter to the Romans, Paul stated that "on the human level [Jesus] was born of David's stock" (Rom. 1:3). A generation later, when the myth of the Virgin birth was already established, it was blended in a curious way with that of the Davidic descent of Jesus. The birthplace of Jesus was shifted from Nazareth to Bethlehem, the birthplace of David, and a fictitious genealogy was established which made Jesus (through Joseph) a descendant of David, although Joseph was not supposed to have fathered Jesus (see Matt. 1 and 2:1; Luke 1:32, 2:5, 3:23–32).[9]

Peter's second speech introduced into Christianity the belief in the suffering Messiah (Acts 3:18). This was the logical consequence of the fact that Jesus' disciples, having witnessed his passion and his tragic death, at the same time believed that he was the Messiah who had ascended into heaven. Peter interpreted Deutero-Isaiah's poem of the suffering servant of God as the prophecy of a suffering Messiah.

In Peter's speeches the Messianization of Jesus had not yet reached the stage of interpreting the suffering of Jesus as an expiatory act for the sins of mankind. In other words, the Messianic nature of Jesus, in the view of the earliest Christian community, did not consist in expiating the sins of mankind, but in what Peter believed to be a fact, namely, that God had raised Jesus, exalted him at His right hand, and made him both Lord[11] and Messiah (Acts 2:32−36). Jesus' Messianic mission also seems to have been conceived in a similar way as that of the messenger in the Book of Malachi: to prepare the way for God when the day comes. Peter in his second speech described Jesus' mission nearly in the same way as Malachi by saying to the "men of Israel": "The Lord [in this case God] may grant you a time of recovery and send you the Messiah He already appointed, that is, Jesus. He must be received into heaven until the time of universal restoration comes, of which God spoke by His holy prophets" (Acts 3:19−21).

The core of the Messianic belief of the early Christian community was thus *parousia*,[11] the return of the risen Jesus to earth, and the close connection of this event with the coming of the kingdom of God. This was entirely different from the earlier belief (in Jesus' lifetime) that Jesus was the savior-king of Israel. But it was also different from Paul's belief in the preexistent, divine Christ.

The first Gospel, that of Mark, was written many years after the establishment of the Christian community in Jerusalem, and also after Paul's Letters, which were addressed to Christian communities outside Jerusalem. Mark's Gospel, nevertheless, constitutes a bridge between the Jerusalem community and Paul. Mark's Messianic faith was more transcendental than that of the Jerusalem community, but had not yet reached the stage of divinization reflected in Paul's Letters. This transitional character makes Mark's Gospel important for the understanding of the evolution of Christianity.

Mark began his Gospel by presenting Jesus as "son of God." He also asserted that when the spirit descended upon Jesus after his baptism, God's voice from heaven proclaimed him to be His beloved son (Mark 1:1 and 11). But Mark did not yet know the Nativity myth; that is, he had not derived the sonship of Jesus from a physical parentage. To Mark, Jesus appeared to be an adopted son of God. This adoptionist doctrine had been prevalent in the times of the Jewish monarchy when the king was sometimes considered to have been adopted by God as His son, "begotten" by Him on the day of coronation.

Thus, the Gospel of Mark is the oldest source for Jesus' full humanity. It pictured Jesus as a man moved to compassion by human suffering (Mark 1:41 and 6:24) and by the starving crowd (8:2), angered by the obstinacy of the Pharisees (3:5), sighing deeply when the Pharisees expressed their doubts about him (8:12), and above all, in the hour of crisis in Gethsemane, when Jesus had a premonition of his passion and death, overcome by horror and dismay, his heart "ready to break with grief" (14:33–34). In the Christian world Jesus has retained this full human personality.

However, just as Mark went beyond the beliefs of the early Christian community by elevating Jesus to the rank of an adoptive son of God, he also went beyond Peter's designation of Jesus as the suffering Messiah. He did so by adopting Deutero-Isaiah's concept of the suffering servant of God upon whom "the Lord laid . . . the guilt of us all" (Isa. 53:6). Jesus, declared Mark, came "to give up his life as a ransom for many" (Mark 10:45).

From there to the concept of Christ as the expiatory redeemer of sinful mankind was only an additional but decisive step. Although Mark did not take this step, he endowed Jesus with certain superhuman traits. In his Gospel, Jesus performed miracles that go beyond a healer's powers. Moreover, Jesus' parousia was prophesied in the Markian apocalypse in terms reminiscent of the Book of Daniel: the son of man coming in the clouds with great power and glory, sending out the angels, gathering his chosen from the farthest bounds of the earth to the farthest bounds of heaven (Mark 13:26–27).

The Gospel of Mark is an invaluable document, not only as the oldest account of the ministry of the prophet and teacher Jesus, but also as a link between the belief in Jesus as a Jewish savior-king or messenger of God with the belief in Jesus as a reincarnated deity. By retaining Jesus' human qualities, even though as an adoptive son of God, and at the same time by elevating him to the rank of the Messiah who would come in the clouds of heaven to usher in the kingdom of God, the Gospel of Mark succeeded in depicting Jesus as a great, passionate, and revolutionary prophet. Mark's vision of Jesus as the Messiah was, even in his lifetime, supplanted by Paul's belief in Jesus as the preexistent, dying, and risen man-God. But Mark's story of Jesus as the impassioned preacher of the imminent coming of the kingdom of God has remained engraved in the memory of mankind.

In the end neither the Messianism of the original Christian community nor that of the Gospel of Mark prevailed. Yet however ephemeral these beliefs were and however ephemeral was the life span of the community of Jerusalem (it survived just one generation from the death of Jesus until the Jewish War), its profound faith in Jesus as the Messiah and its fervent missionary zeal laid the foundations for the triumph of Christianity. Just as Buddhism could not have become a world religion without the missionary spirit of Buddha's first disciples, so Christianity could not have evolved as a world religion without the missionary spirit of the original Christian community in Jerusalem. In both cases it was a message of salvation for which mankind yearned.

The missionary tradition of Jesus' disciples was grounded in a spirit comparable to that of the classical Jewish prophets and of the two latest Jewish prophets, John the Baptist and Jesus. While in the case of Jesus the symbol of the spirit was a dove (Mark 1 : 10), in the case of his disciples it was "tongues like flames of fire" (Acts 2 : 3). Both symbols were fitting for missionaries: the fast-flying dove which transmits the message, and the tongues through which the fiery message is taught and preached.

There was, however, a new feature in the pentecostal miracle of the tongues of fire. It was not one prophet who received the spirit and spread its message, but a great number (120 according to Acts 1 : 15). Peter aptly referred to the prophecy of the post-exilic prophet Joel (Acts 2 : 16), who had envisioned the age to come as a time in which the spirit would be poured out on all mankind, not only on the sons and daughters, the old men and the young men, but "even on the slaves and slave-girls" (Joel 2 : 28 – 29). The first Christians understood their mission in the same democratic spirit. It should reach not only their sons and daughters but also the slaves and slave-girls. This democratic spirit was the real pentecostal miracle that was to conquer the world. It is only fitting that the Christian Church has bestowed on Pentecost nearly the same rank as is bestowed on Easter, the feast of Jesus' ascent into heaven. That the story of Jesus became the font of hope for salvation for millions and millions of men and women was due to the missionary spirit of his disciples.

3. JESUS CHRIST THE LORD

The early Christians merged two late-Judaic Messianic figures in their visions of Jesus as the savior of suffering mankind: the prophet Elijah, whom God would send back from heaven to earth to usher in the kingdom of God (Mal. 4 : 5); and the son of man coming with the clouds of heaven, to whom sovereignty, glory and kingly power were given (Dan. 7 : 13 – 14). Yet ultimately it was neither Jesus as a new Elijah who would reconcile fathers to sons and sons to fathers, nor Jesus as a new Messiah to whom sovereignty, glory, and kingly power were given, but rather

Jesus Christ as the preexistent Lord, who ultimately emerged in Christianity as the Savior. And it was not in Jerusalem, the cradle of the original Christian community, but in the Jewish Diaspora that the belief in Jesus Christ as the preexistent Lord took hold. The foundations of Christianity, as we know it today, were in fact laid by the Apostle Paul of Tarsus in the Roman province Cilicia in Asia Minor.

Paul represented an ideal synthesis of late Judaism and the cosmopolitan Hellenism which had developed in the post-Alexandrian kingdoms (but which basically was a product of the Hellenistic civilization, dominated by Orphism, Platonism, mystery religions, and an emergent Gnosticism). In his Letters, Paul never referred to his Hellenistic background. Instead, he presented himself as a Jew of Pharisaic background who, like many other Jews, had been converted or, in his own case, had converted himself to Christianity (Phil. 3:5). When as a missionary he addressed himself to Jewish Diaspora communities or to Christian communities that had frequently originated in Jewish Diaspora groups, Paul emphasized his Jewish background. Actually, he belonged to that Jewish Diaspora group whose thinking was a blend of Judaism and Hellenism. Paul called himself "a Hebrew born and bred," and emphasized his "legal rectitude" as a Jew during his pre-Christian life (Phil. 3:6 and Gal. 1:13). But he was in fact culturally and literally bilingual: in Jerusalem, he addressed the crowd in Hebrew (Acts 21:40), but all his Letters were written in a stylistically cultivated Greek. The religion he shaped might also be called bilingual.

The Messiah was a late-Judaic figure, whether as the savior-king who would defeat Israel's enemies and establish the kingdom of God, or as a superhuman savior. The Jewish prophet Jesus, who preached the imminent coming of the kingdom of God and who lived and died a martyr's death for this vision, was not a credible savior to Gentiles, who were familiar with dying and risen gods, but not with crucified and risen prophets. Yet Paul was the Apostle to the Gentiles (though many of his followers may have been Jews or former Jews). While he may have known very little of the person and teachings of Jesus, this knowledge was not of central importance to him. For Paul it was not the life of Jesus that made him worthy of being exalted into heaven, but Jesus' death or, more precisely, his crucifixion. Thus in his Second Letter to the Corinthians, Paul stated that "worldly standards have ceased to count in our estimate of any man; even if once they counted in our understanding of Christ, they do so now no longer" (2 Cor. 5:16).

Because Paul regarded the crucifixion of Jesus as similar in nature to the violent deaths of gods of mystery religions, Jewish and Hellenistic beliefs came to be intimately fused in his concepts. For Paul, Jesus was the Paschal lamb: "Our Passover has begun; the sacrifice is offered— Christ himself" (1 Cor. 5:7). Thus the death of Jesus was an expiatory sacrifice: "Christ died for our sins" (1 Cor. 15:3). It is not clear whether this passage refers to the Deutero-Isaic figure of the suffering servant of God or whether Paul's belief in the expiatory death of Jesus was derived from the mystery religions. For Paul stated that "God put forward [Jesus] as an expiation by his blood" (Rom. 3:25). Thus it is Jesus' blood that unites the believers with him in the sacred communion—a meal similar to that in mystery religions, through which the believers fused with the deity and participated in his eternal life.

Indeed this was Paul's interpretation of the Christian communion meal, the Eucharist. Although his interpretation is the oldest source for this central rite of the Christian religion (1 Cor. 10:16 and 11:23–26), the rite itself must have preceded Paul's ministry because he referred to it as an existing institution (1 Cor. 11:20). New Testament scholars concur that the rite of the communion meal originated in the early Christian community in Jerusalem, where it was a solemn ritual way of remembering Jesus. For Paul, however, it was a mystic ritual through which the believers enter into communion with Christ. Although Paul still interpreted the communion meal as "a memorial" to Jesus, he gave it an entirely new meaning: the bread that is eaten on this occasion is Jesus' body, the cup that is drunk is his blood. By eating the bread and drinking from the cup, the participants enter into communion with Jesus. Although there is no reason to assume that Paul meant a physical consumption of Jesus' body and blood, his interpretation of the communion meal was closely related to the rituals of the mystery religions.

Paul's interpretation of the communion meal was not the only symbol he created of the new conception of Christianity. His concept of baptism was founded on a similar symbolism. It was imbued with the same idea of fusion with the dying and resurrected Christ. Like the Eucharist, the rite of baptism originated in the early Christian community in Jerusalem (Acts 2:38). Yet while for that community baptism seems to have had the same symbolic meaning as for John the Baptist—namely, the purification preparatory to and symbolizing repentance—for Paul this rite meant baptism "into [Christ's] death. . . . By baptism we were buried with him and lay dead in order that, as Christ was raised from the dead in the splendour of the Father, so also we might set our feet upon the new path of life" (Rom. 6:3, 4). Numerous other passages in Paul's Letters confirm that in his view, the new path of life followed by those who "were baptized into union with Jesus Christ" (Rom. 6:3) has a salvational meaning. For according to Paul salvation begins with baptism into the death of the Savior. Thus through the communion with Jesus, which the Christian enters by way of the mysteries of baptism and the Eucharist, he will regard himself "as dead to sin and alive to God" (Rom. 6:11). He can find salvation already in this life although he must still wait for the ultimate salvation, the eternal life with God and Jesus Christ.

To be sure, Paul never denied the humanity of Jesus and never adhered to the docetic belief that Jesus' humanity was only an appearance. "On the human level [Jesus] was born of David's stock" (Rom. 1:3). About the nature of Jesus on the level of the spirit, however, Paul vacillated between an adoptionist Christology and one that came close to the concepts of mystery religions. In the Letter to the Romans, Paul's Christology could be regarded as adoptionist: "On the level of the spirit—the Holy Spirit—he was declared Son of God by a mighty act in that he rose from the dead" (Rom. 1:4). In this passage Paul implied God's adoption of Jesus. This concept clashed, however, with another in which Jesus was elevated to the rank of a divine, preexistent being. In the Letter to the Colossians, Paul did not write of the kingdom of God but of "the kingdom of His dear Son," and he called Jesus Christ "the image of the invisible God, born before all created things." Moreover, Paul presented Christ not only as the first-born of all creation, but "in him everything in heaven and earth was created" (Col. 1:14–17). In the Letter, Paul came even closer to concepts common in Gnostic writings, by making Christ a participant in the *pleroma* ("fullness") of God: "In him dwelleth all the fullness of the Godhead bodily" (Col. 2:9; similarly, Col. 1:19). Thus in Paul's view, Christ, although himself created by God, was fashioned as a co-creator of the universe. Preexistent before anything else was created, Christ existed through all the aeons that had passed since the creation of the world, participating in the fullness of God—in other words, a God himself.

True, the Letter to the Colossians has not been generally recognized as genuine by New Testament scholars. But in his First Letter to the Corinthians (about the authenticity of which there is no doubt), Paul also maintained that "there is one Lord, Jesus Christ, through whom all things came to be, and we through him" (1 Cor. 8:6). In the Letter to the Philippians, also undoubtedly authentic, Paul asserted that "the divine nature was [Christ's] from the first" (Phil 2:6). More specifically about the divine nature of Christ, the First Letter called him "the power [in Greek, *dynamis*] of God and the wisdom [*sophia*] of God" (1 Cor.

1:14). These concepts come very close to those of Philo of Alexandria and the Wisdom of Solomon, with their hypostasization of God as Logos and Wisdom.

If, however, Christ is of divine nature, how and why did he become a man? In Paul's Letter to the Philippians, an attempt was made to explain the mystery of the incarnation of a godlike being in a man who walks on earth. God had a definite purpose in mind with the incarnation of Christ: the redemption of sinful mankind. The redeemer was to be divine but at the same time a humble man. For that reason Christ, although divine, "did not snatch at equality with God, [but] made himself nothing, assuming the nature of a slave. Bearing the human likeness . . . he humbled himself, and in obedience accepted even death—death on a cross" (Phil. 2:6–8).

Paul's Christ, after having humbled himself like a slave, was exalted by God to a rank that God alone had, not only in the Old Testament but also in the original Christian community. Paul used even the symbolism of the Old Testament in order to clarify the elevation of Christ to the rank of a deity who commands worship. While in the Old Testament God exclaimed, "To Me every knee shall bend and by Me every tongue shall swear" (Isa. 45:23), Paul exclaimed that "at the name of Jesus every knee should bow—in heaven, on earth, and in the depths— and every tongue confess, 'Jesus Christ is Lord'" (Phil. 2:10–11).

Thus, Paul's Christ was a godlike, preexistent being who from his timeless existence moved into history for a brief moment, incarnated as a man in order to redeem mankind; by the supreme sacrifice of his life as man, Jesus was to reconcile mankind, which had rebelled against its creator, with God. This divine being, after having fulfilled his earthly mission, returned into God's realm. But he left behind on earth a mankind no longer doomed to rebellion against God and to perdition, but one which had acquired the potential to find the way to reconcile itself with God and the way to ultimate salvation.

Paul's doctrine of the preexistent Lord—who through his earthly suffering, his sacrificial death, and his resurrection became the Savior— was akin to the mystery religions. But Paul also believed in a cosmic dualism, traceable to Zarathustra, that played a great role in some apocalypses and was closely akin to Gnosticism. According to Paul, his age was an age of wickedness, dominated and subjugated by supernatural evil powers which appeared under various names, such as "the elemental spirits of the universe" to which men are slaves (Gal. 1:4, 4:3 and 4:8–9), "the powers that rule the world" (1 Cor. 2:8), and "the God of this passing age" who has blinded the unbelieving minds (2 Cor. 4:4).

These sinister powers were, in Paul's view, the antagonists not only of God, but also of Christ, since the powers that ruled the world crucified him (I Cor. 2:8). But in the end they will be destroyed by Christ. Paul did not personify the demonic powers in a satanic figure. But whether anonymous or personified as Satan, it was the Gnostic "god of this passing age," the Devil, whom Paul introduced into Christianity. The Devil was destined to play a leading role as the antagonist of God, as the evil power who contends with God for man's soul, and as the evil power that resides in all men.

However, the advent of Jesus cleared the path toward salvation for man. God "rescued us from the domain of darkness and brought us away into the kingdom of His dear Son" (Col. 1:13). Those who through the sacraments of baptism and the Eucharist have already fused with the light and the glory which is Jesus Christ are no longer in the grip of the supernatural evil powers which dominate this evil age. The believers are already on the path toward salvation.

Yet this first stage of salvation is still painful: "We, to whom the Spirit is given as first fruits of the harvest to come, are groaning inwardly while we wait for God to make us His sons and set our whole body free. For we have been saved, though only in hope" (Rom. 8:22–23). In other words, the message of Christ is not the ultimate triumph over the evil powers of this age. For that we must wait until the coming of Christ, the parousia. Then the great eschatological battle between the powers of God and those of evil will begin as it was prophesied by Zoroastrianism and Jewish apocalypses. But on the side of the believers the battle will be conducted by Christ. When Christ comes, "he is destined to reign until God has put all enemies under his feet," until Christ has abolished "every kind of domination, authority and power" (I Cor. 15:24–25).

"Then comes the end" (I Cor. 15:24), the end of this world, of this evil age, but also the end of the reign of Christ. For, in Paul's view Christ is not a God in the sense of the Nicene creed, whose reign will never end. Instead, Christ's relationship to God is strictly one of subordination. Paul, rather than Arianism, must be considered the founder of subordinationism: "You belong to Christ; and Christ belongs to God" (I Cor. 3:23). Christ, although divine, remains the messenger of God, charged with a mission. Once that mission is fulfilled, once the supernatural antagonists of God are destroyed, "[Christ] delivers up the kingdom to God the father. . . . When all things are thus subject to [the Son], then the Son himself will also be made subordinate to God who made all things subject to [God], and thus God will be all in all" (I Cor. 15:24 and 28).

Thus, in his innermost soul Paul remained the "Hebrew born and bred" (Phil. 3:5). If belief in the sole God, in His glory, majesty, and omnipotence characterized the Jews, Paul remained a Jew in the same sense as the first Christians remained Jews. True, for every believing Jew, the unique God to whom he daily confessed could have no son, because "the Lord is our God, one Lord" (Deut. 6:4). But it is no less true that Daniel's man coming with the clouds of heaven (Dan. 7:13) was of divine stuff, and this held true even more for some apocalyptic Messiahs. Thus for the Christian community in Jerusalem the elevation of the risen Christ as a preexistent son of God may not have sounded so heretical as it was bound to appear to more orthodox Jews, particularly in view of Paul's belief that Christ's mission on earth after his parousia would be temporary and limited, after which God would be all in all.

The Zoroastrian and Gnostic influences which characterized Paul's vision of the eschatological battle between God and the supernatural evil powers were blended with a doctrine of original sin. Paul obviously derived this doctrine from the Orphic-Platonic dualism between the immortal part of the human soul and its mortal part which, united with the body, is the source of all evil. He made the same distinction as Plato between the two parts of the soul. The terminology he used to distinguish between them can hardly be rendered in English. In the original Greek text he distinguished them as *pneuma* ("spirit") and *psyche* ("soul"). He called the man whose soul is purified by the spirit, *pneumatikos* ("a man gifted with the spirit"), and the man whose soul is unpurified, *psychikos* ("an unspiritual man," 1 Cor. 2:14–15). He went even further by differentiating between a *soma psychikon* ("animal body") and a *soma pneumatikon* ("spiritual body," 1 Cor. 15:44). Thus, it is not the body that is sinful, but the psyche which is united with the body. Yet Paul did not always draw so fine a distinction between two parts of the soul; he made man as a whole sinful. In his Letter to the Romans he made the confession: "I am carnal, sold under sin" (Rom. 7:14).

In any case, and in whatever semantic style, man is inescapably under the bondage of sin, "sold under sin." This doctrine of original sin is Paul's personal contribution to the Christian religion. It was alien to Jewish tradition, as can be seen in the Old Testament Scriptures which distinguished between righteous and wicked men, rather than between good and evil parts of the human soul. Jesus, fundamentally a Jewish thinker, based his message on the same distinction between the righteous and the evildoers. One has only to remember the answer he gave to the scribes who reproached him for eating with sinners: "I did not come to invite virtuous people but sinners" (Mark 2:17).

In spite of the Orphic-Platonic origin of his doctrine of original sin,

Paul attempted to give it the appearance of Jewish origin—the myth of the sin committed by Adam and Eve. He went even further by connecting Adam's sin with death as man's fate: "It was through one man that sin entered the world, and through sin death" (Rom. 5 : 12). Hence sin and death became the heritage of all mankind. Although Paul was convinced of the inescapable sinfulness of man and therefore convinced that moral perfection was an unattainable goal, he imposed upon himself, and upon man generally, the duty to strive toward moral perfection: "I have not yet reached perfection, but I press on. . . . Forgetting what is behind me, and reaching out for that which lies ahead, I press towards the goal" (Phil. 3 : 12–14).

The practical consequences Paul drew from this moral goal were not very remote from the ascetic ideals of the Eastern religions: to strive for withdrawal from all sensual pleasures, which he attributed to man's "lower nature." "That nature sets its desires against the Spirit." Hence he admonished the believers: "If you are guided by the Spirit, you will not fulfil the desires of your lower nature" (Gal. 5 : 16–17). These ethics were derived from Paul's Platonic-Gnostic views of the psyche (as distinct from the spirit) and of the body (with which the psyche is united) as fundamentally evil. The belief that passions and desires of man's lower nature should be suppressed was to become predominant in Christendom based on Paul's authority.[12]

Since in Paul's view man is subject to original sin, man's efforts, however hard he may strive, can never suffice for obtaining salvation. Nevertheless, there can be salvation because the path toward it has been opened through the expiatory death of God's son: "As the issue of one misdeed was condemnation for all men, so the issue of one just act [the event of Jesus] is acquittal and life for all men" (Rom. 5 : 18). It is in this context that Paul's doctrine of grace should be understood. He expounded it systematically in his Letter to the Romans, the most profound document of his religious philosophy. According to this doctrine, man cannot be saved by his own efforts, but only by the grace of God and Christ, poured out on man as a gift (Rom. 5 : 15). Through the redemption that the expiatory death of Jesus has brought to mankind, all those are justified who have faith in him. Their previous sins are forgiven: "In His forbearance [God] had overlooked the sins of the past" (Rom. 3 : 25–26).

Paul's doctrine of divine grace divided Christianity in later centuries. Luther's doctrine of grace through faith alone (*fide sola*) was based on Paul's doctrine of grace—or rather on Luther's interpretation of it—as meaning that good works do not count in the process of salvation. Paul, however, meant that "a man is justified apart from works of law" (Rom. 3 : 2 7), that is, apart from the observation of the Jewish law code. In other words, Paul set grace against the Jewish law code, from which he wanted the non-Jewish Christians to be freed. There is, however, no reason to interpret his doctrine as meaning that a man's conduct during his life does not count in the bestowal of divine grace; for he wrote that before the tribunal of Christ, "each must receive what is due to him for his conduct in the body, good or bad" (2 Cor. 5 : 10).

Paul also derived from his doctrine of grace that of predestination: as God bestows His grace as a gift, He chooses those whom He wants to serve. Paul wrote that "God knew His own before ever they were, and also ordained that they should be shaped to the likeness of His Son . . . and it is these, so foreordained, whom He has also called. And those whom He called He has justified" (Rom. 8 : 29–30). This doctrine also, as will be shown in later chapters, gave rise to deep divisions within Christianity, beginning with the Augustine-Pelagian dispute and culminating in the Calvinist doctrine of the elect and the damned.

Yet Paul never drew fatalistic conclusions from his predestinarian doctrine; he never pretended to know whom God had predestined to be elect or damned. Paul's approach to men can be interpreted as that of a missionary who grants everyone he approaches the benefit of the doubt as to whether or not he can be saved. He wants to help men acquire faith. If he succeeds, he can consider himself as an instrument through which God has fulfilled His purpose: to save men whom God has predestined to be saved. This missionary spirit runs through all the Letters Paul addressed to Christian communities, and it mirrors the spirit in which he performed his missionary work throughout his long, arduous, and perilous ministry. In this respect he proved to be a true disciple of Jesus.

Paul's doctrine of original sin determined his views about ultimate salvation. Although the believer fuses with Christ through the sacraments of baptism and the Eucharist, he must wait for his ultimate salvation until the eschatological day on which Christ will return to meet with those who have shown faith in him. Paul's vision of the ultimate salvation varied. In the First Letter to the Thessalonians (which appears to have been the earliest preserved Letter of Paul, written about twenty years after the death of Jesus), Paul assured the Christians of Thessaloniki (Salonika) that at Christ's coming the faithful Christians, regardless of whether they are still alive, will meet Christ. In mythological language he wrote: "At the word of command, at the sound of the archangel's voice and God's trumpet-call, the Lord [Christ] himself will descend from heaven; first the Christian dead will rise, then we who are left alive shall join them, caught up in clouds to meet the Lord in the air" (1 Thess. 4 : 16–17).

While in this Letter Paul pictured resurrection as being granted to all the Christian dead, in subsequent Letters he asserted that ultimate salvation can be attained only on the basis of a divine judgment on "the day of wrath and revelation of the righteous judgment of God" (Rom. 2 : 5). On that day, "God will pay every man for what he has done. To those who pursue glory, honour, and immortality by steady persistence in well-doing, He will give eternal life; but for those who are governed by selfish ambition, who refuse obedience to the truth and take the wrong for their guide, there will be fury or retribution" (Rom. 2 : 6–8).

By combining the divine judgment at the end of our age with the resurrection of body and soul of the dead, Paul followed the late-Judaic tradition rather than the Hellenic (Platonic) doctrine of the immortality of the soul. In Paul's view ultimate salvation is not granted to the righteous immediately after death. Instead they must wait for the coming of Christ and the last judgment. Yet a sprinkling of Hellenism appeared even in Paul's doctrine of resurrection. The dead will rise, but "we shall all be changed in a flash, in the twinkling of an eye at the last trumpet call" (1 Cor. 15 : 51). He based this vision on the distinction between *soma pneumatikon* and *soma psychikon* which he had borrowed from Hellenic thoughts. He thought that the *soma psychikon*, which had been sown in the earth as a perishable thing, in humiliation and weakness, will be raised as an imperishable, spiritual body, in glory and power (1 Cor. 15 : 42–44).

Thus the resurrected and transformed faithful will attain immortality: "This perishable being must be clothed with the imperishable, and what is mortal must be clothed with immortality" (1 Cor. 15 : 53). In the Letter to the Philippians, probably his last letter, Paul was even bolder in depicting the transformation of the resurrected. He declared that the Lord Jesus Christ "will transfigure the body belonging to our humble state, and give it a form [*synmorphon*] like that of his own resplendent body" (Phil. 3 : 21).

Paul was not consistent in his prophecies about where the resurrected will abide, on earth or in heaven. In the Letter to the Romans he expounded a doctrine which, in the eschatological spirit of Jewish prophets and of Judaic apocalyptical writers, envisioned a "new earth" in which all of nature would be renewed. But he blended this vision with his doctrine of original sin and of the liberation from this heritage through the sacrificial death of Christ: the whole created universe had become the victim of frustration, owing to Adam's fall, and "groans in all its parts as if in the pangs of childbirth" (Rom. 8 : 22). Yet once Adam's sin is redeemed by Christ, "the universe itself is to . . . enter upon the liberty and splendour of the children of God" (Rom. 8 : 21). Thus, as fruit of the parousia of Christ, Paul envisioned a new earth in which there would be a happy life for every living being, not only for men, the "children of God," but also for the animals and plants.

In contrast to this vision, other passages in Paul's Letters seem to indicate that the home of the transformed faithful will be in heaven. Even in the first vision Paul had of the parousia and the resurrection of the faithful, he wrote that the Christian dead and those who are left alive would be "caught up in the clouds to meet the Lord [Christ] in the air. Thus we shall always be with the Lord" (1 Thess. 4 : 17). These two meeting places—the clouds and the air—were obviously meant to be synonymous with heaven. Paul also used the allegory of a building made in heaven that will house us if the earthly frame that houses us today should be demolished (2 Cor. 5 : 1). Thus Paul's Hellenistically colored visions of man's fate after death were very different from Jesus' vision of the kingdom of God on earth into which man, as constituted with body and soul, will enter provided he has proved himself worthy of it.

There is, however, one feature in Paul's visions that comes close to those of Jesus (as can be inferred from the most reliable sources about Jesus' teachings), but that differs from beliefs rather common before and during Paul's lifetime: Paul did not believe in hell as an abode of the evildoers or unbelievers. The "eternal fire that is ready for the devil and his angels" (Matt. 25 : 41) and into which the evildoers will be thrown at the last judgment was absent in Paul's Letters. He envisaged destruction, not hell, as the final punishment inflicted on the evildoers on the day of wrath. He had indicated this already in connection with the day of the Lord: "Sudden destruction will come upon them" (1 Thess. 5 : 3). Likewise, the unbelievers and evildoers "will suffer the punishment of eternal ruin, cut off from the presence of the Lord" (2 Thess. 1 : 9). It is true that in the Letter to the Romans, Paul indicated that on the day of wrath God's righteous judgment will be revealed, and for the evildoers "the fury of retribution, trouble and distress" will be unfurled (Rom. 2 : 8−9). Yet whatever this might mean, the end of the sinners will be destruction. For in the same Letter, Paul contrasted the eternal life in Christ, which would be granted to the faithful believers, with the death of the evildoers: "Sin pays a wage; and the wage of sin is death," not hell (Rom. 6 : 23).

Thus the horrors of hell which have terrified the Christian world for centuries and which still pose a threat, find no foundation in the teachings of Paul, let alone in those of Jesus. When the trumpet blows on the day of the parousia of Christ, Paul prophesied that the evildoers and the other enemies of the cross of Christ will be destroyed; those enemies who have already died will not be resurrected, but they will not be disturbed in their sleep. If the Catholic Requiem Mass culminates in the prayer, *Requiem eternam dona eis Domine* ("Give them eternal rest, oh Lord"), the Apostle Paul envisioned eternal rest even for the evildoers.

Paul succeeded in constructing a synthesis of late-Judaic, Greek, and other Mediterranean religions and philosophies. Other thinkers, such as the author of the Wisdom of Solomon and Philo of Alexandria, also had attempted such a synthesis, but did not achieve more than playing the role of epigones and precursors. Of that group of thinkers, only Paul was profoundly shaken by a personal conversion founded on his belief in a savior who, as the Christian community in Jerusalem claimed, had arisen in the country of Paul's fathers. It was this enlightenment and conversion "on the road and nearing Damascus" (Acts 9:3) that gave Paul the intellectual and moral strength characteristic of all great founders of religions. The tenacity and untiring zeal with which he insisted on his own brand of Christology (foreign to the community that had gathered around Jesus and that continued as the original Christian community in Jerusalem after Jesus' death) could lead to a final victory only because these qualities were matched by unceasing endurance and self-denial. Paul did not teach his doctrines from the safe ground of an academic position or from the pulpit of a richly endowed church. He fought his battles in communion with his fellow-fighters; he faced misery, humiliations, and physical persecutions:

> God has made us apostles the most abject of mankind. We are like men condemned to death in the arena. . . . We are weak. . . . We are in disgrace. . . . To this day we go hungry and thirsty and in rags; we are roughly handled; we wander from place to place; we wear ourselves out, working with our own hands. . . . We are treated as the scum of the earth, the dregs of humanity. (1 Cor. 4:9–13)

Whether Paul died the death of a martyr may never be known, but he certainly lived the life of a martyr. A truly beatific vision of God, of Christ as the Savior of mankind, and of the beatitude of the transformed faithful Christians that would follow the coming of Christ, gave him the strength to survive all hardships and to spread the message of salvation, as he understood it, to all corners of the world.

CHAPTER V

Post-Pauline Christianity

If salvation can be regarded as the most fundamental aspect of all religions, then the
foundation of Christianity should be attributed to the Apostle Paul. As has been noted
in the preceding chapter, Paul's concept of
salvation differed from that of Jesus, who
prophesied the kingdom of God on earth,
and also from that of the original Christian
community in Jerusalem, which sought salvation through a late-Judaic Messiah into
whom it had transformed its teacher Jesus.
But it was Paul's concept of salvation—of
Christ as co-creator of the world, Savior and
leader of the believers into the kingdom of
God—that prevailed in Christianity.

However, Paul's doctrines of Christianity
did not gain recognition without a confrontation with the Messianic beliefs of the original Christian community in Jerusalem,[1] nor
did they constitute the ultimate form upon
which the Christian religion is based. Even
in the brief interval that elapsed between
Paul's mission and the composition of the
synoptic Gospels, the process of divinization
of Jesus, which Paul had initiated, underwent
significant changes. The Logos-doctrine of
the Gospel of John, its hypostasization of the
Holy Spirit, and the apocalyptic fantasies of
the Book of Revelation constituted further

stages in this progression. And the emergence of the Nicene system of Christianity brought the process of divinization of Christ to its apogee: the late-Judaic prophet of the kingdom of God became consubstantial with God.

1. PAULINISM IN THE SYNOPTIC GOSPELS

The Gospel of Mark, the first canonized literary document that succeeded the Letters of Paul, constituted a bridge between the beliefs of the original Christian community and those of Paul, and became a model for the two other synoptic Gospels. Yet the Gospels of Matthew and Luke enhanced Paul's doctrine of Jesus as God's adoptive son by accepting the myth of the Virgin birth of Christ. Moreover, they strengthened the Gnostic elements in Paul's doctrines by introducing a near-Gnostic relationship between God and Christ, expressed in the strange assertion that "no one knows the Son but the Father, and no one knows the Father but the Son and those to whom the Son may choose to reveal Him" (Matt. 11:27 and, slightly differently, Luke 10:22).

The Gospel of Matthew further emphasized the divinity of Christ by alluding to a particular version of the appearance of the risen Christ to his disciples. When the disciples saw the resurrected Jesus, they worshipped him, and Jesus confirmed his divine nature by saying that "full authority in heaven and on earth has been committed to me" (Matt. 28:17–19).

The influence of Pauline dualism and eschatology can also be detected in the Gospels of Matthew and Luke. Just as in Zoroastrianism and the doctrines of the Qumran community, the two Gospels divided mankind between "the children of the kingdom" and "the children of the evil one." In Matthew's words: "The good seed stands for the children of the kingdom, the darnel for the children of the evil one. The enemy who sows the darnel is the Devil" (Matt. 13:38–39). But at the end of the ages the power of Satan will be broken. Matthew in his vision of the last judgment saw "the eternal fire that is ready for the Devil and his angels" (Matt. 25:41).

Pauline influence is also evident in passages in the synoptic Gospels which deal with the resurrection of the dead. Even the Gospel of Mark adopted the Pauline doctrine of the resurrection of the righteous and their transformation upon the coming of Christ, as indicated in the story of the woman who was successively married to seven brothers. When the Sadducees asked Jesus whose wife she would be at the resurrection, he answered, "When they rise from the dead, men and women do not marry; they are like angels in heaven" (Mark 12:18–25). The transformation of the resurrected believer into a spiritual body—which logically would be sexless, as all desires and lusts of the natural body would have vanished—was obviously a Pauline doctrine.

Mark also thought, as Paul did, that the inhabitants of the kingdom of God would have eternal life, and the other synoptic Gospels followed suit.[2] The Gospels of Mark and Matthew, on the other hand, dealt more harshly than Paul did with the fate of the evildoers after death: they continued the late-Judaic tradition of the eternal burning of the evildoers after their death.[3] In the Matthean vision of the last judgment, Christ would mete out eternal punishment on the evildoers (Matt. 25:46). Luke and Paul, on the other hand, believed that only the righteous would be resurrected (Luke 14:14 and 20:35).

In the end the Matthean version of the coming of Christ and of the last judgment won the day. Matthew, as Paul had already done in some of his Letters, envisioned Christ as the judge on the day of judgment. Upon his coming in glory, Christ would separate the sheep from the goats, open the kingdom for the righteous, and throw the evildoers into the eternal fire (Matt. 25:31–42). This Matthean vision took root in the Christian world. Christ as mankind's judge, in his full majesty, with his right hand inviting the righteous into the kingdom of God and with the left hand commanding the fall of the evildoers into hell, was sculpted on the portals of numerous Gothic cathedrals of the Western world, and inspired Michelangelo to crown the Sistine Chapel with one of his loftiest creations. The majestic, awe-inspiring vision of the Gospel of Matthew still arouses fear in the hearts of innumerable Christians who question how they will fare at the end of our age.

2. CHRIST THE LOGOS

The most prominent landmark on the road from the Apostle Paul to Nicaea was the fourth Gospel, that of John, which appears to have been written at the end of the first century. It anchored Jesus' divinization firmly in Christianity. According to John, Jesus was God's son, sent by God into the world, that "through him the world might be saved," and he was simultaneously the Logos who became flesh. The Logos in turn was identified with God: "In the beginning was the Logos, and the Logos was with God, and the Logos was God" (John 3:17; 1:14 and 1).[4]

The Gospel of John followed in substance the Pauline Christology. Just as in Paul's Letters, John's Gospel accepted an adoptionist and subordinationist Christology: Christ is God's son and carries out a mission given to him by God. Paul's belief in Christ as a preexistent co-creator of the world and as representing God's power and wisdom also foreshadowed John's Christology. Yet the Gospel of John deepened the belief in the divinity of Christ by identifying Christ with the cosmological concept of the Logos. This concept was familiar to the Hellenistic-Roman world through the Stoic doctrine of the Logos as the Reason which orders the universe, and was similar to late-Judaic concepts expressed in the writings of Philo of Alexandria. In effect John's Logos, who dwells with God and through whom all things came to be (1:1−2), could have been directly derived from Philo's Logos: the image of God, "through whom the whole universe was framed." 5 Thus Paul's doctrine that all things were made through Christ was paralleled by John's doctrine that all things came to be through the Logos. Moreover, just as John believed that "what God was the Logos was" (1:1), he also believed that Christ, as the incarnate Logos, was one with God: "My Father and I are one" (10:30).

The Logos-cosmology also assumed Gnostic-dualistic features. Like Paul, John perceived the existing world as dominated by the Gnostic "Prince of this world" who would ultimately be driven out by Christ (12:31). He even used the dualistic metaphor of "the light [that] shines on in the dark." "The real light . . . was . . . coming into the world. . . . But the world did not recognize him [the light]" until the Logos became flesh in the person of Jesus (1:5 and 1:9−10). With that event the darkness was dispelled: "I have come into the world as light," said the Johannine Christ, "so that no one who has faith in me should remain in darkness" (12:46). Yet in spite of all conspicuous Gnostic elements in his Gospel, John was not a true Gnostic, and the docetic elements in Christian Gnosticism were foreign to him. For him, the Logos became flesh and dwelled among the people as a man, who even wept at the sight of the dead Lazarus (11:35), and underwent passion and violent death.

At the same time, Jesus appeared in the Gospel of John as both the Savior and the judge of the world. Before he came into the world, men, in Gnostic fashion, "preferred darkness to light because their deeds were evil" (3:19). Through Christ the light came into the world and, with the light, salvation. It was the Gospel of John that coined for Jesus the attribute "Savior of the world" (in the Vulgate, *Salvator Mundi*, 4:42). Thus through the Gospel of John, the title "Savior," which the mystery religions had used for their dying and resurrected god, became Christ's most significant attribute.

With the identification of Christ with the Logos, with the dualism of light and darkness, with the eschatological triumph of Christ over the

Prince of this world, the Gospel of John accentuated the Hellenistic features of Paul's Christology. But the Gospel also drew from the delay of Christ's coming consequences that marked a turning point in the history of Christianity. It did not abandon outright the eschatological belief in the last day when "all who are in the graves shall hear [Christ's] voice and come out" for the resurrection of life or for judgment (5:28). But it contained a number of passages that can be interpreted as a belief in what modern theologians call "realized eschatology," meaning that the eschatological day has already arrived in the person of Christ.[6] Thus when the righteous die, they will not have to wait in their graves for the last day, the day of judgment, because they "have already passed from death to life" (5:24), and "the unbeliever has already been judged" (3:18). "Now is the hour of judgment for this world" (12:31).

Another consequence that the Gospel of John drew from the delayed parousia of Christ was the creation of the Paraclete, which introduced into Christianity the Holy Spirit as a divine entity.[7] A certain tendency to hypostasize God's spirit, comparable to the way late-Jewish literature hypostasized God's wisdom, was already noticeable prior to the composition of the Gospel of John. Paul in his Second Letter to the Corinthians took leave from the Christian community of Corinth by wishing them the grace of Christ, the love of God, and the fellowship of the Holy Spirit (2 Cor. 13:14). In Matthew's lifetime the custom of baptizing in the name of God, Jesus, and the Holy Spirit seems to have been adopted. As noted, the risen Christ in Matthew's Gospel commanded his disciples to "baptize men in the name of the Father and the Son and the Holy Spirit" (Matt. 28:19). The Gospel of John, however, endowed the Holy Spirit with a new personal name—Paraclete—and new functions. The Paraclete would be a gift of God to reside with faithful Christians forever (14:16); he would be a guide and teacher in the spirit of Jesus (14:26 and 16:8), but also a prophet who would make known the things that were coming (16:13).

The introduction of the Holy Spirit as a separate divine entity (though not yet as a person in the sense of the Nicene Creed) was undoubtedly connected with the dawning awareness among Christians that they could not count on the coming of Christ as an imminent event. The Gospel of John recognized the need for closing the gap between the death of Jesus and his parousia, and thus introduced the device of God's sending the Holy Spirit down to earth to continue the work Jesus had begun.

The Gospel of John, like the synoptic Gospels, purported to be an account of the life, ministry, passion, and death of Jesus. But because it was founded upon a spirit that differed from that of Jesus even more than the synoptic Gospels had, it was even less trustworthy. On the other hand, the Gospel of John earned its canonization and its authority as a bridge between the Apostle Paul and the Nicene Creed and as a founding stone of the belief in the divinity of Jesus and the hypostasization of the Holy Spirit. Moreover, it began the process of toning down the fervent hope of Christendom for an early dawning of the kingdom of God and of regarding the Church as an institution substituting in man's daily life for the bliss of the kingdom of God.

3. THE BOOK OF REVELATION

Another Scripture, the Book of Revelation, was composed at about the same time as the Gospel of John, and it bore all the characteristic features of the classical apocalypses. It was originally even called Apokalypsis.[8] Although the apocalyptic spirit was foreign to the theological spirit which inspired the patristic works of the post-apostolic generations, and in spite of the rather uncanonical nature of many of its fantasies, it found admission (although very late and against considerable opposition) to the canonical Scriptures of the New Testament. It proved so popular and mirrored so faithfully the yearnings of Christians for the parousia of Christ and the advent of his reign on earth that its canonization could not be prevented. Vested with this authority, it was able to exert a powerful influence on the thoughts and hopes of many generations of Christians.

Stripped of its fantastic allegories and metaphors, the essential salvational features of the Book of Revelation can be summarized as follows: It shares the Pauline belief in bodily resurrection, but grants to the Christian martyrs the privilege of the immortality of their souls. The soul (*psyche*) of each martyr will dwell "underneath the altar" (obviously in heaven) (Rev. 6:9–11), but at a given moment the martyrs' souls will assemble before God's throne. They will serve Him day and night, guided by Christ "to the springs of the water of life," and they will no longer have hunger, thirst, and tears (Rev. 7).

The end of our age, however, will come later when Christ will descend from heaven with the armies of heaven and will annihilate the hostile armies (19:11–21). Christ's triumph will usher in the millennium, that is, the thousand years' reign of Christ and the martyrs. At the beginning of the millennium the martyrs' souls will be united with their bodies so that they will come to life again. This will be the first resurrection. The resurrected martyrs shall be priests and co-regents of Christ. Satan, however, shall be chained up for the duration of the millennium so that he can no longer seduce the nations. At the end of the millennium Satan will be let loose, and the final battle will be waged when Christ and the saints fight the hostile armies led by Satan. The hostile armies will be consumed by fire and Satan will be thrown into the eternal fire (20:2–10).

Only then, according to the Book of Revelation, will the new age dawn. Earth and heaven will vanish. All the dead will be resurrected (the second resurrection) and "judged, each man on the record of his deeds" (20:11–12). The evildoers, together with Death and Hades, will be thrown into the lake of fire (20:14–15). A new heaven and a new earth will be created, as Trito-Isaiah had dreamed (Isa. 65:17), and the "new Jerusalem" will descend from heaven (21:1–2). That at last will be the earthly kingdom of God (although the Book of Revelation does not use this phrase), where God "will wipe every tear from their eyes; there shall be an end to death" (21:4). And the nations shall walk in the light of the new Jerusalem and "the wealth and splendour of the nations shall be brought into it" (21:24–26).

The grandiose tableau of the age to come culminated in the beatific vision of God. God will dwell in the midst of the people (21:3) and "they shall see him face to face" (22:4). The Book of Revelation did not move the beatific vision of God into a heaven in which only disembodied souls would dwell but left the dwelling place of the blessed ones on earth: God will dwell among the blessed men and women and they will see Him face to face, here on earth.

This towering vision of the age to come seems to have fully responded to the longings of the people for an end to their pains and tears, for peace and harmony in a renewed, eternal life on earth. The fact that the Book of Revelation leaned heavily on the visions of earlier apocalypses, particularly on those of the First Book of Enoch, did not diminish its popularity and authority. On the contrary, by drawing from numerous apocalypses which had been written in late-Judaic and early Christian times, it saved for the following generations the most essential features of a literature that remained apocryphal and soon became virtually inaccessible.

While the Book of Revelation enriched its visions with features found in earlier apocalypses, there were but few sources in New Testament Scriptures from which it could draw, with the exception of one outstanding source: the Apostle Paul's First Letter to the Corinthians, which it resembled in essential features. Both Scriptures believed in bodily resurrection and in an interim reign of Christ that would precede the kingdom of God. There are, however, certain differences between them. The interim reign of Christ that Paul envisioned would be of an indefinite duration, while that of the Book of Revelation would last one thousand years. And in Paul's vision the resurrection would precede the interim reign of Christ, while in the Book of Revelation, it would, except for the resurrection of the martyrs, follow the millennium.

Although the Book of Revelation was written at about the same time as the Gospel of John, their spirits were vastly different. The two Scriptures can, in effect, be considered as representing two poles between which Christianity has been wavering ever since. The Gospel of John attempted to reconcile the Christians with the infinite delay of the coming of Christ and to substitute a realized eschatology for the hope of the advent of the kingdom of God. The Book of Revelation, on the contrary, placed at the center of the Christian religion the longing for the coming of Christ and for the erection of a kingdom of Christ to last one thousand years. This polarity between the Gospel of John and the Book of Revelation, between the realized eschatology and the thousand-year reign of Christ, has remained a constant feature of Christianity and has been the source of incessant friction and divisions in its ranks.

4. THE NICENE CREED

In the more than two hundred years which passed between the Gospel of John and the Council of Nicaea (in 325), Christianity evolved from a modest community to the dominant religion of the Western world. This unprecedented triumphal march was made possible by the continuing process of divinization of its savior figure, a process that had been initiated by the Apostle Paul, had reverberated in the synoptic Gospels, and had been strengthened by the Gospel of John. In the Hellenistic-Roman world Christianity triumphed because it adapted itself to a spiritual environment in which the yearning of the masses for salvation found its most significant expression in the appearance of savior gods and in which even emperors claimed recognition as divine beings.

The process of Hellenization and Romanization of Christianity reached its first climax in the Council of Nicaea. Paul's interpretation of Christ as God's preexistent co-creator nearly elevated Jesus to the rank of a Hellenistic dying and resurrected divinity. The Christ of the Gospel of John, being the incarnated Logos, may have had an even stronger appeal for the Hellenistic world, in which the Logos was a familiar entity. However, Paul and John were still subordinationists. According to the Gospel of John, in the prayer that Jesus addressed to God at the end of his ministry, Jesus declared that God alone is "truly God" and had sent him (John

17:3). Moreover, the Gospel insisted that God is greater than Christ (14:28), and that Christ can do nothing by himself (5:19). Thus Christ became the Savior of the world by commission from God, so to speak: "God sent His Son into the world . . . that through him the world might be saved" (3:17).

This adoptionist and subordinationist doctrine later formed the basis of Arianism, which concluded from it that Christ is created by God, inferior to God, and therefore does not have eternal existence.[9] Arianism, with a more human concept of Jesus than that of the official Church, proved to be popular in many quarters. Later, Germanic tribes (which did not have the Hellenistic-Roman background) invaded the Roman Empire and accepted Arianism. But the subordinationism that Arianism taught could not be reconciled with the Hellenistic-Roman spirit. The Savior of the world had to be a true God who had died and was resurrected. The Council of Nicaea, therefore, branded Arianism a heresy. This was the first profound split within Christianity, one which rent Christendom for hundreds of years.[10]

The creed adopted by the Council of Nicaea constituted only a part of what is popularly known as the Nicene Creed. The doctrine of the Trinity was added by the Council of Constantinople in 381, and that of the double nature of Christ, by the Council of Chalcedon in 451. The Council of Nicaea's contribution to the creed was the formal abandonment of the subordinationism of the Apostle Paul and all four Gospels, and its replacement by a belief in the true godhead of Christ, which took the form of the dogma of "consubstantiality" of God and Christ. More specifically, the council proclaimed that there is one God; one Lord Jesus Christ; Christ is God's Son; Christ was begotten but not made by the Father;[11] Christ is true God from true God; Christ is of one substance (in Latin, *consubstantialis*, in Greek, *homoousios*) with the Father; and through Christ all things were made. While, according to the subordinationist Gospel of John, God sent Christ into the world in order to save it, the Nicene Creed asserted that Christ for our salvation came down (from heaven, as the Council of Constantinople added) and became incarnate.

The Christological controversies were, however, by no means resolved by the Nicene dogma of consubstantiality. The problem of the nature of the Savior remained open. Aside from Gnostic docetism, which believed that Christ is a divine being who only assumed a human appearance, and from Arianism, which believed that Christ is a created being, opinions about Christ's nature were divided. Beside Arianism, the most important deviations from the Nicene Christological doctrine were Monophysitism and Nestorianism. Monophysitism (lit., "belief in one nature") holds that although Christ assumed a physical body as an instrument of salvation, his nature has remained purely divine. Nestorianism on the contrary believes that two persons are united in Christ, a divine person begotten by God, and a human person born of Mary.[12]

The prevailing view about the nature of Christ, which evolved in the patristic writings, held that two natures were united in the person of Christ. This view was derived from Paul's distinction between Christ's descent from King David on the human level, his designation as God's son on the spiritual level (Rom. 1:3−4), and the incarnation doctrine of the Gospel of John ("the Logos became flesh"). The Council of Chalcedon adopted this doctrine which stated that Christ is one person in whom two natures, that of perfect God and that of perfect man, are united. This dogma constituted a substantive addition to the Nicene Creed.

Yet just as Arianism was not extinguished by the dogma adopted by the Councils of Nicaea and Constantinople that Christ was begotten by God before all ages, Monophysitism and Nestorianism were not extinguished by the Council of Chalcedon's dogma of Christ's two natures. Although rejected by the Council of Chalcedon, Monophysitism has remained the prevailing Christian religion in Egypt, Ethiopia, and Armenia, while Nestorianism is alive in Christian communities of Syria, Iraq, Iran, and India.

If the Christological evolution that culminated in the Councils of Nicaea and Chalcedon reflected the integration of Christianity with the Hellenistic-Roman world, the emergence of Trinitarianism reflected the turning away of Christianity from its eschatological roots. As noted, the Gospel of John had de-eschatologized the Holy Spirit by calling it the Paraclete and interpreting it as a substitute for Christ on earth after the death of Jesus. The Gospel asserted that "streams of living water shall flow out from within him" (John 7:38−39). Thus the Holy Spirit began to acquire a this-worldly meaning of salvation within man's lifetime.

Nevertheless, Paul, John, and the Council of Nicaea were not true Trinitarians. The council mentioned the Holy Spirit, but did not yet include it in the consubstantiality of God and Christ. The concept of the Trinity—of the Holy Spirit as a third person in the Godhead—had, however, already spread, beginning with the prominent early patristic writers Tertullian (Quintus Septimius Florens Tertullianus, c. 160−c. 230) and Origen (Origines Adamantius, c. 185−c. 254). As a consequence of this further de-eschatologization process—of the recognition of the Holy Spirit as a sanctifying power on earth—the Council of Constantinople formally elevated the Holy Spirit to the rank of the third person of the deity by addressing him as "Lord" (like Christ), as "life-giver," who proceeds from the Father, and as an object of worship and glorification.

It was one of the strangest incidents in the history of Christianity that in later generations the genealogy of the Holy Spirit became a controversial issue between the Western and Eastern Churches, in effect the only important controversial dogma between them. While the Orthodox Churches accepted the creed as it was adopted in Nicaea, Constantinople, and Chalcedon, it became customary in the Roman Catholic Church to drive the dogma of consubstantiality to its extreme by maintaining that the Holy Spirit proceeds from the Father "and the Son" (in Latin, *filioque*).[13] Indeed, the creed, as now read in Roman Catholic churches, does not follow the text of the creed as adopted by the Councils of Nicaea, Constantinople, and Chalcedon, but uses a text amended by the word *filioque*. This amendment is in obvious contradiction to the assertion, incorporated in the Constantinople version of the creed, that Jesus Christ "was incarnated from the Holy Spirit and the Virgin Mary." Through many centuries the *filioque* was, and has remained, a bone of contention between the Orthodox and the Roman Catholic Churches.

The councils of the "holy Catholic and Apostolic Church" (an addition adopted by the Council of Constantinople) could not remain entirely silent about the eschatological nature of Christianity, which from the beginning had been its very essence. The belief in the coming of Christ—be it as a Messiah, or as a divine being at whose coming the dead would be resurrected and who would usher in the kingdom of God—was inseparable from Christianity. The councils which ruled on the creed of Christendom could not ignore this fundamental belief of all Christians.

Indeed, the Council of Constantinople, more explicitly than that of Nicaea, adopted the doctrines of the coming of Christ, the last judgment, the resurrection of the dead, and the kingdom of Christ (rather than of God), which it called "the life of the world to come." Missing in the creed, however, was the millenarianism of Paul and the Book of Revelation: the belief that when Christ returned to earth, his would be a fighting realm in which Christ would reign until he had destroyed all his enemies (1 Cor. 15:24–25); or in which Christ would reign for one thousand years, after which there would be a last battle with the enemies of the kingdom until the New Jerusalem would come down out of heaven (Rev. 20).

Not only was this eschatological belief missing in the creed, but the Council of Constantinople rejected Paul's subordinationist doctrine that Christ, after having subjected all things to him, would become subordinate to God, and thus God would be all in all (1 Cor. 15:28). In the place of this essentially monotheistic doctrine, the council added to the Nicene Creed the words, "of whose [Christ's] kingdom there will be no end." Thus Christ, consubstantial with God, was elevated to the rank of the ruler of an everlasting kingdom.

5 . THE CHURCH AS MILLENNIUM

According to the Nicene Creed, as amended by the Council of Constantinople, Christ will erect his kingdom when he "will come again with glory to judge the living and the dead." The Council of Constantinople also reaffirmed the belief in the resurrection of the dead and asserted that "we look forward to the life of the world to come."

This then is the ultimate salvation to which all Christians—Roman Catholics, Eastern Orthodox, and Protestants alike—look forward, for all of them have accepted the Nicene-Constantinople-Chalcedon Creed. Yet Jesus' belief that the kingdom of God was "upon us," and the belief of the early Christians that Christ's coming should be expected within the lifetime of the living generation or soon afterward, were bound to vanish as generation after generation passed away without the last trumpet being blown. To be sure, there have always been fervent Christians who are convinced that the kingdom of God is indeed upon us. This belief centers on the vision in the Book of Revelation of the millennium and the descent of the New Jerusalem, so much so that "millenarianism" has become synonymous with the belief that our age will soon end and the life of the world to come is fast approaching.

The Church tried to accommodate itself to the infinite delay in the parousia of Christ, because millenarian beliefs assumed a rebellious character and threatened the tranquillity of the Christian communities. Millenarianism was likely to arise among people in the lower social strata, for whom the descent to earth of the New Jerusalem would mean social and economic liberation from oppression and misery. Thus rebellious religious and social movements were frequently blended together.

The first millenarian movement, Montanism,[14] arose in the second half of the second century. The Montanists believed in the imminent coming of Christ and in the millennium, and were the first millenarians to break with the Catholic Church. Many millenarian rebellions followed in later centuries.

Yet the more the hope in the parousia of Christ receded, with the exception of the millenarian rebels, the more the conviction grew that faith in and devotion to Christ were in themselves a path toward salvation.

Moreover, the Christian communities understood from their outset that faith and devotion can be strengthened by communal institutionalization. Paul's ministry was directed not toward individuals but toward the organized Christian communities, the churches. He extended the saving grace of Christ from the individual believers to their collective, the Church, and recognized the Church as an instrument of grace. In two of his undoubtedly authentic Letters he addressed the Church as Christ's body. In his Letter to the Romans he declared, "All of us, united with Christ, form one body" (12:5); and in his First Letter to the Corinthians, "Now you are Christ's body, and each of you a limb or organ of it" (12:27). If the Letter to the Colossians is authentic, Paul even called Christ "the head of the body, the church" (1:18).

The doctrine of the Church as the body of Christ found its apex in the letter to the Ephesians,[15] in which the Church was not only recognized as Christ's body, but as "the fullness [in Greek, *pleroma*] of him who himself receives the entire fullness of God" (Eph. 1:23). The Church was visualized as the instrument through which "the wisdom of God in all its varied forms" was to be made known, not only on earth but even "to the rulers and authorities in the realms of heaven" (3:10), whoever they might be. The Church was thus glorified, "with no stain or wrinkle, ... but holy and without blemish" (5:26). Thus the Letter to the Ephesians already anticipated the "holy Catholic and apostolic Church" of the Nicene Creed.

From that doctrine there was only one more step to the belief that the Church was the necessary, even the only, instrument of salvation: man cannot find salvation alone. The conclusion that "outside the church there is no salvation" (*extra ecclesiam nulla salus*) was already drawn by Origen and confirmed by the patristic writer and martyr Cyprian (Thascius Caecilius Cyprianus, c. 200–258), and by Augustine (Aurelius Augustinus, 354–430), the greatest Christian theologian of the early Middle Ages.[16]

To understand fully this fateful dictum, which was commonly accepted within the Catholic Church, one must go back to its apostolic claim, as it was finally embodied in the Nicene Creed in the term "apostolic church." With the authority of the Church strengthened, the view arose early that Jesus had delegated to his disciples the authority to forgive sins (Mark 2:5). The Gospel of Matthew maintained that Jesus gave to Peter "the keys to the kingdom of Heaven" and assured Peter that whatever he would forbid on earth would be forbidden in heaven, and whatever he would allow on earth would be allowed in heaven. The Gospel extended this authority to all of Jesus' disciples (Matt. 16:19 and 18:18).

However, no evidence can be found in the authentic New Testament Scriptures for the Church's apostolic claim that the powers Jesus was supposed to have delegated to the apostles were in turn delegated to the leaders of the Church. True, the Pastoral Letters of Paul do contain the apostolic claim.[17] In the First Letter to Timothy the author wrote to Timothy, who seems to have exercised episcopal functions, "This charge, son Timothy, I lay upon you" (1:18). A similar formula was used in the Second Letter to Timothy. However, New Testament scholars have long recognized the Pastoral Letters as pseudonymous writings of a post-Pauline period which, although canonized, cannot claim authenticity. Yet the Pastoral Letters did attest to the fact that the apostolic claim of the Christian hierarchy existed as early as the second century.

A more trustworthy source for the apostolic claim can be found in the so-called First Epistle of Clement to the Corinthians, which has been ascribed to Clement, bishop of Rome (called by the Roman Catholic Church, Clement I, pontificate c. 92–c. 101). In that letter Clement gave a classical definition of the apostolic claim: "The apostles preached the Gospel to us from the Lord Jesus Christ. Jesus Christ was sent from God. Christ then is from God and the apostles are from Christ. They appointed their first fruits . . . as bishops and deacons of those who should believe." [18]

The Church had thus become *the* instrument of salvation and damnation. Since, according to its apostolic claim, Jesus delegated to his disciples the power of forgiving sins, and the apostles in turn delegated this power to the bishops, and the bishops in turn to the priests, the priests of the holy Catholic and Apostolic Church wield the power of forgiving, or refusing to forgive, any man's sins. When the prelates of the Church assembled in Constantinople in 381, they proclaimed their faith in the "one holy Catholic and Apostolic Church."

Soon after the Council of Constantinople had affirmed the sanctity of the Catholic and Apostolic Church, the Church's reign over the conscience of man seemed to be threatened from without and within. From without, the Visigoth conquest of Rome in 410 marked the beginning of the end of the western Roman Empire. With Rome under the heel of barbarians who adhered to the Arian heresy, the dominance of the Catholic Church seemed jeopardized. At the same time the reign of the Church seemed to be threatened from within by Pelagianism. This doctrine, derived from the writings of the theologian Pelagius (born probably in Britain c. 354, died c. 418), denied the dogma of original sin and maintained that man's will is free to choose good or evil: divine grace is not predestined for certain men and refused to others; it has been given to all men, and everyone is free to accept or reject it. Because this doctrine would undermine the claim of the Church to act as the vicar of God and Christ in dispensing or withholding divine grace, Pelagius was excommunicated and his doctrines were condemned by Innocent I (pontificate 401–417) and Zosimus (pontificate 417–418).

Augustine,[19] on the other hand, believed in the dogma of original sin, in divine grace as a gift of God and Christ, in predestination as the instrument of divine salvation and condemnation, and in the supremacy of the Church. In defense of all these doctrines he attacked Pelagianism in several treatises. In the same spirit, and with a view to strengthen the Church during the crisis which Christendom faced due to the fall of Rome, he wrote *De Civitate Dei* ("The City of God"). Thus it was Augustine, a convert from the most extreme form of Gnosticism, who, in his famous treatise, drew the most logical consequences from the sanctification of the Church as the instrument of salvation.

Augustine's doctrine of the saving power of the Church began with his belief in the realized eschatology. In his view Jesus' ministry constituted the beginning of the millennium; Jesus' chief instrument during the millennium would be the Church. Christ and the Church were in effect inseparable from each other: "Christ and the Church are two in one flesh."[20] Christ's millenarian reign, therefore, would be tantamount to the reign of the Church. "The Church even now is the kingdom of Christ and the kingdom of heaven," Augustine asserted in *De Civitate Dei*. "Accordingly even now [Christ's] saints reign with him, though otherwise than they will reign hereafter."[21]

From his doctrine of the Church as the saving instrument of God and Christ, Augustine drew the conclusion that our age is no longer the evil age ruled by the Devil, but a mixture of two cities: Jerusalem, the city of God (*civitas Dei*), and Babylon, the earthly city. "These two cities are made by two loves: the earthly city by love of oneself, even to the contempt of God; the heavenly city by love of God, even to the contempt of oneself." "In truth these two cities are entangled together in this world, and intermixed until the last judgment effect their separation" (*De Civitate Dei* 14, 2 and 1, 35). Although not all members of the Church are saints, the Church as such is holy and those who are outside it or withdraw from it are doomed. "He who puts himself outside the church will be punished by eternal torture even if burned alive in the name of Christ."[22]

As can be seen from these passages, Augustine maintained the belief in the eschatological day of judgment. While the Church is still struggling, often even persecuted, while it still has to contend with the earthly city and its dismal power, eventually, at the end of our age, "the earthly kingdom will be rooted up and the other kingdom will be planted in eternity." [23]

The Manichaean aspect of Augustine's *De Civitate Dei* should not be overlooked. Through all the profound changes his spiritual development underwent he did not totally betray his Manichaean past: there is the construct of the good city and the wicked city, and at the eschatological end of time the good city will triumph over the wicked city. The Manichaean tendencies that have always lurked in the Christian world were doubtless strengthened by the authority Augustine wielded.

Equally strong as Augustine's Manichaean influence was that of his doctrine of the Church as the realization of the millennium. On the basis of this doctrine the Church virtually abandoned the eschatological visions of the Apostle Paul and the Book of Revelation. Christ has already planted his kingdom on earth in the form of the heavenly city of the saints of the Church. Hence, the millennium has already begun. "The Church even now is the kingdom of Christ," the sole dispenser of Christ's grace, of salvation.

If Augustine really believed that the final triumph of the heavenly city over the earthly city would occur within one thousand years, he certainly was mistaken. What happened after that period was the beginning of the deepest and apparently incurable split the Catholic Church ever suffered. Yet Augustine did prove to be right insofar as in the one thousand years following the composition of *De Civitate Dei*, the Church successfully maintained its claim to be the sole font of salvation. Based on this claim, it exerted a tremendous power as the sole dispenser of salvation. Only at the end of that millennium did this power begin to weaken.

6. THE CHURCH AS SACRAMENTAL INSTITUTION

The salvational role that the patristic writers attributed to the Church and that was expanded in the following one thousand years can be understood only if the transformation of the Church into a sacramental institution is recognized. Elements of sacramentalism have existed from the beginning of Christianity. As noted, the Apostle Paul transformed both baptism and the Eucharist into sacraments of a mystic nature. Under his influence these two acts were elevated to the rank of grace-dispensing sacraments. In other words, the originally symbolic acts of baptism and the Eucharist were transformed into a visible form in which divine grace was poured out on the believers.

This sanctification of the sacraments, the belief that they confer *per se* grace on the person who receives them, regardless of the character and conduct of the person who extends them, became a firm foundation of ecclesiastical power. But at the same time the sanctification of the sacraments provoked much resistance, and was destined to become one of the causes of the Reformation.

In early Christianity the resistance to sacramentalism gave rise to Donatism, a North African rebellion against priests who had betrayed Christians in the era of Roman persecution, but who, after the ordeal was over, were allowed to officiate. The Donatists rebelled against the official position, defended by Augustine in several treatises, that the sacraments confer grace, regardless of the worth and faith of the officiating priest or of the receiver of the sacraments. Under the leadership of Donatus (bishop of Carthage from 313 to 347; died c. 355), they insisted that priests be allowed to officiate only if they were in a state of grace, and that sacraments conferred upon persons who defect be made invalid. Although Donatus was later exiled, Donatism remained an active movement in North Africa for more than three centuries, until the Islamization of North Africa.[24]

In the Middle Ages the conflict over sacramentalism was expressed in scholastic terms. The position taken that sacraments confer grace, regardless of the merits of the persons who administer or receive them, was called *ex opere operato* ("by the work done"), while the opposite position was called *ex opere operantis* ("from the work of the doer"). The dispute that split Donatism and Augustinianism in the fourth and fifth centuries was repeated as a dispute between Catholicism and Reformation in the sixteenth century. After the final split between Catholicism and Reformation, the Council of Trent (1545–1563) excommunicated the adversaries of *ex opere operato*. The council confirmed that "the sacraments of the New Testament contain the grace that they signify . . . they are not merely outward signs."[25] The council understood by the term "sacraments of the New Testament" not only the two sacraments of baptism and the Eucharist, which had been established by Paul, but also five additional sacraments—those of the Holy Orders, penance, confirmation, matrimony, and the extreme unction—which had been added later and could be derived from the New Testament only indirectly. The Catholic Church retains to this day the conception of the sacraments as instruments of divine grace, as bringers of salvation. Thus the Second Vatican Council (1962–1965), in the "Constitution on the Sacred Liturgy," proclaimed that "the purpose of the sacraments is to sanctify men. . . . They do indeed impart grace."

The increase in the number of sacraments can be understood as an increase in the powers of the Church over men's souls. Only the Church (with a few extraordinary exceptions) as the mandatory of Christ, could administer the sacraments. Since, according to the apostolic claim, Christ's sacramental authority has been delegated to the priests, ordination became itself a sacrament, the Sacrament of the Holy Orders. By the act of ordaining a person to enter into the ranks of the Holy Orders (to become a priest), Christ himself bestows upon him the sacramental authority to forgive sins, to penalize the sinner, and, consequently, to administer all those acts recognized as sacraments.

Among the sacraments the priest is authorized to confer upon the believers, that of penance affects all Catholics. Like most sacraments, it goes back to an early stage of Christianity. The power to allow and forbid implies the power to penalize those who disregard ecclesiastical prohibitions. The specific form in which the sacrament of penance has been conferred consists of four stages: the contrition of the person who has sinned; the confession of the sin to his confessor-priest; the penitence which the officiating priest imposes upon him; and the absolution which the priest is empowered to grant him.

The more deeply the Church rooted itself in the life of society, the more powerful an instrument of domination did the sacrament of penance become. The most powerful instrument of ecclesiastical domination was the penalty of excommunication: the exclusion from the community of the faithful, meaning that the Church refuses to confer sacraments upon the sinner and denies Christian burial. In the eyes of the Church the excommunicated person loses the access to divine grace which the sacraments give him. He is eternally condemned unless he repents and submits to the Church.

In addition to the four sacraments—baptism, Eucharist, ordination, and penance—which were recognized by the Church in its early period, three ecclesiastical acts—confirmation, matrimony, and extreme unction —were elevated to the rank of sacraments, all very important in a Christian's life, from maturity to death.

The ecclesiastical act of confirmation became important when, as a result of the introduction of the practice of infant baptism, the sacrament of baptism lost its original meaning as a symbol of repentance and forgiveness of sins. Infant baptism was derived from the Pauline doctrine of original sin and has been a common practice since the third century. According to that doctrine, even the newborn infant is burdened by original sin. Since infants are in danger of early death, particularly in preindustrial countries with high infant mortality rates, they can be saved from eternal damnation only by early baptism. Indeed, this was the position Augustine took. It was confirmed by the Council of Carthage in 418, which was held in the midst of the Pelagian attack on the dogma of original sin. As late as 1951, Pius XII (pontificate 1939–1958) ruled that baptism is the only way of imparting to infants the life of Christ.[26] With the spread of infant baptism, the act of baptism could no longer be identified with admission into the ranks of Christian believers. That act requires an age when one is mature enough to understand the essentials of the faith and to assume responsibility for one's actions. It therefore became customary since the third century to add to the rite of baptism that of confirmation, which is conferred by a bishop to each adolescent Christian. The institution of confirmation as a sacrament was created by the second Council of Lyon in 1274.

Whereas marriage in the Jewish and Roman civilizations was considered to be a private affair between the partners, the Christian Church at an early stage held ecclesiastical consent desirable or even necessary. Augustine definitely regarded matrimony as a sacrament, and since his time, this sacrament has been one of the strongest sources of church power. The Church arrogated to itself the right to rule over the requirements for marriages, the validity of marriages, and the dissolution of marriages it considers invalid.[27] As the Church derived from the Gospels the doctrine of the indissolubility of the marriage vows, it succeeded in a number of predominantly Catholic countries to force upon the secular authorities a legal ban on divorce. The sacrament of matrimony thus became an institution through which the Catholic Church effectively intervened in the processes of society. This intervention has become more oppressive as modern society increasingly regards divorce as socially permissible.

Finally, when the end of life approaches, the Catholic Church dispenses the Sacrament of the Extreme Unction (renamed by Vatican Council II, Sacrament of the Anointing of the Sick). Innocent I (pontificate 401–417) was apparently the first ecclesiastical authority to establish rules for this sacrament which soon became generally accepted. The sacrament implies that by forgiving the sins of dying or seriously ill persons, the Church opens to them the portals of heaven, either immediately or after purification in purgatory.

Thus the whole life of a Christian, literally from the cradle to the grave, came to be protected and guided, but also controlled and disciplined by the Church and its ministers. The seven sacraments were the instrument through which this amazing domination was achieved. The foundation of this domination was the doctrine that man can be saved only by the gratuitous grace of God and Jesus Christ; that, however gratuitous this grace might be, it is made visible and operative through the seven sacraments, which work *ex opere operato*; that the Church grants its sacraments through its ministers, who are ordained themselves by way of a sacrament; and that, therefore, there can be no salvation outside the Church.[28]

7. HEAVEN, PURGATORY, AND HELL

The power of the Church to allow and forbid, save and condemn, was magnified and multiplied the more Hellenism prevailed over Judaism in the Christian doctrines about man's destiny after death. The late-Judaic belief in bodily resurrection at the end of our age was slowly pushed into the background by the Hellenic doctrine of the soul's separation from the body after death and the ascent of the soul into heaven or its descent into realms of punishment. As a consequence, man's concern about his ultimate destiny became more intense, and his dependence on the power of the Church to dispense or refuse ultimate salvation became more manifest.

The belief in a post-mortem existence of the soul, separate from the body, grew but slowly in the ranks of Christianity, although traces can be found in its Judaic roots. Some of the Judaic apocalypses—including parts of the First Book of Enoch, a source of inspiration for the Book of Revelation—planted the kingdom of God in heaven, populated by the souls of the righteous.

To the original Christian community, however, belief in the ascent to heaven of the souls of the righteous was still foreign. The kingdom of God, whose dawn Jesus had prophesied, could be nowhere but on earth, to be populated by those men and women who had lived a life worthy of living. As noted, in Paul's vision after death the righteous had to wait in their graves for the coming of Christ; they would then be bodily resurrected although somehow spiritually transformed.

In later New Testament Scriptures, however, a few passages suggest that the belief that the souls of the righteous would dwell in heaven existed even in the early Christian community. The Gospel of Luke related the strange story of the criminal who, crucified along with Jesus, pleaded that Jesus remember him when Jesus ascended his throne in heaven; Jesus answered that the criminal would be with him in paradise "today" (Luke 23 : 42–43). The very word "paradise," being of Persian origin, suggests that the belief in an immediate ascent to heaven of the souls of the righteous was an outside intrusion into late-Judaic and early

Christian beliefs. The Book of Revelation, as noted, asserted that the martyrs' souls would be translated after death "underneath the altar" where they must wait for the resurrection (Rev. 16:9–11). The Letter to the Hebrews crowned its arguments in favor of Christianity with an eschatological scene that unmistakably takes place in heaven, namely in the heavenly Jerusalem where, together with myriads of angels, "the spirits of good men made perfect" assemble before God and Christ (Heb. 12:22–24).

Early patristic literature reflected the same wavering between the belief in bodily resurrection on the eschatological day of judgment and in the ascent to heaven of the souls of the just immediately after death. Justin Martyr (c. 100–c. 165), the first of the great patristic writers, was in spite of his Platonic past strictly opposed to the doctrine of an immediate ascent of the souls of the righteous to heaven. He thought that the spirits of the deceased must wait in Sheol for the day of judgment. He shared, however, the belief of some Judaic sources that in Sheol there are separate dwelling places for the righteous.[29] Similarly, according to Irenaeus (died c. 202) and Tertullian, the only destiny for man after death is the physical resurrection of the "flesh" on the day of judgment.[30] But Tertullian, like Justin Martyr, thought that there were different dwelling places in Sheol for the righteous and the evildoers: one of refreshment and consolation for the righteous and one of pain for the evildoers, while the martyrs would enter Christ's heaven immediately after death.[31]

Origen, on the other hand, blended Platonism with Christianity in a way that may have been partly responsible for the condemnation of some of his teachings three hundred years later, in 553, by the Second Council of Constantinople. He took over from Plato the doctrine of the preexistence of the souls and their continued existence after death. In *De Principiis* he asserted that the bodies of men are doomed to perish after death, that they will not be resurrected (3, 6:1–2), but that after death "the rational being [in man] . . . increasing in mind and intelligence, advances as a mind already perfect to perfect knowledge, no longer hindered by its former carnal senses" (2, 11:7).[32]

Origen's greatest contribution to eschatological thinking, at the same time the most "heretic" one, was his doctrine of *apocatastasis* ("restoration"). The source appears to have been the Apostle Peter's first address to the Jews of Jerusalem. In that speech Peter prophesied that Jesus the Messiah "must be received into heaven until the time of universal restoration [apocatastasis] comes" (Acts 3:21). To that vague idea Origen gave concrete content: All souls after death must undergo a process of purification, a purging baptism of fire until they attain salvation. Yet though there is a fire, there is no eternal hell, for Origen viewed the fire as a purifying process, not as an instrument of punishment. At the end of our age the purifying fire will be extinguished because all souls will have been saved.

If Origen's vision of the purifying fire lay at the origin of the Catholic doctrine of purgatory, his belief in the ultimate salvation of all souls lay at the origin of Universalism.[33] Origen can thus be regarded as the father of both the official Catholic doctrine of purgatory and of Universalism, which has been considered heretic since the Second Council of Constantinople.

The succeeding centuries witnessed the tendency to find an intermediate course among the various doctrines about man's destiny after death. The Hellenic doctrine of the immortality of the soul was widely accepted, but was blended with the late-Judaic and early Christian doctrine of a bodily resurrection on the day of judgment. The belief arose that in the first stage of salvation and damnation the souls of the righteous go to heaven immediately after death, those of the evildoers to hell, while the souls of an intermediate group, who have participated in the grace of God and Christ but whose sins have not yet been entirely expiated, are subject to a process of purification (purgatory), after which they too are admitted to heavenly bliss. The final stage of salvation and damnation, however, would be reached only on the day of judgment when the bodies of all men would be joined with their souls, those of the righteous in heaven, those of the evildoers in hell.

The Hellenic origin of this doctrine is also traceable to subsequent patristic writings, particularly those of Ambrose and his great disciple Augustine. Ambrose adopted the Orphic-Platonic doctrine of the soul's liberation from its prison within the body. "We know," he wrote, "that [the soul] survives the body and that, being set free from the bars of the body, it sees with clear gaze those things which before, dwelling in the body, it could not see."[34] Augustine wrote a treatise "On the Immortality of the Soul" (*De Immortalitate Animae*) immediately after Ambrose had baptized him.

The belief in purgatory also became popular at that time. Augustine accepted it as a process of post-mortem purification of the sinners' souls. Later, Caesarius of Arles (c. 470–542) asserted that venial sins are expiated in purgatory.[35] Gregory I the Great (pontificate 590–604) confirmed this doctrine, and the Second Council of Lyon in 1274 adopted it as an official article of faith. Gregory I also established quasi-officially the doctrine that the souls of the righteous enter heaven immediately after death, while those of the less perfect Christians enter purgatory.[36]

If after death the souls of righteous Christians ascend to heaven, either immediately or after purification in purgatory, what awaits them in paradise? Popular fantasy has always portrayed heaven as a realm of everlasting joys, populated with musician angels and saints whose hymns ascend to God and Christ. The official Church, however, has never indulged in such fantasies, but has attempted to visualize the ascent of the soul to heaven as an act of union with the Triune God, not in the sense of Eastern religions as a fusion with an all-soul, but as a beatific vision of God.

The Church derived this belief from several, if somewhat vague, New Testament sources, above all from Paul's beautiful hymn on love, in which he placed love ("agape," meaning man's love of God and of fellow man) above faith and hope (1 Cor. 13). He crowned that hymn with the vision that while our knowledge is partial, "the partial vanishes when wholeness comes." "Now we see only puzzling reflections in a mirror, but then we shall see face to face" (13:9 and 12).

The patristic thinkers also envisioned heavenly bliss as the wholeness of the knowledge of the Triune God or as a beatific vision of God. Augustine taught that after their purification the souls of the righteous would be granted the vision of the Triune God. Pope Gregory I in his *Moralia* asserted that in the region of blessedness, God would be seen in His glory, which is identical with His nature. The doctrine of the beatific vision culminated in the theology and philosophy of Thomas Aquinas (1224–1274), the leading Catholic thinker of the Middle Ages. He maintained that man has a natural desire to contemplate the divine essence. This desire, however, cannot be satisfied by natural means, but only by a supernatural gift that God bestows upon the souls of the blessed after death. By the light of glory in which the blessed souls dwell and through which they participate in the divine light, they become *deiform* ("Godlike"). Beatific vision, a union of the divine essence with the intellect of the blessed in heaven, reveals God as He is in Himself. The doctrine of the beatific vision was finally canonized by the Constitution of Benedict XII (pontificate 1334–1342). This Constitution, called *Benedictus Dei*, declared that the souls in heaven "behold the divine essence with intuitive and face-to-face vision . . . the divine essence showing itself without covering, clearly and openly."[37]

Dante, in his *Divine Comedy*, allegorized the doctrines of the Catholic Church on the destiny of human souls after death. In a grandiose tableau, he drew an immortal vision of hell, purgatory, and heaven, using the device of the poet's descent from the earth to the lowest depths of the Inferno and of a step-by-step ascent through Purgatory to the loftiest peaks of Paradise. Each of the three realms is divided into compartments. In the Inferno the compartments are populated by sinners whose punishments correspond to their sins; these compartments descend to the center of the earth where Lucifer directs the punishments. In the compartments of Purgatory there are also punishments that fit the sins, but punishment is not eternal because in Purgatory, "the human spirit is cleansed and becomes worthy to rise to heaven."[38] Most remarkable, however, is Dante's belief that even in Paradise there are ascending compartments. Only in the highest sphere, the Empyrean, can the Triune God be seen in beatific vision. Dante explained this hierarchy in heavenly bliss: "I understood then how everywhere in Heaven is Paradise although the grace of the Supreme God does not descend equally on all."[39]

In his compartmentalization of Inferno, Purgatory, and Paradise, Dante allegorized the belief, by then commonly accepted in the Christian world, that not only damnation but also salvation has degrees, that not only the punishments for sins but also the rewards for good deeds are proportionate. "The proportioning of our reward to our merit . . . is a part of our joy," says one of the blessed souls in Dante's Paradise.[40] Earlier, Augustine had asserted that in heaven there are degrees of beatitude, dependent upon the merits of the righteous. The 1439 Council of Florence canonized this doctrine, by declaring that the souls which have incurred no stains of sin or which have been purged of sin "see clearly the one and Triune God, just as He is, yet one more perfectly than another, in proportion to the diversity of merits."[41]

Accepting the doctrine of the soul's sojourn in heaven, purgatory, or hell immediately after death raised a problem: how could this doctrine be reconciled with the original Christian belief that on the last day of our age Christ would come back, the dead would be resurrected, divine judgment would be pronounced, and the kingdom of God would be erected? In spite of the efforts of the Church to keep in the background the original belief in the coming of Christ and in bodily resurrection, it remained an inherent part of the Christian faith, incorporated in the Nicene Creed and in the ritual of the Mass.

Yet how would this decision be arrived at in the indefinite interval between death and the day of judgment, in that interim period which concerns men most immediately and directly, when the fate of their souls will be decided for an aeon of indefinite duration? In Eastern religions no judge is needed for such a decision. Everyone's karma is the determining factor. But the Jewish-Christian belief in God as a personal power, in a judgment imposed by Him (or by Christ) militates against any Eastern-type doctrine. Thomas Aquinas attempted to establish such a doctrine. He taught that the soul of the deceased knows what it deserves and by an internal impulse is carried toward its destiny, in much the same way as a heavy object is carried earthward and a light object, heavenward.[42] But his gravity theory of the flight of the souls after death never found acceptance. A personalistic religion, as Christianity was from its beginning, cannot exclude a divine personal power from the fateful decision about the destiny of man after death.

It follows that each man after death must undergo two divine judgments: one immediately after death, and the second at the end of our age, on the day of resurrection when his soul is reunited with his body. This strange duplication of a particular judgment immediately after death and a general judgment after resurrection has resulted from blending the Hellenic concept of the immortality of the soul with the late-Judaic-Christian concept of bodily resurrection at the end of our age. The doctrine, however, is afflicted with the dilemma that the second divine judgment, which follows after an interval of aeons, cannot but be identical with the first.

The Catholic Church has never been able to find a way out of this dilemma between the particular and the general judgment, which may have been the principal reason that the doctrine of the particular judgment has never been canonized. Although it was established by such authoritative thinkers as Augustine, no council or papal decree has ever stated it officially. Yet it remains one of the Catholic Church's chief sources of ecclesiastical power. The apostolic power of allowing and forbidding, of forgiving and punishing, arrogated by the Church, weighs heavily enough upon each man and follows him to the grave. But the belief in the survival of the souls after death, in their different destinies according to their merits, was bound to become one of the most effective instruments of ecclesiastical power. For the priest as successor of Christ and his disciples is empowered to prejudge the sentence which the divine judge will impose on each man after death. And that sentence will be final, for even on the day of the last judgment it cannot be altered.

Or is the sentence not final? Is the power of the Church strong enough to interfere with a judgment that it has helped itself to impose? The answer, strangely enough, is yes. According to the Church, the divine judge can be swayed by intercessory prayers.

8. THE POWER OF INTERCESSORY PRAYERS

Intercessory prayers are not confined to the Christian religion. Belief in the efficacy of intercessory prayers was rather common in ancient religions, particularly in the Jewish religion, to which Christianity owes so many of its traditions. At first patriarchs and leaders of the Jewish people interceded with God for the forgiveness of its sins. Later, angels were assigned this task.

While in the Jewish tradition intercession remained on the periphery of the drama between God and man, it moved into the center of the Christian religion. After all, Christianity became an intercessional religion from the moment Jesus' death was interpreted as a vicarious sacrifice for the salvation of man. This sacrifice itself was intercession with God on behalf of man. The Apostle Paul stated that "the Spirit itself is pleading for us" and that Christ "pleads our case" (Rom. 8:26). Post-Pauline Scriptures affirmed the belief in Jesus' intercessory role. In the Gospel of John, Jesus at the end of his ministry prayed to God for his disciples and all believers that He may protect them (John 17:9–26). The Letter to the Hebrews asserted that Christ is "able to save absolutely those who approach God through him; he is always living to plead on their behalf" (Heb. 7–25); and to John, Christ appeared "as an advocate with the Father" for anyone who sins (1 John 2:1, King James Version).

In an early stage of Christianity the power of intercession was extended to the angels, above all to the guardian angels. The Gospel of Matthew in particular emphasized intercession by guardian angels (Matt. 18:10). Such great patristic thinkers as Clement of Alexandria, Origen, Ambrosius, as well as Thomas Aquinas, believed that the guardian angels bring men's prayers before God.[43]

Guardian angels have never ceased to play a role in Christian life. But while Christianity shares with other religions the belief in the protective function of angels, it has since very early times had its own saints to whom it has addressed itself for protection and intercession. The belief in the intercessory power of the saints seems to have derived from an intercessory authority that the martyrs acquired during their lifetime: they customarily wrote to bishops letters of recommendation for persons guilty of sins so that church penances would be reduced.[44] Later on, when the saints were moved heavenward and could meet the Triune God face-to-face in all eternity, they became the principal intercessors for sinful man. Cyril of Jerusalem (c. 315–c. 386) stated that the deceased saints were commemorated in order that through their intercession God may receive our petitions. Ambrose advised man to invoke the martyrs because having washed their own sins in their blood, martyrs can intercede for us in our weakness. Augustine, who frequently referred to the saints' intercession, asserted that the martyrs had died in such perfection that they had become our advocates.[45]

Gradually the *Ora pro nobis* ("Pray for us") which the early Christians addressed to the saints became an essential rite of the Catholic Church. Saints have become the protectors of churches, towns, countries, and have even pervaded many professions. Their intercessory function has become marked by the custom of giving names of saints to the newborn. Even such a radical Catholic document as the Dutch *New Catechism* states that "the child . . . is given the name of a saint, under whose particular protection he is placed." [46] With the emergence of the Virgin as "Mother of God" (*Mediatrix*),[47] Mary achieved the highest rank among those blessed ones whose help and intercession is invoked in Eastern and Western Catholicism.

Certainly, every Christian can invoke angels, Jesus, Christ, Mary, or saints to intercede for him. Petitionary prayers issue forth every day from Catholics all over the world. The Church has not superseded this relationship of the believers to the intercessors, but it has intensified, organized, and above all institutionalized it by accepting it in its liturgy. "May Christ . . . enable us to share in the inheritance of your saints, with Mary, the Virgin Mother of God, with the Apostles, the martyrs, and all your saints, on whose constant intercession we rely for help," reads the Canon of the Mass.

With the rise of the belief in purgatory, the belief in intercession reached its climax. No sincere Christian could ever hope that Christ, Mary, angels, or saints would intercede to save the soul of a man who had committed a mortal sin, or to obtain the beatific vision of the Triune God for the soul of a man who had not merited it. Yet Catholics generally believe that the intervention of these holy intercessors may help a poor soul in purgatory achieve an earlier ascent to heaven or subject it to less stringent purifying measures than would be otherwise permitted.

Among early Christian theologians, Augustine taught "that prayer, sacrifices and alms relieve the departed." [48] The Church as early as the seventh century institutionalized prayers for the dead through the Office of the Dead.[49] Funeral masses, which developed into the Requiem Masses, and the ecclesiastical invocation "Hail Mary," with its formula, "Pray for us sinners now and at the hour of death" are likewise of long standing. Since the twelfth century the All Souls' Day (on the second of November) has been instituted as a liturgical day on which the Office of the Dead and Requiem Masses are celebrated in order to help the

deceased attain the purification of their souls. The observance of All
Souls' Day—when Catholics generally visit the graves of beloved ones
who have died, adorn the graves with flowers, and pray for the deceased
—is a particularly striking example of the salvational power of the
Church. The observance of this day is a token of love and remembrance,
but those who observe it also hope that the pains of purification of their
beloved dead will be relieved if they themselves attend the ecclesiastical
rites of the Office of the Dead and the Requiem Mass.

The power of the Church to relieve the lot of the souls in purgatory,
accelerate their ascent to heaven, and relieve the penances for the living
sinners, has been increased by two ecclesiastical instruments: the indulgences and the doctrine of the treasure of merits. Since the eleventh
century, indulgences were grants given by ecclesiastical authorities to living persons for such good works as pilgrimages, crusades, and financial
support of churches or of other ecclesiastical functions. The 1095 Council of Clermont under Urban II (pontificate 1088–1099) granted the
first papal indulgence as an inducement to participate in the first crusade
(1096–1099). The council proclaimed that participation in it "will be
reckoned in place of all penance." [50]

The practice of granting indulgences was first used to relieve the severity of penances imposed by ecclesiastical authorities. But from the fifteenth century on, indulgences were also granted for the souls of the dead
in purgatory. Sixtus IV (pontificate 1471–1484) decreed the first indulgence of this kind in 1476. The difference between an indulgence
for the living and one for the dead is worth noting. In the former case
the Church, for a price to be paid by the sinner, reduces a penalty which
it has imposed itself. But, one may ask, can the Church relieve the terms
of a purification process which, according to Catholic belief, God has
imposed on the sinner's soul after his death? To this delicate question the
Church has given the answer that there is a difference between the effectiveness of the two kinds of indulgences. While an indulgence granted
to living persons is given *per modum absolutionis* ("by way of absolution"), indulgences for the dead are given only *per modum suffragii* ("by
way of petition"). The Church in this case takes over the saints' intercessory role. While in earlier periods saints were invoked to intercede
for the souls in purgatory, the Church later arrogated this role for itself,
either through the rules instituted for this purpose or, in special cases,
through indulgences.

The second instrument that the Church established to relieve the punishments of the living and the dead was the doctrine of the treasure of
merits. This doctrine (also common to Mahayana Buddhism) indicates

that Jesus, Mary, and the saints have stored up a treasure of merits, infinite in the case of Christ, finite in the case of Mary, the martyrs, and the other saints. But in each case the treasure of their merits exceeds the number needed for their own salvation. This excess of merits has been appropriated by the Church for the relief of sinners. The Church alone is entitled to administer this precious treasure by relieving the penances it has imposed on sinners and by interceding for the poor souls in purgatory.[51] The treasure flows, so-to-speak, into its own treasury.

The leading theologians of the thirteenth century, Thomas Aquinas and Bonaventura (Giovanni di Fidanza Bonaventura, 1221–1274) supported the doctrine of the treasure of merits. Canonized in 1343 by Clement VI (pontificate 1342–1352) in the bull *Unigenitus*, it has remained the basis for the Church's authority to grant indulgences. The Code of Canon Law refers to the tie between indulgences and the treasure of merits by defining indulgence as a "remission before God of the temporal punishment due to sins, whose guilt has already been forgiven, which ecclesiastical authority grants from the treasury of the Church." [52]

This involved ecclesiastical system of absolution from sins by the officiating priest and of indulgences based on the Church's treasure of merits provided believers with a feeling of being protected from damnation during and after their life, but at the high price of being spiritually and sometimes politically dominated and economically exploited by the ecclesiastical establishment. In view of the role indulgences played within this machinery, was it a coincidence that in 1517 a young monk and professor at the University of Wittenberg threw out a challenge to the ecclesiastical establishment destined to rend the Catholic Church asunder, a challenge that started with ninety-five erudite theses against the papal interpretation of the validity of the indulgences? The coincidence may have been a greedy prelate's scandalous abuse of the institution of indulgences,[53] but the rebellion against the Catholic Church had much deeper roots than a protest against corruption.

True, the Council of Trent and subsequently Pius V (pontificate 1566–1572) prohibited the corrupt practices which had intruded into the system of indulgences. But they did not touch on the system itself, a system based on the apostolic power of allowing and forbidding, appropriated by the Catholic Church and firmly anchored in the seven sacraments, particularly those of ordination and penance. This power implies that man, inescapably a sinner, can attain salvation in life and ultimate salvation after death only through the apostolic power of the sacramental and sacerdotal Church.

9. THE FIRST REBELLIONS AGAINST SACRAMENTALISM

The Nicene-Augustinian sacramental and sacerdotal church was still an *ecclesia militans* ("fighting church") in the age of Augustine, but transformed itself gradually into an *ecclesia triumphans* ("triumphant church"). It took six centuries—roughly from the fifth to the eleventh century—to Christianize the young European nations (the Germanic peoples, the Slavs, and the Magyars), that is, to inculcate in them the late-classical Hellenic-Roman-Christian civilization. The Church played a leading part in this process. Its prominence invested it with an unassailable authority, which in turn gave to all its doctrines and rites the status of unquestionable truth.

It may have been chiefly for this reason that in the first few centuries of its dominance, the Church succeeded in overcoming not only dogmatic rebellions, such as Arianism and Monophysitism, but also more deep-rooted rebellions, such as the millenarian Montanism and the antisacerdotal Pelagianism. From the sixth to the eleventh centuries, during the settlement and nation-building of the Germanic and Slavic peoples who had invaded most of Europe, the Church was substantially free from major heresies and rebellions.

The original split between the Eastern and Western churches, however, was not of a dogmatic, but of an organizational nature. It grew into a dogmatic split only when the Eastern churches rejected the Roman Catholic belief in purgatory. Moreover, because the elaborate machinery of ecclesiastical penalties and indulgences that was instituted in the West did not develop in the East, the sacerdotal power was always less pronounced in the Eastern Orthodox Churches than in the Roman Catholic Church.

The first rebellions within Western Christianity were not directed against any church doctrines, not even sacerdotalism, but against the Church's worldly wealth and secular power. These rebellions began at the end of the twelfth century when the growth of the cities with their material wealth and more liberal spirit heralded the decline of the feudal age, an age in which the Church had firmly held a position not only of ecclesiastical but also of political, economic, and social power.

The Rebellion of the Monks. The first stirrings of reform movements directed against ecclesiastical worldliness came from within the Church itself. A monk who had been elected pope, Gregory VII (pontificate 1073–1085), led this fight by introducing the so-called Gregorian reforms, aimed at the abolition of ecclesiastical abuses such as simony.[54]

The reform movement began to organize itself with the appearance of the Cistercian order in 1098, founded under the sign of poverty and simplicity, and with the admission into that order of Bernard de Clairvaux (1090–1153), a great monastic leader and ecclesiastical diplomat who never abandoned ascetic life.[55]

The monastic movement at the beginning of the thirteenth century was inspired by the same austere spirit. Both Francis of Assisi (Giovanni Francesco di Bernardone, c. 1182–1226) and Dominic (Domingo de Guzman, c. 1170–1221), based their mendicant monastic orders (the Franciscans in 1210 and the Dominicans in 1216) on the Gospel words preaching renunciation of worldly goods and aspirations: "If anyone wishes to be a follower of mine [Jesus], he must leave self behind; he must take up his cross and come with me" (Matt. 16:24). These stern commandments for Christian discipleship also inspired the third new mendicant order, the Augustinian (or Austin) Friars.[56] The early Franciscans, Dominicans, and Austin Friars remained faithful to the Church. The Dominicans proved this the hard way by leading the Church in its fight against the Cathars and by acting as an important instrument of the Inquisition.

Early Millenarianism. The first profound spiritual rebellion within the Church was directed against the claim to constitute the millennium. In the seven centuries which followed Augustine's proclamation that the Church is the millennium, that it constitutes the kingdom of God on earth, true millenarianism—the belief in a kingdom of God on earth that would be ushered in by Christ's coming—was banned.

However, the Church did not succeed in extirpating millenarianism entirely. From time to time millenarian beliefs stirred up one or the other group of the population. The approach of the year 1,000 gave rise to feverish expectations among great masses of people that God's kingdom on earth would soon be erected. Peasants and lower classes in the rapidly growing cities were particularly prone to transform their yearning for social liberation into millenarian expectations. "Sibylline" oracles about "the emperor of the last days" were believed to be fulfilled in the person of this or that ruler. Preachers who foretold the imminent breaking in of the millennium would stir up large masses.

In the twelfth century, millenarianism found a spiritually prominent advocate in the person of Joachim of Fiori (c. 1135–c. 1201), who significantly was a Cistercian monk of strict observance and later founded an even more austere order. Joachim stated his millenarian belief in the guise of a philosophy of history, which could be interpreted as an eschatological doctrine of progress. He divided history—past, present, and future—into three ages: that of the "Father" (Old Testament), characterized by the law; that of the "Son" (New Testament), ruled by grace; and that of the "Holy Spirit." According to some mystic arithmetic which Joachim applied, the third age was to begin in the year 1260 and would be dominated by the loving spirit. However, in fact, Joachim's third age was to be that of the kingdom of God on earth, where universal love would rule, wars would end, and the beatitudes of the Gospels would materialize. It would be an everlasting kingdom, embracing the whole world, the eschatological culmination and ending of history. In a spirit of apocalyptic prophecy, Joachim envisioned that the third age would be preceded by the fight against an Antichrist and would be initiated by the conversion of the non-Christian peoples. Joachim's millenarian visions were of an outspoken anti-ecclesiastical nature: while the Church was visible in the second age he constructed, it would become spiritual in the third age, ruled not by the ecclesiastical hierarchy but by *viri spirituales* ("spiritual men"), who in his view were represented by monks of the Cistercian type.

The impact of Joachim's millenarian doctrines was tremendous, particularly among the Franciscans. That order underwent several splits between Observants, followers of the austere rules of poverty, and Conventuals, followers of more lenient rules. An extreme group of the Observants became known as the Franciscan Spirituals. They adopted Joachim's doctrines and may have even derived their name from them. They had been protected by Celestine V (pontificate 1294),[57] but were severely attacked by the succeeding popes. John XXII (pontificate 1316–1334) even issued three bulls against them (1317–1318) and openly (in four bulls!) condemned the Franciscan doctrine of evangelic poverty, which asserted that Jesus and the apostles did not own any property.[58]

However rebellious the spirit of mendicant monasticism and Joachimism may have been, none openly challenged the structure and dogmas of the official Church. Although Joachim foresaw his third age ruled by the *viri spirituales*, he did not challenge the rule of the ecclesiastical authorities and the sacramentalism of the official Church during the second age, in which he lived. And although the austere orders challenged the worldliness of the official Church, their criticism of its dogmas did not go beyond the assertion that Jesus and the apostles owned no property.

The Rebellion of the Waldenses. The first real challenge to certain fundamentals for which the Church stood, such as sacramentalism, sacerdotalism, and anti-millenarianism, came from the Waldenser movement. It was based on the teachings and preachings of Pierre Valdes, a French merchant (c. 1140–c. 1217), who emphasized evangelic poverty translated into the reality of religious life. His followers called themselves the *Pauperes Christi* ("poor ones of Christ"). Their heresy became manifest when Valdes and his disciples disregarded a ban on preaching that the ecclesiastical authorities had imposed upon them as laymen. In later stages of their movement their defection from the Catholic Church and its dogmas became more pronounced. They formed their own ministry, with bishops, presbyters, and deacons, and adopted doctrines which two or three centuries later became common among Protestant churches. They rejected all but three sacraments—baptism, Eucharist, and penance —along with prayers to the saints, the belief in purgatory, indulgences, and above all any authority over religious doctrines but the Bible. They were, in fact, the first Protestants. By insisting on the sole authority of the Bible, they undermined the sacerdotal monopoly over the interpretation of the creed. They were also the first reformers who translated the Bible into the vernacular (Provençal), with a view to making it accessible to the lay people.

The rebellion of the Waldenses spread rapidly over large parts of western Europe, simultaneously with the growth of Catharism in southern Europe. This double threat to its ecclesiastical power induced the Catholic Church to organize and use force to fight heresy. The counteroffensive first climaxed in 1184 at the Council of Verona, where the Waldenses and the Cathars were excommunicated and Lucius III (pontificate 1181–1185) issued a bull, *Ad Abolendam*, which instituted a procedure of ecclesiastical trials against the heretics; it included the ill-famed provision of handing over "obdurate" heretics to the secular authorities. This prelude was followed in 1215 by the Fourth Lateran Council's decision (under Innocent III, pontificate 1198–1216) to force secular rulers, under threat of excommunication, to assist the Church in the persecution of heretics. Finally there came the Inquisition, a centralized papal judicial institution established through the Constitution *Excommunicamus*, issued in 1231 by Gregory IX (pontificate 1227–1241). The fight against heresies thus became a bloody civil war that rent Christianity for centuries.

While the Manichaean Cathars succumbed after a cruel warfare, the Waldenses were never subdued, in spite of severe persecution and countless martyred dead. Their movement proved to be seminal for the great Reformation of the sixteenth century, with which they merged.

The Spread of Mysticism. In the century that elapsed between the rise of the Waldenses and the outbreak of the Wycliffe-Hussitic rebellions, there was no other widespread religious movement that could have been considered an organized rebellion against ecclesiastical sacramentalism. That intervening century, however, was marked by a strong wave of mysticism, which in effect constituted a silent rebellion against sacramentalism.

Mysticism was not confined to Christianity. Sufism in Islam and mysticism in Judaism were parallel phenomena. What characterized mysticism in all three religions was the influence of Neoplatonism, an emanative, nearly pantheistic philosophy. Neoplatonism was one of the last products of the Hellenic-Roman civilization. It was founded by Plotinus (205–270 A.D.), who constructed a cosmic hierarchy that descends from the One (the Good) to the Nous (Mind), then to the human souls which are preexistent and immortal, and finally to matter, which emanates from the lowest part of the souls. The aspect of this system that had the strongest impact on Christian, Islamic, and Judaic mysticism was the doctrine that all emanations are longing to return to their source. The human soul can fulfill this longing by uniting with the One through intellectual and moral discipline, that is, through enlightenment and asceticism. By detaching himself from all earthly pleasures, the wise man, in a state of ecstasy, will be absorbed in the divinity—although he still retains his identity and, due to human weaknesses, may not be able to ascend to the divine during his lifetime but intermittently.

This mystical union with the deity in the midst of the ascetic's earthly life, which Plotinus experienced in his visions, was also experienced by numerous Christian, Islamic, and Jewish mystics. The great Eastern thinker Gregory of Nyssa (c. 335–c. 394) could be considered the first Plotinic Christian mystic, although in other ways he remained an orthodox Christian. He believed that, given divine grace, man's soul can enjoy the beatific vision of God during his lifetime.

Whereas the doctrines of Gregory of Nyssa apparently failed to have a great impact on later Christian thought, it is one of the strangest events in Christian history that the writings of a fifth-century, pseudonymous theologian, who called himself Dionysius the Areopagite (later known as Pseudo-Dionysius), were accepted as authentic and authoritative Christian writings of the first century, in spite of their outspoken Neoplatonic nature.[59] In his treatise, "Mystical Theology," the soul in the state of ecstasy ascends to the immediate vision of God and passes into the darkness in which the deity abides. The writings of Pseudo-Dionysius were upheld for more than one thousand years as authentic doctrines of the earliest Christian period. The fact that they were accepted by several popes and by such illustrious thinkers as Albertus Magnus (c. 1200–1280) and Thomas Aquinas, shows the profound susceptibility of Christian thinking and, above all, Christian feeling to mystical influences.[60]

Mystical strains ran through Christianity in all periods, but acquired an outspoken anti-sacramental character particularly in the thirteenth and fourteenth centuries. For his beatitude the mystic did not need the guidance, assistance, and censorship of the ecclesiastical hierarchy. He found salvation through a direct approach to God and Christ. It was no coincidence that some of the most renowned mystics were monks or nuns, particularly of the mendicant orders, who were living in a spirit of austerity which in effect was antithetical to the spirit prevalent in the official Church. Among the luminaries of Christian mysticism, the Flemish mystic Jan Van Ruysbroeck (1293–1381) was an austere Augustinian Canon who castigated the abuses that had arisen within the Church. All outstanding representatives of the German mystical school, such as Johannes Eckehart von Hochheim (Meister Eckhart, c. 1260–c. 1327), and Johannes Tauler (c. 1300–1361), were Dominicans. The great Italian mystic Catherine of Siena (Caterina Benincasa, 1347–1380) was a Dominican nun of the strictest observance.

The doctrines of most mystics were similar to each other, but none was expressed so poetically as Van Ruysbroeck's "Spiritual Espousals." Of the mystic's face-to-face vision of God during his lifetime he wrote: "Those who have raised themselves into the absolute purity of their spirits by the love and reverence which they have for God, stand in His presence, with open and unveiled faces."[61]

Christian mysticism never crystallized in an organizational form comparable to Islamic Sufism and Jewish Hasidism.[62] But in the period that preceded the organized rebellions against sacramentalism, communities arose, particularly in Germany and the Low Countries, with a strong mystical background. Variously known as Brethren of the Free Spirit, as Beghards (male) and as Beguines (female), these communities were partly condemned by the Church (at the Council of Vienne, 1311–1312), partly tolerated, but always resisting its guidance and control. They constituted a base of unrest and anxiety for the Church and may have facilitated the growth of the great reformatory movements with which they largely merged, with the exception of those Beguines whose semi-monastic communities were allowed by the Church.[63]

One of the mystic communities of that period, the Brothers (and Sisters) of the Common Life, even contained germs of the Reformation of the sixteenth century. Its spiritual father was the Dutch priest Gerard Groote (1340–1384). Groote can also be considered as the spiritual father of the Devotio Moderna, a reformist movement which in many respects anticipated the Reformation, particularly in its advocacy of the simple apostolic life and its emphasis on reading the Bible. Like the Waldenses, this movement recommended the translation of the Bible into the vernacular languages.

The outstanding literary product of Devotio Moderna was the "Imitation of Christ" (*De imitatione Christi*), a treatise whose author was probably the German monk Thomas a Kempis (Thomas Hemerken, c. 1380–1471), an Augustinian Canon of the Windesheim Congregation, which had been founded by disciples of Groote in the spirit of Devotio Moderna. The "Imitation of Christ," a collection of guidelines for Christian perfection, centered on the humble, devoted life that has overcome all earthly desires as the way of coming close to God and Christ. It understood this closeness as a loving, quasi-mystical union with the deity. Christ, who himself speaks in the treatise, says to the believer: "If thou couldst perfectly annihilate thyself and empty thyself of all created love, then should I overflow into thee with great grace." [64]

The immense popularity that the "Imitation of Christ" has enjoyed from the time of its appearance (c. 1440) to the present is a testimony to the strong streak of mysticism that runs through the Christian world, blended with the ethical ideal of the simple, apostolic life. In sum, the mystics of the thirteenth and fourteenth centuries were a counterforce to the sacramentalism and sacerdotalism of the official Church.

The Wycliffite-Hussite Rebellions. While the late-Medieval mendicant monasticism and mysticism retained its ties with all institutions of the Church, the English Wycliffite and the Czech Hussite movements grew into open anti-ecclesiastical rebellions.

John Wycliffe (c. 1330–1384), being a cleric himself, never defected from the Church and was never deprived of his ecclesiastical services, although he was from time to time harassed by church authorities. He made, however, decisive contributions to the rebellion against the Church's sacerdotalism, particularly with his attack on papal authority, which constituted the first stage in the dissociation of the English people from the papacy.[65]

Wycliffe's fight against papal authority was only one aspect of his anti-sacerdotal rebellion. He not only attacked ecclesiastical wealth and power but, just as the Waldenses, insisted that the Bible, rather than the priests, be the only source of religious authority. As the Waldenses were the first reformers to translate the Bible into the vernacular, Wycliffe and his disciples (his personal contribution is controversial) were among the first to translate the Bible into English.[66]

As part of Wycliffe's fight against sacerdotalism, he attacked the system of indulgences and masses for the dead and insisted that fundamental church reforms be imposed by the secular authorities.[67] In spite of his radical anti-sacerdotalism, however, Wycliffe did not abandon any official religious dogmas, with the exception of the doctrine of transubstantiation, which had become an official dogma since the Fourth Lateran Council in 1215. He anticipated Zwingli and Calvin by denying that in the Eucharist the substance of bread and wine is changed into Christ's body and blood (transubstantiation).

Like the Waldenser movement, Wycliffism never surrendered, but lived on as Lollardism.[68] That movement originated among Oxford scholars, followers of Wycliffe who were instrumental in translating the Bible into English and in popularizing his doctrines with middle-class groups. After Wycliffe's death, the Lollards produced a creed, the "Twelve Conclusions" (1395), which attacked subservience to the pope, the sacrament of ordination, the temporal powers of the Church, confessions to priests, prayers for the dead, and the dogma of transubstantiation. Although Lollardism turned from time to time to political action (Lollard uprising of 1413–1414; conspiracy of 1431), it never became a real political force. It remained an anti-papal, anti-sacerdotal rebellious group until it merged with the Lutheran movement that was intruding in England and with which it had much in common.

Wycliffe's doctrines were echoed not in the neighboring Low Countries and Germany, where the rebellious spirit had manifested itself in the growth of half-heretical and mystical movements, but in Bohemia. The starting point of Bohemia's anti-sacramental rebellion can be traced to the Moravian priest Jan Milic of Kromerice (d. 1374), who was a follower of Devotio Moderna. As early as 1363 he preached the gospel of the poor and pure church, the coming of Antichrist, and the approach of the millennium.

Jan Hus (c. 1373–1415) grew up in an atmosphere influenced by Milic's preachings. Through his teachings and by virtue of his martyr's death, Hus became the standard-bearer of the religious rebellion in the fifteenth century. Like Wycliffe and Milic, Hus was a cleric. Having familiarized himself with Wycliffe's writings (through the intermediary of Bohemian scholars who had studied in Oxford, the spiritual center of Wycliffism), Hus was determined to fight for church reform within the framework of the Church. Like a number of other Bohemian scholars and clerics, he did not subscribe to all doctrines of his master Wycliffe. But Wycliffe's fight against the wealth, corruption, and worldly power of the clergy and the absolute power of the pope was also his fight. Moreover, embittered about the abuse of the indulgences, which was already rampant during his ministry, he also attacked them. He was supported by powerful nationalist forces in his country and by the popular opposition to ecclesiastical power. But he was also bitterly assailed by conservative ecclesiastical and secular groups and was excommunicated by the Archbishop of Prague in 1411. He became a martyr when he fell into the trap of a royal safe-conduct (issued by King Sigismund I, who reigned from 1410 to 1437), which lured him to the Council of Constance (1414–1418) where he was to defend himself. Although his trial was invested with all the trappings of ecclesiastical procedures, there is no doubt that his execution was a travesty of canonical justice.[69]

The Hussite movement, which sprang up after the execution of Hus, owes its name to the uproar that this martyr's death created in Bohemia and Moravia. But its roots lay in the rebellious spirit which had preceded that of Hus, and it was supported by powerful social and political forces in the cities and even in the nobility. This strong social and nationalist impetus gave the Hussites a power that no previous reform movement had ever acquired. Their goals were formulated in the Four Articles which, while directed against the ecclesiastical power, did not deviate from any religious church doctrines. The Four Articles demanded freedom of preaching, poverty of the priests, the confiscation of ecclesiastical estates, and as a symbol of the Hussites' anti-sacerdotal principles, the communion "in both kinds," that is, in bread and wine: the Church refused the wine to the lay people.[70]

The Hussites proved invincible in the military field, even in the face of the three crusades organized against them. They asserted themselves strongly in their dispute with the official Church. The Council of Basel (1431–1449) negotiated with them on the subject of the Four Articles for the territory which the Hussites controlled, and made concessions to them through the so-called "Compactata," concluded between the Council and the Hussites in 1433 and officially promulgated in 1436. Yet the split between the Hussites and the official Church was never really healed. Paul II (pontificate 1458–1471) annulled the Compactata in 1462 and even excommunicated the Bohemian King Podebrad (who reigned from 1458 to 1471) for recognizing communion in both kinds.

Like the Waldenses and the Lollards, the Hussites never surrendered and their movement never disappeared. The Hussite principles, as enunciated in the Four Articles and in the Compactata, remained in force in the Bohemian and Moravian churches. Later on, Lutheranism acquired a strong foothold in that country. It was not until the fateful battle of the White Mountain in 1620, in which the Czech nation was crushed by the Habsburgs, who imposed the rule of Catholicism for three hundred years, that the force of Hussitism was spent.

However, another religious movement, the Bohemian Brethren (in Latin, *Unitar Fratrum*), had grown out of Hussitism in Bohemia and Moravia. This new group split off from the Hussites in 1457 and formed its own community and ministry, which became a model for later Protestant churches, particularly the Presbyterians. The Brethren too were driven underground by the battle of the White Mountain or emigrated, but they have survived as Bohemian and Moravian Brethren. In 1722 they founded a new center in Germany on the estate of the Lutheran Count Nikolaus Ludwig von Zinzendorf (1700–1760), which they named "Herrnhut."[71] The Moravian Brethren have retained their identity and their communities to the present time. Through missionary activities they founded communities in a number of countries, especially in the United States—with centers in Pennsylvania, where they founded Bethlehem, and in North Carolina. The American community of the Moravian Church has retained its Latin name, *Unitas Fratrum*.

It was thus from many streams that the Reformation sprang. That great religious revolution divided Western Christianity and created religious institutions based on an entirely different relationship of Christian man to his church and its ministers than that upheld by the Roman Catholic Church.

CHAPTER VI

The Reformation:
Moderate and Radical

The rise of the mendicant orders, the spread of millenarianism and mysticism, and the open rebellions of the Waldenses, Lollards, and Hussites signalled the awakening of a new religious spirit, one that rejected the sacerdotalism and sacramentalism of the official church, in favor of the simplicity of the biblical beliefs and of the early church. The final victory of this religious rebellion in a large part of the Christian world was ultimately connected with the personalities of Luther, Zwingli, and Calvin. For it was on the basis of the teachings and activities of these three great religious reformers that a great many of the Protestant churches were founded: the Lutheran churches of Germany and the Scandinavian countries, the Reformed and Presbyterian churches in the English-speaking countries, and the Church of England, which retained certain Catholic features.

Neither the history of the sixteenth-century rebellion against Catholicism nor the structure of present-day Protestantism can be properly understood without taking account of the fact that outside the Lutheran-Calvinist Reformation a more radical rebellion arose—that of the Anabaptists, the Spiritualists, and the Unitarians—which gripped large parts of Europe and influenced religious movements in England and North America from the seventeenth to the nineteenth century. That rebellion in turn gave rise to such powerful Protestant churches as the Baptists, Methodists, Quakers, Unitarians, and Christian Scientists, and to the strictly millenarian churches of the Latter-Day Saints, the Seventh-Day Adventists, and Jehovah's Witnesses.

1. LUTHER AND THE LUTHERAN CHURCHES

The spark that ignited the edifice of Roman Catholic Christianity was kindled in Wittenberg. In 1517, when Martin Luther sent his Ninety-five Theses to his monastic superior,[1] he may not have had much knowledge of the rebellions that preceded his own. But the spirit in which he wrote his theses was the same as that of his predecessors. As a monk, he was akin to Joachim of Fiori, Francis of Assisi, Dominic, and Girolamo Savonarola, all of whom had rebelled against the worldly power and luxury of the Church.[2] But he was also a great scholar, and it was this blend of a monk struggling with his own guilt feelings and of a scholar analyzing Scriptures that inspired Luther to bring a new religion to the world.

In 1512 Luther received a doctor's degree from the newly founded University of Wittenberg. He was subsequently given a chair there and—significantly for his and the university's reformatory spirit—he began to lecture on the Bible, particularly on the Apostle Paul's Letters. It was in Paul's Letters, the Letter to the Romans in particular, that Luther found the spiritual source for his reformatory work.[3]

It so happened that Luther's spiritual development coincided with the Church's implication in some very grave depravations. As a young monk Luther had been commissioned to journey to Rome in 1510, where he witnessed ecclesiastical luxury and corruption in the very center of the Church. A few years later he was shaken by the great indulgence scandal connected with the construction of the papal Basilica St. Peter, as well as the shameless simony of the Archbishop of Mainz and Magdeburg, and the dubious fund-raising practices of the Dominican Johannes Tetzel.[4]

Here then was a particularly crass case of salvation *ex opere operato* ("by the work done"): salvation of souls in purgatory through indulgence money that was actually used to save a corrupt prelate from his creditors. For his impassionate rebellion against this strange concept of salvation through corruption, Luther found spiritual support in the Apostle Paul's concept of salvation. As Luther understood him, Paul taught that man, affected by original sin, cannot be saved by his own efforts, but only by

the grace of God, poured out on mankind through the expiatory sufferings and death of Christ. "God's grace accepted is justification," lec-
tured the young Professor Luther, even before he wrote his Ninety-five
Theses. Paul taught that by faith, rather than by the works of the (Jewish)
law, man can be justified before God. The tenet *Simul justus et peccator,
semper penitens* ("simultaneously righteous and sinner, always peni-
tent")[5] became the nucleus of Luther's faith, and the tenet *Fide sola*
("through faith alone") became the fundamental prerequisite for salvation. Luther was so profoundly impressed by this doctrine, which he
found in Paul's Letter to the Romans, that he even altered the text of
that letter. Whereas Paul asserted "that a man is justified by faith quite
apart from success in keeping the law" (Rom. 3:28), Luther added the
word "alone" to follow the word "faith."[6]

On the basis of this faith Luther conceived the Ninety-five Theses.[7] As
a literary document, they could be regarded as a theological treatise
dealing with the issue of indulgences. But as a political statement, they
constituted an attack on papal authority in one of the central areas of
sacerdotal power, that of forgiving and refusing to forgive. The theses
expressly restricted that power, by asserting that the pope (1) does not
have the power of the keys; (2) cannot remit any penalties other than
those he personally imposed; (3) cannot impose penalties on the dying;
and (4) cannot grant remission to souls in purgatory, but can offer only
intercessory prayers for them.[8] Thus, while not rejecting the authority of
the pope to grant indulgences, the theses deprived them of their chief
attraction, the relief of souls in purgatory.

More fundamental than the quarrel about indulgences was the anti-
sacramental spirit of the theses. What is needed for salvation, they maintained, is not ecclesiastical power to absolve man of his sins, but a life of
faith and repentance. The very first thesis stated: "When our Lord and
Master Jesus Christ said 'Repent,' he willed the entire life of believers to
be one of repentance." Since man is always sinful, he must repent
throughout his life; but, on the other hand, he is always justified: "Any
truly repentant Christian has a right to full remission of penalty and
guilt, even without indulgence letters" (Thesis 36). Thus remission of
guilt through permanent repentance appeared to Luther as the way to
salvation: "And thus be confident of entering into heaven through many
tribulations," exclaimed the last thesis.

Technically it would have proved difficult for an ecclesiastic prosecutor
to find evidence of true heresy in any of the theses, for neither the supremacy of the pope nor any Catholic dogma was formally rejected.
Nevertheless, the Papal Curia undertook a long-drawn-out trial against

Luther. It culminated in an encounter in 1518 between Luther and the great Dominican theologian Cardinal Tommaso Cajetan (c. 1468–c. 1534), in which the only issue that remained controversial was *Unigenitus*, the 1343 bull of Pope Clement VI, which based the practice of indulgences on the doctrine of the treasure of merits. Leo X (pontificate 1513–1521), nevertheless, excommunicated Luther in his 1521 bull, *Decet Romanum Pontificem*. When Luther refused to recant at the historic Diet of Worms, called in 1521 by Emperor Charles V (who reigned from 1519 to 1556), he was outlawed and his writings were proscribed.

Yet even if Cardinal Cajetan had contented himself with Luther's willingness to cease commenting on indulgences, and even if a compromise had been reached, one can argue that the spirit of rebellion against the sacramental church was already too strong to avoid a confrontation between the sacramentalists and the anti-sacramentalists. Luther indeed was willing to be silent about the indulgences, but one could not have expected him to remain silent about the fundamental issue of salvation. His interpretation of the Pauline belief in salvation solely through faith undermined the whole sacramental edifice erected by the Catholic Church. The persecutions to which Luther was subjected may have accelerated his conviction that the Church was in need of a fundamentally new structure. Indeed, within a few years, in cooperation with a group of devoted followers, he constructed the foundations of a church profoundly different from the sacramental structure of the Catholic Church.

It was principally Luther's support of Paul's doctrine of gratuitous divine grace and of justification of the repentant believer through faith that revolutionized the structure of his church. In his view, faith justifies man in spite of sin: "Grace is sufficient to enable us to be accounted entirely and completely righteous in God's sight." [9] But it would be wrong to conclude, as has sometimes been done, that this doctrine encouraged sin, for as the theses show, Luther had a very stern view of the prerequisites for salvation. It would be no less erroneous to conclude from his rejection of good works as an instrument of salvation that Luther considered them unnecessary. For he stated, "Our Christian faith does not free us from works, but from false opinions concerning works, that is, from the foolish presumption that justification is acquired by works." [10]

Being Paulinian, Luther also inherited Paul's predestinarian doctrine: as God pours out His grace gratuitously, He chooses those whom He will save. Earlier than Calvin, Luther adopted the belief in the elect and the damned: "By divine predestination the elect are chosen for eternal happiness, the rest are left graceless and damned to everlasting hell," Luther asserted in *De servo arbitrario* ("On the bondage of the will").[11]

Luther's theodicy was in fact based on the belief that God's justice is unfathomable, that if His justice could be adjudged by human reckoning,
it clearly would not be divine. Nevertheless man remains responsible for
his deeds and thoughts, and his salvation remains dependent on his faith,
which includes life-long repentance.

This concept abolished the priesthood as a sacramental office. It replaced it with the personal relationship of the believer to God, in which
every true believer is a priest himself: "We are all priests. . . . We have all
one faith, one Gospel, one sacrament; how then should we not have the
power of discerning and judging what is right or wrong in matters of
faith?" Hence, priestly privileges were no longer needed, although as
priests ourselves, we may allow or elect certain people "to do that which
we all alike have power to do." [12] Luther's creation was, thus, a new
church, free of the priesthood's dominion over man's soul. But his church
was based on the same Nicene Trinitarian Creed as were the Eastern
Orthodox and Roman Catholic churches. Moreover, the dictum *Extra
ecclesiam nulla salus* remained valid for his new church: "Outside the
Christian church is no truth, no Christ, no salvation." [13]

Luther was one of those rare thinkers who not only revolutionized
the world by the power of his word, but who was also personally instrumental in carrying out that revolution. He was assisted in this task by the
ferment that other religious rebels had created and by the social and
political climate that existed during his lifetime and particularly in his
own country, a climate created by: the rise of the cities to social and
political power; the rebellious spirit of the oppressed peasants (although
Luther deserted them in the hour of crisis, the Peasants' Revolt of 1524–
1525); the fragmentation of the German Empire; the growing power of
the territorial princes; and the readiness of large parts of the "Christian
Nobility of the German Nation" (to whom Luther appealed) to desert
the pope and secularize the properties of the Church.

In 1530, nine years after the Diet of Worms, another imperial diet met
in Augsburg. Under the leadership of Luther's disciple Philipp Melanchthon (1497–1560),[14] a document was submitted to the diet establishing
the foundations of the Lutheran Church. Called the Augsburg Confession,[15] this document did not alter those dogmatic foundations of the
Christian Church that had evolved in the patristic period and culminated
in the Councils of Nicaea, Constantinople, and Chalcedon. Article 1
of the Augsburg Confession retained Trinitarianism. Article 17 confirmed the beliefs in the coming of Christ, divine judgment, general resurrection, "eternal life and everlasting joy" for the righteous, and "endless
torments" for the evildoers (and for the devils!). The sacraments of bap-

tism—including infant baptism—and of the Eucharist were retained (Articles 9 and 10). The Mass was recognized to the extent that it contains the communion under the two forms of bread and wine for the laymen (in accordance with the Hussite rites). Even private confession was recognized, although no longer as a sacral instrument (Article 11). In short, in the field of church dogma the Lutheran Church was conservative. It even retained the Catholic belief that immediately after death, man's soul finds its reward or punishment in heaven, purgatory, or hell. Thus, the men who submitted to the emperor this document of their creed took great pains to emphasize the differences between themselves and the Radical Reformers.

Yet at the same time, the Augsburg Confession set forth the reformed Christian faith and the reformed church structure as Luther had constructed them. It emphasized Luther's fundamental doctrine that God, not for merits' but for Christ's sake, justifies those who believe that they are received in favor for Christ's sake (Article 5). Good works are not a condition for salvation; they are the good fruits brought forth by faith (Article 6).

The Augsburg Confession rejected the Catholic doctrine that the sacraments justify men by the work done (Article 13). The same restriction applied to all ecclesiastical rites: they may be "profitable for tranquillity and good order in the church," but they are not necessary for salvation. Thus, any rites instituted for propitiating God or giving satisfaction for sins were blatantly contrary to the Gospel and the doctrine of faith (Article 15). As prayers to the saints were also banned, Jesus Christ being the only intercessor (Article 21), the Lutheran Church ceased to be a sacramental institution with the power to pour out salvation.

If, nevertheless, Lutheranism continued to maintain that outside the church there is no salvation, the Augsburg Confession understood "church" to mean the assembly of believers in which the Gospel is rightly taught and the sacraments are rightly administered (Article 7), but which has no sacramental authority. While the task of teaching and administering is entrusted to persons rightly called (Article 14), they are not priests in the Catholic sense, but teachers and administrators, or *pastors* (Latin for "shepherds"). While the Augsburg Confession retained confession and private absolution for those who repent (Articles 11 and 12), absolution was no longer contingent on penance.

Although the priestly power of the Lutheran pastor was diminished nearly to the vanishing point, the church retained its power due to its monopoly of ultimate salvation. However, the Lutheran churches were very dependent on the power of the state; they had to pay dearly for the aid the territorial princes had given them during Luther's struggle with the Catholic Church and the emperor. In Germany and in the Scandinavian countries, the Lutheran churches had to recognize the secular rulers as their superiors. The princes established the church orders and installed church superintendents. The principle *Cuius regio, eius religio* ("the ruler's religion becomes that of his territory") was the outcome of the sixteenth-century religious struggle between German Catholicism and Protestantism; it formed the basis of the Peace of Augsburg, concluded between the Catholic and Protestant princes in 1555 by a diet in Augsburg under Ferdinand I (who reigned as king from 1531 to 1556, and as emperor from 1556 to 1564).While that principle sanctioned the Catholic and Protestant churches' monopoly over the creeds of all subjects of the princes and over man's salvation, it also sealed for centuries the subjection of the Protestant churches to the secular rulers. It was not until the 1918 revolution in Germany that the office of the secular rulers as heads of the Protestant churches ended.[16]

2. CALVIN AND THE CALVINIST CHURCHES

The religious revolution which gripped Germany with the appearance of Luther's Ninety-five Theses quickly spread to southern and western Europe, where its character changed perceptibly. In Germany the Reformation was supported by territorial princes on whom the Lutheran churches remained dependent as long as their rule lasted. The same dependence on the secular ruler was imposed on the Church of England. Yet the Reformation received its most powerful impetus neither in Germany nor in England but in Switzerland, which although technically under imperial rule, had in fact achieved independence in 1499.[17] It was first Zwingli, and after his premature death Calvin, who determined the spirit and much of the shape of the institutions of the Reformation in the western countries outside Lutheran Germany and Scandinavia.

Huldrych Zwingli (1481–1531), a Swiss priest since 1506, began to propagate reform ideas simultaneously with and partly independently from Luther. His reformatory views, especially those upholding the sole authority of the Bible, the limitation of sacraments, the symbolic nature of the Eucharist, and the simplification of the religious services, quickly became popular in the Swiss churches. The church of Zurich in particular adopted Zwingli's doctrines, which he formulated in sixty-seven articles in 1523. In the midst of his reformatory activities, however, he was killed in a war against the Catholic cantons. In 1536 the Swiss Reformed churches, guided by Zwingli's disciple and successor, Heinrich Bullinger

(1504–1575), adopted in Basel a reformed creed, the First Helvetic Confession.

The year 1536 also saw in the same Swiss town the publication of Calvin's *Institutes of the Christian Religion*, the fundamental work of the Reformed Church.[18] Jean Calvin (1509–1564), after having completed academic studies in France, left his country for Basel in 1536, shortly after his conversion to the ideas of the Reformation. Soon after the publication of the *Institutes* he moved to Geneva, where (with an interruption from 1538 to 1541) he remained for the rest of his life.

With the establishment of the Swiss Reformed churches, as they were organized by Zwingli and his disciples, and with Calvin's teachings and activities in Geneva, the Western Reformation was firmly rooted. One may indeed regard Switzerland as the native country of the Reformation outside Lutheranism, and Zwingli and Calvin as its founders.[19]

In the field of religious doctrine, the differences between the Lutheran and the Helvetic churches, though minor, were still important enough to prevent a merger of the two main currents of the Reformation. The principal doctrinal difference concerned the nature of the Eucharist. Luther had retained this fundamental feature of Catholic sacramentalism, the belief in the real presence of Christ in the bread and wine of the Eucharist. Although Luther abandoned the Catholic dogma of transubstantiation, he adopted the doctrine of a spiritual presence of Christ in the bread and wine. Zwingli, on the other hand, rejected the belief in Christ's real presence in the Eucharist.[20] In other words, Calvinism, which followed Zwingli's doctrine, removed itself one step further from Catholic sacramentalism than had Lutheranism. In an attempt to heal this split, Luther and Zwingli met personally at the 1529 Colloquy of Marburg in Germany. Although agreeing on fourteen points, they were unable to agree on the issue of Christ's presence in the Eucharist, a doctrinal difference that sealed forever the split between the two principal wings of the Reformation.

Calvinism and Lutheranism also differed over the doctrine of predestination. Both churches were founded on the belief in God's grace which works through faith as the sole instrument of salvation. But Calvin's formulation of the doctrine of predestination, which the Apostle Paul and Augustine had derived from their belief in God's grace, was more rigid than Luther's. Due to Adam's fall, Calvin taught, all men are predestined to be sinners: "God not only foresaw the fall of the first man, and thereby the ruin of all his posterity, but also willed it."[21]

Calvin's doctrine of salvation and damnation can be summarized as

follows: Through the grace of God some sinners are redeemed and predestined to be saved. Yet God also wills the damnation of the others,
who remain fully responsible for their evil thoughts and deeds. "While
God accomplishes through the wicked what He has decreed by His secret
judgment, they are not excusable."[22] On the other hand, where God
pours out His grace, it is certain and inamissible (i.e., incapable of being
lost). Faith, in effect, is imposed by God. From faith springs repentance.
From repentance springs regeneration, which implies an active, pious life.
From regeneration springs justification. From justification springs salvation.

The active, pious life that Calvinism requires is not confined to religious observances, but extends to secular life. In the secular sphere it
means a life devoted to intense work, according to each man's calling.
Hard work and its material results are indicative of belonging to the
elect. These work ethics were well suited to the rising tide of capitalism
in West European and North American countries where Calvinism found
a fertile soil, as particularly the German sociologist Max Weber (1864–
1920) emphasized.[23]

Salvation, in the view of the early Reformed churches, still meant the
ascent into heaven of the souls of the elect immediately after death.
Calvin believed in the watchful wake of the soul of the righteous after
death in an unspecified realm, blissfully anticipating the resurrection of
its body and the last judgment.[24] The doctrine of the immortality of
the soul was confirmed in the First Helvetic Confession (in Article 7).
In the Second Helvetic Confession,[25] those were condemned who believed that the soul will sleep after death. The Heidelberg Catechism of
1563, a German Reformed document generally recognized by the Reformed communities, insisted that "my soul, after this life, shall be immediately taken up to Christ, its head." Even in the Confession of Faith,
adopted by the Westminster Assembly of the English Presbyterians
(1643–1649), it was stated that after death the souls of the righteous
would be "received into the highest heavens, where they behold the face
of God," while the souls of the wicked would be cast into hell (Article 32).

Yet whereas the religious doctrinal differences between Lutheranism
and Calvinism were minor, there was a marked difference in their relations with the secular powers. Lutheran churches were dependent on the
secular authorities, while Calvinist churches were not. Calvinist churches
were governed only by their members. In long-drawn-out struggles with
the civic authorities of Geneva, Calvin succeeded in forcing them to

recognize the complete autonomy of the church. Calvinism's Ecclesiastical Ordinances established four orders of church offices—pastors, "doctors," deacons, and elders—and set up the consistory, an autonomous ruling body of the church composed of pastors and elders. Thus Calvin's Geneva church created the germ of the organization of the Reformed churches.

The Geneva consistory was in charge of church discipline, and imposed a rigid regime of moral-religious duties and prohibitions even upon the civic authorities. Traces of this discipline appear in Calvinist countries to the present time. This strange combination of ecclesiastical autonomy and the imposition of church discipline on the secular authorities characterized the Reformed churches in all those countries where they constituted the ruling church. Church discipline gave the ecclesiastical authorities the power to punish and, in extreme cases, to excommunicate evildoers or persons with "erroneous" opinions; the civic authorities often shaped their laws in accordance with the rules established by the church.[26]

The Helvetic creed, determined by Zwingli, Calvin, and their disciples and formulated in the two Helvetic Confessions, spread from Switzerland to a large part of continental Europe, the British Isles, and the British colonies, principally those in North America. In continental Europe—chiefly in the Netherlands, France (Huguenots), Hungary, and parts of Germany—the Calvinist churches established themselves as Reformed churches, mostly after grave struggles with the secular powers. In England, where the Church of England remained subject to governmental authority, the principal Calvinist communities developed as Presbyterian and Congregational churches. While they differ from each other in matters of ecclesiastical organization, both regard the democratic organization of Calvin's church in Geneva as the common model. Moreover, both churches accepted the Westminster Confession of Faith, which had been adopted under the leadership of the Cromwellian Parliament.[27] In Scotland, Presbyterianism became the established church,[28] while in New England the first settlers established Congregational churches.

Wherever the Reformed, Presbyterian, or Congregational churches achieved recognition as the established or dominant church (as in the Netherlands, Scotland, and some British colonies in North America), they were autonomous in their own government and democratic in their organization. At the same time, however, the churches were intertwined with the secular government. They were a determining factor in secular legislation and practices that dealt with matters of religion and morals.

Salvation was determined both by the church—outside of which there was no salvation—and by the secular government.[29]

When Luther wrote *Von der Freiheit eines Christenmenschen* ("Of the freedom of a Christian man"), he understood freedom to mean the liberation of Christian man from the fetters of sacramentalism and sacerdotalism. This liberation was indeed accomplished by the Lutheran and Calvinist Reformation. However, it was a far cry from true religious freedom as modern man understands it. The Reformation of the Lutheran, Calvinist, and Anglican type bound ecclesiastical and secular authority so closely together, insisted so strongly on the monopoly of its creed and its institutions, watched so anxiously over the observance of its religious and moral laws, that the paths toward salvation were as strictly controlled by these institutions as by the Catholic Church.

3. THE RADICAL REFORMATION[30]

The great Reformers of the sixteenth century had divided Western Christendom by their doctrine of a church freed of sacramentalism and sacerdotalism. However, while they created churches which remained intertwined with the secular powers, a small, despised, persecuted, martyred band of radical Reformers—the Anabaptists, Spiritualists, and Unitarians—introduced the ideal of churches freed not only from the power of an apostolically sanctified priesthood, but also from any ties with secular powers. Moreover, the Radical Reformation introduced religious ideas which challenged dogmas and traditions that had dominated the Christian world for more than a thousand years.

Many currents converged in the Radical Reformation. While it is difficult to distinguish them clearly from each other, they had in common certain features that permit us to classify all of them as radical. The most significant feature they shared was their separatism "from the world," which meant not only being separated from the Catholic Church and the state-bound Protestant churches, but also from the secular powers. These communities in effect constituted the first truly free churches. Many of them took so seriously this principle of separation from the secular powers that their members refused to accept secular offices, to bear arms, and even to offer resistance to their numerous persecutors.

Closely connected with the principle of separation was that of the "ban," as the practice of excommunication was commonly called. While in Catholic and Protestant churches excommunication often served as an instrument of ecclesiastical power, to the free churches it was a symbol of their separation from the world. They were convinced that their freedom could only be preserved if their ranks were kept pure in their beliefs and lives.

A rather common religious doctrine of the Radical Reformation was millenarianism, the conviction of the imminent advent of Christ and his kingdom on earth. The most profound roots of the Radical Reformation probably lay in this deep longing for the advent of a reign of peace and justice on earth. This longing, never quite absent from Christianity, was particularly intense during periods of abrupt economic and social change which characterized sixteenth-century Europe.

While millenarianism traditionally was connected with the expectation of an ultimate, eschatological fight against the forces of the Antichrist, the millenarianism of the Radical Reformation was generally pacifistic. There were exceptions: Thomas Münzer identified the German Peasants' Revolt of 1524−1525 with the Danielic vision of the ultimate fight that would usher in the Fifth Monarchy;[31] and the Anabaptists of Münster firmly believed that their own "kingdom" constituted the beginning of the millennium. All other groups of the Radical Reformation, however, were convinced that their part in the struggle against the Antichrist was to preach the "word" rather than the "sword," as stated by Menno Simons, one of their great leaders,[32] and to trust in God's saving grace, which would bring about His kingdom.

Significantly the millenarianism of the Radical Reformation was generally linked to the rejection of the belief in the immortality of the soul, the ascent of the souls of the righteous after death into heaven, the sojourn of the sinners in purgatory, and the descent of the souls of the evildoers into hell. Doubts in this belief were already prevalent in humanist groups. The Italian philosopher Pietro Pomponazzi (1462−1525), in a 1516 treatise *De immortalitate animae* ("On the immortality of the soul"), maintained that the belief in the immortality of the soul cannot be based on reason but only on faith.

As the Lutheran and the Calvinist Reformation returned to Paul's doctrine of grace through faith, so the Radical Reformation returned to Paul's belief in the "sleep" of the dead in Christ until the day of resurrection (1 Thess. 4:14). For this new "heresy" an elegant Greek word, *psychopannychism*, was created. Psychopannychism was a heresy not only to the Catholic Church, but also to the Lutheran and Calvinist Reformation.[33]

While separatism, millenarianism, and psychopannychism were common features of the Radical Reformation, certain doctrinal differences among its various wings can be discerned. Taking note of the fact that some groups merged two or more doctrinal features, three mainstreams of the Radical Reformation can be distinguished: the Anabaptists, the Spiritualists, and the Unitarians.

The Anabaptists-Mennonites. The Anabaptists were the first group to secede from the state-bound Reformation. After a disputation with Zwingli and Bullinger, and after the City Council of Zurich had ruled that all those who failed to baptize their infant children would be exiled, Conrad Grebel (c. 1498–1526), a layman, baptized George Blaurock, a former priest, in Zurich in 1525. This was apparently the first adult baptism of the Anabaptists. It has been followed by million of others.

The salvational meaning of Anabaptism[34] is obvious: if baptism is the sacrament through which Christ redeems the sinner, it cannot have a salvational effect if performed on infants—who have not yet sinned and cannot yet turn to Christ and repent—but only if performed on those who are able to prepare themselves for redemption through repentance. The Schleitheim Confession formulated this doctrine succinctly: "Baptism shall be given to all those who have learned repentance and amendment of life and who believe truly that their sins are taken away by Christ." [35]

The Swiss Brethren, as Grebel and his followers called their community, organized themselves quickly as a separate church. In 1527, at a synod in Schleitheim, Switzerland, they adopted a Confession which laid the foundation of the Anabaptist creed. That creed comprised: the believers' baptism; the separation from "the world"; the principle of nonresistance to "the devilish weapons of force, such as sword, armour, and the like"; the refusal to take part in secular government and to take oaths; the refusal of communion with other religious bodies; and the practice of the ban to be administered by the pastor.[36] While the belief in psychopannychism was not mentioned in the Confession, the president of the Schleitheim synod, Michael Sattler (born c. 1490, executed 1527), asserted that Mary and the saints were sleeping and awaiting judgment.[37]

The separatism of the Anabaptist community was thus clearly circumscribed: the church should be a community of true believers, which receives only those who have been baptized as repentant believers, not a community to which everyone who was baptized as an infant automatically belongs. This community should also be technically separated from "the world" by refusing community with other religious or secular bodies.

The Anabaptist movement spread rapidly through Germany, Austria, the Low Countries, and northern Slavic lands. It was in the German-Dutch borderland that the millenarian explosion of Münster occurred. The city of Münster was in 1534 spiritually ruled by the Anabaptist Jan Mathys, a disciple of Melchior Hofmann (c. 1495–c. 1543), one of the outstanding Anabaptists, Spiritualists, and millenarians. But while the Melchiorites, as Hofmann's followers were called, rejected violence, Mathys was determined to forcefully introduce the millennium in Münster. After his death in a battle with a besieging army, his follower Jan Beuckelsz of Leiden, Holland (Jan van Leyden) ruled Münster with an iron fist and had himself anointed "King of righteousness over all." He ruled until the kingdom collapsed in 1535 in a mire of blood and tears under the assault of the troops of the Catholic bishop of Münster.

Most Anabaptists were from the outset pacifists, and rejected the belief that the advent of the kingdom of God could be accelerated by secular action. The disaster of Münster strengthened their convictions. In the same German-Dutch borderland where the bellicose branch of Anabaptism had died, Mennonism arose. It has preserved the original Anabaptist beliefs to the present time.

Menno Simons (1496–1561), originally a Dutch Catholic priest, renounced priesthood after the tragedy of Münster and became the spiritual leader of the Anabaptists in the Low Countries. His gospel was that of a peaceful, nonresistant Anabaptism.[38] The Mennonite branch of Anabaptism sought salvation in the hoped-for coming of Christ and refused to be drawn into the secular world. Mennonism spread and survived through the centuries, and is still a living faith in North America and a number of European countries, including the Soviet Union.[39]

One of the American Mennonite communities, the Amish, is particularly well known for its way of life and customs, which have changed little from the pre-industrial society of their origin. That community originated under the leadership of the Swiss Mennonite Jacob Amman (birth and death dates unknown), and resulted from a split within the Swiss-south German Mennonite churches in 1693.

Another branch of Anabaptism which has also survived, although only as a small group of communities within the Mennonite bodies, is the communist Hutterite Church, named after the Austrian Anabaptist Jakob Hutter (birth date unknown, executed in 1536). That community, although not founded by Hutter himself, was organized by him. It derived its strict communist structure from a statement in the Acts of the Apostles that the original Christian community was organized on communist principles (Acts 4:32–35). The leading doctrine of Hutterite communism was aptly defined by Peter Riedemann (1506–1556), the theoretician of the Hutterite community: "All those who have fellowship with [Christ] likewise have nothing from themselves, but have all things with their Master and with all those who have fellowship with him, that they might be one in the Son, as the Son is in the Father."[40] This profound religious foundation enabled that group of originally poor peasants and craftsmen to accomplish the unique feat, in spite of cruel persecutions, of not only surviving but of retaining their character as communist communities to the present time. The Hutterite Brethren are still an active community in some rural areas of the United States and Canada.

The Spiritualists. As mentioned above, certain Anabaptists, particularly Melchior Hofmann, adhered to spiritualist doctrines. The most prominent representatives of Spiritualism were Thomas Münzer and Kaspar Schwenckfeld.

Thomas Munzer, perhaps the most colorful and tragic figure of the Radical Reformation, blended his spiritualism with revolutionary millenarianism. As a millenarian he was an active fighter in the German Peasants' Revolt, and paid for his faith with his life.[41] His spiritualism was characterized by the belief that the foundation of Christian faith is not constituted by the Bible but by the "inner word," with which the believer responds to the "Spirit."

Kaspar Schwenckfeld (von Ossig, 1489–1561) was the only aristocrat within the Radical Reformation. He shared with most Anabaptists the pacifist gospel, and with Melchior Hofmann and Menno Simons the doctrine of the celestial flesh of Christ, thus introducing a streak of Gnosticism into the ranks of the Radical Reformation. The doctrine of the celestial flesh can be summarized as follows: God procreated in Mary pure, celestial, not created, flesh. Accordingly, the Eucharist means the "inward feeding" of the celestial flesh of Christ, and baptism is recognized only as the inward baptism of fire, meaning enlightenment—a belief that prompted Schwenckfeld to abandon the rite of baptism entirely. Like Münzer, Schwenckfeld asserted that man owes his communion with Christ not to an outward authority, not even to that of the Bible, but to the "inward light." Salvation thus becomes an entirely spiritual process, a divinization of the human spirit, which merges with Christ's divine spirit. Schwenckfeld strongly influenced Protestant mysticism (represented especially by Jakob Böhme, 1575–1624, for whom the church existed in the hearts of men), and Protestant Pietism, as well as Quaker and Methodist beliefs. Although Schwenckfeld, in accordance with his doctrine of the inward church, was opposed to founding a church, some of his followers disregarded his hostility and founded another community, at present known as the Schwenckfelder Church, which as a refuge from persecutions in Europe has survived in the United States.

The Unitarians. While the Spiritualists constituted an extreme wing of the Radical Reformation directed toward mysticism, the Unitarians constituted another extreme directed toward rationalism.[42]

Whereas both the Lutheran and Calvinist Reformation adhered strictly to the Trinitarian faith, the Radical Reformation—for the first time since Arianism had vanished—raised the question of whether the sophisticated edifice erected by the Councils of Nicaea, Constantinople, and Chalcedon was really founded on the Bible. More consistently than Lutheranism and Calvinism, the Radical Reformation referred to the Bible. It derived its doubts about the authenticity of the Nicene Creed from the New Testament Scriptures. The Spiritualists challenged the Chalcedonian dogma of the two natures of Christ from a rather docetic point of view, since their Christ was not human and divine, but solely divine. The anti-Trinitarianism of Servetus, the great precursor of Unitarianism, challenged the Trinitarian dogma of Constantinople.

Spanish theologian Michael Servetus (Miguel Serveto, born c. 1500, executed 1553) threw out the strongest challenge to the Catholic-Lutheran-Helvetic Trinitarian faith by publishing in 1531 a treatise which he boldly and provocatively called *De Trinitatis erroribus* ("On the errors of Trinitarianism"). In that treatise he maintained that the Holy Spirit was not a distinct person, but God's power within the hearts of man, and that Jesus was born as God's and Mary's son. While having celestial flesh (a doctrine Servetus adopted perhaps under the influence of the Spiritualists), Jesus was a mortal man who received divine power from God. Servetus in fact revived the adoptionist doctrine of the original Christian community in Jerusalem, but his position did not shake the belief in salvation through faith in Jesus Christ, as established by the Apostle Paul. Servetus was persecuted by the Catholic and Reformed churches alike, not only because of his anti-Trinitarianism, but also because he adopted the Anabaptist doctrine of believers' baptism and psychopannychism. The Reformed Church of Calvin martyrized him; he died on the stake after Calvin, supported by the ecclesiastical authorities of other Reformed churches in Switzerland, had denounced him as an anti-Trinitarian heretic.

Servetus exerted a powerful influence on the Radical Reformation, although he neither founded nor was connected with any religious community. The beginning of an organized anti-Trinitarian, that is, Unitarian movement took place nearly twenty years after the publication of his treatise. The first stirrings came from Italy, obviously inspired by humanist ideas. At a 1550 synod of chiefly Italian Anabaptists in Venice, a radical version of anti-Trinitarianism was adopted. The synod asserted that Jesus was not a god but an exceptional man, Joseph's and Mary's son. The assembly also accepted the doctrine of psychopannychism, according to which the souls of the righteous would sleep until the divine judgment while those of the evildoers would die.[43]

As an organized church Unitarianism arose not in Italy (although Italy contributed to its cause two prominent personalities, Blandrata and Socinus) but on the eastern borders of Western Christianity, in Poland, Hungary, and Transylvania. The history of Unitarianism began in Poland where Calvinism was firmly entrenched, but was split between radical and moderate wings. At a synod of the so-called Minor Reformed Church (the radical wing of Calvinism), Trinitarianism was rejected by some church members who were familiar with the teachings of Servetus. Finally in 1565 the Minor Reformed Church turned Unitarian. Somewhat later, opposition to Trinitarianism was also voiced in Hungary, and in Transylvania by Ferenc David (1510–1579), a bishop of the Reformed Church. He was supported by Georgius Blandrata (Giorgio Biandrata, c. 1515–1588), an Italian physician who had moved to Transylvania. Under the leadership of David and Blandrata, a Unitarian Church was founded in Transylvania; the movement spread rapidly through that country and Hungary.[44]

The great theoretician and spiritual leader of Unitarianism was the Italian Faustus Socinus (Fausto Paolo Sozzini, 1539–1604). In 1578, when Socinus still lived in western Europe, he wrote *De Jesu Christo Servatore* ("On the servant Jesus Christ"), a treatise in which he espoused adoptionist views. He also rejected the belief in atonement through the death of Jesus and asserted instead that Christ showed us the way toward salvation, which we can achieve by imitating him. Socinus moved to Transylvania and later to Poland where he spread his Unitarian doctrines, which became known as Socinianism and which were adopted by the Minor Reformed Church in Poland. In 1605, a year after his death, the Unitarian community in Poland published the so-called "Racovian Catechism,"[45] which appears to have been conceived by Socinus or under his influence.

The Racovian Catechism became the Bible of early Unitarianism. Its principal tenets can be summarized as follows: *God*: God is one. In God's essence there are not three persons, but one. *The Holy Spirit*: The Holy Spirit is not a person of the Godhead, but was sent by God. *Jesus Christ*: Jesus Christ was a man by nature, yet having been conceived of the Holy Spirit and born of Mary, he was God's son. However, he had no divine nature and was not begotten from eternity and from God's essence, but was raised by God after his death and was given power to reform all things. *Christ's role in the world*: Christ did not redeem mankind by his death, but he showed how we could be converted to him and thereby be reconciled with God. *Original Sin and Predestination*: these doctrines were rejected. *Sacraments*: no sacraments are mentioned in the Racovian Catechism. Baptism is an "external rite," not a sacrament. The Eucharist has been instituted in remembrance of Christ, but does not transubstantiate his body and blood. *Ultimate salvation*: Although men are mortal, those who tread in Christ's steps shall "in due time rise from death to come into the society of the same blessed immortality where [Christ] is made partaker." *Resurrection*: When Christ was raised by God, he received a powerful, spiritual, immortal body. Those who will be resurrected will receive a similar body.[46]

Unitarianism in its Socinian form was thus still deeply embedded in beliefs stemming from the original Christian community. But it went further in demythologizing and rationalizing Christianity than any other branch of the Radical Reformation. It shared the adoptionism of the original Christian community and even accepted the Virgin birth of Jesus, but it rejected the transformation of Jesus from man to God, which had been accepted by the Apostle Paul, the Gospel of John, and the Nicene Creed. The Socinian Unitarianism did not accept Paul's doctrine of original sin or share in Paul's sacramentalization of baptism and the Eucharist. Instead, Unitarianism shared with the mainstream of the Radical Reformation the doctrine of the mortality of the human soul. Even the millenarianism of the Radical Reformation was toned down to a belief that at some time there will be a resurrection of the righteous; but there was no clear-cut eschatological program. Thus Socinian Unitarianism prepared the way for currents in Christian thinking which were to mature centuries later.

4. THE HEIRS OF THE RADICAL REFORMATION

The Radical Reformation shared the fate of Buddhism and Christianity: each was defeated in its country of origin but later conquered a world.

The Radical Reformation was unable to withstand the violent and cruel assaults of both Catholicism and Lutheran-Calvinist Protestantism in its countries of origin in central and eastern Europe. But its fundamental ideas survived on foreign soil, mostly in England and North America, from whence they spread through the world.

The Baptists. With the exception of the Mennonites, Anabaptism vanished in continental Europe. However, it was revived in England under strong Mennonite influence. In 1608 a group of Congregationalists emigrated from England to the Netherlands in order to escape the persecutions to which they were subjected as Separatists (from the Church of England). Under Mennonite influence they were converted to Anabaptism. One of their leaders, John Smyth (c. 1554–1612), baptized first himself and then a number of followers. In 1611 one of his followers, Thomas Helwys (c. 1550–c. 1616), returned to England and founded the first Baptist church on English soil.

As it had arisen from Anabaptism, Baptism from the outset accepted the fundamental tenet of Anabaptism: that the church must be an autonomous community of true believers, separated from the world, rather than a community to which everyone, born of parents who are already members of the community, automatically belongs on the grounds of his baptism as an infant. The believers' baptism, confined to those who subject themselves to repentance, is the visible symbol for this exclusive nature of the Baptist Church. The Helwys community stated in a Confession "that the church of Christ is a company of faithful people, separated from the world by the word and spirit of God, being knit unto the Lord, and one unto another, by baptism upon their confession of faith and sins."[47] This foundation has remained unchanged, despite the split between Particular and General Baptists, which occurred at an early stage of its history and ran through a large part of it. This split derived from a conflict within Calvinism originating in the Netherlands.

Based on the writings of the Dutch theologian Jacobus Arminius (Jacob Harmensen, 1560–1609), a movement called Remonstrant Arminianism arose in the Netherlands. It deviated from strict Calvinism in the direction of Pelagianism. The Remonstrance of 1610, in which the doctrines of this movement were incorporated, rejected Calvin's rigid predestinarianism. Arminianism maintained that, while man needs the aid of the Holy Spirit to respond to God's will, grace is not irresistible, as Calvin had taught. Man has the free will to respond to it or reject it. Salvation is thus in the hands of man.[48] The split within Baptism centered on the Arminian controversy. The original Baptist Church in England was Arminian. The Baptists of strict Calvinist observance split off from it in 1638 and were called Particular Baptists because, according to their strictly Calvinist belief, salvation is only open for the select. After the General Baptist Church in England experienced a considerable decline, the split between General and Particular Baptist churches was healed in 1891.

In America, where Baptism first spread under the regime of Roger Williams (c. 1603–1683),[49] Particular Baptism—first along strict Calvinist lines and later modified by modern currents—has been the dominant Baptist branch. Accounting for all branches, Baptism is the most numerous Protestant denomination in the United States, with almost 27 million members in 1977.[50]

The rite of believers' baptism reaches far beyond the Baptist churches. In 1832 the Disciples of Christ (Christian Church) split off from the Baptists in the United States, but retained believers' baptism. Their faith is based on the New Testament, and is similar to that of Unitarianism. The Churches of Christ, which separated from the Disciples of Christ in the beginning of the twentieth century, likewise practice believers' baptism. The two communities have a considerable following in the United States —claiming nearly 4 million members in 1977—and also have members in other countries.

The Quakers (Society of Friends). While Baptism derived directly from Anabaptism, two other great currents of the Radical Reformation— Spiritualism and Unitarianism—arrived in England at a later period. Spiritualism can be regarded as the basis of Quakerism and Methodism, and in a certain sense also of Christian Scientism.

George Fox (1624–1691), the founder of the Quakers,[51] was the son of a weaver and apprentice to a shoemaker. As such, he was hardly acquainted with the Spiritualist writings of Münzer or Schwenckfeld. But his fundamental belief that "the inward light of Christ" reveals to man the spiritual truth and leads him toward salvation is not very different from the doctrines of the sixteenth-century Spiritualists. Fox was from his youth susceptible to "openings," as he called his religious experiences. As revealed in his *Journal*, at the age of nineteen he left his family and friends "at the command of God" in order to seek enlightenment.[52] In one of his early "revelations" he stated: "God opened to me ... that every man was enlightened by the divine light of Christ." Of his own mission he said: "I was sent to turn people from darkness to the light." [53]

Fox rejected Calvinist predestinarianism, asserting that there is no pre-destined election by God of the righteous and damnation of the sinners, but that, on the contrary, anyone ready to receive the divine light of Christ can be saved. Anticipating Methodist doctrines of perfectibility, he even believed that, "to as many as should receive [Christ] in his light, I saw that he would give power to become sons of light." [54]

The community that Fox founded (and that adopted the name "Society of Friends" in the late eighteenth century) has been most consistent in its Spiritualism. This touch of mysticism has made Quakerism a strictly anti-sacramentalist community. Because the divine light of Christ cannot be a privilege meted out by priests or ministers, the Friends abolished not only the priesthood, but even the ministry. In their meetings, the believers receive the light in inspired silence. They can be addressed by whomever feels inspired by the divine light. Consistent with this belief, the Friends recognize only an inner baptism by the Spirit. The sacrament of baptism is, therefore, abolished so that the Quakers, like the Uni-tarians, recognize no sacrament at all.

Although the Quaker community spread to the American colonies at an early date when William Penn (1644–1718) founded Pennsylvania as a Quaker settlement, the Society of Friends has never grown into a large community. Its membership is mainly confined to the United States, England, and some African countries. But its work in the service of humanity and its love of peace have made an enduring impact on man-kind; its members have been performing a work of salvation.

The Methodists. Although the growth of the Quaker community has been confined, their spiritual children, the Methodists,[55] have grown to become the second-largest Protestant denomination in the United States, with almost 13 million members in 1977. Whereas Quakerism grew en-tirely on English soil and had only a spiritual affinity with continental-European Spiritualism, Methodism was at its beginning strongly in-fluenced by spiritual currents that originated in the continental-European traditions of the Radical Reformation. John Wesley (1703–1792), the founder of Methodism, was prior to his conversion in close contact with members of the Moravian Brethren, who had found refuge at the Herrn-hut foundation of Count Nikolaus von Zinzendorf.[56]

Zinzendorf was a disciple of Philipp Jakob Spener (1635–1705) and August Hermann Francke (1663–1727), the founders of Lutheran Pie-tism. The Pietists emphasized the spiritual experience of faith and the emotional devotion to God. With the Moravian Brethren as a nucleus,

Zinzendorf organized a community characterized by particularly strong spiritualist features. The lines from there to Wesley's Methodism were clearly drawn.

Like other religious founders Wesley underwent an experience of enlightenment, which he called an "assurance" of salvation through Christ. He told the story of his conversion in his *Journal*: He owed his enlightenment to a passage from the writings of Luther which was read in 1738 at a Moravian meeting in London. In that passage Luther described "the change which God works in the heart through faith in Christ." [57] To Wesley this change of heart became a personal spiritual experience that brought about the "assurance" of salvation. In the hour of conversion, "I felt I did trust in Christ for salvation; and an assurance was given me that [Christ] had taken away my sins . . . and saved me from the law of sins and death." [58]

From that moment, spiritual experience became the foundation of Wesley's belief and of his assurance of salvation through faith in Christ. In his view the personal, spiritual experience of the salvational faith in Christ is accessible to everyone. Thus what is needed for salvation is not election by God, but the spiritual experience of conversion and the repentance that goes with it. Wesley shared with Fox not only the spiritual foundation of his belief and the rejection of predestinarianism, but also a belief in man's perfectibility: while striving for personal holiness, man can attain sanctification. Hence Wesley defined the Methodist community as "a company of men having the form and seeking the power of godliness." [59]

The missionary spirit which was so powerful in early Christianity was particularly strong in the Methodist community. Wesley's conversion led to his conviction that the communicability of his experience would assure salvation. All that was needed to find the way toward salvation was the guidance of those who had already been converted. To that mission Wesley and his disciples devoted themselves. From 1739 on, Methodist societies were formed, which remained within the Church of England until 1836. In 1743 Wesley and his brother Charles (1707–1788) issued General Rules of the United Societies, which created a firm organizational structure for the Methodist communities. Wesley's missionary activities were stupendous. Reportedly he preached from 40,000 to 50,000 sermons. An even more dynamic force in the work of "evangelization" —as the Methodist conversion was termed—was Wesley's disciple George Whitefield (1714–1770), one of the leading figures of evangelical "revivalism" (another term used for this conversion process) in Britain and its North American colonies. The Methodists were not the first and only Christian community in Britain and North America to preach and achieve conversion, chiefly through their revivalist methods. But together with the Baptists, their great missionary work reaped the most fruit: Baptism and Methodism are the leading Protestant denominations in the United States.

Christian Scientists. Christian Science, although frequently regarded as a religion based on a belief in and method of faith-healing, should rather be understood as the most extreme product of the spiritual currents of the Radical Reformation. Its God is "omnipotent, omniscient, and omnipresent Being, and His reflection is man and the universe" (*Science and Health*, pp. 465–66).[60]

Mary Baker Eddy (1821–1910), the founder and leader of Christian Science, conceived of her religious-philosophical system as the product of a personal enlightenment following her nearly miraculous recovery from a grave, long-lasting illness. Her explanation for her cure became the foundation of a new religion, which has only tenuous ties to Christianity, but close ties to pantheism and to a kind of spiritualist idealism.

The idealism on which Christian Science is based derives from the concept that only mind (spirit) is real: "Spirit, the synonym of mind, soul, or God, is the only real substance" (p. 468). Hence, matter is unreal, is in effect nothing. "When the substance of Spirit appears in Christian Science, the nothingness of matter is recognized" (p. 480). Man's true place in the universe is in the realm of spirit. "Man is not matter. . . . Man is spiritual and perfect" (p. 475). Moreover, as man's physique is unreal, illness and death, evil and sins are likewise unreal. "The only reality of sin, sickness, or death is the awful fact that unrealities seem real to human, erring belief" (p. 472).

If sickness is an illusion, it can be healed through knowledge of the sole reality of spirit. "Mind must be found to be superior to all the beliefs of the five corporeal senses and able to destroy all ills. Sickness is a belief which must be annihilated by the divine Mind" (p. 493). Hence salvation consists in the liberation of the mind from the illusion of the reality of matter, sin, illness, and death. This kind of salvation can be attained neither by faith in the grace of God nor by good works, but by the "knowledge" that only mind is real and that matter is unreal. Christian Science calls that conviction "science."

Such a religious system leaves little room for traditional Christian beliefs. The Catholic belief in heaven, purgatory, and hell as abodes of the souls after death has no place in Christian Science. Neither does the eschatological belief in the advent of Christ, the resurrection of the dead at the last judgment, and the kingdom of God. Nor can Jesus appear as the Savior who by his death atoned for the sins of man. As he appears in Christian Science, Jesus reflects "the highest human concept of perfect man" (p. 242), in whose humanity "the divinity of Christ was made manifest" (p. 25). Christian Science also does not recognize any sacraments, including baptism, and has abolished the priestly office. Instead of priests or ministers it recognizes elected "readers" and practitioners who apply the principles of Christian Science in healing missions.

In 1879 Christian Science was organized as an official church, the Church of Christ, Scientist, in the United States and it grew rapidly. While the church does not publish any membership figures, recent statistics suggest a considerable following with a total of 3,300 churches, two-thirds of which are in the United States, with the balance in Canada, Great Britain and other, mostly European, countries.[61]

Unitarians and Universalists. Like Anabaptism and Spiritualism, the third current of the Radical Reformation, Unitarianism, owed its survival to its transplantation from continental Europe to Britain. The first standard-bearer of Unitarianism in England was John Biddle (1615–1662) who, even before he became acquainted with Socinianism, wrote *Twelve Arguments . . . wherein the . . . Opinion touching the Deity of the Holy Spirit is clearly and fully refuted* (1645). For this heresy he was severely persecuted. Nevertheless, after having studied Socinian writings, he wrote two further treatises which were outright Unitarian. In spite of further persecutions and imprisonments, which continued until his death in prison, he persisted in his Unitarian beliefs. With a small band of followers, he formed a community which met regularly and became the nucleus of Unitarian teachings in England. Into the eighteenth century these teachings were called Socinian or Arian.

For the next two generations Socinian doctrines became known through the Racovian Catechism. They were an object of lively controversies in ecclesiastical and academic circles until 1718, at which time two Presbyterian ministers, James Peirce and Joseph Hallet, having been expelled from their pulpits, organized a Unitarian congregation which survived.[62] From these humble beginnings Unitarianism spread in the eighteenth and nineteenth centuries through England and, above all, America. There it found an intellectual center at Harvard University, in ecclesiastical groups in Boston (under the leadership of the prominent Congregational-turned-Unitarian minister William Ellery Channing, 1780–1842), and in other New England towns. Finally in 1825 a Unitarian Church, the American Unitarian Association, was organized.

Perhaps more than any other Christian community, Unitarianism has undergone a process of demythologization. While certain fundamental principles have remained—such as the rejection of the belief in original sin, of atonement through Christ, and of predestination—the humanization of Jesus has progressed in Unitarian ranks, and humanist ideals have been increasingly emphasized. The 1961 merger of the American Unitarians with the Universalists was a logical step in the same direction. The Universalists were an American community, with its roots in eighteenth-century Enlightenment. Its chief tenet, the ultimate salvation of all men, reaches back to Origen.[63] In 1833 a General Convention of Universalists in the United States was established. In the meantime the Universalists, particularly under the influence of one of their spiritual leaders, Hosea Ballou (1771–1852), had come close to the Unitarian belief in the full humanity of Jesus. The merger of the two communities symbolized the growing kinship between the most rationalist, demythologized forms of Christianity and modern humanist currents. Although many Unitarians and Universalists still adhere to the belief in a sole God, they view salvation as a goal to be achieved through human effort.

Unitarianism has never grown into a large community, but it has had a profound impact on the spiritual development of, particularly, English-speaking peoples. In the United States, Unitarianism was one of the forms in which Enlightenment was intellectually adopted. It was no coincidence that Unitarianism found a refuge at Harvard and sympathy among other intellectual and political leaders of the young United States.

Millenarian Communities. While Unitarianism—the most rationalist wing of the Radical Reformation—flourished on the dynamic soil of America, America also became the haven for millenarianism, the least rationalist current of the Radical Reformation. Millenarian currents ran through most communities of the Radical Reformation. The conviction of the imminent approach of the advent of Christ and the kingdom of God remained alive, particularly in periods of political or social stress, such as that of the civil war in England in the seventeenth century. There was likewise a strong millenarian undercurrent in the German Pietism of the eighteenth century.

However, organized religious communities founded on millenarian beliefs did not appear before the nineteenth century. Virtually all of them, perhaps not coincidentally, were established in the United States. The tremendous dynamism of the United States in that century, the rapidity with which the people of the New World streamed westward and opened up new territories, the stress and strain connected with large-scale immigration, and the misery many of the immigrants experienced, created an atmosphere in which millenarian hopes could thrive.

The Latter-Day Saints (Mormons). It is significant to the link between millenarianism and the pioneer structure of the young American nation that the oldest American-born millenarian community, the Church of Jesus Christ of Latter-Day Saints (popularly called the Mormons), began as a community of settlers on the move. It remained so during the stormy and often tragic period of its westward trek until its members settled down and founded their Zion on the shores of the Great Salt Lake, which in 1896 was recognized by the United States as the state of Utah.

Among all major religious communities, that of the Mormons is the only revealed religion to appear since Islam, and the history of its origin is in many ways analogous to that of Islam. Just as in his visions Mohammed received his revelations from the Archangel Gabriel and made them manifest in the Koran, so Joseph Smith (1805 – 1844), the founder of the Mormon community, received his revelation in several visions. According to Smith's story, these visions culminated in his accepting from a resurrected prophet a book written on golden plates, allegedly buried fourteen hundred years earlier. Smith is said to have translated the book of ancient Egyptian-like characters. This was the Book of Mormon, which became the Bible of the Church of Latter-Day Saints.[64]

Smith wove the chief tenets of his creed into this strange chronicle of an allegedly ancient American people. Based on this faith, in 1830 he organized a church which moved westward with his community. Because the Mormons were harassed in one place after another, they continued their westward trek until they found peace in Utah. A few years before his martyr's death, Smith wrote down thirteen Articles of Faith, which have remained the foundation of Mormon beliefs. The articles confess belief in the Trinity and atonement through Christ, but reject the doctrine of original sin. They culminate in the millenarian belief "that Christ will reign personally upon the earth, and that the earth will be renewed and receive its paradisiacal glory."[65] Even the name Latter-Day Saints which Smith chose for his community attests to his strong millenarian faith. Present-day Mormons, however, do not expect the millennium to be so close at hand as Smith expressed through the name of his community.

Smith believed that the soul is immortal, even preexistent; that after death it rises in an unending eternal progression to ever higher levels; and that the souls in heaven will be reunited with those of their relatives in full conscience. The Mormons' faith in the immortality of the soul is universalist: everyone can hope for salvation in that unending progression after death. Salvation will exist on two levels: in heaven after death, and on a renewed, paradisiacal earth, where Christ will reign after his advent.

Mormonism is universalist even in its church organization. Every man —but not woman—who adheres to Mormon beliefs is to be ordained as a priest. Every man is a "latter-day saint," who even may receive divine revelations, although only the head of the church is recognized as the prophet, seer, and revelator. It is little wonder that a faith promising salvation to everyone—saint and sinner alike, in heaven and on a para-disiacal earth upon the imminent advent of Christ—has grown from a poor handful of farmers in the backwoods of upstate New York into a community of almost three million members in the United States, with a large number of adherents in other countries.

The Seventh-Day Adventists. A similarly impressive growth, particu-larly due to missionary work both within and outside of the United States, occurred in two other millenarian churches: the Seventh-Day Adventists and Jehovah's Witnesses. The history of the Seventh-Day Adventists goes back to the American Baptist William Miller (1782.– 1849), who on the basis of Danielic prophecies (Dan. 8 : 13 – 14) calcu-lated that the advent of Christ and the end of our age would occur in 1844. He attracted thousands of followers (Adventists), but lived to see his prophecy shattered by Christ's failure to appear on the foreordained date. Adventism, however, survived this blow, for soon after, the belief took hold that in 1844 Christ had begun his cleansing work in heaven and would later continue it on earth.[66] Adventism received a further impetus when Ellen Gould White (1827–1915) had a vision of Christ in heaven, preparing for his advent, which would occur at a later, unknown date. Adventism crystallized in 1863 in the organization of the Church of the Seventh-Day Adventists—the term "Seventh-Day" expressing the view that God sanctified the seventh day of the week (Sabbath) rather than Sunday, and made it a symbol of the last day of our age.

While accepting the Trinity, original sin, and atonement through the expiatory death of Christ, the Seventh-Day Adventists derived believers' baptism, millenarianism, and psychopannychism from the Radical Ref-ormation. But they adhere to a unique version of millenarianism: Christ will appear in person, the righteous will be resurrected from their sleep in heaven, the evildoers will continue to sleep, and the earth will be de-void of human life. After one hundred years, the evildoers will be resur-rected on earth, will be gathered by Satan to wage war against Christ, but will be defeated and finally annihilated in a cleansing fire that will restore paradise on earth.[67]

The Seventh-Day Adventists have engaged in intense missionary activities throughout the world, particularly in developing countries, with the result that half a million members in the United States have been joined by over a million adherents in other countries.

Jehovah's Witnesses. The millenarian community which calls itself Jehovah's Witnesses derives its name from a passage in Deutero-Isaiah's proclamation of Yahweh as the sole God of the universe, which reads: "My witnesses, says the Lord, are you, My Servants, you whom I have chosen to know Me and put your faith in Me . . ." (Isa. 43:10). The community was founded in 1872 in Pittsburgh by Charles Taze Russell (1852–1916) under the influence of the Seventh-Day Adventists, but with substantial doctrinal modifications.

The most striking feature of the Jehovah's Witnesses is its particularly strong affinity with the Radical Reformation. It appears as if the spirit of the Radical Reformation had been resurrected in that community. There is the same inexorable separation from the world, with its rejection of any contacts with other Christian faiths and of any dealings with the secular powers. There is the same refusal to bear arms, for which their leaders and adherents, as conscientious objectors, had to suffer innumerable persecutions. There is a Unitarianism comparable to that of the sixteenth century (the Holy Spirit viewed as power of God; Jesus, son of God and born of Mary, viewed as a perfect man and after his resurrection as a perfect spiritual being). And, foremost, there is an indestructible faith in the rapidly approaching millennium.

The failure to prophesy the correct date for the advent of Christ did not impair the propagation of the faith. Russell set that date for 1914, a year in which Armaggedon did indeed break out, although of another kind than that which Russell had prophesied. That failure was later justified by Russell's successor, Joseph Franklin Rutherford (1869–1942), who assured his followers that in 1914 Christ had battled with Satan and had cast him out nearer the earth.

The millenarian variant of Jehovah's Witnesses can be summarized as follows: Life in heaven, in Christ's presence, is reserved for those 144,000 elect who figure in the Book of Revelation (14:1). From among the growing numbers of followers of the community only a very limited number of the faithful have been elected or will still be elected for a celestial existence. All others will have to wait for Armageddon, the day of the battle on earth when God and Christ will fight the forces of Satan.

The battle will end with the annihilation of the evildoers and the ushering in of paradise on earth where the righteous will be resurrected for an everlasting life. In accordance with the Book of Revelation, that period will last one thousand years, after which Satan will be released, a new battle will follow, and Satan will be finally destroyed.[68]

There is hardly a country in the world not penetrated by missionaries of Jehovah's Witnesses, hardly a country in which their literature, particularly the journal, *The Watchtower*, is unknown. In effect, every active member of the community is committed to be a missionary, to spread the gospel of the faith if he is to deserve everlasting life on the renewed earth. As a result, more than half a million Witnesses in the United States have recruited about 700,000 adherents in other countries.

Holiness and Pentecostal Churches. Two additional religious communities which originated in the United States, the Holiness and Pentecostal churches, have blended millenarian convictions with faith in the Holy Spirit. The Holiness churches were an outgrowth of Methodism. They came into being in a period when the official Methodist Church had lost some of the perfectionist fervor of original Methodism. It was then, chiefly after the Civil War, that Holiness churches were founded on the basis of the original Methodist doctrine of perfection (holiness) as the ideal status of Christian man. The Holiness communities are convinced that holiness can be achieved with the aid of the Holy Spirit.

The Pentecostal movement originated at the end of the nineteenth century. Comparable to the Holiness churches' belief in inspiration by the Holy Spirit, Pentecostalists believe that a spiritual experience called "baptism with the Holy Spirit" endows them with extraordinary gifts like those frequently mentioned in the Bible—healing, prophesying, and above all, glossolalia or "speaking in tongues," just as on the day of Pentecost the outpouring of the Holy Spirit (Acts 2:1–4) was believed to have endowed His disciples to speak in other than their mother tongue.

Several Pentecostal communities were organized in the United States.[69] But in the last few years, a new Pentecostal movement has gained considerable strength within both Protestant and Catholic communities in the United States and abroad. Frequently called "charismatic," in accordance with its members' belief in extraordinary gifts bestowed upon them by the Holy Spirit, many of these communities observe services of their own, although they still retain their ties with the official churches.

5. REFORMATION AND CHURCH-STATE RELATIONS

Although the Lutheran and Calvinist Reformation abandoned the sacramentalism and sacerdotalism of the Catholic Church and replaced sacraments and priests with a personal relationship between the believer and his deity, it still claimed to be the sole dispenser of salvation and the sole legitimate religious power in society. Wherever Lutheran and Reformed churches prevailed, they became established churches, that is, religious communities recognized by the state authorities as official churches. This held true not only on the European continent and on the British Isles, but even in the British colonies in America, where established churches were the rule.[70]

The Radical Reformation, on the other hand, adhered from its outset to the principle of religious separation. Religion should be separate from "the world"; it should neither dominate the secular society nor be dominated by it. However, after the Radical Reformation was crushed, its successor religions evolved only slowly and their membership was for a long time limited to England and North America. Progress, therefore, was bound to be slow in loosening the ties between church and state and in establishing religious freedom.

Nevertheless, due to a relaxing of Catholicism's grip on Western society, the principle of religious tolerance and freedom began to take shape. The first stirrings of this freedom were felt in England. Since in England Catholicism, the Church of England, and the Reformed churches alternated in quick succession as dominant churches, and since religious currents of the Radical Reformation gained a following there, it was natural that the English people's allegiance to the principle of monopolistic churches weakened.

Religious tolerance was supported by such an illuminary as John Milton (1608–1674). Outstanding not only as a poet but also as a religious thinker, Milton himself turned from the Church of England to Presbyterianism and later to religious ideas akin to Unitarian doctrines, and was the first prominent writer to plead for religious tolerance.[71] He was followed by John Locke (1632–1704), the greatest philosopher of seventeenth-century England. Locke wrote a number of treatises and letters in favor of religious tolerance.[72] Due to the pressure of the Reformed and the other independent churches, and influenced by the atmosphere of tolerance created by the pleas of these great personalities, the Glorious Revolution adopted the Toleration Act of 1689 which gave the English people a certain measure of religious freedom.[73]

The cultural atmosphere that prepared the way for the final victory of religious freedom was created by the era of Enlightenment. In this period, many intellectual leaders of the Western nations adhered to deistic or even atheistic doctrines, and personalities of the rank of Voltaire and Lessing were protagonists in the fight for tolerance. Thus the principle of religious freedom came to be widely accepted by the public.[74]

Where reigning princes themselves were inspired by the ideas of Enlightenment, their absolute power enabled them to introduce religious tolerance in their domains. Prominent examples are King Frederick II (the Great) of Prussia and Emperor Joseph II. Frederick the Great (who reigned from 1740 to 1786), the friend and protector of Voltaire, established the principle of religious freedom in the first year of his reign. His famous phrase, *Hier muss ein jeder nach seiner Fasson selig werden* ("Here everyone must find salvation as he chooses") became the guiding principle of religious freedom. Joseph II, who reigned in Austria from 1780 to 1790, issued a similar edict of toleration.

Yet it was not the enlightened absolutism of a few European monarchs, but rather the progress of political democracy that ensured the ultimate victory of the principle of religious freedom. As a part of the process of democratization, the political freedoms of speech, assembly, political organization, and the press were extended to the religious sphere. Article 18 of the Universal Declaration of Human Rights, adopted by the United Nations General Assembly in 1948, fittingly combines religious freedom with freedom of thought and conscience. It only confirmed a right that democratic countries have long upheld. Although still severely restricted in some Communist countries, it is a right not entirely denied even there.

The triumph of the principle of religious freedom, however, by no means entailed that of the principle of separation of church and state. In many countries, democratic or not, the ties between the dominant churches and the secular powers were too strong to be entirely severed. It was, in fact, in the United States that a clear-cut separation of church and state was first established.[75]

In the United States the acceptance of the separation of church and state was to a certain extent due to the growing role the successor communities of the Radical Reformation began to play in the American colonies, and thereafter to the millenarian communities of the nineteenth century. The multiplicity of religious communities which settled in the colonies—Presbyterians, Congregationalists, Lutherans, Episcopalians,[76] and Catholics—would in any event have undermined and eventually destroyed the existence of established churches in the American colonies. But, as a number of European examples show, even with a multiplicity of religious communities, close ties between church and state can still be maintained without the existence of an established church. It seems to have been the separatist spirit inherited from the Radical Reformation, rather than the multiplicity of religious communities, that contributed most to the triumph of the principle of separation of church and state in the United States.

Nevertheless, progress in this separation was slow. The First Amendment to the U.S. Constitution adopted in 1791 proclaimed for the federation the principle of religious freedom, and banned the institution of an established church. The states, however, were given the freedom to rule on church-state relations. In fact, the states only gradually abandoned the institution of established churches. With the mass immigration the United States experienced in the nineteenth and early twentieth centuries, it would have been extremely difficult to retain the institution of established churches permanently. Nevertheless, since most immigrants (Catholics, Presbyterians, Lutherans, and Episcopalians) came from countries in which either established churches or close ties between church and state existed, there was often pressure to establish some ties between church and state. It was probably due to the simultaneous, explosive growth of the successor communities of the Radical Revolution that attempts to re-establish some ties between church and state have so far failed, and that the Supreme Court could insist upon an increasingly rigorous interpretation of a genuine separation of church and state.[77]

Thus, the successor communities of the Radical Reformation played a dynamic role in the United States by enriching the scope of religious inspiration and by loosening rigidities in religious doctrines and rites. But their most valuable contribution may have been in the field of religious freedom, which they owe to the separatist spirit of the Radical Reformation.

CHAPTER VII

Modern Trends
in Christian Beliefs

1. THE BELIEFS OF THE OFFICIAL CHURCHES

If Christian beliefs were determined exclusively by the official Christian churches, there would be only meager signs of any marked evolution of Christian faiths. The tremors that shook the Christian world during the last seven generations—beginning with the irruption of the Enlightenment, and continuing with the rapid progress of science and the impassionate fights among theologians over interpretations of the Christian faith—are barely reflected in the expressions of Christian beliefs formulated by the official church bodies.

During the era of anti-modernism and fundamentalism, the Catholic Church waged an impassionate battle both against the secular ideas of progress and liberalism and against modernism in the ranks of Catholic theologians. The battle was waged in two stages. The first was highlighted by the 1864 "Syllabus of Errors" issued by Pius IX (pontificate 1846–1878). Of the eighty theses anathematized in that document, such as naturalism, rationalism, socialism, communism, and the separation of church and state, the last thesis suggested that the pope should reconcile himself with progress, liberalism, and recent civilization. The ban on the last thesis illustrates the degree to which the Catholic Church was out of tune with the liberalizing currents and ideas of progress which then prevailed.

In the second stage, the battle was directed against modernist trends within the Catholic Church. After Bible criticism had spilled over from Protestant Germany into Catholic France, with Ernest Renan's (1823–1892) *La Vie de Jesus* ("The Life of Jesus," 1863), Leo XIII (pontificate 1878–1903) reacted by issuing the 1893 decree *Providentissimus Deus*. It established norms for historical Bible analysis based on the doctrine of the divine origin of the Scriptures. In disregard of this decree, such outstanding Catholic theologians as the French priest Alfred F. Loisy (1857–1940) and the English priest George Tyrrell (1861–1909) published critical writings that continued to undermine the doctrine of the inerrancy of the Scriptures.

Pius X (pontificate 1903–1914), nevertheless, intensified his predecessor's fundamentalist policy by issuing three anti-modernist documents: the decree *Lamentabili Sane Exitu* (1907), anathematizing sixty-five propositions of the modernists; the encyclical *Pascendi Dominici Gregis* (1907), analyzing and condemning their doctrines; and the motu proprio *Sacrorum antistitum* (1910), introducing the redoubtable oath against modernism and forcing it upon all Catholic clerics.

In the Protestant world, fundamentalism played a role similar to that of anti-modernism in the Catholic Church, for it was also based on the doctrine of the inerrancy of the Scriptures. Protestant fundamentalism started in 1876 with the Bible Conferences in the United States, and crystallized in the Niagara Bible Conference of 1895 proclaiming "five points" of fundamentalism which have remained its pièce de resistance: the deity of Christ; the Virgin birth of Jesus; the atoning death of Christ; his resurrection; his advent and divine judgment. In the first three decades of the twentieth century, fundamentalism became an aggressive force in the United States, leading to the ouster of liberal theologians, the fight against liberal-minded theological seminaries, the anti-evolutionary laws in some Southern states, and finally the formation of fundamentalist associations.[1]

This violent reaction against modern trends in Christian beliefs has lost much of its impetus. Critical Bible research, once blocked by anti-modernist decrees, was officially encouraged by Pius XII (pontificate 1939–1958) in the 1943 encyclical *Divino Afflante Spiritu*. In the Protestant churches, fundamentalism could not seriously challenge the critical spirit which had characterized Protestant theology since the beginning of the nineteenth century.[2]

In spite of this liberalizing trend, the official positions of Christian churches have not wavered. The Catholic Church's position is entirely unequivocal: the Nicene Creed constitutes the very foundation of the faith and is an inherent part of the liturgy. Thus Vatican Council II (1962–1965), despite all its revolutionary innovations, proclaimed the traditional belief of the Catholic Church in the salvation, purification, or damnation of the souls after death. In the Dogmatic Constitution of the Church, *Lumen Gentium*, it was stated that the souls of the righteous "have been received into their heavenly home and are present to the Lord." Moreover, the blessed souls in heaven communicate with the "wayfarers" on earth. They exchange spiritual goods and "do not cease to intercede with the Father for us." A vital fellowship even exists between the righteous on earth and the souls in purgatory, while the soul of the wicked and slothful servant is condemned "to go into eternal fire . . . where there will be weeping and gnashing of the teeth."

Although the Protestant churches have no central authority empowered to determine the fundamentals of the faith, the World Council of Churches[3] is also based on the Nicene Creed. This is even alluded to in the official designation of the World Council as "a fellowship of Churches which accept Jesus Christ our Lord as God and Saviour." Moreover, the Assembly of 1961 confessed the Trinitarian faith, by adding, "according to Scriptures and therefore seek to fulfill together their common calling to the glory of the one God, Father, Son, and Holy Spirit." Finally, the Second World Conference on Faith and Order (Edinburgh, 1937), which preceded and prepared the way for the organization of the World Council of Churches, founded its Christology on the doctrine of Christ as the preexistent Logos: "In the fullness of time," proclaimed the report of the conference, "the Word, the Eternal Son of God, is manifested in Christ our Lord, the Incarnate Word, and His redeeming work . . . in whose name alone salvation is offered to the world."[4]

Although thirty years elapsed between the Edinburgh conference and the 1967 World Conference on Church and Society, the latter conference retained the fundamental doctrine that Christ is man's divine Lord, his redeemer and Savior, in whom all things hold together and who is all, and in all. The 1967 conference also drew an eschatological picture of the end of our age and the kingdom of God based on the visions of the Apostle Paul and the Book of Revelation, and exclaimed:

> The Christian lives in the world by the hope of the final victory of Christ over the powers of this age. . . . In the fulfillment of time all nature, all the forces of human society, and human life itself will be transformed in a way beyond the imagination. . . . The kingdom of God broke into human

history with the coming of Christ and will extend over the whole of creation. In the war between the risen Lord and the demonic powers, the latter
cannot be victorious. Jesus the Messiah has come and will come again.[5]

2. THE LIBERAL THEOLOGIANS

A deep cleavage exists between the fundamentalism of both the official
Catholic and Protestant churches, and the trends that have prevailed in
Christian thought since the beginning of the nineteenth century. The
revolution in Christian thinking began with the so-called liberal theology,
whose roots lay in Romanticism and in the general atmosphere of the
Enlightenment. Romanticism's contribution to liberal theology was its
emphasis on sentiments and feelings. In the religious sphere, among the
fathers of liberal theology were the Spiritualists and the Lutheran Pietists,
who stressed religious experience.

German philosopher and theologian Friedrich Schleiermacher (1768–
1834) can be regarded as the founder of liberal theology. His emphasis
on feeling and experience as the source of religious beliefs bordered on
mystical pantheism, with its feeling of oneness with the infinite. The
strong deist trends of the Enlightenment had reduced Christian doctrines
to vague beliefs in a provident Godhead or to the belief (propagated by
Kant) in God as a moral postulate. This left no room for the belief in
the divinity of Christ and his expiatory death as the salvational eschatological event. Salvation was no longer the fruit of gratuitous divine
grace poured out on sinful man and mediated through the expiatory
suffering of God's son. Rather, it was attained through the union of the
believer with the divine. That union was mediated through Jesus, not as a
deity but as the one who was perfectly holy, because perfectly one with
God.

Though Schleiermacher was not a deist but a Christian, his Christianity was neither based on a belief in God's gratuitous grace nor in
Christ as consubstantial with God. Instead, his Christ was the ideally
God-conscious man, absolutely perfect, sinless. While "in the origin of
Christ a supernatural activity was operative," and while Schleiermacher
even accepted the Virgin birth of Jesus, his Christ remained a man.
Christ's redeeming power did not stem from his sufferings and his death,
which Schleiermacher did not consider as expiatory, but from the free
will of Christians to assume fellowship with him, to share his God-
consciousness: "The activity by which [Christ] assumes us into fellowship with him is . . . a creative production in us of the will to assume him
into ourselves."[6]

Schleiermacher did not initiate a thorough demythologization process which characterized a later phase of critical theology, but he did regard the eschatological features of Christianity as myths created by Jesus' disciples: "We cannot conclude that because God was in Christ, [Christ] must have risen from the dead and ascended into heaven, or that because he was essentially sinless he must come again to act as the judge. Rather [these beliefs] are accepted only because they are found in the Scriptures." [7]

If Schleiermacher was the founder of liberal theology, German theologian Albrecht Ritschl (1822–1889) was its greatest representative. Like Schleiermacher, Ritschl was profoundly Christian, but he intensified the demythologization process. He rejected the myth of original sin, the preexistence of Christ, and Christ's vicarious sacrifice. He also asserted that the apostles' original beliefs in the kingdom of God, divine judgment, the resurrection of the righteous, and the advent of Christ were not maintained by the Church; "that a consistent eschatological theory cannot be gained from the New Testament data, and that the hints of the New Testament as to the condition of the blessed and of the lost lie beyond the possibility of a clear presentation." [8]

At the center of Ritschl's faith lay the Kantian concept of God as a postulate of the moral imperative, rather than Schleiermacher's concept of God-consciousness. Religion in Ritschl's theology is based on our moral values, which were perfectly embodied in Jesus. By perfectly understanding God's purpose, Jesus triumphed over his own death, and mediated God's purpose to us. Ritschl did not deny the divine role of Christ as "the mediator of the highest conceivable fellowship between God and man." But it was "by his morally effective teaching and by his gracious mode of conduct," that Christ paved the way to the kingdom of god. [9]

Ritschl's ethical concept of Christianity culminated in the kingdom of God, not as an eschatological but as an ethical ideal. This in effect is a commitment to ethical action: "The kingdom of God is the divinely vouched for highest good of the community founded through His revelation in Christ; but it is the highest good only in the sense that it forms at the same time the ethical ideal for whose attainment the members of the community bind themselves together through their definite reciprocal action." In other words, Ritschl's kingdom of God can be characterized as a social ideal and the Christians can be defined as a community which seeks to realize it. The ideal is social both in the sense that the community members have bound themselves together in order to achieve it, and that it is based on the idea of brotherly love among all men: "The righteous conduct in which the members of the Christian community share in the bringing in of the kingdom of god has its universal law and its personal motive in love to God and to one's neighbour"—"neighbours" to be understood as "moral beings." [10]

Ritschl's kingdom of God does not exist as an actual community, but "in so far as the Christian community is active in its realization, is in the process of growing." The kingdom can never be perfect because man can never become perfect. At this point, however, Ritschl fell back on eschatology: "Christian faith . . . rests upon the hope that the perfecting of the kingdom of God as the highest good will be realized upon conditions which extend beyond this world of experience." [11]

Ritschl did not deny the potential of salvation for the world of experience, for he still believed in divine redemption through the forgiveness of sins or through justification: "Sinners are given by God the right to enter into communion with Him and into cooperation with His final purpose, the kingdom of God, without their guilt and their feeling of guilt forming a hindrance thereto." But in reality this reconciliation is based on ethics rather than eschatology: "These effects of divine redemption . . . find practical application only on the condition that the believer takes at once an active part in the recognized purpose of the kingdom of God and has given up the following of selfish ends and inclinations." [12]

3. THE SOCIAL GOSPEL

Ritschl's doctrine of the kingdom of God was in effect the doctrine of the social gospel. While he admitted that the perfection of this kingdom could not be expected in history, he conceived of its growth as a historical process and a social commitment of Christian man. Living in an age that had seen enormous political, economic, and social changes and powerful social movements for the betterment of society, he conceived of the kingdom of God as an ethical ideal for which men must strive as members of a community.

Ritschl was not the only Christian thinker to assign a social meaning to the concept of the kingdom of God. The social movements which swept through the nineteenth century were echoed in the churches, where they created a powerful impetus for Christian social movements, even for a fusion of Christian and socialist ideas. In the 1850s a Christian socialist movement arose in England, propagated by John Frederick Denison Maurice (1805–1872), Charles Kingsley (1819–1875), and John Malcolm Forbes Ludlow. In Germany Paul Johannes Tillich (1886–1965) and Eduard Heimann (1889–1967), and in Switzerland Hermann Kutter (1863–1931) and Leonhard Ragaz (1868–1945), were the leaders of

Christian socialist movements.[13] Within the ranks of Catholicism an outstanding representative of Christian socialism was French philosopher Emmanuel Mounier (1905–1950). His philosophical starting point was to merge personalism—which insists on the priority of the person over material and collective needs—with the social ideal of a community oriented toward justice, love, and creation.[14]

In the United States the concept of the social gospel was given momentum through the writings and activities of two prominent clergymen, Josiah Strong and Walter Rauschenbusch. Josiah Strong (1847–1916) was a dynamic personality who blended strong religious convictions with vigorous action in their service. He was convinced that the kingdom of God, as Jesus understood it, is a social order of love and justice, and that the Church's mission is to work for the realization of this social ideal: "By the kingdom of heaven or the kingdom of God, of which Christ speaks so often, he does not mean the abode of the blessed dead, but a kingdom of righteousness which he came to establish on earth, of which he is the king, and whose fundamental law is that of love." Strong declared it "the mission of the church to extend [the kingdom of God on earth] until the kingdoms of the world are become the kingdom of the Lord." [15]

Strong was convinced that the kingdom of God could be prepared only by way of social reforms, and he called upon the Church to "accept her commission to prepare the way for the full coming of the kingdom . . . to become the champion of needed reforms." [16] In this spirit he founded a League for Social Service (later called American Institute for Social Service); organized a parallel institute in England; and helped form the Federal Council of the Churches of Christ in America (1908), one of the founding organizations of the National Council of the Churches of Christ in the United States (established in 1950). The Federal Council understood its mission in the spirit Strong had envisaged. In the preamble to its constitution, the council proclaimed as one of its goals that of securing "a larger combined influence for the Churches in all matters affecting the moral and social conditions of the people so as to promote the application of the law of Christ in every relation of human life." In this spirit the council advocated a number of social reforms.

Walter Rauschenbusch (1861–1918) formulated his doctrine of the social gospel along the same lines of working for "needed reforms." He based it on the conviction that both the individual and the society in which he lives are sinful and in need of redemption. The cardinal sin of the existing society, as he saw it, is that of oppression and extortion. Therefore, the social gospel is the "faith in the will and power of God to redeem the permanent institutions of human society from their inherited guilt of oppression and extortion." The redemption of society is an act of salvation, which for Rauschenbusch was not an eschatological event but a historical process. More specifically, social progress has a salvational meaning: "The kingdom of God implies a progressive reign of love in human affairs." It is in turn this progress, "the development of a Christian social order [which] would be the highest proof of God's saving power." [17]

To Rauschenbusch, the logical way to realize his ideal was to strive for a socialist structure of society. Thus he became a leading representative of Christian Socialism in the United States. He conceived the "Christian social order" as a society "which will best guarantee to all personalities their freest and highest development." He was convinced that these results could best be achieved in a socialist society and that, conversely, the social gospel "constitutes the moral power in the propaganda of socialism." [18]

Yet, the concept of the social gospel, which in one way or another has remained a living force in the American churches, is not identical with Christian Socialism. For instance, Congregational minister and theologian Washington Gladden (1836–1918), one of the earliest fighters for the social gospel in the United States, was opposed to socialism. In fact, the churches remain divided over which societal structure can best foster the realization of the social gospel. The common denominators among all advocates of the social gospel have been a strong belief in the social responsibilities of society and a feeling that society has failed to shoulder these responsibilities.

Most advocates of the social gospel and Christian Socialism were found in the Protestant camp. The situation was more complicated among Catholics. While powerful social movements emerged within the Catholic ranks, in Catholic countries they had to contend and compete with Marxist-oriented socialist movements that were basically hostile toward Catholicism. The Catholic-oriented social movements, therefore, tended to organize apart from, and usually antagonistically toward, socialist-oriented political parties and trade unions. [19] These divisions between socialist-oriented and Catholic-oriented parties (and partly also trade unions) still exist in the Catholic parts of continental Europe.

Originally all Catholic social movements evolved without high-level ecclesiastical sanctioning, until a German prelate, Wilhelm Emanuel Baron von Ketteler (1811–1877), bishop of Mainz, emerged as one of the foremost advocates of social reforms and social movements, and spiritually prepared the way for the development of Christian trade unions in Germany. It may have been under his influence,[20] but mainly under the pressure of spontaneous social movements, that Pope Leo XIII, in his encyclical *Rerum Novarum* ("On the condition of workers," 1891), established an official Catholic position on the social order of society.

Rerum Novarum was not a social gospel; it did not profess that ordering the social life would help or hinder the achievement of the kingdom of God. On the contrary, the encyclical asserted that man, in his life on earth, is bound to suffer: "To suffer and to endure is the lot of life" (para. 14). The encyclical also adhered to the Paulinian concept that human life is an exile from which we yearn to escape, and that real life will begin only after Christ has led us into the kingdom of God. Yet *Rerum Novarum* did not preach indifference toward the social order. It sharply attacked exploitation of labor and any other social injustice. And it vigorously endorsed attempts to improve social conditions by social action, through the practice of charity and the promotion of social justice, and through social movements, such as trade unions. The encyclical also insisted on the duty of the government to regulate economic and social conditions. However, it sharply criticized the socialist movement as violating the "natural rights" and functions of property. The encyclical amounted to the Catholic hierarchy's official support of Christian trade unions in their competition with the socialist-oriented trade unions. At the same time it was a signal that the Catholic Church no longer sided with the socially conservative forces but recognized the need for social reforms.

When forty years later, in 1931, Pius XI (pontificate 1922–1939) issued the encyclical *Quadragesimo Anno* (significantly called, "On reconstructing the social order and perfecting it conformably to the precepts of the Gospel"), the world had gone through a world war and found itself on the threshold of the most devastating economic depression. In this grave social crisis the encyclical recognized that the existing social order was based on an "open violation of justice" and was in need of "a radical and speedy reform" (para. 4 and 84). While the encyclical still rejected the socialist movement because of its purely secular goals (para. 129–131), and even rejected Christian Socialism (para. 131),[21] and while it upheld Pope Leo XIII's concept of the transient and perishable nature of temporal happiness, it adopted the doctrine of progress in the secular sphere of society as progressive steps toward the "final end of all." The positive recommendations of the encyclical were not too different from those of *Rerum Novarum*.

Again a generation later John XXIII (pontificate 1958–1963), the great leader of forward-looking Catholicism, issued two encyclicals dealing with the societal problems of our age—*Mater et Magistra* in 1961, and *Pacem in Terris* in 1963. These two documents form a unity: that of a rather comprehensive programme for the desirable political, economic, and social ordering of modern society along national and international lines. These two documents consider issues of human rights, democracy, economic and social policies, cooperation between economically advanced and developing countries, a rational world order, and world peace, issues that could be endorsed by any progressive political or social group.

Of particular interest under the aspect of Christian eschatology is the adherence of these encyclicals to the view that progress in the secular ordering of the world is a step toward the kingdom of God. *Mater et Magistra* pronounced this view categorically: "If each one of you does his best courageously, it will necessarily help in no small measure to establish the kingdom of Christ on earth" (para. 261). But the encyclical did distinguish between the kingdom of God on earth and in heaven: "And this [kingdom on earth] we shall some day leave to go to the heavenly beatitude for which we were made by God" (para. 231).

Vatican Council II emphasized more strongly than the encyclicals the need for profound changes in order to make society more humane: "This social order requires constant improvement. . . . In freedom, it should grow every day toward a more humane balance. An improvement in attitudes and widespread changes in society will have to take place if these objectives are to be gained." [22] Yet the eschatological aspect of societal progress still lay at the center of the council's social programme. In the council's view, societal progress would extend the kingdom of God, but that perfection would have to wait for the end of time. Although the council asserted that the kingdom of God "is of a heavenly and not of an earthly nature," [23] it will descend upon the earth: "God is preparing a new dwelling place and a new earth where justice will abide." And although "earthly progress must be carefully distinguished from the growth of Christ's kingdom, nevertheless, to the extent that the former can contribute to the better ordering of human society, it is of vital concern to the kingdom of God." [24]

The council even agreed to certain concepts about the ordering of society which revealed the influence of Teilhard de Chardin on official Catholic thinking and on the council's phraseology.[25] Whereas the word "socialism" remained taboo, the council held that "socialization," defined as an intensification of reciprocal ties and of mutual dependencies, would give rise to a variety of public and private associations and organizations. It would also tend to increase the qualities of the human person, to safeguard his rights, and to foster the evolution toward unity.[26]

This brief analysis of the four encyclicals and of the documents of Vatican Council II concerning social problems shows that in the course of the last three generations, which witnessed enormous societal changes, official Catholic thinking also changed substantially. The last stage of this evolution confirmed the chief thesis of Rauschenbusch's social gospel: that the better ordering of society is of vital concern to the kingdom of God. Moreover, what is needed to achieve a more humane balance in society are changes leading toward a gradual improvement of the social structure.

As the logical consequence of the de-eschatologizing trend of liberal theology, the social gospel was its crowning glory. Yet the evolution of the social gospel both in the Catholic and Protestant camps grew out of eschatological foundations. Indeed, among the most prominent modern theologians who adhered to eschatological positions, Paul Johannes Tillich was a religious socialist and Reinhold Niebuhr was closely connected with social democratic movements.[27] Liberal theology began to fade only when the demythologizing consequences of nineteenth-century Bible criticism induced theologians to adopt eschatological rather than rationalist positions.

4. THE ERA OF BIBLE CRITICISM

Bible criticism has a long history, going back to the eighteenth century, when German philosopher and theologian Hermann Samuel Reimarus (1694–1768) rejected all miracles; asserted that Jesus was but a man with Messianic illusions who preached morality to prepare for the immediate coming of the kingdom of God; and that Jesus' resurrection was an invention of his disciples.[28] More systematic Bible criticism began in the nineteenth century, parallel to the demythologizing views of Schleiermacher and Ritschl. Critical writings began with Ferdinand Christian Baur (1792–1860), the founder of the Tübingen school of historical Bible criticism.[29] Under Hegel's influence, Baur interpreted the fight between the Apostle Paul, representing Gentile Christianity, and the Apostle Peter, defending Judaizing Christianity, as Hegelian thesis and antithesis, a fight resolved by the Catholic synthesis as a compromise between the two wings of Christianity.

German theologian David Friedrich Strauss (1808–1874), the first of the "Life of Jesus" authors, thoroughly applied a demythologizing method to his analysis of the Gospels and denied the historicity of all supernatural elements.[30] For him, Jesus was a great religious teacher. Bruno Bauer (1809–1882) doubted even the existence of Jesus, and credited the rise of Christianity to the consciousness of its early disciples rather than to a historical Jesus. Ernest Renan was among the writers who, in *La Vie de Jesus* ("The Life of Jesus," 1863), supported the conception of Jesus as a moral teacher.[31]

A leading representative of liberal historical criticism was German theologian Adolf von Harnack (1851–1930). Von Harnack regarded Jesus as the supreme teacher and revealer of God, and analyzed the history of Christian dogma that culminated in the Councils of Nicaea, Constantinople, and Chalcedon.[32] He concluded that "the claim of the Church that the dogmas are simply the exposition of the Christian revelation, because derived from the Holy Scriptures, is not confirmed by historical investigation. On the contrary, it becomes clear that dogmatic Christianity . . . was the work of the Hellenic spirit of the Gospel soil." [33] Although few scholars today would disagree with this statement, in those days his analysis of the history of Christian dogma was a bombshell.

German theologian Ernst Troeltsch (1865–1923) was another leading exponent of liberal historical criticism. He understood Christianity as a historical phenomenon, whose doctrines were meaningful only in their historical framework and which were subject to an evolutionary process. In his view no revelation on which a religion has been based can claim eternal validity. While Troeltsch did not deny the occurrence of divine actions in the various religions, he stated that "the divine reason, or the divine life . . . constantly manifests itself in always new and always peculiar individualization—and hence . . . its tendency is . . . toward the fulfillment of the highest potentialities of each separate department of life. . . . Christianity is a historical individuality." [34]

Bible criticism received a strong impetus from the methodology of "form criticism" (*Formgeschichte*), developed by two German Bible scholars, Johannes Weiss (1863–1914) and Martin Dibelius (1883–1947). Weiss expounded this method in 1912, and Dibelius first applied it.[35] Form criticism consists of a critical, literal analysis of the structural forms of the Scriptures, of tracing their history, traditions, and derivations, and then finding the so-called *Sitz im Leben* ("historical setting") of the various parts of the Scriptures.

Prominent German theologian Rudolf Bultmann (1886–1976) used this method in his earlier writings in an attempt to separate the real ministry of Jesus from the accretions that the early Christian community contributed.[36] He concluded that while Jesus believed in the coming of a Messiah, he did not consider himself the Messiah, nor did he believe in his impending death as the vicarious sacrifice of the son of God, which would have a salvational significance. To understand Jesus' message today, it must be freed from its mythological veils, said Bultmann. The essential myths which must be abandoned are those of the preexistence of Jesus, his nature as the incarnate son of God, his sinlessness, his vicarious assumption of the sins of the world, and man's deliverance from sins through him.[37]

Both Harnack's critical analyses of the dogmas adopted by the Councils of Nicaea, Constantinople, and Chalcedon, and Bultmann's form criticism, appeared to establish the fact that Trinitarian Christianity could not be derived from the person and the teachings of Jesus. The Bible criticism written by Reimarus, Strauss, and Renan appeared to be vindicated.

5. THE EXISTENTIALIST THEOLOGY

A strong reaction against the liberal school of theology set in at the beginning of the twentieth century. This new, fundamentally eschatological theology has dominated Christian thought in forms variously called "crisis theology," "dialectical theology," or simply "neo-orthodox theology." However, its characterization as "existentialist theology" seems the most appropriate.

There is doubtless a close connection between world conditions and these new trends in Christian thinking. The relative peace and prosperity that characterized the Western world in the second half of the nineteenth century drew to a close. World War I threw its shadow over the world, and brought with it a feeling of crisis and anxiety, a feeling that continues to plague mankind. Salvation was no longer expected, as liberal theology had assumed, from the teachings of a superior human being— the role that liberal theologians had given to Jesus.

These changes in religious thought were preluded by a 1906 treatise, *Geschichte der Leben-Jesu-Forschung*, written by the great Alsatian theologian and philosopher Albert Schweitzer.[38] In confronting the critical analyses which the liberal theologians had undertaken, Schweitzer concluded that the Jesus constructed by that school had never existed. "He is a figure designed by rationalism, endowed with life by liberalism, and clothed by modern theology in a historical garb."[39] Schweitzer's Jesus appeared as an eschatological prophet and Messiah who was convinced that the kingdom of God was so close at hand that it would arrive before the return of his disciples whom he sent on a mission, and that he could be the Messiah whom God has chosen to usher in His kingdom.

Schweitzer was further convinced that when Jesus realized that the time of Messianic woes had not yet arrived, he went to a sacrificial death in order to introduce the Messianic woes.

Schweitzer arrived at the conclusion that Jesus is significant for our time and can help us not as he is historically known, but as he spiritually affects men. Schweitzer wrote his treatise eight years before the outbreak of the First World War, when the prevailing mood of his generation was one of optimism. He contrasted this world-affirming spirit with the world-negating spirit which in his view was characteristic of Jesus' teachings. Nevertheless, Schweitzer insisted that the affirmation of the world must be based on a Christian spirit, that salvation must come from work on earth in a Christian spirit. It was in this spirit that he opened his hospital in Lambarene, Africa.

The final break with liberal theology was initiated by the outstanding Swiss theologian Karl Barth (1885–1968). Barth rejected liberal theology in favor of existentialist philosophy which originated in the writings of Danish religious philosopher Sören Aabye Kierkegaard (1813–1855). Kierkegaard's basic premise was that man has the freedom of choice, but that since he does not really know himself or his destiny and cannot trust himself, his freedom is a source of guilt, anxiety, and despair. "There is no living man," he asserted, "who is not in some degree the victim of despair; no man in whose inner life there does not dwell an unrest, a dispeace, a disharmony, the dread of something unknown, of something on which he dare not look, a dread of the possibilities of his own being, a dread of himself."[40] Man cannot rationally overcome this fundamental dread. He cannot become an "authentic self" by any means other than by making the personal decision to face God in lonely isolation, to trust in Him although He remains unknown, and to commit himself to faith in God, however absurd this might appear, and although he can never know whether he will be saved or condemned.

Because Kierkegaard lived when society was at the threshold of its greatest scientific, technological, and economic triumphs, it is no wonder that his philosophical and religious positions were for a long time virtually unknown outside his native country. Not until nineteenth-century optimism was shaken by world tensions that finally broke into the First World War did existentialism gain ground.

Barth's fundamental work, *Der Römerbrief* ("The Epistle to the Romans"), appeared in 1919, immediately after World War I.[41] In it he launched a scathing attack on liberal theology and propounded his crisis theology. It constituted the reintroduction of Paulinism into modern theology without attempting to "modernize" Christianity by any process of demythologization or de-eschatologization. On the contrary, the triune God of Barth's theology is beyond our scientific comprehension, "the unknown God dwelling in light unapproachable" (p. 35). Christ, being God Himself, whom "God sends . . . from the realm of the eternal, unknown world of the beginning and of the end" (p. 277), cannot be understood within the confines of history, as little as his resurrection can be understood within history.

According to Barth, man is the eternal sinner: "Sin is the characteristic mark of human nature as such. . . . It is the Fall which occurred within the emergence of human life" (p. 173). Nevertheless, we shall be saved by grace, the gift of Christ, who bridges the gulf between God and man. Grace alone will save us; "achievement is of no value and has no independent validity in the presence of God" (p. 59). However, since man is by nature a sinner, grace cannot save us as long as we inhabit a mortal body. We must wait for the kingdom of God, the day "when mankind will be dissolved and the new era of the righteousness of God will be inaugurated" (p. 97). This will be "no moment in time, no temporary event, no telluric or cosmic catastrophe" (p. 500). It will simply be the end. We must wait for it; we cannot force it upon history. Barth was a consistent Paulinian even in rejecting the doctrine of the immortality of the soul: "Redemption can only take place at the coming Day when there shall be a new heaven and a new earth" (p. 169). On that day body and soul will be resurrected, something not understood within the confines of history (p. 204).

The Barthian theology was the most radical Christian response to the changes marked by World War I, World War II, and the grave international tensions that followed. The world crisis was reflected in Barth's crisis theology. It is "inevitable," he asserted, "that human life shall be thwarted, undermined, and finally denied, by insecurity, limitation, suffering, and at the last by death" (p. 170). There is no salvation before the trumpet calls us from our graves. In later years Barth attempted to "humanize" God and to gain more distance from existentialism, but the foundation of his theology remained unaltered: Christianity must be understood on a nonrationalist basis and can be maintained only as an eschatological creed.

This theology, based on existentialist premises, dominated the Protestant world for the period between the two world wars and immediately following World War II. Among the best-known existentialist theologians (aside from Barth), Paul Tillich and Reinhold Niebuhr of the

United States are of particular interest because of their attempt to reconcile the eschatological features of existentialist theology with ideas of a socialist regeneration of society.

Paul Tillich, as a religious socialist, showed much sympathy with Marxism, and recognized the structural analogies between Marxism and Jewish prophetism.[42] Tillich agreed with much of the Marxist analysis and criticism of the existing society, but found fault with the absence of an eschatological aspect in its historical prophecy. While Marxism remains within history, existentialist theology professes that demonic forces of history can never be eliminated and that a secular kingdom of justice and peace can never be established. In contrast, "religious socialism, in the spirit of prophetism and with the methods of Marxism, is able to understand and to transcend the world of today."[43] Tillich expounded his theological system in his comprehensive work *Systematic Theology*.[44] This work represented the thoughts of many modern Protestant theologians, and illuminated their views of salvation.

In spite of a thorough demythologization, which he called "deliteralization," Tillich firmly upheld the Christian belief in God and "Jesus as Christ." God is "the active ground of being," on whom "man is continuously dependent because he is eternally rooted in the divine ground." Although Christ is God-like, Tillich replaced the Nicene doctrine of the divine nature of Christ with the concept of "eternal God-Manhood" (vol. 2, p. 148). Christ remained the Savior, not through a vicarious death, but as the "New Being," the "new aeon," the universal regeneration (vol. 2, p. 127). In the old aeon man is estranged from God, living in a world ruled by evil structures that produce anxiety. The Messiah's mission is to conquer these structures and establish a new reality. While man can participate in the New Being, the initiation of the new aeon, "the transition from the temporal to the eternal, the 'end' of the temporal, is not a temporal event" (vol. 3, p. 399). Salvation and damnation are eschatological events.

Like Barth, Tillich rejected the belief in the immortality of the soul, which he termed a "non-Christian pseudo-Platonic popular superstition" (vol. 3, pp. 409–10). But man's participation in the eternal life will depend on the ultimate judgment, which will be based on the degree of the "negative" in the life of each person. To the extent that a person has chosen to be a "nonbeing," he is excluded from eternal life and is condemned to the extent of his "nonbeing" (vol. 1, p. 284). Tillich rejected the popular belief in heaven and hell, on the ground that "no human being is unambiguously on one or the other side of divine judgment. . . . Nothing is merely negative, and consequently no being can ultimately be annihilated, that is, excluded from eternity" (vol. 3, pp. 408, 399).

In temporal life those who have faith in Christ participate in the "New Being," but only "under the conditions of man's existential predicament and, therefore, only fragmentarily and by anticipation" (vol. 2, p. 118). For full participation man will have to wait for the advent of Christ. Tillich also accepted the belief in general resurrection, along the lines of Paul's doctrine of the resurrection of a "spiritual body," as "a body which expresses the spiritually transformed personality of man" (vol. 3, p. 412). The kingdom of God, in the new aeon of eternal life, will be a realm of universal and perfect love, where there is no need for morality and law. In this kingdom there will still be individual life, but "in eternal life the centre of the individual person rests in the all-uniting divine centre and through it is in communion with all other personal centres" (vol. 3, p. 402).

The life and work of existentialist philosopher Reinhold Niebuhr (1892–1971) were characterized by a tension between history and eschatology. Although he was a social activist striving for social and political progress, Niebuhr was convinced that history "is incapable of fulfilling itself and, therefore, points beyond itself to the judgment and mercy of God for its fulfillment." This is fundamentally due to man's innate sinfulness, the result of his self-love and self-centeredness, an innate spiritual defect. Niebuhr blamed man's defectiveness on his hybris, that is, on the refusal "to admit his creatureliness and to acknowledge himself as a member of a total unity of life." [45]

Since man is, and must remain, imperfect, his society must remain imperfect. Yet Niebuhr admitted that moral progress is possible: "There are no limits set in history for the achievement of more universal brotherhood, for the development of more perfect and more inclusive mutual relations." [46] Indeed, Niebuhr's practical work was chiefly devoted to assisting in the achievement of moral progress in society. He insisted, however, that the defects in human life are to too high a degree constitutional to be eliminated by a reorganization of society.

In the end salvation cannot be attained within history. "The culmination of history must include not merely the divine completion of human incompletion, but a purging of human guilt and sin by divine judgment and mercy." This process necessarily transcends history. The advent of Christ must be understood as the end of history, as the final supremacy of love over all forms of self-love. Man, and society as a whole, will be subject to the last judgment: man will be judged according to his own ideal potentiality, but sinful civilizations will be destroyed. [46]

The theological views of Rudolf Bultmann were rooted in existentialist foundations no less than those of Barth, Tillich, and Niebuhr, but contained fewer eschatological features because of the thorough demythologization process he applied to Christian beliefs. In the spirit of existentialism he asserted that the real substance of Jesus' message was the absolute certainty that man is faced with an inescapable, existential decision which allows no delay.[48] Man must decide whether he wants to obey God's will. Every belief Jesus expressed, every rule of conduct he established, was based on the imperative of the immediate decision, the existential commitment. Hence, Jesus demands that man find his "authentic existence," that is, the commitment to live consciously and act responsibly.

Although Bultmann thoroughly demythologized Jesus' life and message, he remained Christian on the basis of his existentialist philosophy. If human existence means living in anxiety, man can alleviate his anxiety by understanding his own authentic existence, and by committing himself to his future. For Bultmann this liberating act meant accepting Jesus' religious and ethical message. Bultmann accepted the cross "as an eschatological event in and beyond time," and Jesus as mediator between God and man,[49] and he saw in this eschatological event the foundation for man's authentic self-understanding.

Bultmann's theology is, in fact, a theology of realized eschatology. In *Jesus und Paul* he stated that

> according to [Jesus'] proclamation, God's reign is indeed the sovereignty of His will, but it is a reign that is perfectly realized throughout the entire world and over every man—namely God's own act at a specific time. And this time is immediately at hand; indeed, it has already broken in with the coming of Jesus himself.[50]

In a later treatise Bultmann further clarified his doctrine of the realized eschatology. He stated that what Jesus and the Christian community understood as the end of the old aeon and the breaking-in of the new aeon, was the

> certainty of the unconditionedness of the divine demand and the divine grace, and the certainty that he, Jesus has to proclaim these two realities as something new . . . and definitive. . . . That man stands in this 'interim' expresses his paradoxical existence before God as the Judge and the gracious Father; for him who lets God be his God, the past is extinguished and the future is open.

More concretely stated, "the past that is ended" is "my particular past in which I was a sinner. And the future for which I am freed is likewise my future." Sin in this context means "to want to live out of one's self . . .

rather than out of a radical surrender to God. . . . It is from this sin that the grace of God frees the man who opens himself to it in radical surrender, that is, in faith." [51]

If eschatology means the belief in the end of our aeon, that is, of history itself, the question arises whether the realized eschatology can even be considered as eschatology. Bultmann expressly stated that Jesus' proclamation of divine demand and grace "clothes itself for him in the mythological notion of the end of the old and the beginning of the new aeon." [52] Certainly, if eschatology is understood as the doctrine of the last things, then eschatology reduced to the mythological notion of the end of the old aeon would vanish together with that myth. Eschatology, as Bultmann understood it, must therefore mean the tie which connects man with his ultimate "authentic existence" in God. Bultmann maintained that this tie was established by Jesus' "proclamation" about the ultimate divine command addressed to man's conscience, and that man's unconditional obedience to this command is the sole prerequisite for his salvation. Moreover, he saw Jesus not only as the messenger appointed by God to proclaim this message, but also as the mediator who, through the cross, sealed that tie between God and man.

The question arises, however, whether this link between God and man is essential to the existentialist concept of authentic existence or whether it is in need of demythologization itself. This question was raised by Schubert M. Ogden, a prominent disciple of Bultmann. Ogden maintained that, in accordance with Bultmann's rules of demythologization, Bultmann's "claim that authentic historicity is factually possible only in Jesus Christ must be regarded as just as incredible and irrelevant as the other myths with which it properly belongs." [53] Ogden holds that as a saving act in the face of man's fall, and as a means of establishing man's authentic existence, God's love alone "is omnipresently efficacious as a redemptive possibility," if only man grasps the chance that God gives him. Ogden thereby does not eliminate Jesus' proclamation from Christianity: while God's primordial love is the only ground of salvation, it is "decisively revealed in Jesus." In this sense, Jesus is indeed God's work of salvation, the unqualified manifestation of God's love.[54]

When demythologization reaches this stage, Christianity understandably reverts to a strictly monotheistic faith in which Jesus not only ceases to be consubstantial with God, but even loses the role Bultmann still conceded to him, as the Messiah who mediates man's salvation. Jesus becomes a voice through which God once spoke to man. The Savior, however, is no longer Christ but God alone (Ogden's position). Yet if that stage is reached, the existentialist theology must recognize that the commitment God demands of man was pronounced not only by Jesus, but also by Zarathustra, the Jewish prophets, and Mohammed; each maintained that he had received from God a mandate to proclaim man's commitment to Him.

6. THEOLOGY IN A SECULARIZED WORLD

An important group of theologians has centered on the problems which the secularization of modern society has created for Christianity. Their concern has been systematically expressed by Harvey Cox in *The Secular City*. His point of departure is the secularization of modern life, which he interprets as "a historical process . . . in which society and culture are delivered from tutelage to religious control and to closed metaphysical world-views." Modern life in state and society has undergone a process of desacralization and deconsecration. Modern man's goals, both in society and in his personal life, have become pragmatic: "Life for him is a set of problems, not an unfathomable mystery. . . . He wastes little time thinking about 'ultimate' or religious questions. And he can live with highly provisional solutions." [55]

Cox asserted, nevertheless, that in spite of all his secularity, profanity, and pragmatism, modern man is still a Christian. He is still guided by the goal of the kingdom of God, as Jesus proclaimed it. Jesus "is [the kingdom's] representative, its embodiment, and its central sign." Thus there is still God who, through Jesus, has committed man to strive for His kingdom, which remains eschatological since it can never be achieved in history. For modern man the kingdom has a secular meaning. He understands Jesus' call "as a summons to leave behind the society and symbols of a dying era and to assume responsibilities for devising new ones." For modern man, not only the kingdom but also the commitment to it have a secular meaning: "Today the Gospel summons man to frame with his neighbour a common life suitable to the secular city." [56] Yet this secular commitment is at the same time a divine commitment. In summary, Cox posits that the Savior is not God or Jesus or man. Rather all together are partners on the road to secular salvation in a secular city.

German theologian Dietrich Bonhoeffer (1906–1945) and American theologian Paul Van Buren likewise assumed a secular setting of Christianity in the modern world. Imprisoned and finally executed, Bonhoeffer was prevented from publishing his thoughts. His chief work, *Ethics*, and his statements, letters, and an *Outline for a Book*, which he sketched in prison, were published posthumously. He emphasized that the Church should accept man's maturity in a "world come of age." Man in modern society can relate to Christianity if he understands that the essence of Jesus' message and mission is that "Jesus is there only for others. . . . It is only this 'being for others' . . . that is the ground of his omnipotence, omniscience, and omnipresence. Faith is participation in this being of Jesus." In the same vein, Bonhoeffer stated that "our relation to God is not a 'religious' relationship to the highest, most powerful, and best Being imaginable . . . but is a new life in 'existence for others,' through participation in the being of Jesus." [57] Bonhoeffer not only preached this social understanding of Jesus and God, but lived and died for it. He was a leader of the anti-Nazi wing of the Protestant Church (*Bekennende Kirche*) and conspired clandestinely against the Hitler regime. By suffering a martyr's death, he showed that Christian existence is "being there for others."

In *The Secular Meaning of the Gospel*, Paul Van Buren attempted to prove that Jesus' message, which for nearly two thousand years had a transcendental meaning, also has a secular meaning. Although modern man is secular, he need not abandon the Gospel since it can have a secular meaning for him. In Van Buren's view the substance of Jesus' message was freedom and the commitment to use it in the service of others: "Jesus . . . stands out as a remarkably free man. . . . The evangelists . . . indicate this freedom in many ways: . . . his 'authority,' his openness to friend and foe; free from familiar claims, free to disregard rites . . . but also free to serve others." The impact of this freedom in the midst of fear and servility, the impact of fearlessness even in the face of death, converted his disciples and set them free. Van Buren interpreted the Easter event on this basis: "The disciples were changed men. They apparently found themselves caught up in something like the freedom of Jesus himself, having become men who were free to face even death without fear." [58]

Thus Van Buren remained Christocentric: Jesus the man showed men what freedom means; he made freedom the meaning of life; he admonished us to found our individual and social life on freedom from fear, anxiety, and slavery. This freedom, however, rests on a secular, nontranscendental basis. Sin likewise has a secular meaning: "Being bound by fear and anxiety, mistrust and self-concern." [59]

From that point there is only one step to a secular existentialist interpretation of salvation through Jesus. To Van Buren, Jesus appeared as the Savior by freeing us from life's anxieties: "Our fears may be calmed by the presence of one who is unafraid and free from the fears and anxieties which bind us." [60] If Jesus is a Savior in a secular way, however, the salvational message can be understood without using the word "God" or similar terms: "In the language of faith a statement about God is really a statement about man. . . . What faith speaks of is . . . man and his self-understanding." [61] Van Buren clarified his understanding of a godless Christianity as follows: "Christianity is fundamentally about man . . . its language about God is one way—a dated way, among a number of ways—of saying what it is Christianity wants to say about man and human life, and human history." [62] If, however, the language about God is dated, it follows that the language about salvation and damnation through God's judgment at the end of our aeon is no less dated. Christianity is thus reduced to "a certain form of life-pattern of human existence, norms of human attitudes and dispositions and moral behaviour." [63]

If in Van Buren's theology, Jesus' message and mission have been secularized to such a degree that their divine roots have withered away and Christians no longer need to believe in God, two other American theologians, William Hamilton and J. J. Altizer, have formally proclaimed a Death-of-God theology: "We are not talking about the absence of the experience of God, but about the experience of the absence of God," Hamilton stated. Altizer similarly exclaimed that "the contemporary Christian must accept the death of God as a final and irrevocable event." [64] But the two theologians asserted that although God has disappeared, the word of Jesus has not. Thus according to Hamilton, "Our worldly work is Christian . . . for our way to our neighbour is not only mapped out by the secular social and psychological and literary disciplines, it is mapped out as well by Jesus Christ and his way to his neighbour." Hamilton understood the word of Jesus in a strictly secular way, as meaning that "the human conditions that create despair, whether they be poverty, discrimination, mental illness, or fear of death, can be overcome." Altizer likewise believed that the word of Jesus is "present wherever that which has been becomes anew." But he retained an eschatological perspective; he spoke of the present age as seeking "fulfillment in a redemptive and eschatological future," and he was prepared to "celebrate the death of God as an epiphany of the eschatological Christ." [65]

Thus in the Death-of-God theology, Jesus' message is no longer founded on God. His message does not point to the coming of a kingdom of God, but to a secular kingdom. The freedom in which Jesus lived and which he taught means a secular freedom and service to one's neighbors. Moreover, the call to repentance which Jesus proclaimed is a call to turn away from a self-centered and slavish life toward a life of freedom and self-chosen service to others. But the question arises whether this post-theistic Christianity differs in any substantive way from the ideal of striving for the humanization of man and his society which has evolved on secular foundations. In other words, are not these two currents, that of Christianity-without-God and that of secular humanism, in fact parallel to each other and bound to merge?

7. MODERN CATHOLIC TRENDS

Although modern theology has been predominantly Protestant, the need to establish new avenues in Christian thinking has not been confined to Protestantism. There have been significant developments in Catholicism which, in spite of the differences in the spiritual and ecclesiastical structure and traditions between Catholic and Protestant churches, point toward similar currents in the two main branches of Christianity.

As noted, the official pronouncements of the Catholic Church, stated in the papal encyclicals and the Constitutions of Vatican Council II, were progressively concerned with the imperfections of the existing society, increasingly emphasized the need for social reform, and expressed the belief that the *Populorum Progressio* ("progress of the peoples") toward a better society is possible and necessary.[66] Thus secular goals have increasingly preoccupied the Catholic Church.

There has even been an important evolution in Catholic dogma. The concept of ultimate salvation has been especially broadened, obviously in response to the growing ecumenical movement. As the Roman Catholic Church became less isolated from the other Christian churches, it could hardly maintain its claim as the sole receptacle of salvation. Vatican Council II not only formally abandoned the doctrine "Outside the [Catholic] Church there is no salvation," but even opened the promise of salvation to the non-Catholic Christians, to the Jews and Muslims, "who . . . along with us adore the one and merciful God," to those "who seek the unknown God," and finally to those "who have not yet arrived at an explicit knowledge of God, but who strive to live a good life."[67] If this formula is taken literally, it is doubtful whether even atheists and Death-of-God theologians are excluded from the hope of ultimate salvation.

Extending potential ultimate salvation to non-Catholics and even to non-Christians has not weakened the official Catholic Church's belief in the ascent of the souls of the righteous to heaven, and in purgatory and hell as the destiny of the souls of sinners. It was chiefly against this rigid traditionalism of the doctrine of salvation and damnation that the Dutch

Catholic Church rebelled. While the famous New Catechism of the Dutch Church remained orthodox in many respects—such as its belief in the Trinity, the immaculate conception and the assumption of Mary, the indissolubility of the marriage vows—its doctrines of salvation and damnation deviated markedly from those enunciated a year earlier by Vatican Council II.[68] The doctrine of original sin was considerably diluted, in a near-Pelagian sense: man is free to sin, and "there is no necessity [for sinning] imposed on man from above or from below." [69] The New Catechism adhered to the Pauline belief that man is unable to effect his own delivery, yet it maintained that while contact with God broken off by sin cannot be reestablished without Him, man can reestablish this contact in cooperation with Him.

The eschatological doctrines of the New Catechism are a blend of realized eschatology and resurrection. In the spirit of the realized eschatology the advent of Christ in the traditional sense was replaced by his presence "with us": Christ "does not actually 'return' since he is already with us. When he does 'come,' his presence will be completely manifest." The "coming" of Christ "includes his perpetual, hidden and gladdening coming in our daily existence." [70]

The New Catechism interpreted resurrection as something which does not wait indefinitely for the coming of Christ; instead men can rise immediately after death, outside time as we know it. The New Catechism did not reject the belief in heaven, purgatory, and hell, but interpreted it in an unorthodox way: After death man will be converted to God's light and love. Bad will, indifference, and rebellion "will be cleansed away and purified." But the man who has lived in grave sin, in enmity toward God, will be doomed to a state of eternal callousness in which he will be "entirely closed in on oneself, without contact with others or with God." [71]

These deviations from the official Christian dogma had important implications for the extent of ecclesiastical power. Although the New Catechism conceded that funeral prayers, prayers for the dead, prayers during the Mass, and even prayers for healing may have good effects, its interpretations of Christian doctrines considerably diminished the believer's dependence on the priest. By man's own efforts and by his faith in God, he can be received, through the grace of God, into the beatific communion of the faithful believers, even if only after purification. Even if he has lived in grave sin, he does not have to fear the fires of hell.

The Commission of Cardinals, charged by the Vatican with commenting on the New Catechism, emphasized these dogmatic differences in its 1968 Declaration. The Declaration insisted on the doctrine of original sin, and also stated that "while the pilgrim church still awaits the glorious coming of the Lord and the final resurrection," the souls of the just, having been thoroughly purified, "already rejoice in the immediate vision of God."

The discussion in the Catholic camp about man's destiny after death has not been confined to that of the Commission of Cardinals. Considerable differences of opinion regarding the immortality of the soul also arose among the scholars who contributed to the *New Catholic Encyclopedia*. M. E. Williams and H. Dressler supported the official Catholic belief in the existence of the disembodied soul after death and its beatific vision, purification, or damnation. But H. M. McElwain referred critically to the intrusion of Platonic and Neoplatonic thoughts into the core of Christian theology, which led to the belief in the immortality of the soul, with its neglect of the human person (body and soul). It is not the soul, but "the person in Christian reality [who] is the object" of redemption and salvation. "Until such time as [the resurrection of the person] comes to pass, every man in some sense is in a state of expectation." [72]

Yet the Catholic intellectual world has been preoccupied for the last twenty years less by theological debates than by the theories of Teilhard de Chardin, a religious philosopher who propounded a metaphysical system foreign to any doctrines and concepts in Christianity. Although a priest, his system has only tenuous contact with traditional Christian beliefs.

Pierre Teilhard de Chardin (1881–1955), a French Jesuit, was a distinguished paleontologist and geologist, but his chief concerns were metaphysical speculations about the direction and meaning of evolution. He expanded the theory of evolution from the firm ground of biological evolution to the much less firm ground of human evolution. He was convinced that evolution is directed toward the unification of mankind, which he also called "socialization." [73] He held that evolution takes place in what, in analogy to the biosphere, he called the noösphere, that is, "the thinking envelope of the Earth," which has evolved with the rise of man. The direction of this process is toward a superconsciousness of mankind as a whole which in effect would transform mankind into a collective being. In his chief work *The Phenomenon of Man*, in which he systematically expounded his theory of evolution, he stated that

> the noösphere tends to constitute a single closed system in which each element sees, feels, desires, and suffers . . . the same things as all the others. . . . We are faced with a harmonious collectivity of consciousness, equivalent to a sort of super-consciousness. The idea is that of the earth not only

becoming covered by myriads of grains of thought, but becoming enclosed in a single thinking envelope so as to form, functionally, no more than a single grain of thought on the sidereal scale." [74]

If evolution has led to the rise and growth of the noösphere, that sphere itself is evolving in the direction of convergence toward a spiritual center, the "Omega Point":

> The noösphere—and more generally the world—represents a whole that is not only closed but also centred. Because it contains and engenders consciousness, space-time is necessarily of a convergent nature. Accordingly its enormous layers, followed in the right direction, must somewhere ahead become involved to a point which we might call Omega, which fuses and consumes them integrally in itself. [75]

Thus man, in Teilhard's view, is still evolving, from a species in which he sees, feels, desires, and suffers individually, toward a collective being, a single vast grain of thought. Man's salvation on earth consists in the unification of mankind, as opposed to individualization. Teilhard wrote that "the first essential is that the human units involved in the process shall draw closer together," and shall be motivated by "a sense of universal solidarity based on profound community." He envisioned "a new kind of love, not yet experienced by man, which we must learn to look for as it is borne to us on the rising tide of planetarization." [76] Although in his view evolution toward "profound community" will occur spontaneously, the loss of individuality it implies moves it close to totalitarian systems. Teilhard indirectly recognized that his evolutionary doctrines tended in this direction, for he regarded modern totalitarianism as the distortion of something magnificent, but still quite near to the truth. [77] He obviously envisioned that the unification of mankind, which totalitarianism attempts to achieve through force and indoctrination, will be accomplished by "the new kind of love."

The convergence of the universe toward the Omega Point forms a tenuous link with Christianity. Teilhard envisioned Omega, the "point of convergence at the end of the world," as a hyper-personal entity, which must be "a spiritual centre, a supreme pole of consciousness." This "universal centre of unification," under whose influence the noösphere evolves in convergent direction, must be conceived of as preexisting and transcendent. [78]

This evolutionary doctrine could be considered as a variant of strictly monotheistic religions. But Teilhard attempted to reconcile his personal faith with that of the Christian doctrine of the triune God by substituting Christ for God as the occupant of Omega Point and introducing the

Holy Spirit as Christ's organ.[79] In his personal credo,[80] he stated: "The universal Christ is a synthesis of Christ and the universe. He is . . . an inevitable deployment of the mystery in which Christianity is summed up, the mystery of the incarnation." Teilhard attributed to Christ even the traditional role as Savior: "In a universe of 'conical' structure Christ has a place ['the apex'] ready for him to fill, whence his spirit can radiate through all the centuries and all the beings. . . . In such a world Christ cannot sanctify the Spirit without . . . uplifting and saving the totality of matter." [81]

Teilhard's vision of ultimate salvation was entirely different from that of traditional Christianity: At the end of time mankind as a whole, although not individual man, would be saved by being obliged "to abandon its organo-planetaric foothold so as to pivot itself on the transcendent centre of its increasing concentration. This will be the end and the fulfillment of the spirit of the earth." [82] In other words, the traditional Christian beliefs in man's ultimate salvation have been replaced by a belief in the submergence of mankind as a whole, or rather, of the collective spirit of mankind, at the end of time in the Omega Point, the transcendent center of the universe.

Teilhard's cosmic vision of man's evolution and ultimate destiny at the end of time made a deep impression on the intellectual world far beyond the Catholic camp. But neither the personal God of Christianity nor Christ himself could be recognized in Teilhard's Omega Point. Moreover, his vision of the ultimate fusion of a planetarized mankind with the Godhead could not be reconciled with the Christian belief in the divine judgment and the resurrection at the coming of Christ.

The ecclesiastical authorities' reaction to Teilhard's writings was a modernized version of the traditional anathematization process. His ecclesiastical superiors refused permission for the publication of his major writings and cut off his academic career. The Vatican (through the Congregation of the Holy Office), in a *Monitum* of 1962, labeled Teilhard's and his disciples' writings dangerous on the ground that they contained ambiguities and "so grave errors that they offend the Catholic doctrines." [83] Nevertheless, Teilhard's ideas spread throughout Catholic circles. His doctrines and visions became so popular among Catholic intellectuals that Teilhard associations were even formed in some European and American cities. The attraction of his writings seems to have been due to his attempt—as a priest and an assiduous worker in the field of natural science—to reconcile scientific theories of evolution with Christian beliefs. This attempt was not entirely successful, for his speculations about the noösphere and its convergence toward a transcendent spiritual center could not contribute much to the scientific research on evolution, nor could their association with Christian beliefs increase their authority.

In any case, the popularity of Teilhard's system is symptomatic of the need of religious groups to harmoniously link the modern theories of evolution with the Christian faith. Both Catholic and Protestant churches in the last few decades have strongly insisted upon drawing lines of demarcation between science and religion. Consequently they insist that scientific hypotheses are on a level different from religious beliefs and therefore cannot affect these beliefs. But this position could not block man's natural urge to integrate these two fields of human experience. That Teilhard de Chardin made such an attempt made his writings popular; and that he had to suffer exile and enforced silence gave him the well-deserved aureole of a martyr.

Both the Dutch New Catechism and the writings of Teilhard de Chardin were symptoms of a severe crisis in the ranks of Catholicism which affects not only marginal issues, such as birth control, the indissolubility of the marriage vows, the celibacy of priests, and even the language of the liturgy, but also the fundamentals of Catholic beliefs. The Catholic Church has officially recognized the existence of this religious crisis. In an "Apostolic Exhortation" issued in 1970, Pope Paul VI stated that many Catholics were "troubled in their faith by an accumulation of ambiguities, uncertainties and doubts about its essentials," among which he enumerated the Trinity, the real presence of Christ in the Eucharist, the Church as an institution of salvation, and the sacraments. Moreover, he referred critically not only to such disintegrating trends, but also to modernizing currents. He noted "a tendency to reconstruct . . . a Christianity cut off from the unbroken tradition which links it to the faith of the apostles." [84]

A year after the pope raised his warning voice, Swiss theologian and priest Hans Küng (born 1928) published a treatise attacking the innermost citadel of Catholicism, the sacred nature of the priesthood. He preceded this challenge with a sharp attack on the dogma of the pope's infallibility.[85] But while the offensive against the sacred nature of the papal office was directed against a comparatively recent institution, Küng's views on the priestly office struck at the core of Catholic sacramentalism. His fundamental thesis was that "a Christian does not need the mediation of a priest in order to enter the innermost sanctuary of his temple, that is, to reach God Himself." [86] The priest should be a leader of his community, but his ordination should not be of a sacramental nature. The apostolic succession is that of the Church in general, but should not be considered as adhering to any church function.[87] Consequently all church members should share all responsibilities and elect their leaders, from the lowest to the highest levels.

The Catholic hierarchy could not remain silent about doctrines that threatened to undermine the foundations of Catholic sacramentalism. The Sacred Congregation for the Doctrine of the Faith repeatedly reprimanded Küng for his views, which were further expanded in a more recent work, *On Being a Christian*.[88] But the Catholic crisis obviously cannot be eased by disciplinary measures. The painful process of adjustment to the "secular city" of modern man, both in the Catholic and Protestant camps, has apparently not yet run its course.

8. THE THEOLOGY OF SOCIAL CHANGE

The evolution of Christianity from a fundamentalist religion toward one that embraces a variety of beliefs tending to diminish the gap between Christianity and secular humanism, has been paralleled by an evolution of the societal goals of Christianity and humanism. Until recently, the hierarchy of the Christian churches tended toward the conservative side of society. This was true both of Catholicism, from the pope down to the village priest, and of the major Protestant churches. As late as the 1930s the Catholic hierarchy in countries like Spain and Austria actively supported those forces which broke the back of progressive democracy. The Protestant camp's alliance with the throne, particularly in the Lutheran countries, impeded progressive political and social movements. Moreover, in some colonies of European powers, the Christian churches, through their missionary activities, were to a large extent instruments of the conquerors and colonizers.

In all these respects there has been a radical change in the last few decades. In Catholicism this evolution was officially marked by Vatican Council II and the encyclical *Populorum Progressio*. The most significant evolution has taken place in Latin America, where impoverishment, particularly in rural sectors, and the crying need for agricultural and other reforms has moved much of the Catholic hierarchy to switch from the side of the rich to that of the poor.

This change in sympathies is most apparent in Brazil, with its vast starvation belt in the northeast. Helder Camara, "the Red Archbishop of Recife," in northeastern Brazil, was among the first prelates to insist on the need for fundamental societal reforms. In a pastoral letter issued jointly in 1967 with six other Brazilian bishops, Camara even advocated true socialism. Most of the Brazilian hierarchy followed this lead to some extent. The Central Commission of the Brazilian Bishops' Conference issued a pronouncement in 1963 sharply attacking the existing social order and calling for agrarian reforms and expropriations. In a similar statement adopted in 1968, the Brazilian bishops protested against the suppression of civil rights.[89] Many Brazilian priests who supported the fight for political and social reforms paid heavy tribute for their activities with imprisonments and tortures.

The bulk of the Catholic hierarchy of other Latin American countries have adopted similar positions. This new current manifested itself at the international Eucharistic Conference of 1968 in Bogota and at the General Conference of the Bishops of Latin America in Medellin, Colombia. The bishops' conference affirmed the need for social and political change in that continent, and declared: "We will not have a new continent without new and reformed structures, but above all not without new men who know how to be truly free and responsible in the light of the Gospel."[90] The following Conference of the Bishops of Latin America, which was held in Puebla, Mexico, in 1979, likewise condemned the existing societal structure for not having adequately solved the problems that challenge us, and it appealed to "all without distinction of class to accept and take up the cause of the poor." Pope John Paul II, who opened the conference, while warning of priests' direct participation in liberation movements, spoke out warmly in favor of their activities in the struggle for social betterment.

Prominent Catholic representatives of the theology of social change are also found in European countries, such as the Netherlands, Germany, and France, where the spirit of the Catholic Church is generally liberal. Theologians Schillebeeckx, Metz, and Laurentin represent this spirit. Dutch Jesuit Edward Schillebeeckx (b. 1914), strictly adhered to the belief in the kingdom of God as an eschatological event beyond human history, but insisted that "the God of the promise . . . gives us the task of setting out toward the promised land that we ourselves, trusting in the promise, must reclaim and cultivate." Whereas past history has not afforded us salvation, we can assure the triumph of salvation by making society more humane, by transforming "the terrestrian event" into a history of salvation. As human society is ordered at present, a change from a history without salvation to a history with salvation cannot be made without a revolution. Although wary of the concept of a "theology of revolution," Schillebeeckx was "inclined to go along with those who . . . wish to investigate the ethical implications of an active Christian participation in a revolution which a past history, offering no human salvation, has made inevitable."[91]

German theologian Johannes Baptist Metz (b. 1928) based his radical societal ideas on an eschatological foundation. "An eschatologically oriented theology," he wrote, "must place itself in communication with the prevailing political, social and technical utopias and with the contemporary maturing promises of a universal peace and justice." While his starting point was Christian love, he emphasized its societal dimensions, which he interpreted as "the unconditional determination to bring justice, liberty and peace to the others." He did not exclude revolutionary action from the domain of Christian love. "If love is actualized as the unconditional determination to freedom and justice for the others, there might be circumstances where love itself could demand actions of a revolutionary character." [92]

French theologian René Laurentin took as the starting point of his theology of social change the vision of the last judgment in the Gospel of Matthew (25:32–46). In the Gospel, the Son of Man (Jesus) will admit to the kingdom all those who have given food, drink, hospitality, and clothing to any of his brothers. Laurentin transformed this eschatological prophecy into a call for social change. In Laurentin's vision Jesus exclaims: "When you changed those structures that generate hunger, thirst, nakedness, and loneliness, when you created and operated structures through which men could finally feed themselves . . . in a community of justice and love, it was to me that you did it." This change of structure can be expected only through revolution: "If we consider the structures that have to be transformed, this conversion can also be called a 'revolution' if present structures do not allow us to foresee any real solution worthy of the name—as it now seems." [93]

The theology of social change has also found ardent partisans in the Protestant camp. Just as in the Catholic camp, the Protestant theology of social change went back to the eschatological roots of Christianity. German theologian Jürgen Moltmann clarified this renewed eschatological spirit by contrasting it with the doctrine of realized eschatology. In his view, accepting the doctrine of realized eschatology neglects the element of promise that is contained in the life and teaching, dying, and rising of Jesus. In a renewed eschatological spirit Moltmann insisted on the need for a transformation of the existing society. "Christian hope is itself summoned and empowered to creative transformation of reality." He broadened the concept of salvation from one of individual rescue from the evil world to one of "the realization of the eschatological hope of justice, the humanizing of man, the socializing of humanity, peace for all creation. . . . In practical opposition to things as they are, and in creatively reshaping them, Christian hope serves the things that are to come." [94] In a later treatise, Moltmann defined the social ideals which he derived from the crucifixion of Jesus: The crucified God "is the God of the poor, the oppressed and the humiliated." He accepted socialism as "the symbol for the liberation of men from the vicious circle of poverty." [95]

In the vast spectrum of Christian communities there is an infinite variety of strata with very different political, economic, social, and cultural compositions and aspirations. Moltmann's goal of "the socializing of humanity" is not shared by the politically and socially conservative strata, which constitute a large sector of the Christian world. However, an ever-increasing sector of the Christian hierarchy and theology, in accord with the secular humanists, has opted for a humanizing transformation of present-day society.

CHAPTER VIII

The World of Islam

In the area west of the Indus, we have traced the quest for salvation along several paths: first, the Zoroastrian beliefs in the ultimate triumph of good over evil; second, the Orphic-Platonic doctrines of an immortal soul which originates in heavenly spheres and ultimately winds its way back to them; third, the late-Jewish beliefs in a sole, omnipotent God who would erect His kingdom on earth and open it to resurrected man; and fourth, Christianity's faith in Jesus Christ, the Savior, who with God and the Holy Spirit, forms a triune divinity. Christianity was born within the confines of the Roman Empire, which it eventually conquered. It then spread to all nations which inherited the Roman civilization as well as to those parts of the world where Latin and Germanic peoples established a firm foothold. Yet the Zoroastrian-Greek-Jewish modes of seeking salvation were transformed not only by Christianity but also by Islam. The belief in a sole, omnipotent God and in His kingdom originated in Israel but spread over wide areas of the globe by way of Islam. Thus man's hope for salvation through the grace of God—either the sole God or the triune God—became the dominant faith of more than half of mankind.

Almost from its inception, Islam triumphed in a large part of the Eastern Hemisphere. This success, however, was not exclusively due to the military ascendancy of the Muslim peoples. It is true that the unprecedented military achievements of the Arab Muslim warriors—who destroyed the Sassanid Empire, decimated the Byzantine Empire, and swept through North Africa and the Iberian peninsula—and in later centuries the Muslim Ottomans' conquests in the west and the Muslim Moguls' in the east played an important part in the Islamization of vast regions. The prestige of the conquerors and the material advantages the Muslims enjoyed (particularly in government services and taxation) were important reasons to convert to Islam. But even under the strongest military pressure, forcible Islamization was the exception. Vast areas—particularly in Southeast Asia and in Africa south of the Sahara—were converted to Islam not by the conquerors' sword but by the peaceful influence of traders and missionaries.

To spread so rapidly, a religion must have a unique salvational appeal. Islam's chief appeal apparently lay in its strict, uncompromising, millenarian monotheism, which withstood well the competition from Hindu devotionalism, late-Zoroastrian apocalyptic beliefs, and even Christian eschatology, particularly since in the Christian world, millenarianism had been largely neglected or abandoned by the official churches. The striking success of Islam in the Christian, Zoroastrian, and Hindu countries it penetrated can be regarded as a kind of victorious Protestant movement, not unlike early Unitarianism. And, like the conversion of Catholics to Protestantism, converting to Islam required dedication to a belief in the "Book," without a sacerdotal intermediary for the attainment of salvation.[1]

I. MOHAMMED THE PROPHET

The Bible of the Islam world, the Koran, was composed by one of history's foremost religious creators, a unique personality who combined the qualities of a great religious founder with those of a great political and military leader.

The life of Mohammed (Abul-Qasim Muhammad ibn 'Abdullah, c. 570–632),[2] is not enveloped in legends and miracle stories like those attributed to some other great religious founders, because his personal life, his teachings, and the propagation of the religion he created are well-established fact. There is no question that he was a native of Mecca, at that time an important trading center in Arabia; that he was orphaned at an early age, and slowly rose from poverty to moderate wealth; that his first religious experience, at about the age of forty, appeared to him as a divine revelation; that in the next twelve years or so he composed the first parts of the Koran and preached his message; that he met with growing opposition, chiefly from Mecca's wealthy sector; that he was forced to emigrate (the *Hegira*) to Medina in 622 A.D.; and that in the last ten years of his life, he became the unchallenged religious, political, and military leader of Medina and later on, through military conquest, of Mecca.

Mohammed firmly believed that the Koran was not his own work, but that it was slowly—over twenty years—revealed to him by God through the intermediary of the archangel Gabriel (Koran 2:91 passim).[3] He did not even pretend that the revelation was fundamentally new. It was only "confirming what was before it" (2:91), namely revelations God had bestowed on the Jewish prophets from Abraham to Jesus.

Mohammed did not consider himself a Messiah, but a prophet, a man with a God-given mission, "a mortal the like of you" (18:110 and 41:5). He was aware of his fallibility perhaps more than any other prophet in the Judeo-Christian line: God had found him erring and guided him. But whatever his failings were, from the day of his enlightenment Mohammed carried out his ministry with a tireless energy, an unyielding tenacity, an unfaltering zeal, and strict consistency.

Mohammed's teachings were closely akin to those of Jesus. Like Jesus, Mohammed believed in the one God as the sole creator and ruler of the world. He too preached the coming of the kingdom of God, and admonished men to make themselves worthy of being admitted to it. Like Jesus, he insisted that nothing stands between God and man to bring about the kingdom or determine man's admission to it. He believed that his supreme mission was to preach the—Jewish—belief in the unity of the deity. Indeed, he addressed the Jews directly on this issue and assured them, "Our God and your God is one, and to Him we have surrendered" (29:45). To the believers he proclaimed, in a way reminiscent of Deutero-Isaiah, "Your God is one God: there is no God but He" (2:158). God alone on the day of judgment will decide on the ultimate fate of all men.

The thousand years of Zoroastrianism, late Judaism, and Christianity did not leave Mohammed unaffected; there is hardly a sura in the Koran which does not refer to angels and devils—aside from the *djinns* ("demons"), who were inherited from pre-Islamic, pagan Arabia—and to the supreme Devil.[4] However, none of these semidivinities is attributed with any power over man or any intermediary functions between God and man. All are subordinate to God, either as His messengers (*angeloi*) or as tempters. In a dialogue between God and Satan, God rules: "Over my servants thou shalt have no authority, except those that follow thee" (15:42). Yet the fact remains that, as in Christianity, Satan has played an important part in the Islamic world. To balance Satan there are, just as in Christianity, guardian angels who watch over man and return him to God after death (6:61–62).

Man's ultimate fate, however, depends on his conduct and on his faith in God. Both are intertwined. The very word "Islam" means submission to God's will, "Muslim" meaning the person who surrenders to God. Being submissive to God means being virtuous. The five pillars of faith which the Koran established center upon the symbols of the profession of faith: (1) reciting the confession; (2) the five daily prayers; (3) the month of fasting (*Ramadan*); (4) the pilgrimage to Mecca (*Hadj*); and (5) a social duty, the *zakat* tax, which is "for the poor and needy, those who work to collect it, those whose hearts are brought together, the ransoming of slaves, debtors . . . and the travellers" (9:60). This social duty symbolizes an entire social and ethical system. It was not a communist system of communal property, but one of benevolence and neighborliness in which usury was strictly prohibited (cf. 2:276–78); slaves were given the means to liberate themselves; and part of one's private possessions was to be distributed to parents and other relatives (a system of social security which has endured to the present time in pre-industrial societies), to orphans, the needy, and travellers (2:211 and 4:400). Thus, being pious and virtuous, that is, being worthy of entering the kingdom of God, means being submissive to God, fighting for the faith, and being of a social and brotherly spirit.

However, the Koran does not entirely subscribe to a doctrine of good works. There is a pronounced incompatibility between the doctrine of free will and man's responsibilities stemming from his free will, on the one hand, and the belief in predestination, on the other. These two doctrines have been the source of profound disagreement among Islamic theologians. The Pauline concept of gratuitous divine grace can be found in numerous Koran passages, such as "[God] leads astray whom He will, and guides whom He will" (16:95). Mohammed was so deeply convinced that God's power over the entire creation is limitless that in some passages he attributed even man's will to God's grace. Yet there are also numerous passages which stress man's responsibility. Indeed, the whole Koran can and should be understood as a fiery call to feel and act responsibly. In a particularly beautiful passage God says: "We offered the trust to the heavens and the earth and the mountains, but they refused to carry it and were afraid of it; and man carried it" (33:72). True, the Koran adds that man "is sinful, very foolish"[5]; he is not up to his task. But the fact remains that he has shouldered his responsibilities. Having done so, if man wants to obtain God's grace he must take the initiative: "God changes not what is in a people until they change what is in themselves" (13:12). Repentance, a change in the direction of one's life, then, is the condition for God's grace, just as repentance was the call that the Jewish prophets, John the Baptist, and Jesus sent forth to men.

In spite of the vacillations between belief in predestination and freedom of will, the Koran teaches that man's ultimate destiny depends on his "works," which embrace his thoughts and deeds: "God may recompense them for their fairest works and give them increase of His bounty" (24:38). Thus God may pour out more grace than man actually deserves, because God is merciful and compassionate: "Praise belongs to God, the Lord of all Being, the All-merciful, the All-compassionate," exclaimed Mohammed in one of the first suras he composed.[6] And almost all suras begin with the exclamation, "In the name of God, the Merciful, the Compassionate."

God's mercy assures man that he can attain his salvation without being overburdened by his duties: "God charges no soul save to its capacity. . . . Our Lord, do Thou not burden us beyond what we have the strength to bear. And pardon us and forgive us and have mercy on us" (2:286). Yet the Koran stresses that however merciful and compassionate God might be, His grace is not gratuitous, but is in one way or another commensurate with man's conduct, with his thoughts and deeds.

Nor can God's judgment be swayed by the intercession of another power, as there is no power but God Himself. God's oneness excludes intercession. He has no partners. Neither angel nor saint can intercede for man: "How many an angel there is in heaven, whose intercession avails not anything, save after that God gives leave to whom He wills and is well-pleased" (53:26–27). While the Koran speaks of guardian angels, their plea is acceptable only as it pleases God—and it will please God only if man's thoughts and deeds justify it.

At the end of our age, God will judge all men. That end is strictly apocalyptic, for although the Koran does not envision an apocalyptic fight between God and Satan, the world as it now exists shall be destroyed. The sun shall be darkened, the stars shall be thrown down, the mountains shall be set moving, the seas shall be set boiling (81:1–10), the heaven shall be split and the earth shall be crushed (69:14–16). This will be the day of judgment when the trumpet will be blown, the angels shall carry the throne of God, man shall be exposed, and none of his secrets shall be concealed (69:17–18). For those who have died this will be the day of resurrection, "when souls shall be coupled [with their bodies]" (81:7). The living and the dead will be judged by their thoughts and deeds, as God has "numbered [them] in a clear register" (36:11).

The judgment will be either salvation or damnation. Muslim evildoers will be punished in hell with all its terrors, certain features of which, however, are similar to those of the Catholic purgatory. One belief that took hold among Muslims was that a section of hell is reserved for Muslim sinners. There they would be able to reconcile themselves with God so that in the end, that section of hell will be wiped out and, ultimately, the entire Islam community will become sacred.[7]

The recompense for the righteous believers will be eternal life on a rejuvenated earth, the paradise. Many suras of the Koran depict, with all the exuberant fantasy of Middle-Eastern poetry, the joys and delights of paradise, distinctly a kingdom of God on earth. After having been destroyed at the end of our age, the earth will be renewed. It "shall shine with the light of its Lord" (36:69). Then the righteous believers, the living and the resurrected, will be admitted into paradise. Its gates will be opened and the gatekeepers will say to the blessed ones, "Well you have fared; enter in, to dwell for ever." And the blessed ones will exclaim: "Praise belongs to God who . . . has bequeathed upon us the earth" (39:73–74).

The post-Pauline doctrine of the immortality of the souls of the deceased and their abode in heaven, hell, or purgatory, was alien to Mohammed. His doctrine was outright psychopannychistic: When "the trumpet shall be blown . . . the dead are sliding down from their tombs unto their Lord. They say, 'Alas for us! Who roused us out of our sleeping-place?'" (36:51–52). It was this psychopannychist belief that was revived by the Radical Reformation nine hundred years later.

2. UMMA—THE RELIGIOUS-SECULAR COMMUNITY

Mohammed did not create a church. No church with a strictly hierarchic organization has ever been organized in the Islamic world. There are no ecclesiastically ordained priests who, upon the authority of their sacerdotal functions, have the power to grant or withhold salvation. The mosque, although a sacred place of assembly, is not a church which exerts disciplinary power over believers. The *imam* who leads the service in the mosque, and the *khatib* who preaches there, are not ordained priests. They are delegated mainly by government, not ecclesiastic, authorities.

However, while no sacerdotal hierarchy stands between God and the individual to influence his state of grace or damnation, Islam did create a unity of religious and secular organization unknown to any other major society. It ruled the Muslim world for thirteen centuries and has only hesitantly and incompletely yielded to modern forms of society. This religious-secular community, called the *umma*, has ruled as effectively over Muslim souls as the Christian Church has ruled over Christian souls. Salvation and damnation in the Islamic world are bound up not with mosque, imam, and khatib, but with the umma as an awe-inspiring religious-secular community. Thus as Christianity matured under the tenet *extra ecclesiam nulla salus* ("outside the church there is no salvation"), so the umma replaced the ecclesia in Islam so that there could be no salvation outside it. Hence, one could state: *extra ummam nulla salus*.

The unity of society's religious and secular organization was deeply rooted in the history of the original Muslim community. As soon as Mohammed arrived in Medina, he became, in addition to his religious ministry, the secular leader of an emerging nation.[8] Consequently in that part of the Koran he conceived in Medina, many laws and regulations can be considered secular. Thus the Koran became the law of the land.

However, with the spread of Islam over a large part of the world and with the evolution of Muslim society, the Koran—once the law of a simple society in an isolated part of the world—could no longer suffice as the foundation of the legal, political, social, and moral structure of society. *Shari'a* (lit., "the path to the watering place"), the totality of God's commandments, comprising both the canon law of Islam and the rules of human conduct, had to adapt itself to the variegated conditions of societies much more differentiated than that of seventh-century Arabia. This could be achieved only by incorporating in Shari'a rules far more encompassing than those established by the commandments of the Koran.

To adapt Shari'a to new societal conditions, its base was broadened to include not only the Koran, but also three other sources: *Hadith* or "tradition"; *Idjma*, the consensus of recognized scholars on the interpretation of the Koran and of Hadith; and *Idjihad*, the analogical deductions from all three sources. One drawback of this system was that "tradition" was confined to what Mohammed allegedly said or did outside of what he said in the Koran itself, and to what his companions allegedly said or did with his approval. Another drawback was that the rule of Idjma was narrowed down to the interpretations given by the scholars who lived during the first few centuries of Islam's existence.

Yet however rigid and cumbersome this machinery might have been, it functioned fairly well until modern society irrupted in Muslim countries and shook Islam to its very foundations.

An important aspect of this system was the absence of any central ecclesiastical authority, comparable to the central authority in Catholicism, which could make final decisions on Shari'a rules. Outside the Shi'ite Shari'a (see section 3, below), only four collections of Shari'a were recognized by the Muslim communities as authentic: the Hanafi, Shafi'i, Maliki, and Hanbali rites. Yet this system still left enough leeway for the day-to-day interpretation of Shari'a. It was as interpreters of Shari'a that the *ulama*, the Muslim theologians and scholars, fulfilled their most important function. In this capacity they wielded a certain position of power which they still exert, although almost everywhere on a much-reduced scale.

Shari'a was never the official law of the land in any country, but in all Muslim lands it was the foundation on which the law was based.[9] Vital sectors of social and personal life like marriage, inheritance, and civil contracts were always governed by Shari'a. Yet it never embraced the Muslim's entire social and personal life: for example, most commercial relations were governed by laws outside it. Whatever rules, practices, and interpretations were used to adapt Shari'a to the ever-changing political, economic, social, and cultural conditions in the vast expanse of Muslim lands, or to transcend Shari'a in limited spheres, the characteristic Islamic unity between religious and secular life was always preserved.

As long as the Muslim community dominated its huge empire from its center, the head of this unified state, the caliph, was simultaneously its religious and secular leader.[10] Only when various parts of the empire split off from the whole did the caliphate cease to constitute the unity of the religious and secular leadership of the entire Muslim community. It gradually became a shadow office, particularly after the fall of the 'Abbasid caliphate in 1258, when the Mongols conquered Baghdad.[11] Secular and religious authority, however, resided in the heads of the successor states.

However authoritarian the regimes of many of the heads of Muslim states might have been, they were not religious dictators. In the religious sphere, regimes were subject to the authority of Shari'a and of those religious leaders who were entitled to interpret Shari'a. It was, in effect, a secular-religious condominium that ruled, and to a certain extent still rules, the Muslim countries. This close interdependence between secular and religious authority was evident in the old Ottoman Empire. The Ottoman sultan,[12] either directly or by delegating authority, built and maintained most of the country's mosques and appointed their imams and khatibs. Above all, he appointed the Shaikh-al-Islam, who, although dependent on the sultan for his office, exerted unchallenged religious authority. By issuing legal opinions, the Shaikh-al-Islam not only shared in the preparation of legislation, but possessed a veto power over new legislation. By exercising authority over the ulama, and by his right to make recommendations for the appointment of judges, he and the ulama balanced the authority of the secular ruler and his administration with an equally powerful religious authority.

Thus, even after the disintegration of the unitary Muslim state, and after the demise of the caliphate as a living institution, the umma was preserved as a religious and secular community. Ideally, this community was identical in all countries which adhered to Mohammed's Sunna, the totality of the Prophet's words and actions, as written down in the Koran and collected in the Hadith. However, the secession of the Shi'ite communities from the mainstream of Muslim communities broke the unity of the umma. The Shi'ite umma developed along different lines from that of the mainstream Muslims, who claimed to adhere to the Prophet's true Sunna and who therefore called, and still call, themselves Sunnites.[13]

With that reservation, however, it can be stated that the umma's religious and secular rule over all its members provided a definite framework into which the lives of all Muslims had to fit. If the Christian Church had the authority to watch over the conduct of its adherents and rule over their salvation and damnation, the Muslim umma exerted the same or an even greater authority. The individual Muslim cannot hope to attain salvation unless his conduct agrees both with the five pillars of faith and with the positive legal and moral institutions and rules established on the basis of Shari'a—including all those modifications to which Shari'a was subjected over time.

3. ISLAMIC MESSIANISM

The appeal of Islam's monotheism, with its millenarian element of bodily resurrection and paradise on earth for the righteous, was from its inception overwhelming and has to a certain degree remained so. However, its austere doctrine of the sole God, reigning in His unapproachable majesty above His creatures, invited Messianic and mystical deviations, just as Jewish monotheism produced late-Judaic and Christian Messianism and mysticism.

Although the Koran impassionately fought against the belief in a savior figure, Messianism evolved early in Islamic history, first in the form of Shi'ism. Soon after the death of Mohammed, Shi'ism originated from conflicting claims to the caliphate. The Shi'ites (lit., "'Ali's party," Shi'at 'Ali) claimed that Mohammed, through divine ordinance, appointed 'Ali (c. 600–661), husband of the Prophet's daughter Fatima, as the spiritual and secular leader—the caliph or Imam—of the Muslim community. 'Ali was elected fourth caliph in 656. After his assassination, his powerful rival Mu'awiya from the Umayya clan claimed and acquired the caliphate, which remained in his family (the Umayyad dynasty) until 750.[14]

The political conflict over Mohammed's successor generated a profound religious and political split. The Shi'ites believe that the Imam is given divine guidance which renders him sinless and infallible. They also believe that the office of the divinely appointed Imam must remain in the hands of the Prophet's family. Hence, the Shi'ite doctrines were from the outset Messianic. Unable to block Mu'awiya's accession to the caliphate, the Shi'ites also failed to have 'Ali's son Husain elected as caliph after the death of Mu'awiya. They refused to recognize the newly elected caliph and induced Husain to rebel against him. But Husain's forces were defeated and he was killed in battle at Karbala (in present-day Iraq) in 680. Because the Shi'ites regard his death as that of a martyr, the belief in a suffering savior arose, closely resembling ancient mystery religions and Christian Messianism. Passion plays, akin to medieval Christian passion plays, are performed in Shi'ite regions on the anniversary of the battle of Karbala. These plays present the death of Husain as vicarious. In one such play, Mohammed says to his daughter Fatima, Husain's mother: "Thou are right to weep for thy slain child . . . but as the price of the martyrdom God on the day of judgment will give into our hands the keys of paradise and hell."[15]

Husain's line survived his death. The Shi'ite recognize its heads as Imams, one of whom—the seventh according to the "Seveners," the twelfth according to the "Twelvers"—is regarded as the last Imam. The Shi'ites believe that the son of the Seventh Imam or the Twelfth Imam did not really die, but "withdrew"; he will return as *Mahdi*, as savior of suffering mankind, on the eve of the day of judgment, and will establish justice on earth. The Shi'ite Mahdi gradually acquired other Messianic features. He became an incarnation of the preexistent divine light, which descended from Adam to all prophets recognized by the Koran and finally to Mohammed. Moreover, the Mahdi will be sinless and infallible —qualities which Mohammed had rejected as pagan.

Shi'ism was from the outset a rebellious movement supported by social, political, or ethnic groups opposed to their ruling groups. Yet it has always been inclined to splinter into different sects, nearly all of which go back to the first centuries of Islam. Remarkably, most of these sects are still alive. The most successful variant of Shi'ism, religiously and politically, was that of the Isma'ilis, also called the Seveners. The name Isma'ilis is derived from Shi'ite history. It seems that the sixth Imam refused to recognize his elder son Isma'il as his successor because of intemperance. But the Seveners insist that Isma'il, being an Imam, must have been sinless and must therefore be recognized as the seventh Imam. They claim that after the death of Isma'il in 762, his son Mohammed "withdrew" and will return to earth as the Mahdi savior.

The most active and dynamic group among the Seveners was the Karmatians.[16] Organized in Mesopotamia in 877, they constituted a peasant- and artisan-supported social-revolutionary movement, based on communal property of those initiated into the community proper. Their religious doctrines (as well as those of the Isma'ilis) showed marked Neoplatonic and Gnostic influences. They rapidly gained ground, formed militant groups, and founded a state in Arabia in the first half of the tenth century. They became so strong that they united Arabia and captured Mecca in 930. But soon afterward they fell under the control of the Isma'ili dynasty of the Fatimids.

The rise of the Fatimids constituted a spectacular upheaval in Muslim history. Their story is connected with that of Isma'il, the seventh Imam. One of the alleged descendants of Isma'il, 'Ubayd Allah-Sa'id, was persecuted by the ruling Sunnite 'Abbasid caliphate. As a result, he emigrated to North Africa, where in 909 one of his followers conquered Ifriqia (present-day Tunisia and eastern Algeria). Proclaimed Mahdi and caliph, 'Ubayd Allah-Sa'id founded the Fatimid dynasty (named after Fatima, Mohammed's daughter, whose descendant he claimed to be) in Ifriqia. The Fatimids in quick succession conquered all of present-day Algeria, Morocco, and Egypt, where in 969 they founded Cairo. After having extended their dominion over North Africa and Syria, they reigned for two hundred years. However, they never succeeded in converting the bulk of the population to Isma'ilism. One by one, their conquered lands fell away until in 1171 the great Muslim warrior Saladin (Salah al-Din Yusuf ibn Ayyub, 1138–1193), a zealous Sunnite, overthrew the Fatimid dynasty and brought about the end of Isma'ilism in North Africa.

This was, however, not the end of Isma'ilism. One of its branches, the Nizari, still exists. It derived its name from Nizar, son of a Fatimid caliph. Nizar was assassinated but his grandson was proclaimed Imam in Persia, thus founding the Nizari Imamate. In the thirteenth century the Nizari-founded state collapsed under Mongol pressure, but the Nizari

Isma'ilis have survived as an important Shi'ite community, particularly in India. After their forty-sixth Imam was forced to flee from Persia to India in 1840, his heirs became the Aga Khans of Isma'ilism, recognized as Imams to the present time.

From its beginning Shi'ism found strong sympathies in Persia (present-day Iran), perhaps as a symbol of opposition to the Arabs who had overrun and destroyed the independent nation of Sassanid Persia. As a result of the foundation of Iran as a state, Twelver Shi'ism became its leading Shi'ite community. The foundation of Iran was the work of Shah Isma'il (1487–1524), the first ruler of the Safavid dynasty. His family had led a Sufi order founded by Shaikh Safi al-Din, from whom both that order—Safawiyya—and the Safavid dynasty derived their names. Shah Isma'il inherited the leadership of the order and became its military leader in the fight against the Ottomans and Uzbeks. Because his enemies were Sunnites, he apparently used Shi'ism as a weapon. Having gained control over most of present-day Iran, he succeeded, partly by force, in converting a large part of the population to Shi'ism, and in establishing Twelver Shi'ism as the state religion of Iran. So it remains to the present time.

In addition to the Twelvers and the Seveners, other Shi'ite sects emerged which, although presently active, have not attained more than local importance. The Alawi is one sect which goes back to the first centuries of Islam. Its founder was Ibn Nusair from Basra, who in 843 proclaimed himself to be the chief disciple of the tenth Shi'ite Imam. He adopted an extreme Neoplatonic emanationist doctrine, combined with secret initiation rites, which have been retained by the Alawi community. The Alawis have survived through eleven centuries and constitute an important religious community in present-day Syria, Lebanon, and Turkey.[17]

Another Shi'ite sect, the Druzes, broke away from the Isma'ilis. Their origin lies in Mahdist claims of the Fatimid caliph al-Hakim (who reigned from 996 to 1021). His followers, led by Al-Darazi (from whom the name "Druzes" is derived), were convinced that al-Hakim would produce the Messianic age. After his death the Druzes, in Shi'ite fashion, believed that he had "withdrawn" and would soon return to fulfill his divine mission. The Druzes later settled in present-day Syria. They have survived as a closed, secret community for more than nine hundred years and are still active, principally in Syria, Lebanon, and Israel.

Latecomers in the array of Shi'ite sects were the Babis, the forerunners of the modern Bahai religion. Their founder, Mirza 'Ali Mohammed (c. 1820–1850), was an Iranian who claimed descent from Mohammed.

He called himself *Bab* ("Gate," meaning gate to the divine truth), and proclaimed himself to be the Imam Mahdi. The Babis were a revolutionary group opposed to the Shi'ite establishment in Iran. In 1848 they openly declared their secession from Islam and from the Shari'a. A bloody civil war followed during which thousands of Babis were killed and the Bab was executed.[18] The Babis gradually grew apart from the Islamic world and transformed their sect into the Bahai religion. The founder of the modern Bahai community was Abdu-l-Baha' ("Servant of the Glory," 1844–1921). A follower of the Bab, he proclaimed himself to be a manifestation of God, was persecuted, and died in prison.

Bahai's fundamental doctrine is that all founders of the great religions (the Bab among them) are manifestations of God, so that all religions have the same substance. The Bahais consequently believe in the brotherhood of man and world peace, and they strive for social progress. As a result of intense missionary activities, initiated on a worldwide scale by Abdu-l-Baha', the Bahais have many followers not only in Iran and other Asian countries, but also in North America, Europe, and Africa.

Islamic Messianism has not been confined to the Shi'ites. It appeared from time to time in Sunnite Islam, mainly as a millenarian creed, often accompanied by social and political rebellion. It has always been connected with the figure of the Mahdi, the eschatological savior who is central to Shi'ism. But even in Sunnite communities the ulama, guardians of the faith, could not always inhibit the rise of Mahdist movements, however unorthodox they might have appeared. Thus North African Muslim historian 'Abd al-Rahman Ibn Khaldun (1332–1406) stated that the Sunnite masses commonly believed that at the end of time a descendant of Mohammed, who would be called al-Mahdi, would aid the faith, make justice triumph, and reign over the Muslim world. Ibn Khaldun even recounted the legend that Isa (the Arabic name for Jesus) would descend upon the earth, kill al-Dadjdjal (the Muslim counterpart of antichrist), and follow the Mahdi.[19]

Several revolutions in the Muslim world were directly connected with Messianic Mahdism. The first in 750 resulted in the 'Abbasid overthrow of the Umayyad caliphate. The 'Abbasids claimed descent from Mohammed's uncle, al 'Abbas ben 'Abd al-Muttalib (566–652), and derived a Mahdist claim from this alleged kinship with the Prophet. The revolution which brought them to power was actively supported by Shi'ite groups and showed distinct Mahdist features.

The rise of the Almohad dynasty in Morocco in the twelfth century constituted another Mahdist revolution. The Almohad movement was a strange blend of puritanical, strictly monotheistic beliefs and Mahdism.[20]

Its founder, Abu 'Abdullah Ibn Tumart (c. 1080–1130) proclaimed himself a sinless Imam, who would institute a reign of justice and faith. In revolt against the ruling dynasty he and his successors conquered the whole Maghreb (Morocco, Algeria, and Tunisia) and the Muslim-controlled regions of the Iberian peninsula.

The last Mahdist revolution and conquest was that of Mohammed Ahmed ben 'Abd Allah (1844–1885), the Mahdi and liberator of the Sudan. Like many other Islamic saviors, he claimed descent from Mohammed. He was a deeply religious, ascetic personality who opposed both the worldly attitudes prevailing in the order he had joined and the Egyptian-British occupation of his country. He became the leader of a nationalist-religious rebellion and proclaimed himself the Mahdi, whose coming was to signal the purification of Islam and the destruction of the unbelievers. Under this authority he conquered the Sudan, annihilated the Egyptian army, and in 1885, conquered Khartoum. The Mahdist regime survived Mohammed Ahmed for thirteen years, after which it was crushed by the British-Egyptian army. But the Mahdist movement survived the military collapse. Under the leadership of the Ansar,[21] a Mahdist confraternity, the Sudan gained independence from Egypt (officially in 1956). The Mahdist Party (which called itself the Umma Party) was a determining force in the governments of the Sudan until the military coup of 1969.

Although Mahdism, even outside the Shi'ite sector of Islam, has shown itself to be a vital force into the twentieth century, it is questionable whether it will remain so. While in the past Mahdism often displayed a rebellious nature and constituted a vehicle for nationalist upheavals, in the last few decades nationalism has more and more become an autonomous secular force in Muslim countries. In Muslim lands from Morocco to Indonesia, struggles for independence were waged under the banner of national self-determination, a foundation more solid than that of Mahdism.

4. SUFISM—ISLAMIC MYSTICISM

However dramatic and forceful millenarian Mahdism might have appeared, it has not had a lasting impact on the evolution of Islam, with the exception of the Shi'ite sector. The more powerful and enduring force in this evolution has been mysticism. Whereas Mahdism sought salvation through the coming of a Mahdi, Sufism, the Islamic form of mysticism, sought salvation through mystic union with God. Yet interpenetration between Mahdism and Sufism did occur, particularly among the Shi'ites, where Sufism found an easy access.

Mysticism could not be legitimately derived from the Koran, because Mohammed's God, in His majesty, can never be reached by man. Any mystic view of man's relationship to God was foreign to Mohammed. But in so immense a literary document as the Koran, it was inevitable that one or another passage could be interpreted in the spirit of mysticism. The lyric exaltation with which the Koran frequently speaks of God lends itself to such an interpretation. A famous Koran passage, "Withersoever you turn, there is the face of God" (2:109), could be interpreted in a pantheistic way. Another passage, "We [God] are nearer to [man] than the jugular vein" (50:15), could be interpreted as a mystical union with God. In any case, Sufism has never regarded itself as a deviation from Islam, but as its deeper meaning.

Sufism apparently evolved not as a mystical, but as an ascetic movement, as even the origin of its name suggests—*sufi* is the rough woollen robe of the ascetic. Like mysticism, asceticism was foreign to Mohammed, whose piety was eminently social. There is a natural bridge from asceticism to mysticism which has often been crossed by Christian and Muslim ascetics. By meditating on the Koran and praying to God, the Muslim ascetic believes that he draws nearer to God. By leading an ascetic life, he imagines that he paves the way for absorption in God, the Sufi way of salvation.

While the orthodox Muslim hopes that devotion to God and good works will lead to paradise, the Sufi path to salvation leads from a beatific vision of God to absorption in God, and sometimes even to pantheistic beliefs. These stages were marked by many prominent Sufi thinkers. Among the first Sufis was a great poetess, Rabi'a ab-Adawiya of Basra (c. 714–801). In a poem she confronted the "selfish" love of God, which seeks enjoyment in loving God, with the true love of God, which leads to the beatific vision of God. In a prayer she directly implored God "to withhold not from me Thine eternal beauty." She already appears to have reached for the mystical union with God: "My hope is for union with Thee, for that is the goal of my desire."[22]

The most prominent Sufi of the early period—and the only Sufi martyr —was the Persian al-'Halladj (c. 858–922).[23] He interpreted the mystical union with God (*ittahad*) in a more rationalist way: God is "the essence whose essence is love." The union of the mystic with God is not one of substance but of faith and love. In his poetry, however, al-'Halladj appears to have been much less cautious than in his theological writings.

In his poetic ecstasy he exclaimed: "[God's] Spirit has mingled itself with my spirit as amber mixes with fragrant musk." His mysticism met with bitter opposition, not only from the more rationalist-minded Mu'tazilis,[24] but even from the Shi'ites. His tragic end, however, seems to have been due to his political activities, which were suspected of having been inspired by the revolutionary Karmatians. In any case, he was accused both of heresy and Karmatism, and was executed. He died a true martyr who stood fast to his mystical faith to the bitter end.

Like Isma'ilism and Christian and Jewish mysticism, Sufism was strongly influenced by Neoplatonism. This influence was strengthened by the authority of prominent Islamic philosophers of the tenth and eleventh centuries, such as al-Farabi and Ibn Sina, both of Turkestan. Abu Nasr Mohammed al-Farabi (c. 878–c. 950) was the first of those courageous Islamic philosophers to recognize religious doctrines only as symbols of philosophical truths. His philosophical system blended the Aristotelian concept of God as the first cause with the Neoplatonic doctrine of the emanation of all intellects from God, from the stellar intellects down to man; the bridge was formed by the "Active Intellect," a link between God and the human intellect. Man can acquire intellectual knowledge only when illuminated by the Active Intellect. Deviating from the Koranic belief in resurrection at the end of time, al-Farabi taught that after death the souls of the knowers (the philosophers) merge with the Active Intellect, while the souls of those who know the truth but act against it survive in hell. All other souls perish after death.

On the same basis of philosophy's supremacy over religion, Abu 'Ali al-Husain Ibn Sina, known in the West as Avicenna (980–1037), continued and expanded al-Farabi's Neoplatonic doctrines of emanation: Through emanation from God a gradual pluralization of intellects takes place, on the lowest level of which man's intellect emanates. While man's soul is immortal, his destiny after death depends on the degree of perfection attained during life. Souls that have led pure lives will attain eternal bliss, while imperfect souls will be eternally tormented. However, Avicenna held that the mystic, through spiritual exercises, could attain a direct vision of God during his lifetime.[25]

The reception given these philosophical systems varied. They were apt to strengthen Sufi mysticism, but the heterodoxy of their doctrines and their claim to philosophy's superiority over religion aroused strong opposition in orthodox ranks. The great Persian theologian Abu Hamid Mohammed Al-Ghazali (1058–1111), on the basis of Sunnite orthodoxy, launched the strongest attack against the Islamic philosophers in his famous treatise, "The Incoherence of the Philosophers." The bitter condemnation from such an authoritative source had the effect of discrediting philosophy in the Muslim world for many centuries.

However, the philosophical school found a great defender in the person of Spanish philosopher Averroes (Abu al-Walid Mohammed ibn Ahmad ibn Rush, 1126–1198). Held in high esteem in the medieval Western world, chiefly as the author of a detailed commentary on Aristotle, Averroes continued the Neoplatonic emanational philosophy of al-Farabi and Avicenna. He wrote an anti-Ghazali treatise called, "Destruction of al-Ghazali's Destruction." Yet even Averroes's authority could not prevail over religious dogma and the deeply rooted Muslim belief in the unassailable truth of the Koran. The seeds of medieval Islamic philosophy found more fertile ground in the Western world, where an Averroist school arose that adopted his tenet of philosophy's supremacy over religion. That school remained active for several centuries and later merged with Renaissance currents. But its conviction that the intellect is a source of knowledge independent of, and superior to, religion gradually acquired dominance in the West.

In the ranks of Sunnite Islam, the only deviation from Koranic orthodoxy that has survived to the present time, aside from later reformist currents, has been Sufi mysticism. Even al-Ghazali fell under its spell. In his great theological work, *Revival of Religious Sciences*, he included mystical training and ecstasy in the religious training of the Muslims.

Soon after the era of al-Ghazali, Sufism found two of its most prominent representatives in Egyptian poet al-Farid and in Spanish philosopher al-'Arabi. The poetry of 'Omar Ibn al-Farid (c. 1182–1235) reflected an ecstatic mysticism, a union with the "Spirit of Mohammed," which in fact stood for a union with God. The following verse shows the degree to which al-Farid's mysticism approached pantheism (of which he was accused): "My spirit is a spirit to all spirits, and whatsoever thou seest of beauty in the universe flows from the bounty of my nature." [26]

Abu 'Abd Allah Mohammed Ibn al-'Arabi (1165–1240) was perhaps the greatest philosopher of the extreme Sufi school. In a work on Sufi doctrine he interwove Platonic, Neoplatonic, and pantheistic strains. His fundamental doctrine was in fact pantheistic: The existence of created things is nothing but the very essence of the existence of the creator. Before phenomenal things were created by God, they preexisted in Him as ideas. Mohammed occupies a place in this pantheistic universe as God's Logos. If ultimate salvation consists in unity with God, the mystic is saved, for he is one with God. Al-'Arabi distinguished the path of mysticism, which alone leads to salvation, from that of reason. The highest knowledge is not that attained through reason, but "the knowledge which the soul blows into the heart." This knowledge comes from God and is acquired only after thorough mystical training.[27]

Al-'Arabi's system was not the last word of Sufism. A succession of Sufi teachers followed who agreed with or criticized one another. As al-'Arabi had blamed other Sufi writers for holding pantheistic views, his doctrines were in turn denounced as pantheistic. What unites all Sufis, however, is their belief that there is a path toward salvation which leads to the vision of or union with God during one's lifetime. Mysticism tends to separate those who partake in the esoteric knowledge of the mystical path to God from the common people to whom this path is closed. It was, therefore, consistent with the spirit of Sufism that esoteric communities resembling Buddhist and Christian monastic orders grew in their ranks, although Mohammed considered monasticism to be foreign to the spirit of Islam (Koran 57:27).

The Sufi orders originated in the twelfth century as loose communities of teachers and their disciples. They soon became fraternities with a monastic nucleus, based on strict—although not celibate—discipline, and a large following of lay members. The orders quickly spread over the entire Muslim world and are still important to it. They share with the Buddhist and Christian orders the principal feature of monasticism: the faith that through their discipline, their rites, and their ceremonies they constitute a path to salvation.[28] Sufi fraternities have been inclined to elevate their founders (*shaiks*)—or one or another of their successors —to the near-divine rank of saints able to perform miracles and, being in communion with God, to intercede for their followers. These saints are invoked to protect their followers from all kinds of dangers and afflictions and to guide them toward salvation.

The cult of the saints, *wadis*, is older than the Sufi orders among Muslim peoples. It is based on the popular belief that God has equipped with miraculous powers the great ascetics, teachers, and heroes who excel in piety, religious profundity, or fortitude. Being in contact with God, the wadis may be able to control the weather, cure the diseased, revive the dead, and pave the way to paradise for the faithful. Since early times Muslims invoked and implored wadis to intercede for them, even though the belief in intercession is as foreign to the Koran as are Messianic beliefs.

The growth of the Sufi orders furnished the strongest impetus to the cult of the saints. The origin of the first major Sufi order, the Kadiriya, is a typical case. Founded by a prominent Persian Sufi, 'Abd al-Kadir al-Djilani (c. 1078–1166), the order spread rapidly through many Muslim countries and is still one of the most important Sufi fraternities. But whereas al-Kadir defined sainthood in classical Sufi fashion as a quality acquired by a man who has overcome his accidental self and has reached his essential being, the members of his order attributed to him such miraculous powers as raising the dead, extinguishing fire, crushing mountains, punishing sinners, assisting the oppressed, and bestowing grace on man.[29]

As Sufi orders spread over Islam lands, as the number of founder-shaiks and successor-shaiks multiplied, as other pious men and secular rulers and heroes became the objects of veneration, the cult of the saints became—and has remained—a common feature of the Muslim world. Shrines, mausoleums, pilgrimages to tombs of the saints, memorial festivals, gift offerings, prayers, dancing, and other rites celebrate the saints. Saints are invoked to cure particular diseases, protect against specific dangers, and act as guardian angels of specific towns and professions. The Koran's strong injunction against companion gods, intercessors, and mediators has been forgotten. God the Merciful and Compassionate is assisted in his functions of mercy and compassion by innumerable wadis who also dispense salvation.[30]

5. ISLAMIC REFORM MOVEMENTS

If Shi'ite and Sunnite Mahdism, Sufism, and the cult of the saints had triumphed in the whole Islamic world, the spirit of Islam, as Mohammed had conceived it, would have vanished. But while Islam generated mystical and, in substance, polytheistic tendencies, reform movements emerged from time to time which aimed at a more purist conception of Islam. These movements, however, never resulted in a split within Sunnite Islam comparable to that between Roman Catholicism and Protestantism.

Reform movements were almost as old as Islam itself. The oldest centered on the problems of divine grace and predestination. As has been noted, the Koran is characterized by a distinctive tension between the belief in divine grace and predestination on the one hand, and the full responsibility of man on the other, a tension that has given rise to many doctrinal debates and clashes. Islamic reform movements fought for positions opposite those taken by the mainstream of the Christian Reformation. While Luther and Calvin revived the Pauline doctrine of justification by grace and divine predestination, Islamic reform movements emphasized man's full and exclusive responsibility for his conduct and faith, and ultimately for his salvation or damnation. They have thus assumed positions characteristic of Western Pelagianism, existentialism, and secular humanism. The enemy of Islamic reform movements was obviously different from that of the Christian Reformation. The chief enemy of the early Islamic reform movements was the caliphate which was based on divine grace, and the ulama who in turn depended on the caliph. The chief enemy of the Christian Reformation was the power of the ecclesiastical hierarchy which was largely based on the "good works" of the laity that flowed into its treasuries.

Early Islamic reformism was carried on the waves of several movements: the Kharidjis and their successors, the Ibadis; the Kadaris; and the Mu'tazilis. Each movement was characterized by a strong faith in man's free will and responsibilities. The oldest movement, the Kharidjis, surfaced during the period of the fourth caliph, 'Ali, Mohammed's son-in-law. When 'Ali agreed to have the murder of his predecessor arbitrated rather than revenged, the Kharidjis, a fierce nomadic group, disagreed and "seceded" (thence their name). They constituted a powerful guerilla movement which became a dominant military power during the era of the Umayyads, to whose downfall they contributed. They represented a democratic opposition to the caliphate, insisting not only on the popular election of the caliph (which had been abolished by the Umayyads), but on the duty of the people to depose any caliph who deviated from Islamic law and morals. Thus in contrast to the tendency within Islam—most strongly pronounced by the Shi'ites—to attribute to the ruler divine sanction, these early reformers held that the ruler should be allowed to keep his office only if his conduct is equal to its sanctity. The right to rebel against an unworthy ruler, a principle upheld by Western humanism since the seventeenth century, was claimed by an Islamic community one thousand years earlier.

Another significant feature of the Kharidji movement was its rejection of the doctrine of justification by divine grace. The Kharidjis held that man can be saved only if he deserves it by virtue of his deeds. Their movement, with its strict puritan ethics, was in fact an early attempt at an Islamic Reformation. Though the Kharidjis disappeared, one of their offspring, the Ibadis (or Abadis), has survived. Named after their founder, 'Abd Allah b. Ibad, the Ibadis conquered part of Arabia and founded an Imamate in Oman in 751. They have retained a strong following in that country, in Oman's daughter country Zanzibar,[31] and in other parts of Africa. Their Kharidji spirit lent strong support to the Wahhabi movement.

Another early reform movement, the Kadaris, appeared in the seventh century and is recognized as the immediate precursor of the Mu'tazilis. The Kadaris preceded the Mu'tazilis in their rejection of predestinarianism and in the conviction that man possesses power, *kadar*, over his own actions, whereas the predestinarians attributed kadar to God alone. Considered heretics by the Umayyad caliphate, a Kadari leader, Ma'had al-Juhani, was executed in 699.

The early Mu'tazili movement adopted the chief doctrine of the Kadaris, that of man's free will. Two theologians, Wasil Ibn Ata (699–749) and 'Amr Ibn 'Ubayd (d. 762), are credited as the founders of the early Mu'tazili school. One of their followers, Abu al-Hudhayl (died c. 841) was the real founder of the Mu'tazili theological system. A prominent Islamic thinker, he was the true father of Islamic rationalism. Shi'ism and the incipient Sufism were the chief enemies of Abu al-Hudhayl. He countered these doctrines with a pure and strict monotheism and a more rationalist approach than that of the Koran. He began, in fact, the process of demythologization, which has become common in modern Christian theology: God, although a personal God, has no attributes and dwells not in one place, but everywhere; moreover, the abundant anthropomorphism of the Koran—such as, "God's face," "God's hands"— must be understood allegorically; and there can be no beatific vision in a literal sense.

Abu al-Hudhayl's rationalist monotheism was reflected in his concepts of God's justice and man's free will: Man, not God, creates the good and the evil in himself. Divine predestination is incompatible with God's justice. Instead, God's justice requires that man's will be free to obey or disobey the divine order and that those who choose to obey it will be rewarded and those who disobey it will be punished. In other words, salvation and damnation, although dispensed by God, depend on man's free will. The strongest challenge that Mu'tazilism posed to Muslim orthodoxy was its assertion that the Koran was not eternal—as orthodox Islam claimed, and still claims—but was created.

Due to the resurgence of orthodoxy from the late ninth century on, Mu'tazilism did not survive as an organized movement. However, its spirit has not disappeared from Islam. Theologians generally attempt to prove that faith in God and His laws is compatible with reason. In fact, *Kalam*, the Arabic term for speculative theology, has always been based on this tenet.[32] Islamic theology owes this kind of rationalism to Mu'tazilism.

Thus orthodox theology, which acquired ascendancy in the following centuries, retained some Mu'tazili features. The most prominent theologians of the leading orthodox school were Hanbal, al-Ashari, and Ibn Taimiya. While Ahmad Ibn Mohammed Ibn Hanbal of Bagdad (780–855),[33] rejected rationalist arguments in matters of religious doctrine and retained the anthropomorphism of the Koran, he taught that understanding the mystery of God's nature must be left to God. In his view, service to God is the fundamental prerequisite of salvation, as opposed to the Messianic beliefs of the Shi'ites and to the trust of the Sufis in absorption in God as a path toward salvation. His brand of strict and pure monotheistic beliefs and ethics has survived in the Islamic reform of the Wahhabis.

Abu al-Hasan al-Ashari of Basra (c. 874–c. 935) was first a Mu'tazili and only later converted to orthodoxy. Yet he retained an essential feature of Mu'tazilism, the doctrine of the rationality of religion and the permissibility of rational arguments in religious matters. Thus, while ascribing to God eternal attributes, he insisted that their nature is unknown to man. While believing in the doctrine of beatific vision in paradise, he asserted that its nature cannot be known. Although retaining the doctrine of divine predestination, he taught that God wills both good and evil, but has bestowed upon man the power to acquire the will to do good.[34]

Taqi al-Din Ahmad Ibn Taimiya of Damascus (1263–1328) gained lasting fame for the indomitable courage with which he attacked both Sufism and the cult of the saints. That cult had become so popular in his lifetime that he was persecuted for opposing pilgrimages to the tombs of the saints. He died in prison.

The climate of the next few centuries was hostile to the spirit of reform. In that period of further expansion, people who were converted to Islam either adhered to beliefs similar to Sufi doctrines or, due to an animistic background, were attracted to the cult of the saints and the belief in their magic powers. It appears that Islam owed its triumphs in Asia and in Africa south of the Sahara largely to the kinship of its mystical and magical wings with the religions it met in its new territories.

Later, when territorial expansion had spent its force, Muslim countries either had to defend themselves against or surrender to Western imperialism. When Western civilization threatened to engulf Islamic culture, reform movements emerged once again in the Muslim world. They surfaced first in nomadic areas on the periphery of Muslim states, where freedoms were not in immediate danger.

The first of these new reform movements was Wahhabism, born in Arabia. One thousand years later, Wahhabism revived the old revolutionary fighting spirit of the Kharidjis, who in large part had been nomads themselves. As noted, the Ibadi branch of the Kharidji movement directly influenced the Wahhabi movement. The ideological substructure of Wahhabism lies in the Hanbali school of Islamic law. Just as the Protestant Reformation sought a return to the pure world of the Bible, Wahhabism sought a return to the pure word of the Koran, as it appeared to be most faithfully interpreted by Hanbalism. Above all, Hanbalism rejected all the mystical and magical additions which had deprived Islam of its character as a pure monotheistic religion. Significantly for this reformatory spirit, the Wahhabis hold in high esteem the Hanbali theologian Ibn Taimiya, who was martyred in his heroic fight against the intrusion of magic into Islam.

Wahhabism's Westernized name derives from Mohammed Ibn 'Abd al-Wahhab of Arabia (1703–1792), one of Islam's greatest religious reformers. The reformation he advocated was based on the return to the Koran and Hadith, with its strict monotheism. The Arabic name of the Wahhabi movement is indeed Muwahhidun ("Unitarians"). Like Mu'-tazilism and Hanbalism, Wahhabism believes that salvation and damnation lie in God's hands alone, and that no human being, whether saint or prophet, has the power of intercession. Guided by the doctrine that "all objects of worship other than God are false," the Wahhabis reject the veneration of saints and prophets. In order to stop the pilgrimages to the saints' tombs, they destroyed such tombs and mausoleums in every region of Arabia they dominated. Their purist spirit extends even to the architecture of their mosques, which have no minarets or decorations.

The triumphant march of the Wahhabis through Arabia was largely due to the fact that 'Abd al-Wahhab succeeded in persuading a local ruler, Mohammed Ibn Sa'ud, to fight for the cause of the reform. The Arabian peninsula, nominally part of the Ottoman Empire, was at that time dominated by a number of territorial rulers. In long-drawn-out wars, in which victories alternated with defeats and retreats, Mohammed Ibn Sa'ud and his successors expanded their territorial rule until one of the most gifted Muslim rulers, 'Abd al-'Aziz Ibn Sa'ud (c. 1880–1953) succeeded, by way of conquest, in uniting a large part of the Arabian peninsula under the Sa'udi dynasty (Saudi Arabia). Thus in the heartland of Islam, in the country in which Islam was born, the pure faith of its founder has been restored. The Ka'ba, to which every faithful Muslim must make a pilgrimage during his life, is in the hands of Islam's most faithful sons. The hundreds of millions of Muslims believe that salvation can be assured only if they make a pilgrimage to Saudi Arabia, the country where pure, unadulterated Islam reigns and where Shari'a, the law of Islam, is still the law of the land.

The impact of Wahhabism on the Islamic world was profound. It resulted in a well-ordered state, independent both of the Ottoman Empire and of Western imperialism, which has been able to exploit an unprecedented treasure of oil. Thus Wahhabism demonstrated that an Islamic commonwealth could be built on the foundations of a purified

Islam. But because this purification adhered to strictly fundamentalist lines, with Shari'a remaining the law of the land, the Wahhabi type of Islamic reform flourished only in areas whose cultural and social structure was similar to that of Arabia.

In the first half of the nineteenth century, the Senussi reform movement arose in the nomadic area of eastern North Africa, comparable to that of the Wahhabis in Arabia but based on a Sufi order. In 1837 an Algerian sharif,[35] Mohammed Ibn 'Ali al-Sanussi (1791–1859), founded the Senussi order on principles of purification similar to those of Wahhabism. Al-Sanussi established several lodges of his order in present-day Libya, and the Senussi order became the nucleus of a Bedouin community in eastern North Africa, under Ottoman suzerainty. During World War II, after Turkish rule in Libya was replaced by Italian rule, the Senussis fought on the side of the British against the Italians. After independence was achieved, their leader, Sayyid Mohammed Idris al-Mahdi al-Sanussi (b. 1890), a grandson of the founder of the order, was elected king of Libya by the National Assembly in 1950. He was overthrown by a military coup in 1969. The leader of the military coup, Colonel Mo'ammar Mohammed al-Qadafi, as president of the Libya Revolutionary Command Council, has introduced a policy that can be interpreted as a return to the austere spirit of the original Sanussi regimes. It is not only in her oil riches, but also in her Islamic puritanism, that present-day Libya resembles Saudi Arabia, although radical Libya's political and social system greatly differs from Saudi Arabia's conservative political and social system.

While Wahhabis and Senussis reformed Islam along fundamentalist lines, most Islamic reform has been influenced by modernistic concepts. In the last hundred years, the modern Western world descended upon the world of Islam in two ways: it brought modern science and technology to the Muslim countries, but at the same time it subjugated most of them in one form or another.[36] Western penetration also tended to produce a fundamentalist reaction in Muslim lands. The natural reaction to Western imperialist expansion was to cling fiercely to Islam. Although just as in Christian countries, religious indifference, agnosticism, and atheism may be found in some chiefly urban areas, no overt attempts have been made to discard any of Islam's fundamental tenets.

On the other hand, Islam has been very receptive to modern science, due above all to an array of outstanding spiritual and political leaders. This movement was opened by the great religious and political leader of Asian Islam, Djamal al-Din al-Afghani (1839–1897). He was a bitter opponent of Western imperialism, and dreamed of unifying the entire

Muslim world, including the Shi'ites, under a true caliphate (as distinguished from the fictitious caliphate of the Ottoman Empire). But he also aimed at a reformed Islam and advocated the introduction of liberal institutions. In all Muslim countries in which he lived—and he lived in many of them—he supported the movements opposed to foreign domination and in favor of Islamic reforms. He was also the first in the school of modern Islamic thinkers who insisted that Islam (an Islam purified of superstitions, to be sure) is a religion of reason and therefore compatible with modern science.[37]

The outstanding spiritual leaders of Indian Muslims—above all Sir Sayyid Ahmad Khan (1817–1898), Sayyid Amir 'Ali (1849–1928), and Sir Mohammed Iqbal (1876–1938)—went much further than al-Afghani. They too insisted that Islam is compatible with modern science and modern institutions: Ahmad Khan stated that the work of God—meaning nature and its laws as they are discovered by modern science—is identical with the words of God—meaning the Koran. But these spiritual leaders in India realized that for Islam to open itself to modern science, it was imperative to introduce modern education in place of traditional Muslim education. Ahmad Khan acted on this theoretical position by founding in 1875 the first modern Muslim institute of higher learning, the famous Muslim Anglo-Oriental College in Alighar, which was elevated to the rank of a university in 1920.[38]

The modernism of these Indian Muslim thinkers did not stop at the recognition of modern science and education, but extended to the Islamic faith itself. While unquestionably loyal to the fundamentals of Islam, they engaged in a liberal interpretation and even demythologization of certain of its tenets. Thus the poet-philosopher Mohammed Iqbal, one of the spiritual leaders who propagated a Muslim state on the Indian subcontinent, affirmed that heaven and hell are not localities but states of being: heaven is the joy of triumph over the forces of disintegration; hell is the painful awareness of one's failure as a man. He shared, moreover, the universalist doctrine (which had become rather common among Muslims) that hell is not a state of eternal damnation but a corrective experience which may make a calloused ego sensitive to divine grace.[39]

Iqbal was in effect a Mu'tazili in his belief that man is the master of his destiny. Moreover, he regarded the concept of predestination as incompatible with Islamic ethics: "A being whose movements are wholly determined cannot produce goodness. Freedom is thus seen to be a condition for goodness."[40] Iqbal extended man's freedom to his social world in declaring that not only individual, but also social and political freedom lies in man's hands. A child of his era, he blended political liberalism with a faith in progress, and imputed all these concepts to Islam: "The teaching of the Koran that life is a process of progressive creation necessitates that each generation ... should be permitted to solve its own problems."[41] He considered that the chief problems his generation was called to solve in the spirit of Islam were those of equality, solidarity, and freedom. To these ideals he contrasted India's colonial status.

While India's exposure to Western cultural influences was more intense than that of most Muslim countries, modern concepts were not confined to that country. A prominent Egyptian reformer, Mohammed 'Abduh (1849–1905), assumed similar if less radical positions that lastingly influenced Muslim thinking. He followed and for a while collaborated with al-Afghani. When they both lived in Paris, they published a periodical on behalf of a secret Muslim society which advocated unity and reform of Islam. Like the Asian reformers, 'Abduh propagated democratic reforms, particularly in the juridical and educational fields. Later he was able to implement certain reforms as a member of the Administrative Committee of the renowned Islamic university al-Azhar in Cairo, where he helped introduce modern sciences, and ultimately as the Grand Mufti of Egypt (from 1899 to 1905).[42]

'Abduh also insisted upon Islam's compatibility with modern science, based on the primacy of reason. "The Muslims are agreed that if religion can reveal certain things to us that exceed our comprehension," he wrote in his chief work *Risalat al-Tawhid*, "it cannot teach us anything that is in contradiction with our reason."[43] He aimed at a purified Islam founded on reason, an Islam which "does not astonish you with miracles nor extra-ordinary occurrences nor heavenly voices."[44] 'Abduh was thus opposed to the popular distortions of Islam, such as the worship of saints. In the same spirit, he was intent on modernizing the legal, political, and educational institutions of the Muslim world. Reason should prime tradition, was his leading principle.

Strangely, the reform movement 'Abduh initiated later became a hearth of fundamentalist reaction. If 'Abduh considered reason as the foundation of Islam, his followers—whose Salafiya movement gained great spiritual power in Egypt—emphasized the fundamental doctrines of Islam in their confrontation with the secularizing tendencies which slowly entered Muslim countries. The periodical *Al-Manar*—which 'Abduh's principal disciple Mohammed Rashid Rida (1865–1935) founded in 1898 with the purpose of promoting 'Abduh's reformist views—became an instrument of fundamentalism and was later taken over by the fundamentalist Muslim Brotherhood.[45]

6. THE PROCESS OF SECULARIZATION

The era of the great Islamic reformers, the al-Afghanis, the Ahmad Khans, the Mohammed Iqbals, and the Mohammed 'Abduhs, is now over. While their memory is revered by Muslim intellectuals,[46] the problems confronting the present-day Muslim world are concerned with what effects the secularizing process has had on the fundamentals of religion.

Secularization in Islamic society has changed the most fundamental institution on which it was founded, namely, the umma, the unity of the religious and the secular community. It has, above all, meant the diminution of the role of Shari'a, which had been Islam's central institution for thirteen centuries. As a consequence of this process, secular ideas have seeped in from the West, above all those of nationalism and socialism. The Islam of today, therefore, cannot be understood without taking into account the specific nature of its process of secularization.

While secularization has been going on in almost all Muslim countries, it has been carried out most consistently and thoroughly in Turkey, without, however, undermining the Islamic character of that country. Turkey's transition from a traditional Muslim country to a modern, but still Islamic commonwealth occurred in the wake of a fundamental political revolution. The modernization of the Islamic institutions was first carried out in the nineteenth century, due to pressure from the West and military defeats. Under the regime of *Tanzimat* ("reform legislation"), modern law codes were introduced from 1850 to 1870. But a grave setback occurred under the authoritarian regime of Sultan Abdul Hamid II (who reigned from 1876 to 1909). Successive waves of revolutionary movements culminated in the revolution of 1908–1909: the Constitution of 1876, which had been suspended, was restored; Sultan Abdul Hamid II was dethroned; and under the leadership of Mustafa Kemal (1881–1938)—best known as Ataturk—Turkey was transformed into a modern state. In quick succession Ataturk abolished the caliphate (1924) and the office of the Shaikh-al-Islam, replaced Shari'a with a complex of legal codes based on Swiss, German, and Italian law codes (1926), secularized the schools, and finally disestablished Islam formally (1928).

However, while Ataturk did away with religious institutions which Islam society had considered sacred and immutable for thirteen centuries, he did not carry out a genuine separation of state and religion. On the contrary, he took measures designed to purify and reform, in a direction which might best be described as Mu'tazili. He dissolved the Sufi orders[47] and banned the pilgrimages to the tombs of saints and princes. On the other hand, he established two government organs deal-ing with religious matters—a Department of Religious Affairs and a Department of Pious Foundations—as instruments for directing the reli-gious life and the religious institutions of the Turkish people in a spirit of reform.

Ataturk's religious reforms met with considerable resistance from politically and religiously conservative groups during his lifetime. After his death his own party, the Republican People's Party, which retained power for another twelve years, began to weaken some of his religious reforms. Thus religious instruction in the public schools was reintro-duced in 1948–1959. The opposition party, the Democratic Party, which swept the elections in 1950, was determined to undermine the religious reforms of the Ataturk era. Under the leadership of Adnan Menderes (b. 1899, executed 1961), the government rescinded the ban on visits to the tombs of saints, extended religious instruction in the public schools, and permitted the establishment of religious schools.

The danger that the Menderes regime might sabotage the religious re-forms initiated by Ataturk seems to have been a factor that moved the army to overthrow Menderes in 1960. The constitution, adopted by ref-erendum in the following year, proclaimed that Turkey is a secular and reformist state. Although chosen to counteract the religious policy of the Menderes regime, the constitution does not reflect the actual relations between state and religion in present-day Turkey. If the term "secular state" implies the separation of state and religion, then present-day Tur-key is not a secular state. Islam, although formally disestablished, is in fact closely intertwined with the state, through government control over religious personnel and over religious instruction in the schools, the operation of government-run religious training institutions, and the con-struction and maintenance of mosques. Moreover, the ban on religious orders, which has been maintained, constitutes another intervention by the state in the structure of religion.

Yet the constitution describes the relationship between state and reli-gion correctly when it declares that Turkey is a reformist state. As a democratic state—however difficult it has proved from time to time to live up to democratic principles—and as a modern state in its legislation, judiciary, social welfare, land reform, and education, Turkey is a reform-ist state.[48] By making serious efforts to return religion to Islam's original principles, Turkey has been carrying out a truly Islamic reformation.[49]

No other Muslim country has effected the Islamic reformation so thoroughly and consistently as Turkey. In almost all Muslim countries, however, the identity of religious and civic life which characterized Islam from its beginning has been substantially weakened. Shari'a has been reduced step by step in virtually all Muslim countries, with the exception of Saudi Arabia. This process has even spread to spheres such as marital relations in which religion traditionally determined human conduct. Civil and penal law codes based on European models have been adopted, and Shari'a courts have been secularized or their influence curtailed. In education, modern primary and secondary schools have gradually over-shadowed or replaced traditional Islamic schools. In higher education, secular universities successfully compete with the ancient Islamic universities.[50]

This does not mean that the Muslim countries have ceased to be Islamic and that their peoples are no longer true Muslims. Their personal lives are still imbued with the spirit of Islam, and their personal relations with that of Shari'a. Even in such strongly nationalist countries as Iraq and Egypt, the Islamic nature of the community is still emphasized. Thus the Constitution of Iraq (adopted in 1964 after the seizure of power by the socialist Ba'ath Party) declares that Iraq is a democratic socialist country, based on its Islamic spirit. The Egyptian Constitution of 1971 states that "Islam is the religion of the state . . . and the principles of the Islamic shari'a are a major source of legislation." Religious instruction is obligatory in all Egyptian schools. Moreover, in 1960 the Egyptian government established a Supreme Council for Islamic Affairs which has been making intense efforts to propagate modern Islamic ideas, both in Egypt and in other Muslim countries, by way of literary publications and magazines.

Yet in most Muslim countries secular currents have become the most important driving forces. Among them nationalism and socialism have turned out to be the strongest and most effective. The liberation of most Muslim countries from foreign rule was based on national rather than religious aspirations. Even on the Indian subcontinent, where the Muslims insisted on being liberated separately from areas in which the Hindus prevailed, it took only twenty-three years (1947–1970) until Islamic Pakistan split along national lines.

The fact that the nationalism of the Muslim countries is of a secular nature can be illustrated by Arab nationalism. Arab countries are deeply divided among themselves over their economic, social, and political structures. But when Lebanon and Iraq attained their independence in 1945, an Arab League was formed as an instrument of Arab solidarity —and was successively joined by all Arab countries. The basis of this solidarity was the conflict with Israel. It became a common cause for an entire generation, in spite of sharply divergent interests among its member states. Only when Egypt decided to seek ways to end its conflict with Israel did the raison d'être of the league appear questionable for the foreseeable future.

The secular spirit fostered by the forces of nationalism has at times been on a collision course with religious forces. Prior to the 1978–1979 revolution in Iran, the most striking case of a clash between these two forces occurred in Egypt in the 1950s. Egypt was the birthplace of the Muslim Brotherhood, *al-Ikhwan al Muslimum*, an organization based on fundamentalist Islamic reform ideas, blended with a political liberation movement. The Brotherhood was founded in 1928 by Hasan Banna' (1906–1949) and was directed by him until his assassination. The Brotherhood spread from Egypt, where it maintained the strongest popular support, to other Arab countries. In Egypt it agitated for resistance to British domination and helped organize the fight against it, but on a religious rather than nationalist basis. The Brotherhood opposed the modernistic movements which had received a strong impetus from the Turkish revolution. It advocated instead an Islamic system of government, as distinct from the modern democratic party system. When the old Egyptian regime was overthrown in 1952, the Muslim Brotherhood emerged as a powerful organization with which the new regime attempted to cooperate. But the fundamentalism of the Brotherhood clashed with the nationalism of the revolutionary forces, led by Gamal Abdel Nasser (1918–1970), and open warfare broke out between them. The movement was banned in 1954, and after an attempt on Nasser's life, it was severely persecuted. Although driven underground, the Brotherhood was not completely crushed. In 1965 it organized another attempt to overthrow the Nasser regime.[51]

The Iranian revolution constitutes the most violent conflict our generation has experienced between the forces of Islam and those of modernization. There were a number of factors that aggravated this conflict. Iran is the largest of those Muslim countries whose social, economic, and cultural structure has been exposed to the sudden influx of oil revenues. It was dominated by a dynasty which grew not organically, but in conflict with radical elements, which it could overcome only with foreign assistance (ouster of the Mussadegh regime in 1953). It secured its own regime only through a ruthless dictatorship, with the assistance of a privileged military caste and secret police. The maltreatment of the religious institutions in fact added only one element to the growing opposition which the dynasty faced. In the last phase of this fight the Messianic element of Shi'ism seems to have played an important part. Ruholla Khomeini is one of the Ayatollahs (supreme ulamas) who by their elevated position acted as elements of organized opposition. But because Khomeini had been exiled for many years and because he excels by a stern and ascetic life, he was nearly given the rank of a Messianic Shi'ite Imam—which he certainly never claimed. It was this heightened authority that decisively helped to unleash the forces of revolution and to assure their victory. Whether and to what extent this will determine the nature of the societal system that will emerge in Iran remains to be seen. The allegiance of the Iranian people to Shi'ite Islam and its institutions will doubtless be deepened. But the highly developed economy and technology of an oil-centered system are also bound to play an important role.

If nationalism is one of the driving secular forces in the Muslim world, socialism, although different from that of Western societies, is another. In Muslim countries socialism is generally allied with a strong nationalist trend and is considered a constituent of national liberation. Since a large part of the industrial and financial sectors of the economy in these countries was in the hands of foreigners, socialism meant its transfer into the custody of the nation; the agricultural sector, which occupies most of the population in virtually all Muslim countries, has more or less preserved its traditional structure. Another feature of Muslim socialism is the authoritarian structure of the regimes promoting it. This feature, to be sure, is not specifically Islamic but common to many countries that are economically and socially similar to Muslim countries.

Socialist policies of this kind have been initiated in a number of Muslim countries, ranging from Indonesia to Algeria. Under Sukarno (1901–1970) the principal political parties of Indonesia adhered to socialist principles, including the Masjumi Party, the leading Muslim group. Even under the Suharto regime, which acquired power by a military coup in 1965, the public sector of the economy has remained strong. The first rulers who emerged after the separation of Pakistan and Bangladesh —'Ali Bhutto in Pakistan and Sheikh Mujibur Raman in Bangladesh— declared their allegiance to socialism; but the overthrow of both regimes seems to have left the societal systems of these countries in a state of suspense.

In Syria and Iraq a pronouncedly socialist movement, the Ba'ath Party, has attained power. It was founded by a non-Muslim socialist, Michel Aflak (b. 1910), who was also a committed Arab nationalist. The party, which was founded in 1946, immediately after Syria had achieved independence, has been based on a blend of socialism and Arab nationalism. "Socialism," states the Constitution of the Syrian Ba'ath Party, "constitutes . . . the ideal social order which will allow the Arab people to realize its possibilities and to enable its genius to flourish." [52]

In 1963, the Ba'ath Party acquired power in Syria and Iraq, in both countries in alliance with military forces. But in spite of its declared goal of resurrecting the Arab nation, it has never been able to attract many Muslims in other Arab countries. Socialist policies made their way to Egypt and Algeria through indigenous forces. In Egypt, Nasser first had to overwhelm the fundamentalist forces led by the Muslim Brotherhood before he could embark on a socialist programme. In the Interim Constitution of 1962 the National Assembly declared Egypt to be a socialist state, and the National Union (the governing party) was replaced by the Arab Socialist Union. The Constitution of 1971 proclaimed in its first article that "the Arab Republic of Egypt is a democratic socialist state."

Just as Egypt blended its version of socialism with a modern version of Islam, Algerian socialism was also built along Islamic lines. The country's leader, Houari Boumedienne (1925–1978) acquired power in 1965, and tried from the outset to transform Algeria into a socialist state. He regarded socialism as a means to end foreign economic domination and to develop the Algerian economy as fast as possible with a minimum of foreign capital. And Boumedienne was also convinced that under modern conditions socialism is the logical consequence of Islam. Like many other modern Muslims, he insisted that "Islam is not only a spiritual path but a social and political programme. . . . It exceeds all other religions in equality and in its struggle for the liberty of men." [53]

The world of Islam is a world in transition. It has lost the religious-secular unity of the umma. Secular forces vie with religious ones. Modern concepts of Islam and the heritage of Mu'tazilism struggle with fundamentalist beliefs, which are still strongly embedded in rural areas and in small urban communities. Yet the example of Turkey shows that while the umma has been weakened, Islam itself has not lost its vitality. Religious indifference may be widespread, particularly among intellectuals and urban groups who oppose the Sufi orders and superstitions which Sufism has nourished. But this opposition does not touch the fundamentals of Islamic faith. Whereas part of the population is still devoted to Sufi cults, to the belief in salvation through magic and the intercession of saints, the educated strata of the population seems to follow the rationalist Mu'tazili concepts of the turn-of-the-century Islamic reformers.

What may baffle Western observers of contemporary Islam is the fact that these reformist leaders have no outstanding successors; that the intense battle about a renewal of the faith that has marked Christianity for more than a century has been missing in Islam. Islam has no Barths, Bultmanns, Tillichs, or Niebuhrs. Some Western scholars of Islam are inclined to infer from this absence of theological discussions that fundamentalism is still predominant.[54] Yet what is in fact predominant is an astonishing capacity to reconcile modern science and modern political and social ideas with Islamic religious beliefs. Many Muslims look forward to a socialist order of society, a world of social justice and equality, a perfect society. But even they base their egalitarian ideals on the social tenets enunciated or implied in the Koran. They have never ceased to look forward to the end of time when the trumpet will blow and God will awaken the sleepers to erect His kingdom on earth.

CHAPTER IX

Secular Humanism

Secular humanism grew out of the Jewish-Christian eschatological vision of the kingdom of God as an age of unending peace and welfare, justice and love. This vision, secularized in the form of a perfect society, has been the goal for which humanists have aimed. They believed that this goal would be achieved through natural laws and rights rather than through divine intervention. Humanists also believed in a law of human progress to the effect that society tended naturally toward this goal. Only in the last few decades has the faith in the existence of laws ensuring progress toward the perfecting of society been shaken and even lost. It has been replaced by a conviction that progress is never assured, but must be fought for, and by a determination to wage this fight.

1. THE DAWN OF SECULAR HUMANISM

Secular humanism could not arise as long as there was a general acceptance that the gratuitous grace of God was the indispensable prerequisite for salvation. For the ultimate goal of secular humanism—the perfection of society through human efforts—presupposes not the gratuitous grace of God, but rather the full responsibility of man for his own thoughts and deeds.

A weakening of the belief in the gratuitous grace of God occurred in the late Middle Ages within the ranks of Christian theology. Thomas Aquinas accepted man's responsibility and freedom of will, as is expressed by his famous tenet, "Will and freedom of choice are not two powers but only one." [1] Man, after having deliberated on a course of action (*voluntas deliberata*), is free in the act of decision. Two prominent English theologians, Duns Scotus (c. 1266–1308) and William of Ockham (c. 1285–1349), went even further in asserting man's responsibility for his thoughts and deeds. Duns Scotus wrote of "the will which is a free power by its essence." [2] Ockham also considered the human will to be an active power that is absolutely free: "A man experiences the fact that however much his reason dictates some action, his will can will, or not will, this act." [3]

However, the decline of predestinarianism in favor of an emphasis on the freedom of the human will, while characteristic of some of the leading medieval theologians, had yet to result in any humanist currents. The beginnings of humanism had to await the spiritual transformation of human thinking, which accompanied the economic, social, political and cultural rise of the cities in medieval Europe and eventually culminated in the Renaissance. Two thinkers of the Renaissance, Giovanni Pico della Mirandola (1463–1494) and Desiderius Erasmus (c. 1466–1536), were particularly important in laying the foundations for the humanism which later flourished in the Age of Enlightenment—Pico through his stress on the dignity of man, Erasmus through his emphasis on the freedom of the human will and on reason as the guide toward greater perfection.

Italian philosopher Giovanni Pico della Mirandola based his concept of the dignity of man on the absolute freedom of the human will. In the *Oration on the Dignity of Man*, he asserted that man determines his place in the universe through his own free choice; as "the molder and maker" of himself, man can "grow upward . . . into the higher natures which are divine" or "grow downward into the lower natures which are brute." [4] Pico was not a modern humanist aiming at the perfection of society. In his view, the ideal life was not one of action for the sake of mankind, but rather one of contemplation, the highest activity in which man could engage. Nevertheless, the germs of humanism can be traced to his faith in man's capacity to aim at perfection through his own efforts.

The most outstanding Renaissance philosopher, Desiderius Erasmus, was a Dutch cleric who—although the Council of Trent placed his works on the index, and although he himself did not spare the Church in his attacks on the "follies" of contemporary society—nonetheless always remained a faithful Catholic. Yet, at the same time, he paved the way for humanist ideas. Luther was correct in stating of Erasmus, "Human concerns prevail in him more than divine ones."[5] It was no coincidence that the final parting of the ways between Luther and Erasmus was occasioned by their disputation on the problem of free will—Erasmus attacking Luther's predestinarianism in his treatise *De libero arbitrio* ("On the free will"), and Luther retorting in *De servo arbitrio* ("On the bondage of the will").[6]

While Luther and Calvin founded their hope for salvation on the gratuitous grace of God, Erasmus chose the humanist path of reason. "What is the proper nature of man?" he asked rhetorically in *On a Firm and Appropriate Education of Boys*, and his reply was: "Surely it is to live the life of reason."[7] In fact, the whole treatise, written in 1527, long before the Age of Enlightenment, manifested the spirit of enlightenment. Its chief theme was perfection through education: "Nature has implanted in us the instinct to seek for knowledge." If through proper education we make good use of this instinct, we will attain our goal of happiness. If we are fortunate enough to receive the proper education, we will be nearly as perfect as God. Modern man may be amused at the extent of Erasmus's faith in education. But the belief in man's perfectibility through reason became a source of inspiration for the Age of Enlightenment.

Both Pico and Erasmus still thought in terms of the individual man searching for his own salvation and happiness. The quest for perfectible man had yet to become the quest for a perfectible society. It took another century before the intellectual leaders began to search for the societal conditions necessary to the building of a just and humane society.

2. THE DOCTRINE OF MAN'S NATURAL RIGHTS

Humanist writers of the seventeenth to the nineteenth centuries based their faith in the perfectibility of human society on two doctrines—the doctrine of man's natural rights and the doctrine of a law of progress.

The doctrine of man's natural rights was derived from the doctrine of natural laws inherited from Greco-Roman antiquity. Beginning with Heraclitus, Greek philosophers, particularly Aristotle and the Stoics, held that the universe is ruled by reason; hence the laws of nature are the laws of a rational universe. The Cynics taught that one will be virtuous and happy by following the laws of nature and rejecting the artificial values of social conventions.[8] Christianity also emphasized the rule of natural law, but subordinated it to the will of God. The classical Christian doctrine of the relationship between God and natural laws was stated by

Thomas Aquinas: Everything in the world is ruled by eternal law, which itself is subject to the rule of God. Natural law, by which the world of man is ruled, is therefore part of God's eternal law.[9] Thus the doctrine that the world is ruled not by an arbitrary power, but by an eternal law, arose in Greek philosophy and was revitalized by Thomas Aquinas before being adopted by the philosophers of the Enlightenment.

With the Enlightenment, however, the concept of the laws of nature underwent a significant transformation. The belief arose that the laws of nature which guide human behavior imply natural rights and duties that should guide human conduct and institutions. As long as natural laws had been interpreted as divine laws, human rights and duties had been understood as derived from divine commandments. The reinterpretation of these rights and duties as natural rights and duties was an important step in the process of secularization which occurred during the Age of Enlightenment. Enlightenment thinkers held that once these natural rights and duties were generally recognized and became the foundation of society, the path toward a perfect society would be opened.

The beginnings of the doctrine of man's natural rights can be traced to the treatise *Defensor pacis* ("Defender of peace," 1324) by Italian political philosopher, Marsilius of Padua (c. 1280–c. 1343). Marsilius proposed some of the fundamental rights of man which several centuries later became the basis of the revolutionary political movements of the Age of Enlightenment, and which eventually became the basis of the principles of modern democracy: the right of the people to legislate, either directly or through an elected body, and to choose the ruler of the state; the responsibility of the ruler toward the people; and the right of the people to "correct" or depose a ruler who betrays their trust.[10]

Marsilius's doctrines were revived more than two hundred years later, under the impact of the revolutionary changes brought about in Europe by the growth of individualism, Renaissance humanism, and the Reformation. The first written expressions of these doctrines can be found in the writings of Scottish humanist George Buchanan (1506–1582) and German political philosopher Johannes Althusius (1557–1638). Probably in connection with his struggle against Mary Queen of Scots, in *De jure regni apud Scotos* ("On public law in Scotland," 1579), Buchanan advanced the doctrines of the sovereignty of the people, the general will of the people as the basis of kingly rule, and the right of the people to resist tyrannical rulers.[11]

Johannes Althusius was the first writer to propound a doctrine of popular sovereignty based on a theory of the social contract, which was to become the prevailing political tenet of the Age of Enlightenment. Althusius defined the social contract as follows: "Politics is the art of associating men for the purpose of establishing, cultivating, and conserving social life among them. . . . The subject matter of politics is, therefore association . . . in which the . . . associates pledge themselves each to the other, by explicit or tacit agreement, to mutual communication of whatever is useful and necessary for the harmonious exercise of social life." [12] The sovereignty of the people, as exercised by their local, provincial, and commonwealth corporations, flows from the social contract: The ruler, elected by the commonwealth, contracts with the associates and is responsible to them. He can also be deposed by them if his rule is unlawful.

With the exception of atheistic writers, the humanists of the Enlightenment generally retained Thomas Aquinas's doctrine of God as the source of natural laws and rights. But the emphasis they placed on the rationality of nature and on the strictness and inescapability of its laws tended to restrict, if not entirely eliminate, God's role. Thus Dutch jurist Hugo Grotius (Huigh de Groot, 1583–1645), in the famous treatise *De jure belli et pacis* ("On the law of war and peace," 1625), defined the law of nature as "a dictate of right reason, which points out that an act, according as it is or is not in conformity with rational nature, has in it a quality of moral baseness or moral necessity; and that, in consequence, such an act is either forbidden or enjoined by the author of nature, God." However, God's commandments are subordinate to the law of nature. "The law of nature . . . is unchangeable—even in the sense that it cannot be changed by God." [13]

When contrasted with the traditional and conventional legal structure of the feudal era, the doctrine of man's natural rights was inherently revolutionary. Nonetheless, the weakening and dissolution of the feudal system initially led to a strengthening of the rulers' centralist power. In countries with particularly strong centralist tendencies, such as France and England, the doctrine of man's natural rights led some political philosophers to conservative centralist conclusions. This is exemplified by two outstanding political writers—Jean Bodin (1530–1596) in France and Thomas Hobbes (1588–1679) in England.

In *Six livres de la Republique* ("Six books on the commonwealth," 1576), Jean Bodin, on the basis of the natural rights of citizens, expounded a doctrine of absolute sovereignty which gave the monarchical ruler unlimited power and freed him from the obligation to seek the consent of his subjects. Thomas Hobbes, important as both a philosopher and a political thinker, developed his political doctrine in several books, of which *Leviathan* (1651) became the most widely read. Hobbes is commonly credited with having founded the doctrine of the social contract (as Althusius's earlier exposition of that doctrine had received very little attention). He arrived at his doctrine from a mechanistic view of primitive man: Natural man is self-centered and dominated by his drive for self-preservation, beyond good and evil. Natural man's self-preservation constitutes a natural right, but if allowed to prevail results in perpetual insecurity. Thus the striving for self-preservation forces men to found a state. In every state there must be a sovereign power to enforce the social contract, that is, to safeguard the natural right of self-preservation. But once men have entrusted this function to a ruler, his power becomes absolute and irrevocable.

In Hobbes's youth, the divine right of the kings was still uncontested in England, although the struggle between king and people broke out during his lifetime. But by the time John Locke (1632–1704) was a young man, England no longer upheld the divine right of kings; during his lifetime, the people's natural right to choose their ruler and to depose any ruler who broke the trust placed in him was established and applied twice. In effect, Locke became the political philosopher of the Glorious Revolution of 1688. In *Two Treaties of Government* (1690) he anticipated the fundamental theses of the French Enlightenment, the American Declaration of Independence, and the *Droits de l'homme* of the French Revolution: By nature, all men are free, equal, and independent. In forming communities, men do not abrogate their freedom and equality; on the contrary, "the end of law is not to abolish or restrain, but to preserve and enlarge freedom." Locke emphasized the democratic principles of majority rule and the separation of powers, in which the executive branch of government is subordinated to the democratically organized legislative branch. Since a government acts as the trustee of the people, it can be removed or changed by the people should it violate their trust.[14] Locke did not claim that a society based on these principles would be perfect. But since he held that the natural law on which society should be founded is identical with the law of reason, the perfection of society was implied as a societal goal.

While England's Glorious Revolution was influenced by Locke, the spiritual precursors of the French Revolution were the *philosophes*, the leaders of the French Enlightenment, many of whom were contributors to Denis Diderot's (1713–1784) *Encyclopédie*.[15] Their political doctrines were similar to those of Locke, both in substance and in their derivation from the natural rights of man.

The foremost political philosophers of the French Enlightenment were (Charles Louis de Secondat, baron de la Brede et de) Montesquieu (1689–1755) and Jean-Jacques Rousseau (1712–1778). Montesquieu's most important contribution was the systematization of the doctrine of the separation of powers in *De l'esprit des lois* ("On the spirit of the laws," 1748). Starting from the doctrine of natural rights and taking contemporary England as his model, he insisted that the preservation of liberty requires the separation of legislative, executive, and judicial powers. Although Montesquieu was an aristocrat at heart, his doctrine of the separation of powers, by limiting the power of the ruler, constituted a great step in the evolution of the principles of democracy.

Rousseau's principal contribution to the political doctrines of the Age of Enlightenment was contained in his *Contrat social* ("The social contract," 1762). The revolutionary turn that he gave to the doctrine of man's natural rights was proclaimed in the opening statement, which denounced the violation of human rights in contemporary societies. Echoing Locke's doctrine that man is born free, Rousseau opened his treatise with the famous sentence: "Man is born free, and everywhere he is in chains." [16]

It would be erroneous to attribute a back-to-nature philosophy to Rousseau, as has so often been done. The liberty that Rousseau believed should be established was not the natural liberty of primitive man, but civil liberty which can exist only in democratic communities. In his *Contrat social*, Rousseau attempted to trace the principles of that liberty. He held that democratic communities of that kind are ruled by the general will (*volonté générale*) and that, since all men are committed to obey this general will, their liberty is voluntarily limited. From the existence of civil liberty follows the moral, juridical, and political equality of all citizens, which requires a democratically structured state.

Rousseau's doctrine of the general will as the foundation of democracy in later stages of democratic development proved to be a grave obstacle to the recognition of the rights of minorities. In his time, however, that doctrine constituted a powerful argument in favor of the sovereignty of the people, and was even recognized as such by the French Revolution: The *Droits de l'homme* expressly stated that "the law is the expression of the general will."

Locke and Rousseau, like most other leaders of the Enlightenment, defined equality in terms of its moral and political aspects. They did not consider its economic aspects, which were to arise as a fundamental issue in the nineteenth century, when the industrial revolution created an impoverished and exploited working class. Nowhere did the leading spirits of the Enlightenment envisage economic and social equality as an ideal. On the contrary, the protection of private property was a basic component of the social contract and was among the freedoms for which they strove. Socialist philosophers, such as Morelly, Gabriel Bonnot de Mably, and François Babeuf, were outside the mainstream of the French Enlightenment.

The leading figures of the Enlightenment did hold, however, that the right to property should not be unlimited. Locke viewed the protection of property as the protection of the products of a man's labor. Rousseau proposed to limit economic inequalities, stating that "no citizen should ever be wealthy enough to buy another, and none poor enough to be forced to sell himself." Condorcet (marquis de Caritat, 1734–1794) was convinced that "fortunes tend naturally toward equality and that their extreme disproportion either could not exist or would quickly cease if positive law had not introduced factitious means of amassing and perpetuating them." [17]

The doctrines of the leading figures of the Enlightenment in England and France became a living force which has survived in the democratic communities of our age. The American Revolution reflected the ideology, and even the phraseology, of the Enlightenment era. The appeal in the American Declaration of Independence to the "laws of Nature," the Declaration's "self-evident truths . . . that all men are created equal, that they are endowed by their Creator with certain unalienable rights, that among these are Life, Liberty, and the pursuit of Happiness," that governments derive their just powers from the consent of the governed, and "that it is the Right of the People to alter or abolish" destructive forms of government "and to institute new Government"—were directly derived from the teachings of the political philosophers of the Enlightenment. The Declaration of the Rights of Man and Citizen, which the Constituent Assembly of the French Revolution adopted in 1789, was based on the same doctrine of the natural, inalienable, and sacred rights of man.

While these doctrines spread rapidly and often became a vital instrument in the fight for democracy, and while democratic systems of government were indeed established in a number of countries, defeats alternated with victories. The same European countries that established the democratic rights of liberty and political equality within their own borders, founded colonies in which indigenous populations were denied these rights. In the place of the modest social and economic inequalities Locke and Rousseau had allowed for, huge inequalities in economic and social status sprang up with the growth of the capitalist system. Authoritarian systems—such as military dictatorships and fascist and communist regimes—arose, either supplanting democratic systems or preventing their development. Even within the last generation, although fascist regimes in Germany and Italy were defeated and most colonies were liberated, military dictatorships and communist regimes have assumed power in a number of countries.

Today the issue hangs in the balance. On paper, at least, the democratic doctrine of the rights of man, as established by the Age of Enlightenment, has found more recognition than ever before. Communist regimes frequently call themselves "people's democracies." The United Nations, on its founding day (26 June 1945), reaffirmed in the preamble to its charter, "faith in fundamental human rights, in the dignity and worth of the human person, in the equal rights of men and women and of all nations, large and small." Indeed, in Article 55 of its charter, the United Nations assigned itself the task of promoting "universal respect for, and observance of human rights and fundamental freedom for all." The Universal Declaration of Human Rights, adopted by the United Nations General Assembly in 1948, even employed the phraseology of the Age of Enlightenment. The preamble states that "recognition of the inherent dignity and of the equal and inalienable rights of all members of the human family is the foundation of freedom, justice and peace in the world." The first article states that "all human beings are born free and equal . . . in dignity and rights" and have the right of "rebellion against tyranny and oppression."

The United Nations has committed itself, as one of its fundamental tasks, to promote the implementation of these doctrines; and even in its most essential task—"to maintain international peace and security"— it is the heir of the Age of Enlightenment. The political philosophy of the Enlightenment treated the attainment and maintenance of peaceful relations between nations as an intrinsic humanist goal. The ideal of perpetual and universal peace can be traced back to Desiderius Erasmus. To this ideal he devoted a treatise, *Querela Pacis* ("The complaint of peace"), in which he praised peace as "the fountain, parent, nourisher, augmenter and defender of all good things," and condemned war as "the seed of all evils." In an impassioned appeal to princes, priests, magistrates, and to Christians generally, he urged them to support the cause of peace.[18]

The following period with its series of European wars, culminating in the Thirty Years' War (1618–1648), was not conducive to the development of the idea of perpetual peace. Hugo Grotius—the great advocate of the law of nature as the basis of positive law, who wrote *The Law* of *War and Peace* during the first stages of the Thirty Years' War—recognized as fundamental the right of states to conduct wars. This right was to be restricted only by certain principles, such as that of the freedom of the seas.[19]

At the time the doctrine of the social contract became popular, some writers advocated a contract between states as a way of ending war and establishing a perpetual peace. Just as the state had been formed with a view to safeguarding peace among its people, the individual states should federate in order to safeguard peace among themselves. In 1713, at the end of the War of the Spanish Succession, one of the early protagonists of the French Enlightenment (Charles Irenee Castel) Abbé de Saint-Pierre (1658–1743) published a "Project for rendering peace perpetual in Europe" (*Projet pour rendre la paix perpetuelle en Europe*). The Abbé even submitted this "Project" to the Peace Congress of Utrecht. A blend of very radical and reactionary ideas, the "Project" proposed, on the one hand, the establishment of a permanent organization of Christian states,[20] equipped with the power to arbitrate all disputes between member states and with a joint army to enforce arbitration; on the other hand, it excluded non-Christian states, and protected member states against internal rebellion and revolution.

The most constructive proponent of the idea of perpetual peace was Immanuel Kant (1724–1804), who may be regarded as the spiritual father of the concept of the United Nations as a peace-keeping instrument. He devoted two treatises to this idea: *Idea of a Universal History from a Cosmopolitan Point of View* (1784), and *On Perpetual Peace* (1795). In the first essay, he maintained that "the problem of establishing a perfect civic constitution is dependent upon the problem of a lawful external relation among states and cannot be solved without a solution of the latter problem." Lawful external relations among states require the creation of a League of Nations,[21] through which "even the smallest state could expect security and justice, not from its own power and by its own decrees, but only from this great League of Nations . . . from a united power acting according to the decisions reached under the laws of their united will."

When Kant wrote the first treatise, the Western world had recently witnessed the American fight for liberation from colonial rule, waged under the aegis of the philosophy of Enlightenment, and it was on the threshold of the French Revolution, which was to shatter the feudal regime under the same banner of Enlightenment. The feeling was strong among the men of the Enlightenment that a time of general human fellowship was approaching. The great German poet Johann Christoph

Friedrich von Schiller (1759–1805) in the hymn *An die Freude* ("Ode to joy," 1787) exclaimed: "Every man a brother plighted where thy gentle wings are spread" (*Alle Menschen werden Brüder, wo dein sanfter Flügel weilt*), and he broke into the exalting words: "Millions in our arms we gather, to the world our kiss be sent!" (*Seid umschlungen, Millionen, diesen Kuss der ganzen Welt!*)—a dithyramb which, immortalized by Beethoven's Ninth Symphony, still reverberates throughout the world.[22] In 1792, the French National Assembly granted honorary citizenship to Schiller himself, as well as to George Washington, Thomas Paine, and the English utilitarian philosopher Joseph Priestley. On that occasion, the assembly declared that "friends of freedom must be dear to a nation which has . . . proclaimed its desire for the brotherhood of nations"[23]—only to become embroiled immediately afterwards in the most devastating wars Europe had ever experienced.

It may have been under the sobering impression of the wars between revolutionary France and the anti-revolutionary powers that Kant in *On Perpetual Peace* proposed to severely limit access to the League of Nations: perpetual peace could not exist at the beginning, but only at the end of a progress toward a more perfect world. As he expressed this in the spirit of his philosophy, perpetual peace would be the fruit of a "reign of pure practical reason": "Seek first the reign of pure practical reason and its justice and your end—the blessing of perpetual peace—will necessarily follow."[24] He believed, however, that this blessing could be achieved only if every state had a constitution derived from the concept of the social contract and established on principles compatible with liberty and equality. Such states, Kant believed (naïvely, as it turned out), would always prefer peace to war. If they were to form a federation, designed to straighten out differences among them, peace would be preserved. Kant was, however, not so naïve as to hope that perpetual peace would be established immediately. He blended his faith in the eventual attainment of perpetual peace with a faith in the endless progress of the human race: "If the hope could even be conceived of realizing, though by an endless progress, the reign of public right, perpetual peace . . . is not then a chimera, but a problem of which time, probably abridged by the uniformity of the progress of the human mind, promises us the solution."[25]

3. THE DOCTRINE OF THE LAW OF PROGRESS

From Francis Bacon to Utilitarianism. Kant's faith in the "uniformity of the progress of the human mind" and in the eventual achievement of perpetual peace points to the two pillars on which rested the hopes of the Enlightenment for the evolution of a perfect society: the doctrine of man's natural rights and the doctrine of the law of progress.

The belief in a law of human progress was much slower in developing and in gaining acceptance than was the belief in man's natural rights. This was largely a consequence of the respect for the cultural achievements of ancient Greece and Rome, a respect which had been nourished by the Renaissance. The same spirit of humanism that evolved during the Renaissance and became instrumental in paving the way for the Age of Enlightenment had also resulted in a tendency to elevate ancient civilization over that of contemporary Europe.

It took considerable time as well as marked cultural and material progress, before this assessment changed, before trust in the ability of civilization to renew itself and to progress was finally established. The great English humanist philosopher Francis Bacon (1561–1626) argued that science is self-progressing and that, consequently, modern man stands on the shoulders of antiquity.[26] Nonetheless, the debate over whether to attribute superiority to the ancients or to the moderns continued during most of the seventeenth century. It was only in the age of Louis XIV that recognition of contemporary achievements caused the balance in the "quarrel between the ancients and the moderns" to begin to shift in favor of the moderns. French poet Charles Perrault (1628–1703), who attributed superiority to the moderns and expressed his trust in the continuous progress of the human mind, was influential in this shift of opinion.[27]

However, most important in the triumph of the doctrine of the law of progress were the striking advances in the field of science. This became the main argument advanced by exponents of the doctrine of the law of progress. The "age of science"—the period which began with the great discoveries in the natural sciences—was heralded by the leading rationalist philosophers of the sixteenth and seventeenth centuries, particularly Francis Bacon and René Descartes.

However problematic Bacon's own method of induction, his conviction that only the method of scientific research is a valid tool for the progress of knowledge—and thereby an efficient instrument of the progress of human welfare—was of crucial importance. In *The Advancement of Learning* (1605), he held that learning is the decisive contribution to progress in human welfare and an instrument of human power: "The sovereignty of man lieth hid in knowledge." Significantly, Bacon's utopian commonwealth, "New Atlantis," was to be ruled by scientists and was to contain a research institute to foster scientific discoveries which would improve the human lot.[28]

René Descartes (1596–1650), notwithstanding the marked differences between his concept of scientific method and Bacon's inductive method, like Bacon, based his scientific system on the conviction that all knowledge of the world must be obtained through scientific methods. Descartes attempted to find a uniformly valid method to utilize in the search for scientific truth. Any assertions of knowledge about objects are subject to doubt until all necessary tests for their verification have been undertaken; but the certainty of one's own existence constitutes a basis for valid statements. One's own existence is proved by the capacity to think, the famous *cogito, ergo sum* ("I think, therefore I am"). This insistence on applying rationalist methods for understanding the world proved to be a valuable instrument for the progress in science.

Descartes's first work, *Discours de la methode pour bien conduir sa raison et chercher la vérité dans les sciences* ("Discourse on the method of properly guiding the reason in the search for truth in the sciences," 1637), gave direction to modern science. Descartes was firmly convinced that by applying rationalist methods of science, men can become "masters and owners of Nature." It is significant that he had originally planned to entitle the *Discours*, "The Prospect of a Universal Science which can elevate our Nature to its highest Perfection." [29] In Descartes's view, as in Bacon's, science opens the door to human perfection.

The firm conviction of these two leading philosophers that scientific understanding of the world is the key to progress heralded the stupendous scientific progress achieved in the following period. The scientists of the seventeenth and eighteenth centuries laid the foundations for most natural sciences, with their leading discoveries in astronomy and physics (Galileo, Kepler, Huygens, Newton, Halley, Reaumur, and Laplace), chemistry (Boyle and Lavoisier), and biology (Harvey and Linnaeus). Was it any wonder that the faith in human progress, which Bacon and Descartes had sparked through their insistence on applying scientific methods in the search for knowledge, found its confirmation in the visible progress that took place in the natural sciences?

The basis for the progress of the sciences was the faith of the Age of Enlightenment in the ineluctable reign of the laws of nature. The greatest and most influential scientist of that age, Isaac Newton (1642–1727), stated: "These principles I consider not as occult qualities, but as general laws of nature, by which the things are formed." [30] It was in this spirit and under the impact of the visible progress in the sciences that the doctrine of the law of human progress arose. As Bacon had equated knowledge with power, progress in scientific knowledge was now held to be instrumental in producing progress toward the perfection of society.

The French writers of the Enlightenment were the foremost proponents of the doctrine of progress through science. The brilliant succession of French writers of the Enlightenment era began with Bernard le Bovier de Fontenelle (1657–1757). In *Digression sur les anciens et sur les modernes* (1688), he continued Perrault's argument in favor of the moderns and insisted that human reason progresses continuously, although slowly, and that posterity would surpass the present generation. The Abbé de Saint-Pierre also upheld the continuous progress of universal reason.[31] And Voltaire in his fight against obscurantism insisted that "reason and industry will always progress more and more; of the evils which afflicted men, prejudices will gradually disappear." [32] After all, the vast enterprise of the *Encyclopédie* was based on a faith in the supremacy of knowledge in man's struggle to perfect society. (The popularity of encyclopedias, summaries of knowledge compiled by the most competent and modern sources, illustrates the rapid acceptance of the idea that knowledge is a tool for perfecting society.[33]) The contributors to the *Encyclopédie*, like other French *philosophes*, were strong adherents of the doctrine of the law of progress. Even the strict economist Turgot (baron de l'Aulne, 1722–1781) insisted that the human race is marching continuously toward perfection, and believed, moreover, that he had discovered a law of acceleration of progress.[34] In his brief career as finance minister of France (1774–1776), he attempted to put his doctrine of human progress into practice, carrying out truly revolutionary measures, which became a model for the French Revolution. When he was dismissed and his reforms abandoned, the path toward a nonrevolutionary change of the feudal system was all but barred.

Like Turgot, Condorcet was a revolutionary. Directly involved in the French Revolution, his life ended tragically. He was persecuted and arrested as a partisan of the Girondins, and died in prison. While hiding prior to his arrest, he wrote *Esquisse d'un tableau historique des progrès de l'esprit humain* ("Outline of a historical tableau of the progress of the human spirit," 1793), which has become a classic of the doctrine of the law of progress. Starting from his belief in the goodness and grandeur of man, he expounded a historical scheme of man's ascent from primitive beginnings to the age of enlightened reason as the outcome of an irreversible progress and an infinite process of perfection. He thought that from his knowledge of history he could derive ten stages, the tenth and last being the age ushered in by the French Revolution. This would be an age in which intellectual progress would be advanced enough to produce a reign of freedom, virtue, respect for human rights, and equality, including equality of the sexes and of all human races.

The doctrine of stages of human progress survived far into the nineteenth century. French philosopher Auguste Comte (1798–1857) constructed three ages through which mankind was to pass: the theological age; the metaphysical age; and the positive (scientific) age, in which sociology, the science of society, would enable mankind to predict and control its own future. The doctrine of stages of societal development also appeared in Marx's historical materialism, although on an entirely new basis.

The doctrine of the law of progress was strengthened by the religious beliefs which prevailed in the Age of Enlightenment. While that period witnessed the first major incursion of avowed atheists into the Christian world,[35] deism prevailed among the men of Enlightenment. That creed never supplanted Christianity as an official religion, but constituted a congenial expression of the religious feelings of the men of Enlightenment and underlay their trust in human progress. Deism was in effect a new monotheistic religion. Like the Jewish and Islamic religions, it believed in one all-powerful God, sole creator of the world, who would reward the virtuous and punish evildoers. Voltaire (1694–1778), the most aggressive among the deists, expressed this belief in nearly Koranic terms: "One God alone, a God who rewards the good and avenges evil, a God who cannot . . . have had associates."[36] Deism considered itself a natural religion, adverse to anything that disturbed the natural order of the universe.

Deism as a religion was first defined and expounded in the writings of English philosophers, such as Herbert of Cherbury (Edward Herbert first Baron, 1582–1648), John Toland (1670–1722), and Matthew Tindal (1657–1733).[37] In the minds of many leaders of the Enlightenment the triune God of Christianity was replaced by a deistic God. The God of Leibniz and Kant was undoubtedly a deistic God. The outstanding leaders of French Enlightenment, such as Montesquieu, Rousseau, and Voltaire, were deists; Voltaire was even fanatical in his hatred of Christianity.[38] The chief architects of American Independence and of the Constitution were likewise deists; the Declaration of Independence can be read as a deist document. Similarly, the National Assembly of the French Revolution asserted in the preamble to the *Droits de l'homme* (August 1789) that it declared these rights "in the presence and under the auspices of the Supreme Being [*Être Suprême*]." Moreover, in its final stage the French Revolution officially elevated deism to the rank of an established religion.[39]

While deism did not deny the existence of evil in the world and in the human mind, it rejected the Christian doctrine of original sin. As the deistic God is gentle and benevolent, He also steers man's mind in this direction. Man, being a son of God, has an innate disposition toward goodness. Most representative of the doctrine of man's innate goodness was a group of English philosophers, the so-called Cambridge Platonists. They propounded a doctrine of the innate moral sense of man, based on Christianity but supported by rationalist concepts.[40] Under the influence of that school Anthony Ashley Cooper, Third Earl of Shaftesbury (1671–1713) taught that man's moral sense is innate, although it can be improved by training and education. In a strictly deistic manner, Shaftesbury held that the providential "Universal Mind" had established a general harmony in which man participates through his social feelings and his sense of partnership with mankind as a whole. Thus the moral sense is essentially a social sense. There is a natural harmony between the individual and society, between individual happiness and general welfare.[41]

English philosophers of the eighteenth century were inclined to blend Shaftesbury's doctrine of the moral sense as the basis of human progress with utilitarian theories. Francis Hutcheson (1694–1746) can be regarded as the father of utilitarianism. He thought that he had found a guiding principle for the action of the moral sense, namely, the promotion of the general welfare of mankind, which he equated with the greatest happiness of the greatest number of men.[42] Utilitarianism thus proposed a simple formula for the perfection of society: Men can achieve the goal of establishing a perfect society if they succeed in founding a social system in which the greatest number of men will experience the greatest happiness.

Utilitarianism as a social and political doctrine was first expounded by Joseph Priestley (1753–1804) and Jeremy Bentham (1748–1831). Priestley was an outstanding liberal thinker, advocate of religious tolerance and of the abolition of slavery, and a friend and honorary citizen of the French Revolution. In his *Essay on the First Principles of Government* (1769), he proposed a utilitarian majority rule of government: "The good and happiness of the members [meaning, of the majority of the members] of any state is the great standard by which everything related to that state must be determined."[43] Bentham, a philosopher and prominent jurist, applied utilitarian ethics to the governance of society in his *Introduction to the Principles of Morals and Legislation* (1789): The greatest happiness of the greatest number should be the object of all legislation. The pursuit of this goal should be the object of moral action and education. Bentham believed he had found an answer to the thorny question of how to measure happiness in order to determine the greatest happiness of the greatest number of men: "The value of pains and pleasures must be estimated by their intensity, duration, certainty, proximity, and extent. The greater amount of any of these qualities may counterbalance the lesser amount of any other."[44]

Utilitarianism suffered from weaknesses which either prevented its application or even rendered it dangerous. Its principal conceptual weakness lay in the impossibility of defining and measuring happiness. Bentham's criteria clearly begged the question—intensity of feelings is a quality which can hardly be measured objectively.[45] The fundamental weakness of utilitarianism, however, stems from the fact that societal action whose sole goal is the happiness of a majority might simultaneously endanger the happiness of a minority. There is obviously a conflict between the utilitarian goal of the greatest happiness for the greatest number and another leading principle of the Age of Enlightenment, the dignity and equality of man. The three great revolutions which originated in the spirit of Enlightenment—the Glorious Revolution of England, the American Revolution, and the French Revolution—attempted to resolve this conflict by combining the majority principle with that of inalienable human rights. This fusion is reflected in the Bill of Rights of the Glorious Revolution, the *Droits de l'homme* of the French Revolution, and the first ten amendments to the American Constitution.

From Leibniz and Kant to Hegel. The specific contribution of German Enlightenment was its emphasis on the moral aspects of progress. For the central figures of the German Enlightenment, the central issue was not happiness itself, but the striving for perfection—perfection being understood as the moral perfection of mankind, rather than of individual man.

The origin of German Enlightenment philosophy can be traced to Gottfried Wilhelm (Freiherr von) Leibniz (1646–1716), who understood the relationship between God—the central monad—and all individual monads as a prestabilized harmony.[46] Despite the existence of evil, the world, in harmony with God's eternal plan, is as perfect as any world could be. However, this perfection is not static, but is a perpetual, never-ending progress toward absolute perfection of the universe, a progress in which man participates. Leibniz described this process as follows: "Although many substances have already attained a great perfection, yet on account of the infinite divisibility of the continuous, there always remain ... slumbering parts which have yet to be awakened, to grow in size and worth, and in a word, to advance to a more perfect state. And hence no end of progress is ever reached." [47]

Philosopher and poet Gotthold Ephraim Lessing (1729–1781) proclaimed moral progress to be the aim of divine Providence. "Go thine inscrutable way, Eternal Providence," he exclaimed in *The Education of the Human Race*. He viewed the slow pace of Providence as the movement of a "vast slow wheel which brings mankind nearer to this [moral] perfection. . . . It will come, it will surely come, the time of perfection when man . . . will do the good because it is the good." [48]

The foundations of German Enlightenment philosophy were established by Lessing's great contemporary, Immanuel Kant. Kant derived a doctrine of progress from his distinction between pure and practical reason. Whereas pure reason cannot make any meaningful statements about anything that transcends the finite world of appearances, practical reason—that is, moral reason—follows certain postulates which must be considered as moral laws. The most important postulate for the moral world order is Kant's categorical imperative: "So act that the maxim of your will could always hold at the same time as the principle of a universal legislation." [49] Man's will being free, he may or may not act in accordance with this imperative. But whether he does so or not, he is conscious that it would be his duty (*Pflicht*) to do so, an obligation not imposed by an external power or divine will, but derived from man's inner freedom. However, Kant did not consider this concept, close as it comes to Shaftesbury's innate moral sense, as a safe basis for man's progress toward a perfect society. He remained faithful to the deistic belief in divine providence as an instrument of moral progress.

Kant revealed his belief in *Idea for a Universal History from a Cosmopolitan point of view*, in which he also expounded his idea of a League of Nations. [50] In that treatise, he defined the goal of the perfection of society as the achievement of "a universal civic society which administers law among men," and as "a society in which freedom under external laws is associated in the highest degree with irresistible power, that is, a perfectly just civic constitution." In that context, Kant introduced his doctrine of "the secret plan of Nature," which was to play a crucial role in Hegel's system and which also found its way into Marx's system. [51] Although Kant maintained that "Nature has willed that man . . . should partake of no other happiness or perfection than that which he himself, independently of instinct, has created by his own reason," he obviously doubted whether man can be trusted to bring about his perfection solely by his own reason. It was in this context that he fell back on divine Providence, the deistic deus ex machina, who was so often conjured by the writers of the Enlightenment: "The history of mankind can be seen, in the large, as the realization of Nature's secret plan, to bring forth a perfectly constituted state as the only condition in which the capacities of mankind can be fully developed." [52]

While Kant maintained his faith in human progress as leading to the perfecting of society, post-Kantian philosophy in Germany deviated increasingly from this position, but without ever abandoning it entirely. This deviation was already apparent in the writings of Johann Gottfried von Herder (1744–1803). Herder understood progress in a more relativistic way than did the writers of the Enlightenment. In contrast to the rationalism of the Enlightenment, he held that each historical period and each people had its specific character. This theory, which was the starting point of German romanticism, excluded any belief in unilinear progress.[53] However, even Herder, particularly in *Ideen zur Philosophie der Geschichte der Menschheit* (1784–1791),[54] considered history to be a product of divine providence which aims at the development of humanity, with the victory of reason as the ultimate goal.

Johann Gottlieb Fichte (1762–1814) departed even further from Kant's rationalism by his absolute idealism and, in his later years, his mysticism, with its pantheistic tendencies. Thus in *Die Bestimmung des Menschen* ("The vocation of man," 1800) he invoked God as the "sublime will" and stated that "there is a spiritual bond between Him and all finite rational beings, and He Himself is that spiritual bond of the rational universe. . . . This will unite me with Himself. It also unites me with all finite beings like myself and is the universal mediator between us all." Fichte even exclaimed, in words reminiscent of Christian and Islamic mystics, "Sublime and living will! . . . I may well raise my soul to Thee, for Thou and I are not divided!" [55]

Fichte was convinced that "the sublime and living will" planted mankind firmly in this world and, comparable to Kant's vision, through a foreordained world plan is guiding mankind from primitive beginnings toward perfection: "An idea of a foreordered, although only gradually unfolding accomplishment of time, in which each successive period is determined by the preceding . . . presupposes a world-plan." Hence Fichte's link with the Enlightenment was his conviction that the "world-plan," through constant progress, leads mankind from primitive states to perfection, one of whose essential features is "endless peace on earth." Within the continuous progress Fichte distinguished (comparable to Condorcet's ten ages) five ascending epochs, ending with "the age in which humanity with more sure and unerring hand builds itself up into a fitting image and representative of reason." [56]

When Fichte published *The Vocation of Man* in 1800, the world was a battlefield between revolutionary France and the European powers opposed to the French Revolution. But in the midst of this bloody war Fichte looked toward the future of mankind, and he envisioned as the fifth epoch the age of humanity, in which the ideals of the French Revolution would be achieved: Liberty—"The end of the life of mankind on earth is this: that in this life they may order all their relations with freedom, according to reason"; Equality—"In an ideal state all have equal civil privileges or civil freedom . . . all are citizens and subjects in like manner" [57]; Fraternity—"It is the vocation of [the human race] to unite itself into one single body, all the parts of each shall be known to each other, and all possessed of similar culture. . . . We may surely calculate that this end, which is the condition of all farther social progress, will in time be attained." Added to these ideals was that of universal peace (in a more optimistic vein perhaps than Kant): "By reason of the existence of some really free states will the empire of civilization, freedom, and with it, universal peace gradually embrace the whole world." [58]

Thus Fichte always remained faithful to the doctrine of progress toward freedom, equality, and universal peace, as it had evolved in the Age of Enlightenment. In spite of his appeal to the German nation to free itself from French domination,[59] he recognized fully the progress which the French Revolution had brought about.

It was Georg Friedrich Wilhelm Hegel (1770–1831), with his overpowering authority, who diverted the philosophy of progress into idealistic and politically reactionary channels. However, Hegel retained one aspect of the German philosophy of Enlightenment without any transformation: the doctrine of divine Providence as an instrument of progress and, ultimately, of the perfection of society. Kant's "secret plan of Nature" and Fichte's "world-plan" appeared in Hegel's philosophy as "the cunning of reason" (*die List der Vernunft*). While Nature and individual man follow their own aims, they act ultimately as the instruments through which the world-plan is carried out: "This may be called the cunning of reason—that it sets the passions to work for itself." [60]

The world-plan must be understood in the terms of Hegel's idealistic philosophy, which saw all objects as they appear to our senses as being ultimately the manifestations of the "World-spirit" (*Weltgeist*).[61] Hegel understood the history of the world as the unfolding of the Absolute Mind through a process leading from the unconscious (Nature) to the conscious (man), and from primitive stages of human consciousness to its more perfect stages in modern society. His philosophy was thus no less based on the doctrine of a law of progress than was that of the philosophers of the Enlightenment. Even his idealistic interpretation of history as the unfolding of the Absolute Mind did not differ greatly from the widespread belief among the writers of the Enlightenment in a benign Supreme Being who steers mankind in the direction of unending progress.

The distinguishing feature of Hegel's philosophy of progress was his claim to have discovered the law that governs the unfolding process, namely, infinite progress by an infinite number of steps, each of which is characterized by a dialectical process. By propounding this doctrine, he widened the traditional concept of dialectic as a tool of logic. Dialectic was traditionally understood as a method of the discovery of truth of an argument through a three-step procedure: (1) the assertion that an argument is true (thesis); (2) the attempt to refute that assertion or to discover contradictions within it (antithesis); (3) the agreement on a new statement which may constitute a synthesis of the opposing views. Hegel added to this traditional concept the doctrine that the historical process itself, in each of its infinite phases, that is, in the unfolding of the World-Spirit, operates as a three-step dialectical process. In each phase of history, contradictions and conflicts arise which "negate the existing structures, and out of these conflicts a new structure arises." "Spirit is at war with itself," wrote Hegel. "It has to overcome itself as its most formidable obstacle. That development, which in the sphere of Nature is a peaceful growth, is in that of spirit a severe, a mighty conflict with itself." More specifically, "the dialectical nature of the Idea in general" is constituted by the fact that "[the Idea] assumes successive forms which it successfully transcends; and by this very process of transcending its earlier stages, gains an affirmative and in fact a richer and more concrete shape." [62]

While Hegel's doctrine of dialectic was compatible with the idea of human progress, his own understanding of human progress was limited by his equivocal doctrine of freedom. As long as he dealt with freedom in general terms, he cleaved to the concepts of freedom as they had evolved in the Age of Enlightenment. He even elevated these concepts to a transcendental principle: "The substance, the essence of spirit is freedom." The Western nations have attained the consciousness "that man, as man, is free." Consequently, history is a process of the unfolding of freedom: "The history of the world is none other than the progress of the consciousness of freedom." [63]

Hegel was, however, not only a child of the Age of Enlightenment but also of the continental-European counterrevolution that followed the French Revolution. Its influence appeared in the form of a deification of the state, which implied the crushing of the freedom of man as individual: "The State is the divine idea as it exists on earth."[64]

> The state is the actuality of the ethical ideas. It is ethical mind qua the substantial will, manifest and revealed to itself.... Self-consciousness... finds in the state ... its substantive freedom. The state is absolutely rational inasmuch as it is the actuality of the substantial will which it possesses. ... This substantial unity is an absolute end in itself, in which freedom comes into its supreme right. On the other hand, this final end has supreme right against the individual, whose supreme duty is to be a member of the state.[65]

The state, being the final end, has supreme right vis-à-vis the individual. Man's supreme duty is no longer, as Kant had maintained, to obey the moral law, but to obey the state. While the philosophers of the Enlightenment had also conceded that the law of the state takes precedence over individual subjectivity, they had included the condition that the law has been instituted either by the general will of the people or by democratic procedure. But Hegel categorically rejected democracy in favor of absolute monarchy. "Opposed to the sovereignty of the monarch," he stated, "the sovereignty of the people is one of the confused notions based on the wild idea of the 'people.' Taken without its monarch and the articulation of the whole which is the indispensable and direct concomitant of monarchy, the people is a formless mass and no longer a state."[66]

To do justice to Hegel, it should be added that he did not deify all states, regardless of their form and the quality of their rulers. Specifically, he defended not arbitrary monarchic rule, but the rule of "enlightened monarchy." He stated that "[the will of kings] is regarded as deserving of respect only so far as, in association with reason, it wisely contemplates right, justice, and the weal of the community."[67]

Hegel's philosophy had a profound impact on the contemporary world, as an expression of the romantic spirit that prevailed in the first half of the nineteenth century. But its reactionary features, so obviously contrary to the idea of human progress as it was then understood, were bound to arouse a vigorous reaction. The reaction came from the left wing of his disciples and was destined to develop into one of the strongest forces of history, comparable only to the French Revolution in its impact on world history.

4. THE SOCIALIST WING OF HUMANISM

As a contemporary movement, socialism is essentially an offspring of the Age of Enlightenment. It arose in France, one of the leading countries of the Enlightenment, partly as a forerunner of the French Revolution, partly in its aftermath. In the first decades of the nineteenth century the socialist movement was still centered in France, and the revolution of 1848 was strongly influenced by it.

Five years prior to that revolution, the young Karl Heinrich Marx (1818–1883), attracted by the socialist movement of France, spent a short time in Paris and contributed to its literature. Shortly thereafter, the European socialist movement was to become dominated by this great thinker, who blended the political philosophy of the Enlightenment with left-Hegelian ideas, but who at the same time was a dynamic revolutionary activist. Marx himself defined his activism by the famous phrase: "The philosophers have only interpreted the world in various ways; the point, however, is to change it." [68] It was only in the post-World War I period that Western socialism loosened its ties with Marxism and sought new ways of achieving its goals.

The French Socialists. The origins of French socialism can be traced to two little-known writers of the pre-revolutionary period: Morelly and Gabriel Bonnot de Mably. In 1755, Morelly (of whom not even his full name and personal data are known) wrote a treatise which, significantly, was entitled, *Code of Nature or the true Spirit of its Laws always neglected or misunderstood*.[69] The treatise advocated a communist economy, motivated by the doctrine that man is essentially good but corrupted by existing institutions, and the belief that man will again become good through the establishment of a society that would eliminate private property, the principal cause of evil. For his communist society, Morelly proposed that private property be limited to what is necessary for consumption, and that every person be sustained by public funds and work according to his own capabilities.

Gabriel Bonnot de Mably (1709–1785) entitled his principal treatise, *Doubts expressed about the Philosophers-economists concerning the Natural and Essential Order of Society*.[70] The "philosophers-economists" about whose wisdom Mably expressed his doubts were the Physiocrats, whose "natural order" was that of a society guided by the profit incentive and based on the private property of land as the only source of national wealth. In contrast to the natural order of the Physiocrats, which, he maintained, fostered the most vicious egotistical instincts,

Mably advocated an order of equality which would encourage mutual love, the highest human quality. Like Morelli, Mably envisioned a society in which all means of production would be commonly owned and consumers' goods communally distributed.

Until the French Revolution, however, the socialist version of the concepts of freedom and equality was still uncommon. The peasants in the country, the craftsmen in the towns, the businessmen in the cities all wanted not to communalize their land and enterprises, but rather to liberate them from feudal and monarchical fetters. Socialist ideas began to spread and to arouse men to concrete action only under the impact of the Revolution itself. A genuine revolutionary, François Noël (Gracchus) Babeuf (1760–1797) became the first fighter for, and martyr of, the modern socialist cause.

Babeuf was not a theoretical thinker. He represented a blend of journalist and political activist that later became important in the propagation of socialist and communist ideas. In the journal *Défenseur de la liberté de la presse* ("Defender of the freedom of the press"), which he founded in 1794 and later rebaptized *Le tribun du peuple* ("The tribune of the people"),[71] Babeuf advocated absolute equality of incomes and attacked the economic inequalities which had survived, or even emerged from, the Revolution. The political group he founded was called the "Society of the Equal Ones" (*Société des égaux*). In 1796, planning to take revolutionary action against the Directoire, he had posters put up in the streets of Paris announcing that "Nature has given to every man the right to enjoyment of an equal share in all property." Soon afterwards Babeuf's conspiracy against the Directoire was discovered and he was executed.

Babeuf was a revolutionary who interpreted literally the promise of equality the French Revolution had inscribed on its banner. But he did not advocate terror or dictatorship, having himself witnessed their effects in the course of the Revolution. On the contrary, he advocated the implementation of the democratic Constitution of 1793, which, before it had even been put into effect, had fallen victim to the Comité National du Salut. Hence, Babeuf, in spite of his reputation as a terrorist extremist, should be regarded as a democratic socialist humanist.

In the period of reaction against the French Revolution—which began with the Directoire and ended with the Second French Revolution of 1830—socialist humanism developed on what Marx and Engels called a utopian basis, which was, however, rich in ideas that were eventually to come to fruition. The most important figures of that stage of the socialist movement were, in France, Saint-Simon (Claude Henri, comte de

Rouvrai, 1760–1825) and François Marie Charles Fourier (1772–1837), and in England, Robert Owen (1771–1858). Saint-Simon was inspired by the vision of an organized and planned industrial economy, in which competition among industrialists and among farmers would be replaced by cooperation among industrialists, farmers, scientists, and workers, designed to enhance the commonweal through scientifically organized production. There would be no differences in social standing, only differences in economic functions and capabilities. The state would lose all but its administrative functions.[72] Later, more strictly socialist ideas were propagated by the Saint-Simonists, while Saint-Simon's planning ideas were not revived until the contemporary economic era.

The utopias which Fourier and Owen envisioned were in fact cooperative schemes. These two utopians may be regarded as spiritual fathers of the cooperative movement—Fourier being more of a visionary, Owen, more of an activist. What Fourier envisioned as a harmonious society was a system of producers' cooperatives. The units of that economic system, the "phalanges," were to be producers' cooperatives of a moderate size (1600 persons), each of which would occupy a housing unit (*phalanstère*). Within the phalange, class distinctions (between capitalists, directors, and workers) would be partly eradicated by the workers' contributions to the capital outlay of the phalange. In any case, the profit from the capital invested in the phalange was to be distributed among the three productive factors.[73]

Robert Owen was a man of humanist social ideals which he fought for untiringly, endeavored to realize through his own action, and for which he sacrificed his sizable fortune. A wealthy manufacturer who had personally witnessed the misery of the English working class,[74] Owen initiated and carried out social schemes in his own factory, propagated a number of social reforms, and proposed a plan to establish cooperative communities that would be financed by the state. The unit of the community was considered to be the foundation of the economic system. Each community was to comprise about 1,200 persons and to remunerate its members on the basis of labor-time, which anticipated Marx's doctrine of labor-time as the basis of value. When the public authorities failed to respond to his plan, Owen financed a project in the United States (New Harmony in Indiana, from 1825 to 1828), whose failure cost him his fortune. Yet he continued with his social work and was closely connected with the early British trade unions. Owen's followers formed some producers' cooperatives; and his ideas prepared the ground for the Rochdale Pioneers, the founders of the modern cooperative movement.

In France, in the interval between the revolutions of 1830 and 1848, a new generation of socialist writers and activists arose, the most prominent of whom were (Jean-Joseph Charles) Louis Blanc (1811–1882), Pierre-Joseph Proudhon (1809–1865), and Louis Auguste Blanqui (1805–1884). In his magazine *Revue du Progrès*, founded in 1839, Louis Blanc printed his treatise *L'organisation du travail* ("The organization of labor") which advocated a kind of communal socialism, based on a communist principle which he formulated in the famous phrase: "To each according to his needs, from each according to his abilities." This principle was to be realized by way of social workshops (*Ateliers sociaux*) whose initial capital would be advanced by interest-free loans and whose profits would be distributed to the workers for social schemes, reinvestments, and investments in other social workshops. Blanc's ideas became popular in France, particularly when he broadened them to include "the right to work," that is, the principle of full employment. In the revolution of 1848, he played a prominent role as a member of the revolutionary government which he committed to adopting and implementing the right to work. The government created national workshops, which amounted to public works for the unemployed. But, as the French economy was poorly organized at that time, the experiment failed. Disappointed workers rebelled; and Blanc fled to England.

When Marx moved to Paris in 1843, the leading socialist writer there was Pierre Joseph Proudhon. Although the ideas of these two thinkers soon clashed, they were alike in certain respects. Proudhon in *What is Property?* (1840)—a question to which he gave the now-famous answer: "Property is theft" [75]—derived his condemnation of capitalist property from the same doctrine of the exploitation of labor by capital which Marx later adopted. Moreover, in his *System of Economic Contradictions or the Philosophy of Misery* (1846), Proudhon started from the same left-Hegelian doctrine of the contradictions in capitalist society as did Marx. Finally, Proudhon's view that all persons should be equally remunerated for their work on the basis of time worked was akin to Marx's doctrine of labor value.

On the other hand, Proudhon's ideas of economic structure differed from those held by Marx. "Mutualism," the system Proudhon advocated, resembled those of the other utopians of his era: An "exchange bank" would grant interest-free credits to the worker-producers and would buy and distribute the goods and services produced by them. One of the principal features of Proudhon's mutualism was the absence of any role for the state. All economic transactions involved in this system would be between the bank, the producers, and the consumers. In 1849,

Proudhon was involved in the founding of such a *Banque du Peuple*, but it failed. He showed great courage during the revolution of 1848, contributing articles to radical journals and, as a member of the Constituent Assembly, proposing a steep tax on rents and interests. From 1849 to 1852, he was imprisoned for his revolutionary activities.

Marx was critical of Proudhon's *System of Economic Contradictions*; and, even in that early stage of the socialist movement, a deep split arose over the methods through which a socialist society should be achieved. Proudhon was an avowed anarchist;[76] Marx was also an anarchist with respect to the ultimate societal goals. But while Proudhon rejected the use of violence both by the government and partisans of anarchist socialism, Marx regarded revolution, even violent revolution, as an indispensable instrument for profound structural change. His anti-Proudhonist essay, *The Poverty of Philosophy*,[77] revealed this clash in the doctrines of the two socialists. Georges Sorel (1847–1922) related that, in a letter to Marx in 1846, Proudhon rejected force as a means for achieving socialism. The last sentence in Marx's *Poverty of Philosophy* asserted that in any transformation of society, the final word is "combat or death, bloody struggle or extinction." [78]

Of all the French socialists, Louis August Blanqui most consistently and actively fought for the cause of freedom and equality, and he frequently paid for his revolutionary activities with his own freedom. Early in his life, he concluded that the socialist ideals could be achieved only by revolutionary force and dictatorial power. At that time he joined the Carbonari.[79] In the revolution of 1830 he fought on the barricades and —literally—unfurled the red banner of revolution. Cofounder of a secret society which organized a coup in 1839, he was sentenced to death after its collapse, but was later amnestied. In the following decades, he was in and out of prison (over a period of more than forty years), hailed by his followers as *le martyre*. Blanquism is still part of the French political scene. Blanqui's followers remained organized throughout the numerous splits in the French socialist movement and were one of the two constituent groups that merged in 1905 to form the Parti Socialist Unifié under the leadership of Jean Jaurès.

Marx and Engels. The writings and activities of the French socialists made a profound impression on the young left-Hegelian scholar and activist Karl Marx and strengthened his socialist convictions. He blended the impulses received from the French socialists with those he received from his upbringing in the atmosphere of Hegelianism. To the socialist movement that was growing in Western Europe, he contributed two new elements derived from a transformation of Hegel's philosophy—the concept of alienation and the doctrine of the dialectical process of history —which were to become of decisive importance for the movement. For Marx, these two concepts became indispensable tools for analyzing and criticizing the capitalist society, reasons for its overthrow, and vehicles to bring about a socialist society.

Hegel's concept of alienation was one of the dialectical forms in which the process of the unfolding of the World-Spirit can be understood. By creating Nature, the World-Spirit alienates himself from himself. The process of man's acquiring self-consciousness and the evolution of history is a process of overcoming the original alienation. Marx demystified Hegel's concept of alienation by transforming it into a sociological concept: In the capitalist society the worker is alienated from the product of his work. In a manuscript written in 1844,[80] Marx stated that in the capitalist society "the worker is related to the product of his labour as to an alien object" and "sinks to the level of a commodity." The manuscript analyzed in detail the alienation, devaluation, and externalization of labor in the capitalist society.

From this concept of alienation the young Marx derived his conviction that the workers would strive for emancipation from the capitalist yoke: "The emancipation of society from private property is expressed in its political forms as the emancipation of workers. . . . In their emancipation is contained the universal human emancipation." In *Private Property and Communism*, he defined communism as "positive overcoming of private property as self-alienation . . . therefore as the complete and conscious restoration of man to himself . . . as a social, that is, human being. This communism . . . is humanism."[81]

In later years, Marx concentrated his fight against capitalism on the economic aspects of the capitalist system: the exploitation of the worker through the employer's appropriation of part of the value created by the worker, as well as the creation of an "army of the unemployed," which further depresses workers' living standards. However, in the same fundamental work *Das Kapital* in which Marx analyzed the economic aspects of capitalism, the concept of alienation also found its proper place. In the capitalist society the products of the worker's labor appear as commodities which have assumed an objective character: "A commodity is . . . a mysterious thing, simply because in it the social character of men's labour appears to them as an objective character stamped upon the product of that labour." The products of labor are reified: "There is a definite social relation between men that assumes, in their eyes, the fantastic form of a relation between things." In this reification of the social relations between men, in this "fetishism of commodities," as Marx termed it,[82] the alienation of the worker is crystallized. It would require the transformation of society into "a community of free individuals, carrying on their work with the means of production in common, in which the labour-power of all the different individuals is consciously applied as the combined labour-power of the community" to dissolve the fetishist character of social relations between men and to liberate them from alienation.

The second Hegelian doctrine that Marx transformed was that of the dialectical evolution. Here again he undertook a process of demystification, taking the Hegelian doctrine of the dialectical nature of the universe and of its evolution and turning it from its metaphysical head "rightside up again." [83] He transformed this Hegelian doctrine into one of historical evolution which he termed "historical materialism" (*materialistische Geschichtsauffassung*), in contrast to Hegel's idealism.

Historical materialism was first expressed in writing in 1845, in Friedrich Engels's and Karl Marx's joint essay, *The Holy Family*.[84] Marx had met Friedrich Engels (1820–1895) first in Cologne and later in Paris; and Engels became his lifelong friend, collaborator, and popularizer. Their essay contained a fundamental aspect of historical materialism, namely, the doctrine that the economic relations constitute the basis of society on which the juridical, political, and spiritual relations and institutions rest as a superstructure. In *The Poverty of Philosophy*, Marx elaborated on this aspect of historical materialism, making men's productive forces the prime element to which the social relations between men correspond, and contending that changes in the productive forces are the dynamic element for changes in social relations, on which, in turn, the superstructure rests. By productive forces he meant the techniques of the economic process, and consequently he considered technological change as the dynamic factor in social relations: "The handmill gives you society with the feudal lord; the steam mill, society with the industrial capitalist." The social relations determine the ideological structure of society: "The same men who establish their social relations in conformity with their material productivity, produce also principles, ideas and categories in conformity with their social relations." [85]

In 1848, Marx, together with Engels, wrote *The Communist Manifesto*, a document that was destined to revolutionize the world. *The Communist Manifesto* was not intended to be a scientific treatise, but the political programme of the Communist League, a small socialist group with a central committee in London and branches in a few other European countries.[86] But while *The Communist Manifesto* was conceived as a beacon for the international socialist movement, it was also an important sociological document, based on a historical analysis from the point of view of historical materialism. Its chief thesis was that the modern productive forces are revolting against the property relations that are the conditions for the existence and power of the bourgeoisie. Moreover, the manifesto pointed to economic depressions—which have continued to disturb the capitalist economy from its early days—as a symptom of the contradictions which plague capitalist society. In this situation, the class struggles between bourgeoisie and proletariat become a dynamic force that determines history at the moment when the revolt of the productive forces against the existing economic and social relations becomes strong enough to force a decisive change upon society.

Marx formulated the doctrine of historical materialism more comprehensively in the preface to *A Contribution to the Critique of Political Economy*,[87] which in effect constituted an outline of *Das Kapital*. In this preface, Marx stated:

> In the social production of their life men enter into definite relations that are indispensable and independent of their will, productive relationships which correspond to a definite stage of development of their material productive forces. The sum total of these relations of production constitutes the economic structure of society, the real foundation on which rises a legal and political superstructure and to which correspond definitive forms of social consciousness. The mode of production of material life conditions the social, political and intellectual life process in general. . . . At a certain stage of their development the material productive forces of society come in conflict with the existing relations of production. . . . From forms of development of the productive forces these relations turn into their fetters. Then begins an epoch of social revolution. With the change of the economic foundation the entire immense superstructure is more or less rapidly transformed. In considering such transformations a distinction should be made between the material transformation of the economic conditions of production . . . and the legal, political, religious, esthetic or philosophic—in a word, ideological forms in which men become conscious of this conflict and fight it out.

The Communist Manifesto was not only the first work in which Marx expounded the fundamental elements of historical materialism; it was, above all, the first socialist programme to claim that the socialist movement could, and should, rest on a scientific basis. Historical materialism was to reveal the necessity of the socialist revolution as the end product of the revolt of the rapidly developing productive forces against economic and social relations that fettered them. At the same time, historical materialism was to reveal that the working class would acquire the will and the power to revolutionize society, since the capitalist economy was transforming the overwhelming majority of the population into proletarians. "The proletarian movement is the self-conscious, independent movement of the immense majority, in the interest of the immense majority." The rise of the proletariat, in turn, is bound to produce the revolution. "The proletariat, the lowest stratum of our present society, cannot stir, cannot raise itself up, without the whole superincumbent strata of official society being sprung into the air." Historical materialism claims to prove the inevitability of this revolution. "What the bourgeoisie ... produces, above all, are its own gravediggers. Its fall and the victory of the proletariat are equally inevitable."

The Communist Manifesto outlined the evolution of society subsequent to the revolution: (1) The proletariat will make itself the ruling class—a vague formula, interpretable either as a dictatorship of the proletariat or, since the proletariat would constitute the immense popular majority, as the democratic rule of the majority;[88] (2) The supremacy of the working class will be transitory, for its revolution cannot have any other result but that of sweeping away all classes; (3) The classless society that the victorious proletariat will create will be an association of free people; (4) The state, which in all class-ruled societies is an instrument of the ruling classes, will lose this function, as a corollary of the disappearance of the classes. "When ... class distinctions have disappeared and all production has been concentrated in the hands of a vast association of the whole nation, the public power will lose its political character."

Marx has often been reproached for having failed to produce any concrete programme for the functioning of a socialist economy. In fact, however, *The Communist Manifesto* contained a blueprint of the measures which a revolutionary regime would be likely to adopt, such as: abolition of property of land; centralization of credit and of the means of communication and transport; a steeply progressive income tax; abolition of the right to inheritance; equal obligation of everyone to work; combination of agriculture with manufacturing industries; free education of all children in public schools; and integration of education into the industrial production. Parts of this programme were characteristic of an early stage of socialism, but all the measures envisaged were conceived as transitional devices. The fundamental goal of the communist movement was to establish "an association in which the free development of each is the condition for the development of all."

Thus the revolutionary spirit of *The Communist Manifesto* was based on a profoundly humanist ideal: the free development of each individual, which is prevented by the social relations characteristic of the capitalist society, namely, the exploitation of the worker, the transformation of labor into a commodity, the alienation of man from his work, and the depersonalization of the relation of man to the goods he produces and consumes. The same humanist spirit manifested itself in the General Rules of the First International (International Workingmen's Association), which were also written by Marx. The rules stated that "all societies and individuals adhering to [the International Workingmen's Association] will acknowledge truth, justice and morality as the basis of their conduct towards each other and towards all men, without regard to colour, creed, or nationality."[89]

The foundations of Marx's thoughts were thus clearly revealed in all his writings, beginning with those of his early youth and culminating in *Das Kapital*. There was, on the one hand, the heritage of the radical wing of the Age of Enlightenment, reflected in the profoundly humanist ideal of the perfect society as a society of equals, a human community without classes and class antagonisms, and without the coercive force of the state. There was, on the other hand, the heritage of the Hegelian philosophy, which supplied the specific form to Marx's doctrine of the evolution of human society.

In Marx's philosophy of history, in particular, certain fundamental elements of Hegelian philosophy can still be detected, in spite of their radical transformation. Hegel's "ideas" were replaced by the productive forces of society. The World-Spirit, with His cunning of reason, was replaced by the dialectical course of history, with its own cunning. In the dialectical drama of history, the thesis was constituted by the productive forces; the antithesis, by the contradictions between productive forces and social relations which necessarily arise at a certain stage of the development of the productive forces; and the synthesis, by the new society that emerges from the revolution and resolves these contradictions.

Hence Marx saw each stage in the history of mankind as a dialectical process. He emphasized the determinism involved in this doctrine by his assertion that the social relations between men are necessary and independent of the human will, and that social existence determines men's consciousness. The dialectical process between productive forces and social relations shapes the juridical, political, and cultural superstructure, thereby determining the course of history. The philosophies of Hegel and Marx were also analogous with respect to the end product of the historical process. According to Hegel, the end product would be the ultimate realization of the World-Spirit in a perfect society. According to

Marx, the end product would be the classless society, realized by the victory of the proletariat.

Thus both Hegel and Marx, each in his own way, remained faithful to the doctrine of progress that had prevailed in the Age of Enlightenment. Far from denying Enlightenment laws of progress, historical materialism was an attempt to give these laws a firm foundation by revealing the mechanism through which they work. Each of the successive systems of economic relations constitutes progress over the preceding one: "The Asiatic, the ancient, the feudal, and the modern bourgeois modes of production can be indicated as progressive epochs in the economic system of society." [90]

The millenarian note in this concept of progress should not be overlooked: Each step from one structure of society to the next is the outcome of a gigantic class struggle, comparable to the struggles prophesied in the Jewish-Christian apocalypses. The end product of the historical process will be a perfect society, free from oppression and from the antagonisms which have plagued all historical societies—in other words, the secularized form of the kingdom of God.

When confronted with the realities of world history, historical materialism shares the difficulties faced by all philosophies of history: it attempts to reduce to strict laws something that defies any law. Marx's great contribution to the understanding of the dynamics of society was that, in an age of tremendous technological, economic and social change, he was the first to draw attention to the role played by the technological, economic, and social structure of society. However, whether the productive forces have ever been the sole determining factor in the economic and social structure of society and the principal determining factor in its juridical, political, and culture structure cannot be proved. The primitive watermill (to use Marx's example) served ancient as well as feudal societies; modern turbine-driven mills are used in both free-enterprise and communist societies. Social relations are certainly reflected in the juridical, legal, and political structures of all societies, but that does not imply that they unilaterally determine that structure. There are numerous examples in history of social relations that were determined by other, above all political, factors. Modern history abounds in examples where political forces determined economic and social relations without having themselves resulted from a conflict between productive forces and social relations.

The Russian and Chinese revolutions offer perhaps the best examples of the impact of political forces on social structures. According to Marxist doctrine, these two revolutions, arising in countries that had a prevailing feudal structure with a thin capitalist veneer, should have resulted in the rise of capitalist societies. Yet although Lenin and Mao Tse-tung were fervent Marxists, the revolutions they directed defied the historical law of their teacher. Instead, these two revolutionary leaders proved that ideas fermenting in the minds of men can acquire such an overwhelming force as to be able to determine economic, social, political, juridical, and cultural structures.

Thus the claim of Marx and Engels to have based the socialist movement on a scientific foundation cannot be proved; no religious or secular movement promising salvation or a perfect society can prove a claim to have discovered the necessity of that happening. Nevertheless, historical experience shows that movements can be greatly assisted by claims that they rest on scientific or other rational grounds. The history of the socialist movement constitutes a classical case of the power which claims of this kind can exert, however problematic their foundation. The tremendous impetus the socialist movement received from *The Communist Manifesto* and from the later writings of Marx, Engels, and their disciples was undoubtedly a strong contributing factor in the transformation of capitalist societies into Western welfare states and of preindustrial Eastern societies into communist states.

The impact of Marx's doctrines and personality was so strong that socialist movements everywhere accepted his doctrines and for generations remained faithful to their spirit, even while modifying their content and while being subjected to other influences. There was, however, one element in Marxist doctrines which quickly became a source of discord within the socialist movement and has divided it to the present time. This was Marx's concept of the nature of the socialist revolution. As noted, this discord had already appeared in the correspondence between Marx and Proudhon and in Marx's *Poverty of Philosophy*. The anarchist Proudhon rejected force as a weapon for achieving socialism, while Marx resigned himself to "bloody struggle" as the only way of transforming society.

After the defeat of the liberal and socialist forces in the French, German, and Austrian revolutions of 1848, an attempt was made to revive the idea—which had inspired the Communist League and its *Communist Manifesto*[91]—of an international alliance of all socialist forces. When the International Workingmen's Association was formed, Marx won its leaders over to his concept of the socialist revolution. The General Council of the International, at its meeting in 1864, approved the General Rules, drawn up by Marx, and the first Congress of the International (Geneva, 1866) adopted them. These rules stated that the proletariat would act as a class "to ensure the triumph of the social revolution and of its ultimate goal, the abolition of classes" and that "the conquest of political power becomes the great duty of the proletariat."[92]

Within the International, the conflict between Marxists and Proudhonists flared up again over the issue of using force to change the society. After the death of Proudhon, his disciple Mikhail Aleksandrovich Bakunin (1814–1876) took up the banner of anarchism. An anarchist activist in his native Russia, Bakunin had become a member of the revolutionary government in Dresden in 1849. He was condemned to death and extradited to Russia, but had been able to flee to Western Europe. Although Bakunin's goal was to achieve a socialist economy and classless society, he was opposed to the seizure of political power by the victorious proletariat, that is, to the institution of a new governing authority, even in a transition period. He insisted that the socialist society be built on local communal groupings rather than on any central authority.

In 1868, Bakunin organized the International Alliance of Socialist Democracy, which quickly found followers in the Latin countries of Europe—Italy, Spain, Belgium and the French part of Switzerland.[93] Bakunin's organization joined the International at its Basel Congress of 1869 in an attempt to gain control. Three years later, at the Hague Congress of the International, Marxists and Bakuninists fought openly for control of the organization. While the Bakuninists were expelled, the headquarters of the International were transferred to New York, marking the end of the first attempt to found an international organization of the socialist movement.

The anarchist movement continued its existence within the Latin countries of Europe. After the First World War, it was temporarily strengthened by its fusion with syndicalist trade organizations, which were based on doctrines similar to those of the anarchists. But anarcho-syndicalism was dealt a severe setback by the Spanish civil war of 1936–1939. With Franco's victory in Spain and the fascist regime in Italy still in power, the strength of anarchism was exhausted, and has never since been regained.

The split between socialism and anarchism apparently induced Marx and Engels to modify their views on the way in which a stateless society would be achieved. Shortly after the split with the anarchists, Marx, in *Critique of the Gotha Programme* (1875), introduced a doctrine of two phases of the communist society, a doctrine which was to become an important element of official communist ideology. The doctrine asserted that, even after all capitalist income had been abolished, in the initial phase of communism, no genuine equality of incomes would be achieved. The communist economy would still be based on factors making for inequality of incomes. It was only in a later, higher phase of communist society—after the enslaving subordination of individuals to the division of labor had vanished; after labor, from being a mere means of life, had become the prime necessity of life; and after the productive forces had increased with the development of individuals—that the narrow horizon of bourgeois right would be left behind and society would inscribe on its banner, "From each according to his ability, to each according to his needs." [94] In other words, the perfect society, as Louis Blanc had envisioned it, would not automatically emerge from the socialist revolution, but would be the end product of a social and economic development affecting the nature of work and the productivity of labor.

His two-stage doctrine did not lead Marx to the conclusion that the disappearance of the state would have to await the perfection of the communist economy. But Engels did conclude that the vanishing of the state could be expected only as the result of a—presumably slow—process, for which he used the famous phrase, the "withering away" of the state. Confronted with the anarchists' insistence that the socialist revolution abolish the state and create a stateless system, Engels declared that "as soon as class rule, and the individual struggle for existence based upon the present anarchy in production . . . are removed, nothing more remains to be held in subjection—nothing necessitating a special coercive force, a state." But he qualified this prediction by adding: "State interference in social relations becomes, in one domain after the other, superfluous, and then dies down of itself. . . . The state is not abolished. It withers away." [95]

This retreat from the ideal of a perfectly egalitarian, stateless society served the communists as a justification for their own form of the socialist community. While the entire socialist movement rejected the anarchist ideal of the abolition of the state in the wake of the socialist revolution, the split between socialism and anarchism was replaced by a split between the socialist and communist movements over the methods of acquisition of power and the subsequent nature of the state.

The Communist Version of Marxism. As was noted, the communist revolution in Russia (and subsequently in China) contradicted the predictions of historical materialism. Furthermore, the authoritarian state that arose from the revolution was contrary to the humanist spirit of Marxism. When the Bolsheviks took power in November 1917, eighty-five percent of the Russian population were peasants. It is true that workers were the leading force in the soviets of Petrograd and Moscow, which constituted the spearhead of the Bolshevik revolution. But the November upheaval was the product not of a revolt of the industrial productive forces against the thinly spread capitalist class, but of hunger, societal disintegration, and a longing for peace after a succession of military defeats and the disorganization of the Russian state machinery. None of the criteria that historical materialism had established for the outbreak of a socialist revolution applied. If there were a socioeconomic motive for revolution, it was the land hunger of the peasants. Indeed, they began to appropriate feudal estates months before the communist revolution succeeded. The first act of the Soviet government, one day after the seizure of power, was to issue a decree giving all land to the peasants without payment or rent. The expropriation of industrial and commercial enterprises proceeded much more slowly. It took more than seven months until all large industrial and commercial enterprises were nationalized. One of the great paradoxes of history is that Lenin (Vladimir Ilyich Ulyanov, 1870–1924), who had been one of the most faithful partisans of historical materialism,[96] led a revolution that refuted the laws under which, according to historical materialism, a socialist revolution would occur.

After Marx and Engels had modified their original anarchist ideal of the stateless society, Lenin had to go only one step further to interpret Marx's two-phase doctrine as meaning that the disappearance of the state had to await the higher phase of the communist society. After having quoted Engels's phrase of the gradual withering away of the state and Marx's two-phase doctrine, Lenin concluded: "Until the 'higher' phase of communism arrives, the socialists demand the strictest control by society and by the state over the measure of labour and the measure of consumption. . . . Communism in its first phase retains 'the narrow horizon of bourgeois right.' Of course, bourgeois right in regard to the distribution of consumer goods inevitably presupposes the existence of the bourgeois state." Yet the statement which he made about the continuation of the "bourgeois state" was still based on the conviction that the end product of the socialist revolution would be a stateless society: "The dictatorship of the proletariat . . . will for the first time produce democracy for the people. . . . Communism alone is capable of giving a really complete democracy, and the more complete it is, the more quickly will it become unnecessary and wither away of itself."[97]

There is no reason to doubt the sincerity of Lenin's conviction. He was intent upon establishing a political system in which workers and peasants would rule. He was also aware of the danger that the bureaucracy might overwhelm the workers' democracy.[98] Yet, within his lifetime, his hope that, after a transitional period, the communist revolution would produce a non-authoritarian, classless society, was shattered. In all countries in which the communist revolution succeeded, it has, while annihilating the old ruling classes, produced a hierarchy of new classes in which the political leadership and the upper echelons of the bureaucracy, technocracy, and military rule autocratically over all other classes. This development has been recognized, not only from outside the communist orbit, but also from within,[99] particularly by critics who originally played a major role in the system, but who later were either defeated in power struggles, such as Leon Trotsky (b. 1879, assassinated 1940) in the Soviet Union, or who rebelled, such as Milovan Djilas (b. 1911) in Yugoslavia.[100]

In the Soviet Union, no efforts have ever been made to change this rigid elitist system. When reform efforts were made in certain Soviet bloc countries (Hungary and Czechoslovakia), they were crushed by the Soviet power. Communist countries which have loosened their ties to the Soviet Union (Rumania), or even severed them (Yugoslavia, Albania, China), nonetheless retain authoritarian governments.

In societies that consist of upper and lower classes whose social, economic, and political status differs considerably, the state cannot be reduced from an instrument of power to a purely administrative organ. Moreover, state power is used not only within a class-structured society, but also in relations between states. This holds true for communist societies no less than for other societies. Not only has state power (particularly military power) remained an essential element in the relations between communist and noncommunist states; even in relations among communist countries, military state power has constantly been used. It was, as noted, used twice by the Soviet Union against satellite states and is permanently in evidence along the Soviet-Chinese border.

The class and military structure of communist states does not necessarily produce an authoritarian system. It remains, nevertheless, a historical fact that all communist societies have evolved and continued under authoritarian rule and that, in those communist countries in which democratizing tendencies surfaced, the overpowering military superiority of the Soviet Union was used to crush these tendencies. The humanist ideal of freedom that inspired the founders of Marxist socialism, Marx's conviction that socialism would replace the reign of slavery with a reign of freedom and the exploitation of man by man with a free association of free men—these visions have remained unfulfilled in communist countries. Proudhon's and Bakunin's warnings that dictatorship has always a tendency to perpetuate itself and that therefore communist dictatorship is bound to defeat the true goal of the communist movement

—the liberation of mankind from class rule—have so far proved more correct than Marx's hope that the communist revolution, despite its dictatorial beginnings, would pave the way for "humanity's leap from the realm of necessity into the realm of freedom." [101]

West European Socialism. When the Bolsheviks seized power in Russia in November 1917, they destroyed not a bourgeois state, but the semi-feudal czarist system which the revolution of March 1917 had begun to dismantle. The socialist movements of the European industrial countries emerged under entirely different conditions. While semi-feudal and absolutist institutions still existed in some European industrial countries, "bourgeois states," with their system of democratic rule, were on the rise everywhere. This new political order presented the socialist parties with a genuine alternative between a policy aiming at the conquest of the state machinery by democratic means and a policy aiming at the revolutionary destruction of the state machinery and the creation of a dictatorship of the proletariat. A struggle went on continuously between the advocates of these two policies. In the period that ended with the outbreak of the First World War, the pendulum swung several times between those who advocated the moderate course of democratic acquisition of power and those who advocated a revolutionary course; but, in the end, the democratic wing of the socialist movement was victorious.

The German Social Democratic Party of that period, the most powerful socialist aspirant for the conquest of state power, exemplifies the conflict between the two contending wings of the socialist movement. The party originated from a merger of the General German Workers' Organization founded in 1863 under the leadership of Ferdinand Lassalle (1825–1864), and the Social Democratic Workers' Party formed in 1869 under August Bebel (1840–1913). Lassalle was a pre-Marxist socialist who sought to create a socialist commonwealth by democratic means, through a fight for universal suffrage.[102] Bebel, a faithful Marxist, adhered to the doctrine of the revolutionary conquest of power. Yet, the Social Democrats accepted the Lassallean doctrines at the merger congress (Gotha, 1875): the "Gotha Programme" was based on the determination of the new party to come to power by democratic means. Marx was strongly opposed to this turn of events, which ran counter to his political views. In the *Critique of the Gotha Programme*, he insisted on the indispensability of a revolutionary dictatorship of the proletariat. But he could not sway the German party.

The pendulum swung back at the Congress of Erfurt (1891), partly under the impact of Chancellor Bismarck's ban on the socialist movement (1878–1890), which had driven the party underground. The "Erfurt Programme" eliminated the Lassallean features of the "Gotha Programme." Soon afterward, however, the party's revolutionary policy was challenged by a new movement opposed to historical materialism and the doctrine of revolution. Instead, it advocated immediate social reforms and the gradual development of a socialist society by ongoing reforms and coalitions with other progressive parties. The most prominent representative of this doctrine, called Revisionism, was Eduard Bernstein (1850–1932), who propounded his theory in *Evolutionary Socialism* (1899).[103] Bernstein's views were in turn challenged by Karl Kautsky (1854–1938), the principal representative of the Marxist position, in *Bernstein und das Sozialdemokratische Programm* (1899).

However, in spite of its Marxist revolutionary majority, and its strong organization, devoted membership, and impressive strength at elections, the party failed to adopt any of the revolutionary strategies—such as organizing a general strike—that were advocated by a radical wing under the leadership of Karl Liebknecht (1871–1919) and Rosa Luxemburg (1870–1919). This radical wing was to form the nucleus of the German Communist party (under the name of *Spartakusbund*) during the First World War. Luxemburg and Liebknecht, outstanding socialist thinkers in their own right, became martyrs of their revolutionary convictions when they were murdered in January 1919 by reactionary military volunteer groups during a postwar Communist uprising.

Literally from one day to the next, the outbreak of the First World War changed the structure of the socialist movement, not only in Germany, but also in the other European industrial countries. Until that time, the European socialist parties had increasingly opposed the continuous build-up of armaments and the military and diplomatic preparations for war. In their respective countries and at congresses of the International,[104] they had debated using the general strike as a means of acquiring political power and preventing the outbreak of a world conflagration. Yet these intentions were swept away by the outbreak of the war. This happened primarily because, sixty-six years after *The Communist Manifesto* declared that the workers had nothing to lose but their chains, the economic, social, and political conditions of the workers had improved to such a degree that they had acquired a share in the welfare and security of their nations. Therefore, when these were threatened by enemies, the socialist parties of the belligerent countries decided to support the war efforts of their own governments.

This turnabout was not approved by all wings of the socialist movement, resulting in splits, during and after the war, within socialist parties

and the International. The most radical wing of the socialist parties—
largely under the impact of the communist revolution in Russia—
formed communist parties and a communist International.[105] Thus the
advocates of the Marxist doctrine of a socialist revolution and the dictatorship of the proletariat separated themselves definitively from advocates of a democratic transition to a socialist society. This break also
signaled a substantive change in the ideological basis of the democratic
wing of the socialist movement. Rapidly or slowly, tacitly or openly,
socialist parties abandoned the tenets of historical materialism of the
dialectical evolution of society that would culminate in the proletarian
revolution and the destruction of the capitalist state machinery. This
meant a retreat from the millenarian vision of Marxism that—through
troubles and tribulations, intensified class antagonism and class wars,
and a profound social revolution—an everlasting reign of freedom and
welfare, peace and brotherhood, would dawn.

On the other hand, the retreat from millenarianism enabled the socialist movement to concentrate on the humanist aspects of the socialist
ideal that had constituted an intrinsic feature of the early socialist writers,
including Marx and Engels, and that had its roots in the Age of Enlightenment. Socialism was understood as a movement which, in con-
junction with the ideals of liberty and fraternity, emphasizes the ideal of
fullest social justice.

No more significant and dignified pronouncement of the humanist
nature of the post-Marxist socialist movement could be found than the
Declaration of Principle, adopted by the Founding Congress of the Socialist International in Frankfurt in 1951:[106] "The Socialists fight for a
world of peace in freedom, for a world which proscribes the exploitation and enslavement of men by men and of peoples by peoples, a world
in which the development of the personality of the individual is the prerequisite for the fruitful development of mankind as a whole." Thus the
socialist movement has returned to its heritage of the humanist movements of the Age of Enlightenment and has become one of those currents
of modern humanism that emphasize the development of the human
personality, the safeguarding of human rights, and the progress of social
justice.

New Trends in West European Communism. The communist move
ments in the industrial democratic countries have undergone changes that
to a certain extent parallel those in the socialist camp. Outside the Soviet
bloc there are only two European industrial countries, France and Italy,
in which communist parties are mass movements. In both countries,

they have gradually assumed features of democratic parties, in that they are ready to participate, like all other parties, in the governments, even in coalitions with other parties.

In France, the Communist party adopted democratic tactics for the first time in the period from 1936 to 1938 by concluding an alliance—the Popular Front—with the Socialists and the Radical-Socialists.[107] While the Communists remained outside the government, formed by the Socialists and Radical-Socialists under the premiership of Socialist leader Leon Blum (1872–1950), they supported it and thus ensured its existence. The Popular Front government undertook comprehensive social reforms within the limits of the existing economic and social order. Immediately after the Second World War, from 1945 to 1947, the Communist party joined a coalition government under the premiership of General Charles de Gaulle (1890–1970). Through all the vicissitudes of the country's political history since 1947, the French Communist policy has used tactics characteristic of democratic parties. The refusal of the Communist party and the Communist-controlled trade union organization, the Confédération Générale du Travail, during the grave political crisis of May 1968, to join in any attempts to overthrow the de Gaulle regime by revolutionary action was a consequence of its democratic tactics. The conclusion of the Socialist-Communist alliance—which gave its candidate, Socialist leader François Mitterand (b. 1916), almost fifty percent of the vote in the presidential elections of 1974—is an indication of the readiness of the French Communists to adhere to the democratic way of contending for power.[108]

In Italy, a strong Communist party and a strong Communist-controlled trade union emerged after the collapse of Mussolini's fascist regime. As in France, the Communists joined a government coalition under Marshal Pietro Badoglio (1871–1956) in 1944 and under the Christian Democratic leader Alcide de Gasperi (1881–1954) until 1947. From the time the Christian Democrats embarked upon their policy of *apertura a sinistra* ("opening toward the left") in 1961, the Communists have remained willing to participate in a coalition under Christian Democratic leadership. For a while they even supported Christian Democratic governments in the voting process in Parliament in order to prevent a political crisis.

The democratic tactics of the French and Italian Communists received a formal sanction through a declaration adopted by their leaders George Marchais and Enrico Berlinguer in 1975. The statement maintained that the two parties are independent of Soviet control and adhere to the democratic principles of a plural party system and freedom of speech, press, association, and religion. The 1976 Congress of the French Communist party endorsed this policy statement and emphasized that the Marxist-Leninist doctrine of the dictatorship of the proletariat had been abandoned.

Significantly, the changes in the political goals of the communist movement in Western Europe have been accompanied by a retreat from the determinism of historical materialism among communist and left-radical intellectuals. The intellectual leader of Italian communism in its early period, Antonio Gramsci (1891–1937), in essays he wrote in Mussolini's prisons, rejected the fatalist interpretations of Marxism and "the iron conviction that there exist objective laws for historical development of the same character as natural laws, with, in addition, the belief in a fatalistic finalism of a similar character to religious belief: since the favourable conditions are predestined they will come into existence and from these will be determined, in a somewhat mysterious way, regenerative events." French existentialist philosopher, novelist, and playwright, Jean-Paul (Charles Aymard) Sartre (b. 1905), in spite of his strong leanings toward radical activism, likewise rejects the determinism of historical materialism. In his view, the relations between human beings, while of a dialectical nature, manifest themselves in the plurality of human activities, of which economic relations are only one part.[109]

The retreat of Western European communists from the Marxist tenets and their readiness to adhere to the democratic process do not yet indicate that the split within the socialist movement which occurred after the First World War has been healed. But it does indicate that the ties of the Western European communists to the Soviet regime have been loosened and that the wing of the socialist movement that for two generations refused to participate in the transformation of Western European socialism from a Marxist to a democratic movement has abandoned the raison d'être of its separatism.

5. EVOLUTIONARY HUMANISM

While Marxism insisted that societal progress follows a law of a dialectical sequence of tension and revolution, evolutionary doctrines upheld laws of progress of a broader and more general nature. The triumph of evolutionism produced a conceptual revolution comparable to that which had previously been brought about by the theories of Copernicus, Kepler, and Newton about the place of the earth in the universe. In fact, before being extended to the organic world, evolutionism found a firm ground in the reflections about the solar system. Once the aspect of the biblical myth of creation that placed the earth into the center of the universe had been challenged, the other element of the biblical myth—the creation of the organic world by divine fiat—also lost ground.

The first evolutionary theory about the solar system was proposed by Descartes. He thought that all celestial bodies were subject to evolution from a universal matter and that some of them had become attached as planets to large stars such as the sun. A century later Kant and the French mathematician and astronomer Pierre Simon (marquis de) Laplace (1749–1827) proposed a theory of the origin of the solar system that was closer to modern theories. Kant contended that the universe originated from an elementary, rotating matter in which stars were born through condensations. The solar system was itself originally one of these rotating masses, in which planets were formed through local condensations. Laplace expounded a similar theory about the origin of the solar system.[110]

Paralleling these evolutionary theories about the universe and the solar system were discoveries in the fields of geology and biology which were instrumental in the rise of evolutionary theories about the organic world. French naturalist George Louis (Leclerc comte de) Buffon (1707–1788), in *Histoire, naturelle, générale et particulière* ("Natural, general, and particular history," 1749–1789), was important in advancing the idea that not only the solar system, but also the earth and its inhabitants, were the product of evolution. Buffon even cited environmental influences as the motor of evolution.

The great revolution in biological thinking, however, was initiated by French naturalist Jean-Baptiste (Pierre Antoine de Monet, chevalier de) Lamarck (1744–1829). He was the first biologist to derive the theory of organic evolution from sharply defined laws. According to his theory, organic evolution is due to new needs and the ability of the organisms to satisfy them through structural changes that could then be inherited.[111]

Lamarck's theory was plausible enough and could be interpreted as strong support for the belief in a law of progress that was then popular. Lamarckism was, therefore, widely accepted in progressive circles; both Marx and Engels were Lamarckists. However, neither Lamarck nor any other biologist has ever been able to find any evidence for his evolutionary theory, although attempts to do so have continued to the present time.[112]

Nevertheless, English philosopher Herbert Spencer (1820–1903) made a bold attempt to establish an all-embracing doctrine of evolution for the universe, the organic world, and mankind on a Lamarckian basis.

Spencer's evolutionary system was originally based on the identification of evolution with progress. In *Social Status* (1851) and *The Development Hypothesis* (1852), he espoused the doctrine of social and organic evolution. In *Progress: Its Law and Cause* (1857), he broadened his evolutionary philosophy to embrace the entire universe. The fundamental law of evolution that he proposed was that of a process of differentiation from incoherent homogeneity to coherent heterogeneity, which he described as follows:

> The advance from the simple to the complex, through a process of successive differentiation, is seen alike in the earliest changes of the universe . . . ; it is seen in the geological and climatic evolution of the earth; it is seen in the unfolding of every single organism . . . and in the multiplication of kinds of organisms; it is seen in the evolution of humanity . . . ; it is seen in the evolution of society in respect alike of its political, its religious, and its economic organization; and it is seen in the evolution of all those endless . . . products of human activity which constitute the environment of our daily life. From the remotest past which science can fathom, up to the novelties of yesterday, that in which progress essentially consists is the transformation of the homogeneous into the heterogeneous.[113]

That was indeed an all-embracing system of self-induced evolution and progress. Yet in the systematic work on evolution, *First Principles* (1862), Spencer introduced a modification of his theory of evolution although he did not abandon the identification of evolution with progress. He still maintained that as far as man's mental nature and the conditions of his existence are concerned, "evolution can end only in the establishment of the greatest perfection and the most complete happiness," but he attributed evolution in its totality to an "absolute force . . . which transcends our knowledge and conceptions . . . an unconditioned reality, without beginning and end," that is, to an inscrutable, unknown and unknowable entity. Moreover, this mysterious, persistent force produces not only evolution, but also dissolution. Evolution is not a perpetual process, but ends when an equilibrium is attained, and is followed by a period of dissolution. Spencer conceived of an immeasurable period during which evolution goes on universally, followed by an immeasurable period during which the forces of dissolution prevail, followed again by a period of evolution.[114] In other words, Spencer adopted the doctrine of cosmic cycles that had been widespread among Greek and Eastern philosophers and religions. But, as Spencer was familiar with the modern sciences which reckon the universe and organic life in billions of years, his "immeasurable" periods allowed mankind sufficient leeway to dream of perfection. Thus in spite of his mystical interpretation of the forces of evolution and dissolution, he remained faithful to the doctrine of progress established in the Age of Enlightenment.

While Spencer's evolutionism, as far as it concerned the organic world, was still founded on Lamarckism, Charles Robert Darwin (1809–1882) laid the groundwork for the triumph of evolutionism throughout the world on a more solid basis than Lamarck had been able to do, through his epochal work, *On the Origin of Species by Means of Natural Selection, or the Preservation of Favoured Races in the Struggle for Life* (1859)[115] and its sequel, *The Descent of Man and Selection in Relation to Sex* (1871). In making natural selection the principal agent of biological evolution, and in characterizing the "struggle for life" as the prime mover in the evolutionary process, Darwin was undoubtedly a child of the Malthusian era, which ascribed to the tendency toward overpopulation the primary role in the process of "natural selection" among men, and the rugged individualism of the early capitalist society. The rapid acceptance of Darwinism by the intellectual world may to a large extent have been due to the fact that friend and foe of capitalism alike could agree on a theory of evolution which stressed features similar to those that could be found in the existing society.

Thus Darwin succeeded where Lamarck had failed—in convincing modern man that (1) the 3,000-year-old biblical story of the separate creation, by divine fiat, of all existing species of living beings, including man, could no longer constitute the basis of a theory of the origins of the organic world; (2) the theory of the organic evolution of all living beings, past and present, extinct and still existing, was unassailable; and (3) man was part and parcel of the organic world and hence descended from earlier forms of life. The triumph of biological evolutionism was complete and has resisted all attempts to maintain the biblical myth of the separate creation of all species.

In the following decades, Darwin's evolutionary theory was further refined by biological research. Important discoveries, particularly in the field of genetics, clarified the mechanism by which natural selection works. The genetic findings of the Austrian monk and biologist Gregor Johann Mendel (1822–1884);[116] the discoveries of the existence, functions, and chemical composition of genes; the findings about the heredity of mutations which appear in the genetic apparatus—have all been instrumental in placing Darwin's evolutionary theories on a solid scientific foundation.

Biological evolution is not in itself identical with progress. The men of the Enlightenment, who had been the chief proponents of the doctrine of progress, had not included the organic world outside man in their concept of progress. Yet once man was found to be part and parcel of the process of biological evolution, it became natural to apply the doctrine of progress to the organic world as a whole.

Darwin himself understood biological evolution as an aspect of progress. He asserted that for every species there is a tendency of "progress toward perfection" as the result of natural selection: "As natural selection works solely by and for the good of each being, all corporeal and mental endowments will tend to progress toward perfection." [117] Moreover, he viewed the future of man with the same faith in progress toward perfection that he had expressed for the organic world as a whole: "Man may be excused for feeling some pride at having risen, though not through his own exertions, to the very summit of the organic scale; and the fact of his having thus risen, instead of having been aboriginally placed there, may give him hope for a still higher destiny in the distant future." [118] What was still needed for a universal doctrine of progress, embracing both the pre-human organic world and mankind, was a theory of directed evolution. Spencer had already proposed such a theory, which embraced even the pre-organic world: the universe follows a law of evolution from the simple to the complex, through a process of successive differentiations.

Modern biologists, on the basis of thorough observations of the species which evolved in the more than three billion years during which the earth has sustained life, are inclined to agree with the popular belief that life on earth has shown a steady progress from "lower" to "higher" forms of life; in other words, that biological evolution has shown a persistent direction which could be interpreted as a law of biological progress. English biologist Sir Julian Sorell Huxley (b. 1887), on similar grounds as Spencer, holds that the direction of biological evolution is toward greater efficiency, differentiation, and specialization. Thus he defines "higher" organization as "more efficient integration of a greater number of differentiated, more specialized kinds of parts." This higher organization is at work in the organic world as a result of an evolutionary process in which, at every stage, the later dominant groups are distinguished from earlier ones by "efficiency in such matters as speed and the application of forces to overcome physical limitations" and by "greater control over the internal environment." He defines evolutionary progress as "a raising of the upper level of biological efficiency, this being defined as increased control over and independence of the environment." [119]

However, while it might appear legitimate to interpret biological history as one of the advance of the dominant species in the direction of ever-higher degrees of biological efficiency, two closely connected questions arise which have a bearing on the problem of evolutionary direction in the organic world in general and of mankind in particular. First, does the fact that biological evolution has so far moved in a certain direction warrant the conclusion that it will always do so in the future? Against this assumption it can be argued that the understanding of a historical fact must be distinguished from the discovery of a general law. Whereas a general law allows for predictions, the understanding of a historical fact can never become the basis for a scientific prediction for the future course of history.[120] While biologists may be right in asserting that biological evolution has led to greater efficiency, one cannot predict that the geological, meteorological, and other physical conditions (let alone the intervention of man), which allowed for this direction of evolution, will remain favorable to it.

Second, do the facts of human evolution discovered by modern science entitle us to assume that the future history of mankind will be characterized by a similar kind of advance as has so far been the case in biological evolution? There is obviously no more reason for such a belief than there is for the belief in a continuing advance in the evolution of the organic world.[121] For instance, since the sixteenth century, there has been a trend toward rapid progress in natural sciences and, since the eighteenth century, in technology as well, with a concomitant rise in living standards in the industrial countries. But whether conditions will remain favorable for further progress in these domains cannot be predicted. Ecological pressure and a gradual exhaustion of certain non-renewable natural resources, for instance, may create unfavorable conditions for further technological and economic progress.

It was, indeed, the growing doubt in the general validity of the doctrine of progress that led humanists in recent generations to reconsider the foundation of their faith, while the grave political, economic, and social problems of our age led them to search for adequate solutions compatible with the humanist convictions.

CHAPTER X

Humanism Faces the Problems
of Modern Society

I. THE DOCTRINE OF PROGRESS
BREAKS DOWN

The twentieth century has witnessed the breakdown of the belief in a law of human progress, a law that guided the eras of Enlightenment, socialism, and evolutionary optimism. Philosophical trends contributed to this change, but more responsible were the events of this period: two world wars with their cruelty, hecatombs of human victims, and wholesale destruction; the uninterrupted "progress" in perfecting armaments, culminating in nuclear weaponry; the triumphs of communist, fascist, and military authoritarian regimes; and the obstacles in the path of a rational world organization. Even the end of colonial or semi-colonial rule in many areas could not tip the scales in favor of continuous progress, particularly in view of the difficulties facing these emancipated countries on their path toward economic advancement, and of the widespread tendency to turn authoritarian.

Grave doubts in the ineluctability of progress were also induced by features inherent in modern society, especially the growing trend toward mechanization and depersonalization. Long before the world wars, in a period still heralding the triumphs of evolutionism, German philosopher Friedrich Wilhelm Nietzsche (1844–1900) raised a warning voice about that trend. Although he accepted the theory of biological evolution,[1] he refused to equate it with human progress: "Mankind does not represent a development toward something better or stronger or higher in the sense accepted today. . . . 'Progress' is merely a modern idea, that is, a false idea. . . . Further development is altogether not according to any necessity in the direction of elevation, enhancement, or strength."[2] On the contrary, Nietzsche feared "the spectre of the last man, who makes everything small . . . proceeds carefully . . . no longer becomes poor or rich . . . is clever and knows everything."[3]

If Nietzsche feared that scientific, technological, and material progress might bring about a uniformization of man and the loss of his unique personality, later generations also worried about these tendencies. Two well-known expressions of this concern are the great anti-utopian novels, *Brave New World* (1932) by Aldous Leonard Huxley (1894–1953), and *1984* (1949) by George Orwell (1903–1950). Orwell directed his attack against the communist type of society and the political and cultural uniformity it imposes, be it by blatant force or by subtle, mental conditioning. Huxley depicted the nightmare of a completely dehumanized world where babies are born in test tubes, a rigid caste system is established based on differentiated hatching of human and sub-human species, bonds of love and marriage are replaced by sensual pleasure, and every trace of art and creative science has been expunged. The "happiness" of Nietzsche's "Last Man" pervades Huxley's anti-utopia.

Huxley's and Orwell's anti-utopias had a tremendous impact on the Western world. They focused attention on the dangers inherent in increased mechanization, mass production, mass organization, mass propaganda, and mass media. The warnings of these two outstanding anti-utopians have been echoed by modern humanism. After Marx had condemned capitalist society for alienating producers and consumers, the charge of alienation which Huxley and Orwell leveled at modern society strengthened the beliefs of humanists about the need to strive for more humane societal conditions.

Nietzsche's impact should be understood in this context. He was no humanist. His ideal of the good society was aristocratic. He hated democracy's ideals of equal rights and general welfare. The "superman" (*Übermensch*) whom he contrasted to the "Last Man" would be called to command the "herd men." Of the superman he said, "I often reflect how I might yet advance him and make him stronger, more evil and more profound than he is."[4]

Yet what linked Nietzsche to modern humanism was his love of the "earth," his belief that man is responsible for his own destiny, and should hope and strive for a higher destiny. In *Thus Spake Zarathustra* he implored man to "remain faithful to the earth." "We have become man, so we want the earth." Since "God is dead," man's destiny on earth depends solely on himself: "Rather no god, rather make destiny on one's own." Although there is no guarantee that man will progress, and although there is even the danger of regression, "the time has come for man to set himself a goal" above himself. "All that suffers wants to live that it may become ripe and joyous and longing—longing for what is farther, higher, brighter." There is only one path to salvation: man's work on the future that will re-create the past.[5]

To be sure, the roots of modern humanism lie deeper than in the thoughts of this lonely philosopher and his rebellion agaist the mechanization of the industrial era. The humanist ideals of the Enlightenment, of Locke and Kant, Voltaire and Rousseau are as important to modern humanists as Nietzsche's thoughts. What sets modern humanism apart from the Enlightenment and its subsequent evolutionist optimism, and what brought Nietzsche closer to the modern humanists, is the lesson learned from modern philosophers and from the course of modern history: that there is no natural law of human progress; that progress can be achieved only by the will and deeds of mankind; and that progress is always in danger of being lost unless the greatest efforts are made to keep it alive.

A brief consideration of the writings of prominent humanist philosophers will illustrate that an important feature of modern humanism is its denial of the existence of a law of human progress, blended with the conviction that progress can, and should, be the fruit of the most strenuous human endeavors. This awareness of man's responsibility, that man cannot rely on any laws of history to build a more perfect society, is the most significant trait of modern humanism. Among modern philosophers, Karl Raimund Popper (b. 1902) can be considered the most consistent representative of that epistemological school which insists that there can neither be any law of progress in human history, nor for that matter any other evolutionary law.[6] He declared that "the future depends on ourselves, and we do not depend on any historical necessity."[7]

2. DIVIDED VIEWS ABOUT RELIGION

Just as modern humanists abandon the doctrine of a law of progress, so they reject the belief that progress is assured by, or depends on, divine

Providence. Yet modern humanists differ from each other in their religious beliefs just as did humanists of the Enlightenment, when atheism challenged the trust in divine Providence.

The strong atheist wing in modern humanism can be traced primarily to left-Hegelianism. The most prominent representatives of atheism were the left-Hegelians Ludwig Andreas Feuerbach (1804–1872) and Karl Marx (1818–1883). In Feuerbach's view religion constitutes a self-estrangement of man. Man projects his own nature, although purified, outside himself: "Religion, at least the Christian, is the relation of man to himself. . . . The divine being is nothing else than the human being or, rather, the human nature purified . . . contemplated and revered as another, a distinct being." Humanism aims at turning men "from lovers of God into lovers of humanity . . . from lackeys of a heavenly and earthly monarchy and aristocracy into free, self-respecting citizens of the world." [8]

Like Feuerbach, Marx regarded religion as a projection of man's conscience. In his doctoral thesis he stated that "man's conscience is the highest divinity." [9] Soon thereafter, when he began to analyze critically the societal structures, he interpreted religion as a product of the self-alienation of man, in particular the oppressed man of the capitalist society:

> Religion is the self-consciousness and self-esteem of man who has either not yet gained himself or has lost himself again. . . . The wretchedness of religion is at once an expression of and a protest against real wretchedness. Religion is the sigh of the oppressed creature, the heart of a heartless world, and the soul of soulless conditions. It is the opium of the people.

He concluded from this analysis that "the abolition of the religion as the illusory happiness of the people is a demand for their real happiness. The call to abandon illusions about their condition is the call to abandon a condition which requires illusions." [10]

Marx's atheism exerted a powerful influence on the socialist movement, particularly in countries where the Church was an important element of the "establishment" against which the socialist parties rebelled. This was also true of the aggressive atheism of the Soviet regime which was derived not only from Marx's interpretation of religion as an illusory happiness of oppressed people, but also from the role of the Russian Orthodox Church as an instrument of czarism. Once that power was broken, the Soviet Constitution of 1936 proclaimed—officially, at least—religious tolerance.

If Marx regarded religion as an illusion of exploited and alienated man, Sigmund Freud (1856–1939) arrived at a similar conclusion through the instrument of psychoanalysis. Freud traced the origin of religion to the child's need for protection, which he first finds fulfilled by the father, and as an adult, by an exalted father-figure: "When the growing individual finds that he ... can never do without protection against superior powers, he lends those powers the features belonging to the figure of his father; he creates for himself the gods whom he dreads, whom he seeks to propitiate, and whom he nevertheless entrusts with his own protection." Freud recognized that religion has bestowed benefits on mankind: allaying man's anxiety in face of life's dangers, and sanctioning a moral order designed to ensure justice. But he thought that the time should, and would, come when men would overcome the "childhood neurosis" of religion; and that "by withdrawing their expectations from the other world and concentrating all their liberated energies into their life on earth, they will probably succeed in achieving a state of things in which life will become tolerable for everyone and civilization no longer oppressive to anyone." [11]

Atheism, however, does not monopolize modern humanism, not even within the socialist movement. From the moment socialism began to loosen or sever its ties with Marx's historical materialism, the Marxian interpretation of religion as the opium of the oppressed people began to lose its authority, and currents of religious humanism began to appear within the socialist movement. [12]

Among modern humanists who have attempted to integrate religion with their humanist philosophy, Julian Sorell Huxley (1887–1975) and John Dewey (1859–1953) merit mention. Huxley wrote a treatise on religion in which—under the influence of German theologian Rudolf Otto (1869–1937)—he recognized the numinous as an irreducible human feeling of reverence toward the sacred. He regarded as sacred the powers that are behind nature, the great moments of man (birth, marriage, death), the revelations of art and science, the moral ideals, and the practice of good. Similarly John Dewey, one of the founders of modern humanism, recognized the religious attitude as that which connects "man, in the way of both dependence and support, with the enveloping world that the imagination feels is a universe." [13]

Humanist publications of a quasi-official nature tended to emphasize those features of humanism that set it apart from religion rather than those which might ally it with modern religious trends. Thus the "Humanist Manifesto" of 1933, although issued by a group who called themselves religious humanists, viewed the universe as self-existing, not created, and it rejected theism and deism as outdated. The "Humanist

Manifesto II," while conceding that "in the best sense, religion may inspire dedication to the highest ethical ideals," nevertheless rejected the belief in immortal salvation and eternal damnation as harmful, and condemned traditional religions as obstacles to human progress.[14]

Whatever feelings humanists have toward the *mysterium fascinans* and the *mysterium tremendum* of the universe, whether they call it "God" and whether God is dead or alive for them, they categorically deny that man's destiny depends on any external power, call it God or the Universe or Nature. "Dependence upon any external power," Dewey stated, "is the counterpart of surrender of human endeavour." The profoundly humanist conviction of the dignity of man excludes any dependence on external powers. Man, although conditioned by his past, is yet the master of his destiny. It is up to him, alone, to become his own savior. "Humanism," exclaimed leading American humanist, Corliss Lamont (b. 1902), "assigns to man nothing less than the task of being his own saviour and redeemer." [15]

If man is his own savior and redeemer, progress toward this ultimate goal can be measured only by standards established by man himself. As Bertrand Russell (Arthur William, Third Earl, 1872–1970) stated: "We are ourselves the ultimate and irrefutable arbiters of value. . . . It is for us to determine the good life, not for Nature—not even for Nature personified as God." [16]

3. THE FREE PERSONALITY

Because countless political, social, and economic systems have manifested themselves throughout mankind's history, it seems appropriate to ask whether man can ever find universal standards to guide him on the path toward human progress. The answer given by humanists is an emphatic "yes." While Christianity has established as an intrinsic human value the dignity of man as a creature of God, humanism's absolute criterion of human value is the dignity of man as a human being. This criterion is founded on the belief, aptly expressed by John Dewey, "that personality is the one thing of permanent and abiding worth, and that in every human individual there lies personality. . . . His freedom is not mere self-assertion. . . . Liberty is not a numerical notion of isolation; it is the ethical idea that personality is the supreme and only law, that every man is an absolute end in itself." On the basis of this conviction, human dignity acquires the nature of the sacred: "The sense of the dignity of human nature is as religious as the sense of awe and reverence when it rests upon a sense of human nature as a cooperating part of a larger world." [17]

The ideal of the free personality should not be—and in fact has hardly ever been—understood as that of an individuality released from all ties with its social, economic, political, ethnic, cultural, and mostly also religious environment. The same Dewey who elevated personality to the supreme and only law also stated that "assured and integrated individuality is the product of definite social relationships and publicly acknowledged functions." [18] Obviously prerequisite to the development of the human personality is personal freedom, which can be fully realized and maintained only in democratic systems of government. This has been recognized by all humanists, and by none more emphatically than by Dewey in his *Ethics of Democracy*: "Personal responsibility, individual initiation, these are the notes of democracy. . . . Democracy means that personality is the first and final reality. . . . It holds that the spirit of personality indwells in every individual and that the choice to develop it must proceed from the individual." Nearly a hundred years after the French Revolution, Dewey re-emphasized its motto, "Liberty, Equality, Fraternity," and called these ideals "symbols of the highest ethical ideal which humanity has yet reached." [19]

Authoritarian governments cannot ensure to the individual that measure of freedom that the unfolding of personality requires. Such systems are bound to impose on all individuals a uniformity of political and cultural behavior that largely excludes freedom of action. The tragic destiny that has befallen scientists, writers, and artists in the Soviet Union and Eastern Europe proves the irreconcilability of authoritarianism and freedom of personality. It also proves that the human personality is irrepressible and that the strongest personalities are able to resist even the most severe pressures designed to force uniformity upon them.

When the pressure is slightly alleviated within the authoritarian orbit —as in Czechoslovakia prior to the 1968 Soviet invasion, and for a short time in Yugoslavia—voices can be heard which openly proclaim personal freedom as a prerequisite for the unfolding of personality. Thus in an international symposium,[20] two participants from these two countries linked socialism with the ideal of the free personality: Ivan Sviták of Czechoslovakia maintained that the essence of socialism is man's full development and liberation; and Predrag Vanicky of Yugoslavia laid emphasis on the free personality as an element of the socialist community.

While the obstacles to the evolution of free personalities can be easily discerned in authoritarian societies, there are also numerous obstacles in democratic societies which impede the realization of this goal. Modern humanism has directed its complete attention to analyzing these obstacles and to proposing the most humane means to overcome them. The prerequisites for the unfolding of a free personality had been stated by the philosophers and political scientists of the Enlightenment. The French Revolution formulated them succinctly as the societal ideals of liberty, equality, and fraternity.[21] Marx, as a result of his thorough analysis of the capitalist society, added as a prerequisite to the goal of equality that of liberation from social alienation. Modern humanists confront the obstacles to the ideals of liberty, equality, fraternity, and liberation from alienation in several ways, as the following survey shows.

4. THE IDEAL OF LIBERTY:
MAJORITY RULE AND INDIVIDUAL RIGHTS

The emergence of democracy in the industrial countries was a very slow and sometimes painful process. Although the revolutions in the seventeenth and eighteenth centuries had paved the way for the acceptance of the principle of popular sovereignty, it still took many decades to abolish political, social, and economic qualifications for suffrage, and even longer until suffrage was extended to women.

Where democratic rights were established, there arose the problem of how to balance them between the community and the individual. Democratic rights rest on two principles: the sovereignty of the people, from which are derived the people's right to choose a government and to establish the law of the land; and the rights of the individual, either as a person or as a member of a group. These rights include the civil liberties of: religious freedom; freedom of speech, the press, and peaceful assembly; protection against arbitrary arrest; and the right to a fair trial.

These civic rights have always been recognized as essential to democracy. Government by the people presupposes that every citizen, in order to exert his right to participate fully and equally in government, must have the opportunity to express his opinions and to join with others to fight effectively for the realization of his views and interests. In addition, through the instrumentality of a free press and other media, every citizen must have full access to all sources of information.

Modern democracies try to delimit those majority decisions or executive powers that might diminish the rights of the individuals. A compromise between the rights of the majority and those of the individual underlay such important proclamations as the *Droits de l'homme* of the French

Revolution, the first ten amendments to the U.S. Constitution, analogous provisions in the constitutions of other democratic countries, and the Universal Declaration of Human Rights adopted by the United Nations in 1948.

Although democracies recognize these civic rights in principle, limitations on equal and effective participation in government often exist in practice. The right to participate in political decisions is being violated where, because of poverty and lack of education, people can neither exercise their right to vote in accordance with their interests, nor can they gain access to political organizations and propaganda sources.[22] The right to have access to essential information may be infringed where monopolies of information sources exist.

Most of these natural rights—for which humanist philosophers and activitists have fought since the beginning of the Enlightenment consti tute what Isaiah Berlin (b. 1909), English social historian and philosopher, has called "negative" freedom.[23] But within this framework, men and women pursue and fight—alone or as members of political, social, economic, ethnic, national, cultural, and religious communities—for their own goals and ideals. What they need and lay claim to is the right to do so, which Berlin terms "positive" freedom. It is in this field of thought and action that most of the tensions even in democratic societies arise. Political majorities may challenge or suppress what social, ethnic, cultural, or religious minorities may claim as their rights. Hence, the protection of minority rights is a burning issue in modern society.

In the United States, where for historical reasons social, ethnic, and religious diversities are particularly pronounced, some political philosophers have proposed general rules designed to limit or avoid clashes in this field. Robert A. Dahl (b. 1915) suggested that as a general rule in democratic societies, the principle of mutual guarantees "that effectively places certain matters beyond the reach of ordinary majorities" should be constituted through which certain matters would be protected.[24]

John Rawls (b. 1921) in *Theory of Justice* attempted to base minority rights on the concept of justice. He proposed reinstating the doctrine of the social contract as the foundation of the good society. He based his views on "a conception of justice which generalizes and carries to a higher level of abstraction the familiar theory of the social contract, as found, say in Locke, Rousseau, and Kant." His conception of justice— which agrees with that generally held by modern humanists—rested on the principle that each person possesses an inviolability founded on justice that even the welfare of society as a whole cannot override. "For this reason," Rawls added in criticism of utilitarianism, "justice denies that the loss of freedom for some is made right by a greater good shared by others. It does not allow that the sacrifices imposed on a few are outweighed by the larger sum of advantages enjoyed by many." [25]

In spite of these and similar attempts to define the natural, inalienable, and inviolable rights of individuals and minorities, in practice there will always be a compromise between the determination of majorities to govern in accordance with their interests and ideals and the determination of minorities to safeguard those interests they consider vital. There is, however, no doubt that full recognition of the vital rights of minorities is necessary for societal progress.

5. THE IDEAL OF EQUALITY

When the proponents of the French Revolution adopted the principle of equality, they had in mind above all else the abolition of the political and social privileges of the nobility. The status of the *citoyen* ("citizen"), created by the French Revolution, ensured to every person the same legal, juridical, and political rights. Economic inequalities, however, remained. The socialist movement attacked these inequalities but it did not seriously insist on realizing Louis Blanc's egalitarian ideal of a society in which income would be distributed solely on the basis of individual need.

Actually, humanist philosophers and political scientists, past and present, have always recognized that certain inequalities in income and social status are unavoidable in any but very primitive or utopian societies. The ideal of equality is in fact limited to a system of equal social and economic opportunities, a system unimpeded by discrimination of any kind, by crass differences in income and social status, or by economic insecurity.

Minority groups are the ones to suffer most from inequalities resulting from discrimination based on sex, race, ethnicity, nationality, or religion. Abolishing discrimination—be it in employment, in business opportunities, in wages, housing, and education—is of vital interest to minorities. The frequent disregard for this principle of equality constitutes one of the gravest delicts against the "inviolability founded on justice" which Rawls had in mind when establishing his doctrine of justice. Such disregard is based on deep-seated traditions, prejudices, and antagonisms which hinder the enforcement of anti-discrimination laws. However important it may be to wage the fight for equality on legal and political levels, it is just as vital to fight on the moral plane, usually an uphill battle of humanist morality against ingrained traditions and prejudices.

In order to safeguard the right to equal opportunity, quotas and other devices have been instituted to give minorities access to educational or occupational situations which otherwise would be closed to them. This policy—which India has established to help the untouchables, and which the United States has adopted as part of its anti-discrimination legislation and practice—has frequently encountered opposition on the ground that it constitutes inverse discrimination against the best-qualified candidates, and therefore violates the principle of equal opportunity.[26] Granted that this presents a genuine dilemma. Nevertheless, the policy of special favors for the disfavored is rational and justified as long as gross inequalities remain.

While such disparities are particularly glaring, society as a whole is profoundly affected by inequalities that stem from the way modern society developed. In the eighteenth and nineteenth centuries, economic inequalities grew out of feudal societies which had been based on a rigid, immobile class structure. The capitalist economy broke down these rigidities, but failed to create a system that would have kept inequalities to a minimum. The privileges of ownership and education—above all higher education—were sustained. Social and economic inequalities between classes are particularly obvious in the developing countries, which are also victims of crass inequality vis-à-vis the industrial countries.

The days of the excesses of unrestrained capitalism are over. This change was due to two currents, both of humanist origin: (1) the growing power of the working class, and (2) the influence of humanist political leaders and economists. Spurred by socialist ideals and the teachings of Marx and his disciples, the working class organized itself into socialist parties and trade unions, and it grew strong enough to participate in the growing wealth of the capitalist economy. It raised its living standards by forcing society to raise the quality of education and to establish effective measures of social security.

Social security constituted the first step on the road to a welfare state. Those economists and political leaders who advocated the principles of a welfare economy or attempted to carry them out helped transform modern industrial society from the rugged capitalism of the nineteenth and early twentieth centuries to a welfare state society, however rudimentary the application may still be. English economists Arthur Cecil Pigou (1877–1959) and John Maynard Keynes (1883–1946) were the theoretical leaders of the welfare economy, and Franklin Delano Roosevelt (1882–1945) was the first political leader to systematically attempt to implement that policy.

Economists who followed Pigou and Keynes taught that a maximum national product would not be achieved by a laissez-faire policy, as the orthodox schools of economists had advocated. Instead, they believed it would be achieved by a rational policy designed to correct the ill effects of competitive or monopolistic market decisions, and to carry out positive measures for fostering economic and social security and welfare. Pigou's *Economics of Welfare* (1920) was the pioneering work of this school, and Keynes's *General Theory of Employment, Interest and Money* (1936) was its culminating work. In his treatise Keynes argued that economic equilibrium can be maintained in spite of unemployment, and that therefore in periods of recession, government must create purchasing power to realize full employment of manpower and industrial capacities.

Roosevelt's New Deal sparked the policy of the welfare state. The New Deal was designed to heal the immense damage caused by the Great Depression, restore economic equilibrium, stimulate industrial and agricultural production, create employment by public works, and establish a system of social security which had been nonexistent in the United States.[27] Policies similar to the New Deal were practiced first in Scandinavia and then in all industrial countries.

The goals of a socioeconomic system based on welfare-state principles are, in the social sphere, to ensure everyone a minimum income or security in circumstances of unemployment, old age, and illness; and, in the economic sphere, to secure a stable yet dynamic economy, which will ensure full employment and make complete use of industrial capacities. The policy of government intervention in the economic sphere is based on the principles of a welfare economy. But governments intervene not only to help society's lower strata, but also to aid industrial, commercial, and agricultural interests whenever governments consider it necessary for economic and social stability. In spite of this, interest groups are often able to press for economic advantages through state intervention, a process which may destabilize the economy and harm the general welfare.

Although economic theory has determined which principles should be followed in order to achieve stability and welfare within a dynamic economic system, this goal has rarely been attained. True, cyclical movements which have always plagued the capitalist economy have been attenuated; depressions of the disastrous dimensions of the 1930s have not recurred. But the cycles of booms and recessions are still with us and stubbornly persist. The degree of economic and social security which can result only with full employment of all productive resources still escapes modern society. Even if the existing social security systems prevent the worst effects of unemployment in periods of recession, the welfare it ensures is very limited.

Inequalities still exist in industrial countries due to the unequal distribution of wealth and to the concentration of economic power in the hands of a few owners and managers of leading industries. Yet these inequalities are dwarfed by those that exist between economically advanced and lesser developed countries. This disparity results from the fact that the phenomenal economic growth of the industrial countries not only failed to fully benefit their pre-industrial colonies, but the colonial relationship actually masked the crass contrasts in wealth. When the colonies achieved independence, the inequalities became startlingly apparent and even tended to increase due to unusually rapid growth of population, a rapid urbanization process, and unfavorable terms of trade.[28]

The struggle of the pre-industrial countries to reduce and eventually eliminate these inequalities in wealth is in some ways analogous to the persistent struggle for welfare rights and human dignity that has been ongoing within the industrial countries. The industrial democratic countries, which have the financial and technological resources to aid developing countries in their uphill struggle, have been contributing to this goal, both directly and through agencies of the United Nations. The United Nations in fact uses a large part of its resources to foster the economic, social, educational, and technological development of these countries. Nevertheless, accelerating its pace and preventing setbacks remains one of the most difficult and fundamental problems faced by present-day society.

In the industrial countries intense efforts are being made on many levels to reduce economic and social inequalities and the economic insecurity which in turn breeds inequalities: on the level of management-labor relations, chiefly through trade union activities; on that of economic policies, through measures designed to arrive at a more just distribution of the national income and to prevent such disturbances as depressions and inflation in today's economy; on that of social welfare, through political activities designed to strengthen the welfare institutions of society; on that of education, through policies aimed at increasing opportunities for higher education among the lower income strata and minorities.

Rawls offered several guidelines which should be followed in order to achieve a more just and safe society. He held that both free-enterprise and socialist systems could fit into a humanist framework once certain humanizing prerequisites were met. What actually counts is not so much the economic system itself, but the way it is made to work. Rawls established two principles for an equitable societal system: equal prospects for success; and redress. The first principle requires that "those who are at the same level of talent and ability . . . should have the same prospects of success, regardless of their initial place in the social system." The principle of redress states that inequalities resulting from circumstances of birth and natural endowment are undeserved, and thus call for some compensation. Hence, "in order to treat all persons equally, to provide genuine equality of opportunity, society must give more attention to those with fewer native assets and to those born into the less favourable positions." It should follow that "those better circumstanced are willing to have their greater advantages under a scheme in which this works out for the benefit of the less fortunate."[29]

Rawls believed that these principles could be achieved in both free-enterprise and socialist systems, provided certain rules are observed. A just, free-enterprise system requires: equal opportunity in education; equal opportunity in economic activities, by preventing monopolistic restrictions and barriers to desirable positions; the prevention of unreasonable market power, by making markets more competitive; full employment policies; a steeply progressive income tax combined with income supplements for the lowest incomes; inheritance and gift taxes designed to correct the distribution of wealth and to prevent concentrations of power detrimental to political liberties.[30] For a democratic-socialist society Rawls envisaged a market economy in which the enterprises would be publicly owned, and in which the rate of savings and the proportion of production devoted to essential goods would be democratically determined.[31] Rawls's guidelines show that profound changes have yet to be made to achieve the degree of equality that would satisfy humanists.

6. LIBERATION FROM ALIENATION

When the French Revolution proclaimed "liberty" as one of the elements of the perfect society, it understood liberty narrowly as a political and social ideal. It did not consider how liberty is threatened when the worker is alienated from the product of his labor, or when the consumer is alienated from the goods and services he buys. As noted in the preceding chapter, it was Marx who initiated the attack against capitalist society's alienating effects on man. Modern humanism has renewed the attack. A number of humanist writers have focused on this problem, and serious efforts have been made to increase the scope of liberty by undermining such alienation. It should, of course, always be understood that liberty from alienation, like liberty in general, implies recognizing the societal ties which bind the individual to his community.

Two of the sternest critics of modern society were Max Horkheimer (1895–1973) and Theodor W. Adorno (1903–1969), German sociologists and philosophers who reiterated and extended Marx's charges against the "fetishism" of the capitalist economy:

> Since with the end of free exchange, commodities lost all their economic qualities, except for fetishism, the latter has extended its arthritic influence over all aspects of modern life. Through the countless agencies of mass production . . . the conventionalized modes of behaviour are impressed on the individual as the only natural, respectable, and rational ones. He defines himself only as a thing. . . . His yardstick is . . . successful or unsuccessful approximation to the objectivity of his function. But even the threatening collective belongs only to the deceptive surface beneath which are concealed the powers which manipulate it as the instruments of power.

In other words, man has become a puppet of the economic machinery that rules society. The evolution of the machinery turns "into that of the machinery of domination so that technical and social tendencies, always interwoven, converge in the total schematization of man." [32]

German-American political philosopher Erich Fromm (b. 1900) dealt with the problem of alienation under the aspect of the lack of freedom of man's conscience in present-day society. In psychoanalytical terms he distinguished between authoritarian conscience, which he defined as "the voice of an internalized external authority, the parents, the state, or whoever the authorities in a culture happen to be," and a humanistic conscience, which is "our own voice, present in every human being and independent of external sanctions and rewards." "As long as, and to the extent that authoritarian conscience still has a firm grip over men, the freedom attained in modern democracies implies a promise for the development of man rather than a fulfillment." In our present democracy we still bow to too many authorities in the spirit of an authoritarian conscience. In the spirit of Marx, Fromm views the market economy as one of the forces of modern society which fosters the authoritarian conscience: "In the marketing orientation man encounters his own powers as commodities alienated from him. . . . They are masked from him because what matters is not his self-realization in the process of using them, but his success in the process of selling. Both his powers and what they create become estranged, something different from himself." [33]

Among other critics of modern society, German-American political philosopher Herbert Marcuse (b. 1898) and French sociologist Alain

Touraine (b. 1925) emphasized alienation's sociological aspect of domination through reification. Marcuse held that the main instrument of reification in the capitalist market economy is technological evolution, the child of capitalism: "Technology has become the great vehicle of reification—reification in its most mature and effective form." While technological progress has been the source of tremendous wealth that has trickled down to most strata of society, it has at the same time become a new source of domination. It has subjected man to his productive apparatus and thus "perpetuated and intensified unfreedom in the form of many liberties and comforts." In other words, capitalism has replaced "personal dependence (of the slave on the master, etc.) with dependence on the 'objective order of things' (on economic laws, the market, etc.)" [34]

In a similar vein, Touraine emphasized the impersonal nature of domination in modern industrial or, as he calls it, post-industrial society. He held that the modern power elite are the technocrats, who "are not technicians but managers, whether they belong to the administration of the state or to big business, who are closely bound . . . to the agencies of political decision-making." Alienation is the loss of personality in the web of impersonal relations in a society dominated by managers and administrators:

> The alienated individual or group is not only the one left on the sidelines, subject to control or deprived of influence; it also includes the consumer pushed by advertising and credit to sacrifice his economic security for the sake of goods whose distribution is justified by the interests of the producers rather than by the satisfaction of real needs. It includes as well the worker who is subject to a system of organization whose over-all efficiency does not balance its exorbitant human costs. [35]

In a study of alienation of factory workers, American sociologist Robert Blauner suggested the following definition of alienation in the workshop: "Alienation exists when workers are unable to control their immediate work process, to develop a sense of purpose and function which connects their jobs to the overall organization of production, to belong to integrated communities, and when they fail to become involved in the activity of work as a mode of personal self-expression." The lack of control over the work process is a mark of powerlessness; the fragmental relation to the over-all work process is a mark of meaninglessness; the lack of integration into the work community is a mark of isolation; and the lack of personal self-expression is a mark of self-estrangement. [36]

The charge of alienation which modern humanists have raised against the capitalist society applies to the same, if not to a higher degree, in the communist society. Fromm charged communism with alienation on the grounds of its being a bureaucratic society "which transforms man into a thing." Marcuse stated that the Soviet system separates the immediate producers from contact with the means of production—a source of alienation similar to that in a capitalist society.[37]

Even sociologists and political scientists of communist countries, when allowed to speak frankly, have recognized the alienating effects of the present communist system. Thus Predrag Vanicki from Yugoslavia, who participated in a symposium on socialist humanism, admitted that

> the problem of alienation is . . . of vital and historical importance to socialism, not only because practical experience has shown that many deforming aspects of alienation are possible under socialism, but also because socialism must continue on the basis of various social forms which in themselves represent forms of alienation. . . . The political forms in which socialism evolves are essentially particular forms of alienation and are wholly positive and historically progressive only if they tend to dissolve themselves.[38]

Movements designed to overcome the alienation of workers date back to the post-World War I era. The beginning of these movements was connected with the Russian Revolution, in which the workers' councils (*soviets*) played a decisive role. In the initial phase of the revolution, the control over industrial enterprises was left in the hands of the workers' councils, but their influence dwindled until Stalin destroyed the last vestiges of their control. Spurred by the Russian Revolution, workers' council movements sprang up in a number of European countries, and the institution of workers' councils has remained an important feature of modern private and public enterprise systems. However, the degree of the councils' participation in management decisions has varied greatly. In many instances it has not gone much beyond the sphere of working conditions. But with the introduction of a system of "codetermination" (*Mitbestimmung*) in West Germany after World War II, the institution of workers' councils was extended to include workers' participation in the innermost sanctuaries of management, first in the heavy industries (coal and steel) and then in the major establishments of all industries.[39]

Where the workers' council system functions properly, it has become an important factor in the process of liberating workers from alienation. This system alone, however, does not suffice to alleviate the reification of work, which has continuously progressed due to the intensification and fractionation of work (through systems like assembly lines), as well as to the ever-increasing automatization of work processes.

The reaction against the growing mechanization of the work process arose not only among trade unions, but also among social scientists and responsible managers. As a result, work systems have been devised that take into consideration the psychological factors affecting workers and their performance. But the bane of the reification of work cannot be broken by such devices alone. Increasing attention has therefore been given to devising ways to eradicate the chief cause of alienation in the work shops: the authoritarian control of the work process. One solution is to actively engage the workers in shaping and carrying out the work process. In a major study of this problem, undertaken by a Special Task Force of the United States Secretary of Health, Education, and Welfare, the goal of disalienation in the workshop was well defined:

> What the workers want most, as more than a hundred studies in the past twenty years show, is to become masters of their immediate environments and to feel that their work and they themselves are important. . . . An increasing number want more autonomy in tackling their tasks, greater opportunity for increasing their skills, rewards that are directly connected to the intrinsic aspects of work, and greater participation in the design of work and the formulation of their tasks.[40]

Workers' councils, trade unions, and management have experienced a growing awareness of the possibilities of making work more meaningful, through such measures as: self-managing work teams which are given collective responsibilities for larger fragments of the production process; replacing supervisors with team leaders; and establishing rules for the work place based on the collective experience of work teams. Systematic efforts have already been made, particularly in Scandinavia and Japan, to introduce reforms of this kind into industry.[41]

Parallel to the movements designed to overcome worker alienation were movements designed to give the consumer a voice in decisions about the kinds and qualities of products he is to purchase. With the growth of monopolies and oligopolies in the sphere of production and services, the consumer increasingly lost control over the quality and kind of the goods and services offered. But in the last few decades serious and to a certain extent successful efforts have been made both by government regulatory agencies and by consumers' organizations to ensure protective standards of quality from producers of commodities and services.

Just as in the fight for liberation from inequalities, liberation from alienation is a long-drawn-out process which depends on the determination and power of society's progressive forces.

7. THE IDEAL OF FRATERNITY

Humanist ideals are not confined to political, economic, and social spheres. Of the three ideals proclaimed by the French Revolution, that of "fraternity" is an affective one whose realization cannot be achieved by institutions alone. On the other hand, without brotherliness it is doubtful that a society can be a good and a sane one. Such a society requires that *homo homini lupus* ("man is to man a wolf") cede its prevalence to *homo homini frater* ("man is to man a brother").

In proclaiming the ideal of fraternity, the French Revolution was guided by the conviction that once the ideals of freedom and equality were achieved, the non- or anti-fraternal qualities in the human species would give way to feelings of brotherliness. Modern humanists share this hope for the dawn of an age of brotherliness, but they ask some fundamental questions: Does man innately have brotherly feelings that are blocked in imperfect societies, but will surface under favorable societal conditions? Or, in spite of aggressive traits innate in man, will a society based on liberty and equality foster fraternal feelings? Modern humanists advocate both doctrines. Even the psychoanalytic school, which has paid much attention to the problems of brotherliness and hostility, has optimistic and more sober wings that confront each other. Erich Fromm, an outstanding representative of the optimistic wing, is convinced that "man is not necessarily evil, but becomes evil only if the proper conditions for his growth and development are lacking." A good society, in which freedom, economic security and welfare are ensured for everyone, a society organized in such a way that work becomes a meaningful expression of man's faculties, will further each person's growth, thus creating the conditions in which man will become truly productive.[42] Being productive means relating oneself lovingly to the world. "Productiveness is the root of genuine love."[43] Just as Bertrand Russell had asserted a generation earlier that "the good life is one inspired by love and guided by knowledge,"[44] so Fromm trusted that the good society would be held together by a blend of reason and love. He based his optimistic faith in human nature "on the inner experience of each individual, on his own experience of reason and love."[45] He defined the sane society as "a society whose members have developed their reason . . . [and] have the capacity to love their children, their neighbours, all men, themselves, all of nature."[46] "The potentialities of men are such that, given the proper conditions, they will be capable of building a social order governed by the principles of equality, justice and love." Fromm built his vision of a world government on the same foundation of love for mankind, which "cannot be separated from the love for one individual." [47]

Certain other humanists share Fromm's optimistic view of man's potential for perfection. Thus the "Humanist Manifesto" of 1933 concluded with the dictum that "man . . . alone is responsible for the realization of the world of his dreams . . . he has within himself the power for its achievement." Corliss Lamont likewise trusts that man will win in the end: "The humanist philosophy, though granting that man may lose, and lose permanently, is convinced that he has the ability and intelligence and courage to win through." [48]

Freud, on the other hand, was not optimistic about the perfectibility of man and society. In *Civilization and Its Discontents*, he stated that every civilization is built on the renunciation or suppression of powerful instincts; that among man's instinctual endowments are desires for both love and aggression; and that "every civilization has to use its utmost efforts in order to set limits to man's aggressive instincts." [49] He did not expect society ever to overcome the tension between the instincts of love and aggression which characterize human beings. In short, he did not think that man could ever become "good." But he did envisage two possibilities for societal progress. First, to overcome "the inadequacy of the regulations which adjust the mutual relationships of human beings in the family, the state and society," progress could be marked by societal regulations which "should be a protection and a benefit for everyone of us." The second possibility concerns the fundamental tensions between love and aggression. While Freud questioned "whether and to what extent the cultural process . . . will succeed in mastering the disturbance of communal life by the human instinct of aggression and self-destruction," he expressed the hope "that the other of the two 'heavenly powers,' eternal Eros, will make an effort to assert himself in the struggle with his equally immortal adversary." [50] In other words, Freud did not believe that any society could be built on the expectation that all men would be or become good, but he did hope that a society could be established that would be able to strengthen brotherliness and love in the face of aggression and destruction.

Another approach to the problem of building a good society is related to the concept of self-interest that goes back to the theories about the origin of society common during the Enlightenment. According to these theories, the most stable foundation for the good society would be man's self-interest from which, under the favorable conditions created by such a society, fraternal feelings would emerge. These feelings would be based on the mutual advantages all individuals would draw from a society that realized the principles of justice. Rawls represented this cautious approach, and professed that if a society is founded strictly on the principle of justice, the tie that will bind all human beings is that of cooperation, and the prevailing effect among them as members of the community will be one of friendship: "Here is a morality of association in which the members of society will view one another as equals, as friends and associates, joined together in a system of cooperation known to be for the advantage of all and governed by a common conception of justice." The effect of love does not appear in this rational scheme of the good society, yet Rawls does not exclude it: "The sense of justice is continuous with the love of mankind." However, the love of mankind is "supererogatory," going beyond the moral requirements.[51]

The very concept of "love of mankind" implies that realizing the ideal of the good society requires that society expand to embrace a world community. As stated in the "Humanist Manifesto II," "commitment to all mankind is the highest commitment of which we are capable." The dream of modern humanism is indeed that of a world community based on freedom and welfare for all and peace on earth. "What more daring a goal for humankind than for each person to become, in ideal as well as in practice, a citizen of a world community," exclaimed the manifesto. Fromm also visualized a society which "must lead eventually to forms of international cooperation and planning, to forms of world government and complete disarmament."[52]

While a world community and world government are still infinitely distant goals, the shock of two world wars produced the first attempts to realize the more moderate goal of establishing a world organization designed to further peaceful relations among all nations and to foster social, economic, and cultural development. The League of Nations—the world organization created after the First World War—could not stop or itself survive Japan's aggression in the Far East, Italy's conquest of Ethiopia, and Hitler's onslaught on Germany's neighbors. But its successor, the United Nations, has a much broader and more solid basis. While its effectiveness is still very limited, and although in its deliberations, confrontation frequently outstrips cooperation, its vast network of activities and specialized agencies—designed to foster economic, social, and cultural cooperation between the nations and, above all, to give financial, technical, health, and educational assistance chiefly to the developing countries—can be viewed as germs of a fraternal community. Realistically, however, the primary function of the United Nations, that of fostering peaceful relations between nations and of preventing armed conflicts, is still in an embryonic stage. The United Nations can counter threats to peace only when the power constellations between nations favor peaceful solutions. The ideal of fraternity within each nation is far from being realized, and it is even farther removed from fulfillment in the relations among nations.

Thus the problem of how to achieve the victory of brotherliness still remains open for each nation and even more for the world community. No answer can be given to the fateful question of whether Freud was right in his skepticism about man's capability to become good in any society, or whether Fromm's optimistic vision of a sane society in which everyone will be good and brotherly will ultimately triumph.

8. REVOLUTIONARY OR GRADUAL CHANGE?

The prevailing opinion among both secular humanists and modern theologians seems to be that the present-day society is in urgent need of change. Yet there is little agreement about the way a more perfect society can, and should, be brought about. Two conflicting views divide the humanists: should change be revolutionary or gradual?

The hope for a sudden, revolutionary change can be traced to those Jewish prophets who predicted the collapse of their corrupt society by divine action, an end to be followed by the dawn of the kingdom of God. This belief—shared by Jesus, the Apostle Paul, and voiced in the Book of Apocalypse—is deeply rooted in Christianity. Although modern humanism does not ascribe to divine intervention in the destinies of mankind, the hope for a sudden, revolutionary change of society is a powerful force within the humanist movement. The great philosophers of the Enlightenment sanctified rebellion against rulers who violated human rights; the two English revolutions in the seventeenth century reflected this doctrine. The eighteenth century witnessed two great revolutions which produced fundamental changes in the structure of society: the American Revolution created a democratic commonwealth; and the French Revolution abruptly changed the structure of French society and had profound repercussions in a large part of Europe. It was perhaps not by chance that in 1848, on the eve of revolutions which shook western and central Europe, Marx conceived his doctrine of the dialectical evolution of society which proceeds from the maturing of a new society in the womb of an old one, to the revolutionary overturn of the old society upon completion of the ripening process. When war and military defeat virtually destroyed the pre-industrial societies of Russia and China, revolutionary uprisings based on Marxist foundations produced new societies.

Revolutionary changes have continued in the more recent past, be it in the form of revolutionary uprisings, as in the Cuban revolution of 1958–1959 and in the Iranian revolution of 1978–1979; in the authoritarian military form of the Peruvian revolution of 1968, the first phase of the Portuguese revolution of 1974, and the 1974 Ethiopian revolution; or in the democratic form of the Chilean revolution of 1970–1973. Furthermore, radical student and guerilla movements in a number of developing countries have usually been inspired by revolutionary opposition to the "establishment."

The doctrine of revolutionary change has, therefore, remained prestigious in the ranks of humanism. However, in European industrial countries, after the socialist parties were transformed from revolutionary into democratic movements, revolutionary movements have generally been confined to pre-industrial countries. In the present atmosphere of the democratic welfare state, even radical humanists have become more reserved. Thus Marcuse admitted resignedly that "the critical theory of society possesses no concept which could bridge the gap between the present and its future; holding no promise and showing no success, it remains negative." Nevertheless, he saw the beginning of a revolutionary opposition in "the substratum of the outcasts and outsiders, the exploited and persecuted of other races and other colours, the unemployed and the unemployable. . . . The fact that they start refusing to play the game may be the fact which marks the beginning of the end of a period." [53]

The doctrine supporting gradual progress toward the good society likewise has a venerable history. Among the ancients the Roman philosopher-poet Lucretius (first century B.C.) was an outspoken supporter of gradual change. In his great poem *De rerum natura*, he described how civilization advanced—the cultivation of land, navigation, writing, poetry, and the art of peace-keeping: "These were taught slowly, a very little at a time, by practice and by trial, as the mind went forward searching. Time brings everything little by little to the shores of light by grace of art and reason till we see all things illuminate each other's rise up to the pinnacles of loftiness." [54] Thus to Lucretius the "rise up to the pinnacles of loftiness," that is, to the perfect society, appeared as a gradual process: "little by little."

Christian writers had difficulty reconciling the doctrine of gradual progress with their belief in original sin and the last judgment. Yet Augustine skillfully blended these concepts in his belief that man has made wonderful advances, but progress (meaning progress toward God) has been gradual: "The education of the human race, represented by the people of God, has advanced, like that of an individual, through certain epochs . . . so that it might gradually rise from earthly to heavenly things and from the visible to the invisible." [55] The last judgment will, nevertheless, be preceded by decline and destruction.

Philosophers of the Enlightenment also held that human progress is a gradual process. According to Leibniz, one of the most consistent representatives of this doctrine, the development from the most primitive monad to the absolutely perfect one God constitutes a continuous, gradual progress. He pronounced a *lex continui* ("law of continuity") which precludes any leap from one state to another, but permits only gradual change: "It is one of my great maxims that Nature never makes leaps; which I called the law of continuity." [56]

The doctrine of natural evolution enhanced the reputation of Leibniz's law of continuity. Darwin's theory of evolution through natural selection, even in its modern version of genetic mutations, implies infinitely small but continuous evolutionary processes over an extremely long time span. The doctrine of gradual change attracted a wide following among modern humanists. Bertrand Russell stated that "to build up the good life, we must build up intelligence, self-control, and sympathy. This is a quantitative matter, a matter of gradual improvement." He held that this rule applies not only to individuals but also to society, for "the good life must be lived in a good society and is not fully possible otherwise." [57] Ernst Bloch (1885–1976), a prominent German socialist philosopher who visualized hope as the innermost driving force in societal development, accepted the principle of revolution on a dialectical basis, but at the same time recognized the need for gradualism. "How thorny," he exclaimed, "is the path—how often does it require step-by-step movements—that stretches out until the dawn of the regnum humanum." [58]

Among the more recent generation of humanists, two in particular are proponents of gradual change: Karl Popper and Robert Dahl. Popper is most consistent in his insistence on the principle of gradual change. He holds that the distinction between revolutionary and gradual approaches results from a distinction between holistic and rational conceptions of social change. The holistic approach aims at changing society as a whole, according to a blueprint, composed in advance, of a perfect society, while the rational approach considers perfection as a far-distant goal and therefore concentrates on eliminating society's gravest and most urgent ills. He considers the holistic approach as "utopian engineering," and affirms that only "piecemeal engineering" constitutes a rational approach. It is not the speed of social progress that necessarily distinguishes between the two methods of action; it is the approach. Piecemeal reforms may result in rapid advances,[59] but they will always aim at step-by-step reforms of institutions "which can continuously be improved upon . . . carefully comparing the results expected with the results achieved, and always on the look-out for the unavoidable unwanted consequences of any reform." [60]

Robert Dahl, who is concerned with the evolution toward a perfect democratic society, likewise rejects the revolutionary approach in favor of the gradual approach as the most appropriate way to break the power of oligarchies: "Revolutions will probably create from the start a high probability of regression toward hegemonic rule. In the future as in the past then, stable polyarchies . . . are more likely to result from evolutionary processes than from the overthrow of existing hegemonies." [61] To the extent that the "Humanist Manifesto II" can be considered to express the prevailing opinions of present-day humanists, Popper's and Dahl's position is supported by the mainstream of modern humanism. The manifesto, while opposed to "the damming up of dynamic and revolutionary forces," insists that "the true revolution is occurring and can continue in countless non-violent adjustments."

Obviously the doctrine of gradual change is ideally applicable only in truly democratic societies. Authoritarian societies have no political and social institutions which could be used as legitimate instruments of gradual change. Yet, the possibility of gradual change may also exist in these societies; the rulers may respond to social or political pressure without an upheaval.

The political philosophers of the Age of Enlightenment insisted on the people's right to revolt against tyrannical, unjust governments, and revolutions of that kind actually occurred in that period. Modern humanists have not changed their position with respect to revolutions. Thus Rawls insisted that any means for transforming or overturning an unjust and corrupt system are justified.[62] But in truly democratic systems of government, gradual change—which need not be identified with slow change—will be the guarantor for progress toward a more perfect society. As Popper emphatically stated, "Only democracy provides an institutional framework that permits reform without violence, and so the use of reason in political matters." [63]

9. PERSPECTIVES AND PROSPECTS

The point of departure for this study has been the assertion that although not identical, the nonsecular longing for salvation and the secular striving for the perfect society are profoundly akin to one another. Having traced the history of both paths toward these goals, the question to consider now is whether the serious problems confronting today's society have affected the vitality of either the religious or the secular approach.

Regarding the vitality of today's religions, the crisis symptoms in Christian churches should not be overrated. While statistics may indicate a decline in attendance at religious services and in the number of clerics in Western countries, this does not necessarily mean that those strata of society in which religion was once deeply rooted have forsaken their beliefs and lost their trust in ultimate salvation. True, the Catholic Church is in the grips of a serious crisis, due mainly to its rigid support of tenets that ignore what are now widely recognized as necessities, such as modern birth-control methods, the right of divorce and remarriage, and priestly matrimony. But such conflicts do not affect the essence of the faith and need not shake the religiosity of the Catholic community and its longing for ultimate salvation. Moreover, the decline in the membership of the official churches could be compensated by gains made in unorthodox, especially millenarian, movements. There is an unmistakable vigor in such official millenarian denominations as the Latter-Day Saints and Jehovah's Witnesses; and unorthodox religious movements are flourishing, mostly the Pentecostal type which, without necessarily severing their ties with the official churches, assume a sectlike character.

Within the Christian world, secularizing trends have not seriously affected the essence of the faith. In Islamic, Hinduist, and Buddhist societies the secularization process appears to have strengthened rather than weakened the religious faiths. As has been shown, in the case of Islam there has been a growing determination to respond to the impact of Western civilization by reinforcing the ties to the Islamic cultural heritage. Similar currents apparently prevail in other non-Christian countries. Buddhism is influential in Japan and in some south Asia countries, while Judaism has been strengthened by the creation of Israel and by her subsequent confrontations with hostile neighbors.

It can thus be assumed that the quest for ultimate salvation by the historical religions has not subsided, in spite of the secularization process. Religious man still trusts that he can be saved even if his ultimate salvation will not take place in the world as we know it. In the meantime, religious man lives in this world, takes part in the secular society, shows growing interest in its affairs, and longs—no less fervently than secular man—for the perfection of society. Whether society can be perfected is the question that concerns religious and secular man alike.

Moreover, the trend has accelerated toward bridging the gap between the religious yearning for salvation and the secular striving for higher degrees of societal perfection, a trend that has been noticeable since Christian theologians began to preach the social gospel. Pope Paul VI's concern for and indefatigable activities in favor of social justice, economic development, and world peace, were classical examples of the humanism of modern religious life. And the politically and socially radical currents in Christianity are almost identical with those within secular movements which strive for profound societal change. There is, in other words, a growing congruence between religious and secular humanism. Consequently, the question of the perfectibility of modern society is a concern common to all men and women of good will, regardless of their religious beliefs or lack of beliefs.

Unfortunately, the humanist outlook toward society's future has been increasingly challenged by pessimists who have abandoned faith in societal progress. This pessimism has been nourished by simultaneously adverse political, economic, ecological, and demographic trends. In the political sphere, serious doubts exist as to whether a genuinely democratic world, outside the democratic industrial countries, can be expected in the foreseeable future. For in the same post-World War II period in which fascism retreated from most of Europe, and imperialism from most of the colonies, the authoritarian Soviet Union became a superpower which made inroads into democratic central Europe, and an authoritarian communist regime came to power in China. Moreover, after virtually all colonies gained independence, many of them fell under authoritarian rule.

The democratic and communist powers were not content to compete peacefully for the allegiance of the peoples and for economic and social goals. Instead, after World War II the polarization of the world into a democratic and a Soviet power bloc deepened, coinciding with the invention and development of nuclear weapons. In spite of the knowledge that any country that would start a nuclear war would risk self-destruction, a feeling of mortal danger persists and conjures the terror of the potential destruction of human civilization.

Even confidence in economic progress has been severely shaken. Aside from the obstinate business cycle, with its periodic ups and downs, several factors have awakened doubts about the perspectives of economic progress: rapid population growth in the developing countries, resulting from the decline in mortality rates; the sharp rise in oil prices which contributed to the onset of a severe economic recession; growing recognition that there are limits to the exploitation of nonrenewable natural resources; awareness that industrial and population growth produces environmental deterioration unless costly preservation measures are undertaken.

Concern about these factors found an outlet in the so-called "zero-growth" movement. It was supported by a report published in 1972 by the Club of Rome, a loose organization of scientists of various nationalities. The publication, called *Limits to Growth*, regarded as the "predicament of mankind" the consequences of exponential growth of the population and of industrial production. The report concluded that "if the present growth trends in world population, industrialization, and resource depletion continue unchanged, the limits to growth on this planet will be reached sometime within the next one hundred years."[64] The dire consequences which could be expected if these limits were reached— "a rather sudden and uncontrollable decline in both population and industrial capacity"—could be avoided and ecological stability could be achieved only if the growth of population and of capital investment were inhibited.

The report had a marked impact on public opinion, particularly as it was followed by a series of pessimistic publications, of which Robert Heilbroner's *An Inquiry into the Human Prospect* is representative. Heilbroner, an American economist, held that this prospect would be painful, difficult, perhaps desperate. He concluded that in a stationary economy only authoritarian governments would be able to impose upon the people the stern requirements necessitated by shrinking opportunities. Specifically, once the economy stopped growing, the problems of income distribution would become much more severe than they are under conditions of a growing national income, and authoritarian measures would be required to meet these problems.[65]

Menaced by these inroads of pessimism, it is no easy task for secular humanism to maintain its claim that chances are good for progress toward peace, welfare, and social justice, and that it is the duty of all men and women of good will to help bring this about. Yet, a glance at the state of world affairs will show that there is no reason for humanism to abandon its claim.

In the economic sphere, the dynamism which has characterized the economic activities of democratic-industrial, communist, and developing countries alike, has shown no sign of abatement. On the contrary, such adverse factors as the rise in oil prices and the rapid population growth in developing countries have met with a dynamic response. The crisis on the oil market has led to a search for new sites and alternative resources, while unprecedented advances in agricultural productivity have begun to meet the challenge of rapid population growth.

Generally speaking, if the GNP (gross national product) can be considered an index of economic dynamics, this index, aside from an occasional slump in the business cycle, has continued to exceed the growth of population in all three sectors of the world economy—those of the democratic-industrial, communist, and developing countries.[66] One cannot predict whether eventually adverse conditions will weaken or even completely stop the dynamics of the economy. Nor can the social and political effects of such a happening be predicted. If fears are rampant that a stagnant or shrinking production will aggravate class and group struggles, one may as well reason that a downward trend in economic dynamics may strengthen the social and political forces which struggle for a more rational and just ordering of society.

In any case, in the industrial democratic orbit there is an ongoing fight for a more just ordering of society. The fight to improve the economic, social, and political status of minorities—which in the last decade met with growing success—has continued to produce results. The gains made in the field of higher education by minorities—including women—and lower-income classes have been substantial.[67] Higher education is no longer a privileged sanctuary of the male youth of the upper classes.

In spite of the economic progress that has been going on in the developing countries—spectacular in some, much less satisfactory in many others—there is still an immense amount of misery. Many of these countries are plagued by such grave problems as mounting debts, unstable commodity prices, and lack of technical skills and equipment. Yet, there are two trends apt to accelerate their progress. First, the political power of the developing countries has increased due to the formation of power blocs, which loudly and determinedly clamor for the establishment of a "new world economic order." Although reluctant, industrial countries appear to realize that it would be in their best economic and political interest to cooperate with the principal objectives of the developing countries, to the extent that it would not jeopardize the welfare of the industrial countries.

The other favorable trend can be discerned in the field of education. Educational progress in the developing countries—from an extremely low level, to be sure—has far exceeded that in industrial countries.[68] Although serious problems in this field still loom—such as insufficient school buildings and equipment, scarcity and incompetence of teachers, overcrowded facilities—educational progress has nevertheless become an important factor in economic, social, and political development. The authoritarian structure of most of the developing countries is being increasingly challenged by the new strata of educated youth.

The possibilities of evolutionary change should not be ruled out even in the communist orbit. There seem to be two tendencies that may favor such a development. First, it appears that the wave of dissent among intellectuals is mounting. However small numerically this group might be, its moral and intellectual impact seems to be on the rise, and the authorities seem to be less and less able to silence their clamor for civil liberties and cultural freedoms. The other favorable tendency is the growing economic interdependence between the communist and the democratic industrial countries. The continuing or even increasing technological superiority of the democratic countries is likely to attenuate tensions between the communist and democratic camps. Even in China the regime that assumed power after the death of Mao Tse-tung is dedicated to intense technological development, a commitment which will unavoidably produce growing economic interdependence with the democratic countries.

Realistically, there is no reason to nourish illusions about the prospects for perfecting society. The contending forces in human nature and in societal structures—fraternal vs. aggressive, conservative vs. progressive—have always imposed limits on societal progress and will continue to do so. Political tensions within and between countries will not simply disappear. Economic and ecological limitations on progress are bound to persist. But while it is important to be aware of these limiting factors, they tend to be countered by so many favorable trends that the pessimism about the prospects of society, which has lately become so widespread, can be challenged effectively.

If progress toward a more perfect society appears attainable, does modern humanism, both religious and secular, fulfill any function in this scheme of societal development? The answer is that humanism is inseparable from this scheme. The ideals that have inspired religious and secular humanism through the centuries are very much alive and, in our era, their scope has even been increased. While there are no humanist political parties, and it is not likely that there will be any in the foreseeable future, many parties and movements uphold humanist ideals.

Hence the real function of humanism is that of a catalyst in society. Humanists are people who consider progress in the direction of perfecting society to be in their personal interest, and they act and fight accordingly. Taken in this light, there is no difference between religious and secular humanism. The Spanish priests who under the Franco regime were pressing for the democratization and humanization of their society, the Latin American bishops who have publicly proclaimed the urgent need for radical societal change on their continent, each is acting like the secular humanists who raise their voices at universities, in political parties, and through the media to press for those societal reforms needed everywhere.

With an overview of mankind from its remote beginnings, and looking into its future, the perfect society does not seem to lie within reach. Indeed, the quest appears to be eternal. Just as the Judaic-derived religions trust that the kingdom of God will be brought down to earth outside of history at the end of time, secular humanists regard the advent of a perfect society as outside the confines of history as we can conceive of it. Yet both religious and secular humanists are convinced that higher degrees of societal perfection can be achieved, and that tendencies toward perfection do exist, however fragile their roots. They realize that it is up to all men and women of good will to do everything in their power to strengthen these tendencies. Religious and secular humanists alike are endowed with a sacred trust: to actively fight for the perfection of society.

Notes

CHAPTER I

1. All quotations from the Old Testament, the Apocrypha, and the New Testament are from *The New English Bible, with the Apocrypha* (Oxford and Cambridge, 1970).

2. Modern biblical research places the Book of Deuteronomy in the period of King Josiah (640–609 B.C.), with later additions.

3. Homer *Odyssey* 19.

4. The association of Yahweh with wind and weather remained alive in Israel long after His elevation to the rank of the sole God, first of Israel, then of the universe: Yahweh came down in a pillar of cloud to speak to Aaron and Miriam (Deut. 31:15); that cloud came down and stayed at the entrance of the tent when Yahweh spoke to Moses (Exod. 33:9); the Lord filled the temple in a cloud when Solomon's temple was finished (1 Kings 8:10–11). The image of Yahweh "riding on the wings of the wind," as beautifully expressed in the famous Psalm 104, can be found in many Old Testament Scriptures. Even in so late a Scripture as that of Deutero-Zechariah (in the fourth or third century B.C.) did the Lord God "march with the storm winds of the South" (Zech. 9:14).

5. The storm god who scattered the mighty Armada in A.D. 1588, was praised for this deed by the British. Queen Elizabeth I was well aware of this fact when she created a commemorative medal bearing the Old Testament-like phrase, "Yahweh blew with His wind and they were scattered."

6. Henri Frankfort, *Kingship and the Gods*, 4th ed. (Chicago, 1962), p. 51.

7. Martin Buber, *Kingship of God*, 3rd ed. (London, 1967), p. 129.

8. Quoted by Samuel H. Hooke, *Babylonian and Assyrian Religion* (Norman, Oklahoma, 1963), p. 97.

9. Leonard W. King, *Legends of Babylon and Egypt in Relation to Hebrew Tradition* (Oxford, 1918), p. 55.

10. Jan Gonda, *Die Religionen Indiens, I. Veda and Älterer Hinduismus* (Stuttgart, 1960), p. 41.

11. Bhagavad Gita, trans. M. Chatterji (New York, 1960), chaps. 3, 11.

12. Hooke, *Babylonian Religion*, p. 39.
13. Andrew M. Greeley, *The Sinai Myth* (New York, 1972), pp. 46–47.
14. This injunction did not imply that Yahweh ought to be regarded as the only divine personality. Like other Semitic deities, He was always surrounded by a "host" of minor divinities. They were considered "sons of God" or even "sons of the gods," as in Genesis 6:2; or they formed a court (in the manner of Middle Eastern royal courts) such as when the prophet Micaiah saw God "seated on his throne, with all the host of heaven in attendance on his right and on his left" (1 Kings 22:19).
15. The sacrifice of the first-born sons lingered in Israel. Even at the end of the pre-exilic period, Jeremiah accused the sons of Judah of having built a shrine at Tophet "at which to burn their sons and daughters," and to sacrifice them to Molech (Jer. 7:31 and 32:35). There can, on the other hand, be no doubt about the early date of the abolition of the sacrifice of the first-born sons. In the Book of Numbers the initiation of the redemption tax appears as the imposition of a tax to be paid to the Levites, since God declared to Moses that the Levites should be His in substitution of the first-born sons. The Cohen (a descendant of the Aaronite priesthood) to whom this tax is to be paid still asks the father whether he prefers to give the son or the money. See *Universal Jewish Encyclopedia*, New York, 1939–1943, s.v. "Redemption of the first-born."
16. Quoted by Charles S. Branden, *Man's Quest for Salvation* (Chicago and New York, 1941), p. 103.
17. See below, chapter II, section 2.
18. Quoted by Branden, *Man's Quest*, p. 103.
19. Quoted by Francis Cornford, *Greek Religious Thought from Homer to the Age of Alexander* (New York, 1969), pp. 28–29.
20. For Sophocles, see ibid., p. 119; and for Euripides, see ibid., p. 150.
21. Ibid., p. 154.
22. Frankfort, *Kingship*, pp. 278–79.
23. William F. Albright, *From the Stone Age to Christianity*, 2nd ed. (Baltimore, 1957), p. 332.
24. Samuel H. Hooke, *Myth, Ritual and Kingship* (Oxford, 1958), pp. 110–11.
25. Gonda, *Die Religionen*, p. 40.
26. The Book of Leviticus contained a catalogue of transgressions and guilt offerings, combined with confessions (5, 6:1–7). How strong the ritual element in that stage still was can be seen from the cases of David and of King Ahab of the Northern Kingdom (who reigned from c. 874 to c. 853 B.C.). The repentance of David for his sinning with Bathsheba and for the murder of Uriah (2 Sam. 12:3), and that of Ahab as an instrument of his pagan wife Jezebel (1 Kings 21:27), as well as the divine punishment inflicted on their offspring, were still of a strictly ritual nature.
27. "A wounded heart, O God, Thou wilt not despise" (Ps. 51:17).
28. Homer, *Iliad* I, trans. Richmond Lattimore (Chicago, 1962), p. 211.

29. Quoted by Cornford, *Greek Religious Thought*, p. 224.
30. *Encyclopaedia Judaica*, Jerusalem, 1970, s.v. "Sacrifice."
31. For the date of the Letter to Hebrews, see *Encyclopaedia Britannica*, 1972, s.v. "Hebrews, Epistle to the."
32. Dan. 9:16; Wisd. of Sol. 3:16; Tob. 3:3–5; Jth. 7–8.
33. In the Babylonian version, Ea, one of the chief Gods, stated that "on the sinner lay his sin," implying that the community as such was the sinner. Alexander Heidel, *The Gilgamesh Epic and Old Testament Parallels* (Chicago, 1963), p. 88.
34. There are strong indications for the assumption that the passages on individual responsibility and retribution enunciated in the Books of Jeremiah and Ezekiel were added by later editors. *The Interpreter's Bible* (New York, 1954), on Jeremiah, p. 1036; on Ezekiel, pp. 48–49.
35. For the Orphic-Platonic doctrines, see below, chapter III, section 3.
36. The origin of "The Babylonian Job" is uncertain, but in any event preceded the Book of Job probably by some centuries.
37. *Interpreter's Bible*, Introduction to the Book of Job, vol. 3, p. 881.
38. Cornford, *Greek Religious Thought*, pp. 38–39.
39. Ibid., p. 122.
40. Satan plays an important part in the Job epic, but only as a subordinate agent of God.
41. It is rather generally assumed that the bulk of the Book of Job was written in the sixth or fifth century B.C. The atmosphere of utter despair that surrounds it suggests indeed an exilic or post-exilic date.
42. In their books, as they were incorporated in the Canon of the Old Testament, there are a great number of eschatological passages; but Old Testament scholarship has come to doubt that any of these passages go back to the great classical prophets themselves. Most, if not all, were inserted into their books in the post-exilic era when eschatological beliefs had begun to pervade the Jewish people.
43. Some doubts have been expressed, particularly by S. Mowinckel in *He that Cometh*, trans. G. W. Anderson (Oxford, 1959), as to whether those parts of chapters 40 to 55 of the Book of Isaiah which refer to the Servant of the Lord (the so-called Servant's Songs, especially chapter 53) were written by Deutero-Isaiah or by a later author. But the prevailing opinion among Old Testament scholars is that chapters 40 to 55 in their entirety form a unity which strongly suggests one author.
44. The metaphor "Alpha and Omega," which originated in the Book of Revelation (1:8 passim), was doubtless derived from Deutero-Isaiah's "first and last."
45. Examples abound. In the era of the Judges Jephtha declared to the Ammonites: "It is for you to possess whatever Kemosh your God gives you; and all that the Lord our God gave us as we advanced is ours" (Judg. 11:24). Similarly when David was forced into exile by Saul, he blamed Saul for having

banished him "to serve other gods" (1 Sam. 26:19). Solomon saw fit to worship the gods of his seven hundred wives who were foreign princesses (1 Kings 11:4). Even Jeremiah warned those who followed the prompting of their wicked hearts that God "will fling you headlong out of this land into a country unknown to you and to your forefathers; there you can serve other gods day and night" (Jer. 16:13).

46. The belief that God appoints the king as shepherd to guide the people seems to have been rather common in ancient Middle Eastern society. Thus Tiglath Pileser I (Assyrian king of the eleventh century B.C.) proclaimed: "In order that I become the shepherd of the four regions, Ashur (Assyria's paramount God) pronounced my name for the cosmic age." Buber, *Kingship of God*, p. 89.

47. The question of the identity of Deutero-Isaiah's suffering servant has been contested among Old Testament scholars. A number of them held that he was either a historical person, such as one of the classical prophets, or a Messiah figure; but the prevailing view among scholars is that he symbolized the Jewish people.

48. See particularly Helmer Ringgren, *Israelite Religion*, trans. David E. Green (Philadelphia, 1966), p. 293.

49. The stories of Abraham's intercession for Sodom on the eve of her destruction (Gen. 23–32) and Moses' intercession for his people after their apostasy (Exod. 32:11–14) come to mind. Even Amos, in spite of his severe judgment of his sinful people, interceded twice when Yahweh was about to punish them with locusts and fire (Amos 7:1–6).

50. Other insertions in the Books of Isaiah (25:3 and 60:3), Jeremiah (3:17 and 16:19–21), and Zephaniah (3:9–10) made the same prophecies. Zechariah, who was active shortly after Deutero-Isaiah, also prophesied that "many nations shall come over to the Lord on that day and become his people" (Zech. 2:11).

51. The concept of God's kingship in Israel was retained in a number of psalms through the formula: "The Lord is king" (Pss. 47, 93, 96, 98, 99).

52. While Zechariah was active soon after the fall of Babylon and the restoration of Judah, chapters 9 to 15 of the Book of Zechariah were written, at the earliest, two hundred years later. Old Testament scholars have attributed these chapters to one or several authors, who may singly or collectively be called "Deutero-Zechariah."

53. Some Old Testament scholars assume that of the eleven chapters of the Book of Isaiah following the Deutero-Isaiah chapters, several (either chapters 60–66 or 65–66) were written by an author who could be called Trito-Isaiah.

54. In the prophecy inserted in Isaiah 11:6, and in Trito-Isaiah (Isa. 65:25).

55. See Isaiah's oracles about the future king, "upon whom the spirit of the Lord shall rest . . . a spirit of wisdom and understanding, a spirit of counsel and power, a spirit of knowledge and the fear of the Lord" (Isa. 11:2), and par-

ticularly Isaiah's famous oracle about "the boy [who] has been born for us . . . he shall be called in purpose wonderful, in battle God-like, Father for all time, Prince of peace" (Isa. 9:6).

56. That God uses a record of this kind was obviously a common Jewish belief. Originally it may have been a record of all living members of the community. Thus when Moses interceded for the apostate people, he said to God that if God were to refuse to forgive them, He should "blot out my name from Thy book which Thou hast written," and God answered that He would blot out those who had sinned (Exod. 32:32–33). It may have been in a later period that only the names of the righteous were recorded in the book. (See Pss. 40:7; 56:8; 69:28; and Isa. 4:3.)

57. The curse attached to the lack of ritual burial and to the refusal of burial has been characteristic of many civilizations until recent times. Criminals and heretics were, and partly still are, refused burial in sacred burial grounds. The conflict broke out between Creon and Antigone in Sophocles' *Antigone* because Creon refused burial to Antigone's brother Polyneikes and she buried him secretly. The same motive appeared in the apocryphal Book of Tobit, where Tobit secretly buried fellow Jews who had been refused burial by the Assyrian kings Shalmaneser and Sennacherib. Like Antigone, Tobit was sentenced to death for this crime but escaped, like Antigone in one of Euripides' plays (See Tob. 1:16–19).

58. See below, chapter III, section 2.

CHAPTER II

1. The words *moksha*, *samsara*, *karma*, *Yoga*, *Nirvana*, and a number of other words mentioned in this chapter are of Sanskrit origin.

2. The Vedas (lit., "knowledge") are a vast collection of hymns, prayers, ritual and liturgical texts, myths, and philosophical treatises, which were composed through many centuries, beginning with the settlement of the Aryans in India.

3. The Rig-Veda (lit., "Veda of verses") is the oldest of four groups of Vedas which are considered canonical. It consists of a great number of myths and hymns to the gods. See George Benjamin Walker, *The Hindu World* (London, 1968).

4. Quoted by Sten Rodhe, *Deliver Us from Evil* (Lund, 1946), p. 46.

5. Ibid., p. 84. It is interesting to note the parallelism between this Vedic prayer and the eschatological prophecy of Trito-Isaiah: "Every boy shall live a hundred years before he dies; whoever falls short of a hundred years shall be despised" (Isa. 65:20).

6. Quoted by Henry N. Wieman and Walter M. Horton, *The Growth of Religion* (Chicago, 1938), p. 41.

7. The caste system dates back to the earliest Aryan period, but is still very much alive in present-day India. In a late section of the Rig-Veda, it was re-

lated that four groups of men emerged from the body of the God Prajapati: the Brahmins from his mouth, the Kshatrya from his arms, the Vaisya from his thighs, and the Sudras from his feet (see *Encyclopaedia Britannica*, Macropedia, vol. 9, 1974, s.v. "History of the Indian Subcontinent"). The Brahmins constitute the highest priestly caste; the Kshatrya, the warrior caste; the Vaisya, the merchant caste; and the Sudras, the laborer caste.

8. Rodhe, *Deliver Us from Evil*, p. 101.

9. Ibid., p. 117. The Brahmanas were commentaries on the Vedic scriptures which date from the end of the sixth century B.C. See Walker, *Hindu World*, under "Brahmanas."

10. After a Brahmana text, quoted by Rodhe, *Deliver Us from Evil*, p. 93.

11. The Upanishads (lit., "sitting down near," meaning, sitting around a guru or teacher who imparts secret knowledge) were religious-philosophical texts, composed in various periods. The most important Upanishads can be dated from the eighth and seventh centuries B.C. See S. Radhakrishnan, *The Principal Upanishads* (New York, 1953), p. 19 ff.

12. Ibid., p. 497.

13. From the Brhad-aranyaka Upanishads, quoted by ibid., p. 231; from an Upanishadic text, in *Encyclopaedia Britannica*, 1972, s.v. "Brahma and Brahman."

14. From the Chandogya Upanishads, quoted by Radhakrishnan, *Principal Upanishads*, p. 77.

15. Quoted by Rodhe, *Deliver Us from Evil*, p. 35.

16. Ibid., p. 128.

17. Yoga (lit., "joining" or "union") was originally a collection of philosophical writings composed from ancient teachings. Characterized by an Upanishadic spirit, these writings sought release through union with the All-Soul, using various paths. The most significant forms of Yoga are those which base the release on concentration and meditation; bodily postures and breathing practices are some means of this release.

18. From the Brhad-aranyaka Upanishads, quoted by Radhakrishnan, *Principal Upanishads*, p. 273.

19. A passage in one of the Brahmanas reads, "Verily there are two kinds of gods; for indeed the gods are the gods, and the Brahmins who have studied and teach sacred lore are the human gods." Quoted by Samuel G. F. Brandon, in Samuel H. Hooke, *Myth, Ritual and Kingship* (Oxford, 1958), p. 274.

20. *Encyclopaedia Britannica*, 1972, s.v. "Mahavira."

21. Gandhi formulated the Jain principle of nonviolence toward all creatures by stating, "As man has not been given power to create, he has not the slightest right to destroy the smallest creature that lives." *Encyclopaedia Britannica*, 1972, s.v. "Gandhi."

22. Dharma is a Sanskrit term which broadly embraces both the cosmic order

and the religious, civic, and social order; but in Buddhist usage it signifies doctrine, principally Buddha's doctrine. Buddha's Dharma is traditionally symbolized by a wheel, *Dharma cakra*, which sharply contrasts with *samsara*, the wheel of existence. Interestingly enough, whereas Buddhism has vanished from India, Buddha's wheel of Dharma has been enshrined in the coat of arms of modern India.

23. From a discourse in the Majjhima Nikaya, quoted by Charles Eliot, *Hinduism and Buddhism* (New York, 1971) vol. 1, p. 229.

24. *Encyclopaedia of Buddhism*, 1966, s.v. "Arahant." This sanskrit term is usually spelled *arahat* or *arhat*.

25. Krishna has been enveloped in innumerable legends and myths, the most important features of which are that he was a human being, lived a fantastically adventurous and heroic life, was an untiring lover, was accidentally killed by a hunter, and ascended to heaven. The elements of the dying and resurrected fertility god are obvious. See also Walker, *Hindu World*, under "Krishna."

26. *The Bhagavad Gita*, trans. W. Douglas P. Hill (Madras, 1953).

27. Mahatma Gandhi did not oppose the caste system itself, but regarded it as one of his foremost tasks to foster the emancipation of the untouchables, outcasts who did not belong to any of the four traditional castes. He renamed them "Harijans," meaning "children of Vishnu." The Indian Constitution of 1949 legally abolished the disabilities of the Harijans and elevated them to the rank of scheduled castes. Yet the process of integrating them into Hindu society with full social rights is extremely slow. In large parts of India, particularly in rural areas, the disabilities of the Harijans have not disappeared. Many Harijans have sought protection by converting to other religions, chiefly Islam and Buddhism. *Encyclopaedia Britannica*, 1972, s.v. "Untouchables."

28. Charles S. Branden, *Man's Quest for Salvation* (Chicago and New York, 1941), p. 25.

29. A testimony of Gandhi's allegiance to Bhakti Hinduism is contained in a statement made in 1925 in which he said: "My life has been full of external tragedies—and if they have left no visible, no indelible scar on me, I owe it all to the teachings of the Bhagavad Gita." Quoted by W. Douglas P. Hill, as motto for his translation of the Bhagavad Gita.

30. The Hare Krishna sect, which counts a number of devoted followers in the United States and in other Western countries, is directly based on the Krishna cult and specifically on the Bhagavad Gita.

31. Guenter Lewy, *Religion and Revolution* (New York, 1974), p. 278 ff.

32. The word "Mahayana" (lit., "the great vehicle" or "the great career") implies a wide route toward salvation. In contrast, Mahayana Buddhists call Theravada Buddhism the "Hinayana" school (lit., "the small vehicle" or "the narrow route"). Theravada Buddhists reject this name as pejorative.

33. For this Catholic doctrine, see below, chapter V, section 8.
34. This belief, which resembles similar docetic beliefs in Gnostic writings and in some heretic Christian writings about the person of the savior, seems to go back to the oldest controversies about the nature of Buddha. Thus the so-called Mahasanghika school, which was in conflict with the Theravada school, adopted the docetic doctrine that the historical Buddha was only an image of the supermundane Buddha. See Edward J. Thomas, *The History of Buddhist Thought* (New York, 1953), p. 173. About Gnostic docetism, see below, chapter III, section 3.
35. Sutras, (lit., "guiding lines") are doctrinal writings which can be found in Hindu, Jainist, and Buddhist literature. The Lotus Sutra (lit., "Lotus of the Good Law"), most popular of all Mahayana sutras, is of rather ancient Indian origin and was translated into Chinese in the third and fourth centuries A.D. See Eliot, *Hinduism and Buddhism*, vol. 2, p. 53.
36. Thomas, *Buddhist Thought*, pp. 213–17, 223.
37. On Taoism, see section 5 of this chapter.
38. The imperial regime tried to strengthen military discipline by spreading the belief that the Shinto divinities would help the soldiers. When Makiguchi attacked the imperial regime, he was imprisoned. He died in prison.
39. The Pure Land school is of much older, Chinese origin. It goes back to the Infinite Purity Sutra (rendered in Chinese in the second century A.D.) which viewed Buddha Amitabha as the savior who would lead every believer who invokes him into the Pure Land. The Chinese sage Hui Yuan (fourth century A.D.) founded the first Pure Land school.
40. Shin still appears to be by far the largest Buddhist sect in Japan, and Shinran is still one of the most venerated figures in that country.
41. Lewy, *Religion and Revolution*, p. 467 ff. The book to which Lewy refers, *Triumph of Righteousness*, was published in 1953; its author was identified in the body of the book as D. C. Vijayavardhana.
42. The quotations from Confucius's teachings reproduced in this chapter are taken from those parts of the Analects which are most likely to be authentic. For an analysis of the authenticity of the various parts of the Analects, see Arthur Waley, *The Analects of Confucius*, 6th ed. (London, 1971), p. 21. All quotations from the Analects are from Waley's translation.
43. Arthur Waley, *Madly Singing in the Mountains: An Anthology of Arthur Waley* (New York, 1970), p. 231.
44. See, particularly, *Encyclopedia of Philosophy*, 1967, s.v. "Chinese Philosophy."
45. H. G. Creel, *Confucius, the Man and the Myth* (New York, 1949), p. 190.
46. *Encyclopaedia Britannica*, 1972, s.v. "Confucianism."
47. This and the following quotations from Chuang-Tzu are from H. G. Creel, *What Is Taoism?* (Chicago, 1970). The quotation above is from p. 28.

CHAPTER III

1. An example is a thanksgiving prayer offered to the chief god Amon under King Ramses II: "When I cried to Thee in my affliction, Thou didst come to save me." Quoted by William F. Albright, *From the Stone Age to Christianity*, 2nd ed. (Baltimore, 1957), p. 173.

2. See above, chapter 1, section 1. In the New Kingdom the Theban priests identified the local god Amon with the sun-god Re, and merged the two gods.

3. Quoted by Alfred Jeremias, *Die ausserbiblische Erlösererwartung* (Berlin, 1927).

4. Samuel A. B. Mercer, *The Religion of Ancient Egypt* (London, 1949), p. 41 ff.

5. For the history and the description of the various versions of the Book of the Dead, and for the translation of one of its versions, see Sir Ernest A. Wallis Budge, *The Book of the Dead*, 2nd ed. (London, 1940).

6. Quoted from the so-called Theban Recension of *The Book of the Dead*, by ibid., p. xiv.

7. Egypt having been divided into forty-two nomes (provinces), it appears that the forty-two judges were local gods of each of the nomes and that the number of categories of sins was determined after the number of judges.

8. From chapter 125 of the Theban Recension, quoted by ibid., p. 361.

9. Quoted by Albright, *Stone Age to Christianity*, p. 136.

10. Quoted by Jacques Pirenne, "L'au delà dans la religion égyptienne," in *Religions de Salut* (Brussels, 1962).

11. The fable is reminiscent of that of the rich man and the poor Lazarus narrated in the Gospel of Luke (16:19–31). Hugo Gressmann, who related the Egyptian fable, was of the opinion that Luke based his fable on the Egyptian story. See *The Interpreter's Bible*, vol. 8 (New York, 1954), in a comment on the passage of the Gospel of Luke.

12. These Gathas constitute chapters 28–34 and 43–52 of the Yasna. See R. C. Zaehner, *The Dawn and Twilight of Zoroastrianism* (New York, 1961).

13. See Yasna 31: "By His mind, in the beginnings, He fashioned forth corporeal things, consciousness and wills." This quotation, and all following quotations from the Gathas have been taken from Zaehner, *Dawn and Twilight*.

14. These were the so-called "Seven Chapters," containing the Gathas from Yasna 35 to Yasna 42.

15. *Encyclopaedia Britannica*, 1972, s.v. "Zoroastrianism."

16. In later centuries the belief spread, under the influence of Orphism, that the souls of all evildoers would be punished in Tartarus.

17. Plato is the chief source for the Orphic origin of this doctrine. He stated in *Cratylus*: "The Orphic poets . . . were under the impression that the soul is suffering for punishment for certain sins, and that the body is an enclosure or prison in which the soul is incarcerated . . . until the penalty is paid." This

quotation, and all following quotations from Plato's *Dialogues*, are taken from *The Dialogues of Plato*, trans. B. Jowett, 4th ed. (Oxford, 1953). This quotation is from vol. 3, pp. 60–61.

18. Quoted by Francis Cornford, *Greek Religious Thought from Homer to the Age of Alexander* (New York, 1969), p. 63.

19. According to Clement of Alexandria, *Miscellaneous IV*. Quoted by ibid., pp. 72–74.

20. Plato *Phaedrus* 3.246.

21. Plato *Phaedo* 1.80.

22. Plato used the metaphor of a chariot driven by two horses, one of noble, the other of ignoble breed. *Phaedrus* 3.246.

23. Plato *Symposium* 1.212.

24. Plato *Phaedo* 1.66.

25. Ibid., 1.67.

26. Plato *Phaedrus* 3.249.

27. Plato *Phaedo* 1.80–82.

28. Plato *Symposium* 1.205.

29. Ibid., 1.206.

30. Ibid., 1.211.

31. Plato *Theaetetus* 3.176.

32. See Plato *Theaetetus* 3.176: "God is never in any way unrighteous—He is perfect righteousness."

33. Plato *Timaeus* 3.33.

34. Plato *Laws* 10.3.903.

35. Plato *Phaedo* 1.114.

36. Ibid., 1.81, 82.

37. Ibid., 1.114.

38. Plato *Phaedrus* 3.248–49.

39. Plato *Timaeus* 3.40–42.

40. Plato *Laws* 10.904–5.

41. Plato *Phaedrus* 3.250.

42. Plato *Timaeus* 3.41–42.

43. Ibid., 3.42.

44. See section 4 of this chapter.

45. *Encyclopedia of Philosophy*, 1967, s.v. "Aristotle."

46. Quoted by Edwyn Bevan, *Later Greek Religion* (London, 1927), p. 18. It seems that the concept of the *logos*, which was to become important in late-Judaic and Christian thinking, originated in the philosophy of Heraclitus (c. 540–c. 480 B.C.) and was understood by him as the foundation of the order of the universe; but it was through Stoicism that this concept penetrated the ancient Western world.

47. Cleanthes, *Hymn to Zeus*, trans. James Adam, in R. D. Hicks, *Stoic and Epicurean* (New York, 1962), pp. 14–16.

48. Quoted by Bevan, *Later Greek Religion*, p. 25.
49. Proverbs 8:22–23. While a large part of the Book of Proverbs constituted ancient wisdom literature, those parts in which wisdom was personified were most likely composed in the post-Alexandrian period.
50. About Philo of Alexandria, see section 5 of this chapter.
51. According to Orphic literature, Dionysus was killed and devoured by the Titans, and revived by Zeus.
52. *The Homeric Hymns*, trans. Daryl Hine (New York, 1972), pp. 4–16.
53. Lucius Apuleius, *The Golden Ass*, trans. Robert Graves under the title *The Transformations of Lucius, otherwise known as The Golden Ass* (New York, 1951). The quotations in the text are from pp. 264–80.
54. See section 1 of this chapter.
55. Plutarch (A.D. c. 46–119) related that the initiate on his death-bed was clothed with the celestial garments which he had worn in the initiation rites, and that he was united with the deity in the beyond. See Richard Reitzenstein, *Die hellenistischen Mysterienreligionen* (Leipzig, 1909), p. 30.
56. The term "heretic," as used in this and in the following chapters, signifies a deviation from the official doctrines of the Christian Church.
57. The term "docetic" has traditionally been used in connection with the figure of Jesus. Early Church Fathers coined it to signify the heretic belief that Jesus was an entirely divine figure and that his humanity was only apparent.
58. *Encyclopedia of Philosophy*, 1967, s.v. "Philo."
59. *New Catholic Encyclopedia*, 1967, s.v. "Gnosticism, Jewish."
60. The Cabala (Kabbalah) was a late product of Jewish Gnosticism. Of its classics, the earliest, *Sefer Bahir* ("Book of Clarity"), was composed, from earlier treatises and traditions, in the twelfth century A.D. in France, and the *Sefer ha-Zohar* ("Book of Splendor"), in the thirteenth century in Spain.
61. The text of "Poimandres" was published in Hans Jonas, *The Gnostic Religions*, 2nd ed. (Boston, 1963), p. 148–53. The *Corpus Hermeticum*, a collection of religious treatises which seem to have been composed in the first two centuries A.D., belongs to the so-called Hermetic writings. They owe their name to the Egyptian god Thot who in the Greek world was identified with Hermes. In the Hermetic writings he was called "Hermes Trismegistos" (meaning "Hermes, the thrice great").
62. See below, chapter IV, section 3; and chapter V, section 2.
63. It is hardly possible to distinguish the teachings of Valentinus from those of his disciples since his own writings have not been preserved. One of the most important writings, found in connection with the great discovery of Gnostic literature near Nag Hammadi in Upper Egypt (in 1945), was the *Gospel of Truth* (published in 1956), obviously of Valentinian origin. But it cannot be ascertained whether it was written by Valentinus himself.
64. The Aeons—in Greek usage, meaning "periods of the universe"—originally

appeared in Platonic cosmology as phases of the supreme reality, and in the Valentinian Gnostic system as emanations from God.

65. For Marcion and Valentinus, see particularly Hans Jonas, *Gnostic Religions*, and *Encyclopedia of Philosophy*, 1967, s.v. "Marcion" and "Valentinus and Valentinianism."

66. For Manichaeism, see particularly Hans Jonas, *Gnostic Religions*, pp. 206–36, and *New Catholic Encyclopedia*, 1967, s.v. "Manichaeism."

67. The origin of the name "Paulicianism" is uncertain. The name may either go back to the Apostle Paul or to a Manichaean personality by the name of Paul.

68. The name "Cathars" was derived from the Greek word for "pure"; they were also known as "Albigenses," from the town Albi in Southern France, one of their strongholds.

69. This impact was felt even in the linguistic sphere. The German word *Ketzer* ("heretic") is directly derived from Cathar while the French word *bougre*, which has a broad, frequently pejorative connotation, is derived from the heretic Bulgars, that is, from the Bogomils.

70. See particularly Psalms 34 and 91. In the Book of Job, Elihu speaks of an angel, one of thousands, who stands by man, "a mediator between him and God, to expound what he has done right and to secure mortal man his due." The *Book of Tobit*, an apocryphal Scripture which appeared at about the same time as the Book of Daniel, introduced an angel named Raphael as a guardian angel of Tobit and his family.

71. The New English Bible broke with the tradition of translating the Hebrew "son of man" literally into English, as all earlier English versions did, thus acknowledging the fact that the Hebrew term "son of man" is purely idiomatic and has no other meaning than that of signifying "man."

72. Mowinckel, *He that Cometh*, trans. G. W. Anderson (Oxford, 1959), pp. 423–25), held that Daniel's "man" (or "son of man"), who comes with the clouds of heaven (and similar kinds of savior figures in later apocalypses), was derived from Persian and Indo-Persian myths of the "Primordial Man." Thus the savior Saoshyant in late-Zoroastrianism was regarded as an incarnation both of Zarathustra and of Gayomart, the Primordial Man.

73. See Wisdom of Solomon (8:19–20), where Solomon said: "A noble soul fell to my lot; or rather, I myself was noble, and I entered into an unblemished body."

74. The apocrypha were never accepted in the Hebrew Bible, but they constituted part of the Greek Septuaginta. As such they were recognized by the Christian Church and formed part of the Vulgate. The Council of Trent (1545–1563) recognized them officially, but the Roman Catholic Church considers them as "deutero-canonical." The Orthodox and Protestant churches have not given them any official status. Writings "professing to be biblical in character, but not considered canonical or inspired" are com-

monly called "pseudepigraphic." *Random House Dictionary*, unabr. ed. (New York, 1967), p. 1159.

75. Quoted by N. H. Rowley, *The Relevance of Apocalyptic*, rev. ed. (New York, 1964), p. 61. Similar beliefs were expressed in the First Book of Enoch (second century or beginning of the first century B.C.) and in the Assumption of Moses (the first thirty years A.D.). In other apocalypses, however, such as the Similitudes of Enoch (in the First Book of Enoch) and the Psalms of Solomon (around the middle of the first century B.C.), some kind of bodily resurrection was envisioned.

76. In fact, this belief has not wholly disappeared. One of the traditions frequently observed at the Seder rites on the eve of the Jewish Passover consists of setting aside a separate cup of wine for Elijah and opening the door to invite him in.

77. Quoted by A. N. Gilkes, *The Impact of the Dead Sea Scrolls* (London, 1962), p. 53.

78. The Book of Jubilees, *The Testaments of the Twelve Patriarchs* (probably first century B.C.), the Sibylline Oracles, and the Assumption of Moses were particularly rich in fantasies about the misdeeds of Satan and his destruction. The source for most references to post-Danielic apocalypses used in this section is Rowley, *Relevance of Apocalyptic*. Only those apocalypses have been dealt with in this chapter which date from periods prior to Jesus' teachings. References to later Jewish apocalypses, particularly the Fourth Book of Ezra (also called the Second Book of Esdras), the Second Book of Enoch (also called the Slavonic Enoch), and the Apocalypse of Baruch, have been omitted as they were outside the currents which prevailed in the period that gave birth to Christianity.

79. In the "Pittsburgh Platform" adopted by the Central Conference of American Rabbis in 1889, the creed of Reform Judaism, "Israel's great Messianic hope," was interpreted as "the establishment of the kingdom of truth, justice and peace among all men." Similarly the "Guiding Principles of Reform Judaism," adopted by the Central Conference in 1937, pronounced the establishment of the kingdom of God, of universal brotherhood and justice, truth and peace on earth "as Israel's Messianic goal." For the text of the "Pittsburgh Platform," see *Encyclopaedia Judaica*, 1971, s.v. "The Pittsburgh Platform"; for the reference to the "Guiding Principles," see ibid., s.v. "Messiah."

CHAPTER IV

1. The first three Gospels—Matthew, Mark, and Luke—are commonly called synoptic because of the similarities in their accounts of Jesus' life and teachings.

2. Matthew Black, *The Scrolls and Christian Origins* (New York, 1961), p. 94.

3. Significantly the Gospel of John, according to which Jesus was a divine figure, omitted the temptation story.

4. See below, chapter VIII, section 3.

5. Several healings of this kind which were performed during Jesus' lifetime were attested to in the New Testament by his disciples (Mark 6:13), and after his death by the Apostles Peter (Acts 3:2–8) and Paul (Acts 19:12). Paul wrote of signs, marvels, and miracles that he and other faithful Christians performed (Cor. 12:12; Rom. 15:19; Gal. 3:5), and which may have mostly consisted of healings.

6. Cases of healings of this kind were related to three classical prophets: Elijah, Elisha, and Isaiah. Elijah (1 Kings 17:17–24) and Elisha (2 Kings 4:31–35) were supposed to have restored a child to life, while Isaiah was supposed to have lengthened by fifteen years the life of King Hezekiah (who reigned from c. 715 to c. 686 B.C.), by healing him of a deadly disease (2 Kings 20:4–11 and Isa. 38:4–8). In all three cases the restoration to life or the healing were presented as acts of God, combined with magic devices.

7. See Karl Kautsky, *Der Ursprung des Christentums*, trans. Henry F. Min under the title *Foundations of Christianity* (1908; rept. ed., New York, 1953); and S. G. F. Brandon, *Jesus and the Zealots* (Manchester, 1967).

8. Paul M. Van Buren, *The Secular Meaning of the Gospel* (New York, 1963), p. 129, considered the appearances of Jesus to his disciples and followers as "sense-content statements," that is, statements recording sensations: something that I saw, but not what there is for everyone to see. Such statements cannot be verified by commonsense or empirical means.

9. This discrepancy between genealogy and divine origin was of long standing in mythological tradition. In Genesis 21:1–2, Yahweh showed favor to Sarah and she conceived; Isaac was, nevertheless, considered to have been Abraham's son, and Abraham, in Old Testament tradition, remained the patriarch whose descendants became the fathers of the Hebrew tribes. Similar myths preceded that of Sarah in Egyptian mythology, where the queens were shown favor by the chief god Amon-re, but their sons were regarded as the king's sons.

10. The word "Lord" (in the original Greek text, *kyrios*) in the mouth of Peter did not have the same superhuman meaning as it had in the mouth of Paul. In Jewish tradition, *kyrios* meant either God or king, or even any other person of elevated rank.

11. An eschatological event for which, since Paul's Letter to the Thessalonians, the word *parousia* (lit., "arrival") has become customary.

12. The New English Bible translates the Greek word *sarx*, which is used in Gal. 5:16–17, as "lower nature." In the King James Bible and in the Revised Standard Version, sarx is translated as "flesh," a word that has become popular in Christian traditions. However, sarx means not only flesh but also "the seat of the affections and lusts." See *Greek-English Lexicon* (Oxford, 1966); and *Interpreter's Bible*, vol. 10 (New York, 1954), p. 560.

CHAPTER V

1. The Acts of the Apostles, which gave an account of the relations between Paul and the Jerusalem community, concealed this confrontation by presenting Paul as a follower of the Messianic doctrine of that community. (See particularly Acts 17:13 where Paul was supposed to have described Jesus as a man of God's choosing through whom God would have the world judged.) It can, however, be assumed that the Jerusalem community left Paul free to teach his brand of Christianity to the Christian communities in the Gentile world.

2. This is the promise that those who leave home or are persecuted for Christ's sake will receive eternal life in the age to come (Mark 10:29–30).

3. Mark even used the same words as Trito-Isaiah (Isa. 66:24) for the punishment of the evildoers (Mark 9:44 and 48).

4. The meaning of Logos was already distorted by the Vulgate, which translated it with *Verbum*. This wrong translation has been retained in all English versions of the New Testament, which translate Logos as "word," and it can also be found in the French (*Verbe*) and German (*Wort*) versions. It appears most suitable to leave the Greek word Logos untranslated.

5. Quoted from Philo's *Specialibus Legibus*, in *New Catholic Encyclopedia*, 1967, s.v. "Logos."

6. See below, chapter VII, section 5. Rudolf Bultmann was even of the opinion that those passages in the Gospel of John which are based on the "traditional apocalyptic eschatology" rather than on the realized eschatology, were later additions to the Gospel. In *Primitive Christianity in Its Contemporary Setting*, trans. R. H. Fuller (New York, 1956).

7. The Paraclete was translated as "Comforter" in the King James Version, as "Counselor" in the Revised Standard Version, and as "Advocate" in the New English Bible.

8. While the Catholic versions of the New Testament have retained the original title ("Book of Apocalypse"), in the other versions the title varies: "The Revelation of St. John the Divine" in the King James Version; "The Revelation to John" in the Revised Standard Version; and "The Revelation of John" in the New English Bible.

9. Arianism owed its name to the subordinationist teachings of the Alexandrian priest Arius (c. 250–336), who propagated his doctrine in a popular song called *Thalia* (c. 323).

10. In spite of the ban imposed on Arianism, it remained the recognized religion of the Germanic tribes. It did not yield to Catholicism until, with a view to facilitating assimilation with Roman civilizations and institutions, it was abandoned by the Germanic rulers King Chlodwig I of the Franks (in 498), King Sigismund of the Burgundians (in 517), King Reccared of the Visigoths (in 587), and King Pectarit of the Lombards (who reigned from 671 to 688).

11. With a view to stamping out all traces of Arianism, the Council of Constan-

tinople added that Christ was begotten "before all ages." For the semantic difference between the words "made" and "begotten," see Martin Werner, *The Formation of Christian Dogma* (New York, 1957), who notes that the concept of generation ("begotten") was taken over from Gnosticism, and that it appeared as "emanation" (pp. 219–22) first in Christian literature in the writings of Justin Martyr (c. 100–c. 165) and of Tertullian.

12. Nestorius (born c. 400, died c. 451), the founder of Nestorianism, abbot of Antioch and later patriarch of Constantinople, was deposed by the Council of Ephesus in 431 and his teachings were anathematized.

13. Soon after the Council of Constantinople, which stated that the Holy Spirit proceeds from the Father only, Augustine became one of the first protagonists of the *filioque* doctrine. This doctrine soon became popular in the ranks of the Roman Catholic churches and was adopted by the Council of Bari in 1098.

14. Montanism was founded by Montanus, who in 171 began to prophesy that the New Jerusalem of the Book of Revelation would descend in Phrygia. Montanism, which adopted strictly ascetic ethics in preparation for the millennium, was condemned by a synod in Asia Minor (c. 177), but counted even Tertullian among its adherents and remained a strong rebellious force through several centuries. It was destroyed by the anti-Montanist legislation of Emperor Justinian I, who reigned from 527 to 565.

15. In the opinion of competent New Testament scholars, the *Letter to the Ephesians* was not written by the Apostle Paul, but by an unknown author soon after Paul's death. In any case, all Christian communities until the nineteenth century accepted it as authentic and authoritative.

16. See Origen's statement, "Outside the Church, no one is saved," in *Homily 2*, no. 5, quoted in the *World Treasury of Religious Quotations*, ed. Ralph Louis Hoods (New York, 1966), p. 878; Cyprian's pronouncement, "He cannot have God for his father who has not the church for his mother," in *On the Unity of the Catholic Church*, quoted by Henry N. Wieman and Walter M. Horton, *The Growth of Religion* (Chicago, 1938), p. 149; and Augustine's *Sermo ad Cesariensis Ecclesiam Plebem*, quoted from the *Book of Catholic Quotations*, ed. John Chapin (New York, 1956), p. 126.

17. The Pastoral Letters were allegedly written by Paul to Timothy (two Letters) and to Titus.

18. Quoted by Wieman and Horton, *Growth of Religion*, p. 146.

19. Augustine was the son of a pagan father and a Christian mother. In his youth he was attracted by Manichaeism, later by Neoplatonism, and was converted to Christianity in 387 under the influence of the patristic writer Ambrose (c. 339–397), Bishop of Milan. In 395, he was ordained bishop of Hippo (in present-day Algeria).

20. Quoted from Augustine *In Psalmos*, 142, 3.

21. Augustine, *De Civitate Dei*, trans. Marcus Dods (New York, 1948).

22. Augustine, *Ad Donatum*, Ep. 173, quoted by Marcello Craveri, *The Life of Jesus*, trans. Charles L. Markmann (New York, 1967), p. 252.

23. Augustine, *In Psalmos*, 51, 4, quoted in *An Augustine Synthesis*, arranged by Erich Przywara (New York, 1936).

24. The Donatian purity movement was preceded by that of the Novatians. When Cornelius, who favored a lenient treatment of former apostates, was elected pope (pontificate 251–253), the followers of the Roman priest and theologian Novatius (c. 200–c. 258), who was opposed to leniency, elected him anti-pope. The Novatians were excommunicated by the synod of Rome (251), but formed a sect that survived for several centuries.

25. For the text of the council decision and the whole dispute, see *New Catholic Encyclopedia*, vol. 5, 1967, s.v. "Ex opere operantis" and "Ex opere operato."

26. See *New Catholic Encyclopedia*, vol. 2, 1967, s.v. "Theology of Baptism." The fate of infants who die unbaptized has troubled Christianity for many centuries. The prevailing view among Roman Catholics is that such infants dwell in limbo (from Latin, *limbus*, meaning "border"), where there is neither punishment nor heavenly bliss. The doctrine of limbo was developed by Thomas Aquinas and confirmed by Pius VI (pontificate 1775–1799) in his 1794 bull, *Auctorem Fidei*, but has never been proclaimed as a dogma.

27. It may have been no pure coincidence that the Church of England broke from Catholicism when Clement VII (pontificate 1523–1534) quarrelled with Henry VIII about his divorce from Katharine during the years 1527–1533, and the pope excommunicated the king.

28. Although the Eastern Orthodox Church recognizes as ecumenically valid only the decisions of the first seven councils (from Nicaea I in 325 to Nicaea II in 787), it has been observing the same seven sacraments as the Roman Catholic Church. There are, however, certain significant differences. The Orthodox Church permits divorce and remarriage after divorce and does not consider penances as ecclesiastical punishments. See *Encyclopaedia Britannica*, 1972, s.v. "Orthodox Eastern Church."

29. Justin Martyr, *Dialogue with Trypho the Jew*, in *New Catholic Encyclopedia*, 1967, s.v. "Judgment, Divine, in Theology."

30. Werner, *Formation of Christian Dogma*, p. 168.

31. *New Catholic Encyclopedia*, 1967, s.v. "Judgment, Divine, in Theology."

32. All quotations from *De Principiis* are taken from George A. Maloney, *The Cosmic Christ* (New York, 1968), pp. 259–61.

33. For a discussion of Universalism, see below, chapter VI, section 4.

34. Ambrose, *Two Books on the Death of Satyrus*, quoted in *World Treasury of Religious Quotations*, ed. Ralph L. Woods (New York, 1966), p. 470.

35. While the classification of sins as mortal and venial cannot be found in any New Testament Scriptures, it was used since an early stage of Christianity to distinguish between sins which leave the foundations of faith and morals un-

touched (venial) and sins which mark so grave a turning away from God and His commands that they place the sinner outside God's grace (mortal). The Church has never been able to establish an invariant catalogue of sins based on this distinction. The "seven mortal sins" treated in Thomas Aquinas's *Summa Theologiae*, constitute no less an arbitrary selection than the catalogue of mortal sins found in Paul's Letter to the Galatians (5:19–21).

36. See Gregory I, "On the Immortality of the Soul," in his *Dialogues*. See *New Catholic Encyclopedia*, 1967, s.v. "Gregory I (the Great), Pope."

37. For the quotations from Augustine, Gregory the Great, Thomas Aquinas, and Benedict XII, see *New Catholic Encyclopedia*, 1967, s.v. "Beatific Vision."

38. Dante, *The Divine Comedy*, trans. H. R. Huse, Purgatorio, Canto 1, 5–6 (New York, 1954–60).

39. Ibid., Paradiso, Canto 3.

40. Ibid., Paradiso, Canto 7. Goethe at the end of Faust II likewise visualized an ascent to various regions of heaven, populated by various saints, with Mary as Mater Gloriosa in the highest sphere.

41. *New Catholic Encyclopedia*, 1967, s.v. "Beatific Vision."

42. Ibid., s.v. "Judgment, Divine, in Theology."

43. Ibid., s.v. "Angels, Theology of."

44. Ibid., s.v. "Indulgences."

45. For the quotations from Cyril of Jerusalem, Ambrose, and Augustine, see Hippolyte Delehaye, *Les Origines du Culte des Martyrs* (Brussels, 1912), pp. 123–27.

46. Kevin Smyth, trans., *A New Catechism* (New York, 1967), p. 251.

47. Mary was invoked as a mediator since the seventh century in the Eastern Orthodox Church, and since the twelfth century in the Roman Catholic Church. See *New Catholic Encyclopedia*, 1967, s.v. "Mary, Blessed Virgin, Mediatrix."

48. Quoted in *The Office of the Dead* (Dublin, 1820), pp. 154–55.

49. *New Catholic Encyclopedia*, 1967, s.v. "Office of the Dead."

50. Ibid., s.v. "Indulgences."

51. Catholic theologians have derived the Church's authority for appropriating the treasure of merits from one—extremely fragile—scriptural source, a passage in the Letter to the Colossians in which Paul (assuming he wrote that Letter) stated: "It is now my happiness to suffer for you. This is my way of helping to complete, in my poor flesh, the full tale of Christ's afflictions still to be endured, for the sake of his body which is the church" (1:24).

52. *Encyclopaedia Britannica*, 1972, s.v. "Indulgence."

53. See below, chapter VI, section 1.

54. The abuse of buying ecclesiastical offices and other benefices is commonly called "simony." The name is derived from a story, related in the Acts of the Apostles, of a magician by the name of Simon, who offered the apostles money in order to receive the Holy Spirit (Acts 8:18–29). With the growth

of the power and wealth of the Church, simony became increasingly widespread in spite of repeated ecclesiastical bans on it.

55. The Cistercian order grew out of the Benedictine orders, founded by St. Benedict in 520. The austere community of the Cistercians was preceded by that of the Carthusians, founded in 1084. An even stricter community, which branched off from the Cistercians are the Trappists ("Cistercians of the strict observance") founded in 1664.

56. The Austin Friars derived the rules of their order from the austere Augustine's monastic teachings and life style which had inspired a number of monastic observances. Some of those orders which were based on Augustinian rules united and formed the Order of the Hermits of St. Augustine (popularly called Austin Friars) in 1256.

57. Celestine V, the first pope whose pontificate ended in abdication, was an ascetic monk who sympathized with the orders of strict observance. After his abdication he was interned by his successor, Boniface VIII (pontificate 1294–1303), and died in prison.

58. The Franciscan Spirituals were absorbed by the Observants (Friars Minor of the Observance), who officially separated from the Conventuals in 1517. Another Franciscan order of strict observance, the Capuchines, was founded in 1525. All three orders—Observants, Capuchines, and Conventuals—are still in existence. Another Franciscan community, the Fraticelli, were followers of Joachim like the Franciscan Spirituals. After having severed their ties with the official Church, they were cruelly persecuted. Their remnants joined the Friars Minor of the Observance in 1473.

59. Pseudo-Dionysius (Dionysius the Areopagite) claimed to be identical with the Dionysius mentioned in the Acts of the Apostles (17:34) as having been converted by the Apostle Paul.

60. The authenticity and authority of the writings of Pseudo-Dionysius remained unchallenged until the Renaissance, although theologians did not recognize the forgery before the seventeenth and eighteenth centuries. In the Eastern Orthodox churches the authority of Pseudo-Dionysius is still accepted. See *Encyclopaedia Britannica*, 1972, s.v. "Pseudo-Dionysius."

61. Jan Van Ruysbroeck, *De altero verae contemplationis modo* [On another way of true contemplation], quoted by Maurice Maeterlinck, *Ruysbroeck and the Mystics* (London, 1894).

62. Hasidism—which owes its name to the pious men (Hasidim) of strict observance in the Seleucid-dominated era of Israel—originated among eighteenth-century East European Jews, as a distinct way of religious life rather than as an intellectual movement. It has always centered on the teachings and activities of inspired, charismatic rabbis, to whom miraculous powers frequently were ascribed. The first of these rabbis was Israel ben Eliezer (Ba'al Shem Tov, "Master of the Good Name," c. 1700–1760). The religious basis of Hasidism has from the outset been a mystical feeling of nearness to God. It is that highly emotional relationship to God on which the

joyful rites of the Hasidim are based. A strain of Kabbalah, particularly of the Lurian Kabbalah, goes back to the teachings of Isaac ben Solomon Luria, born in Jerusalem (1534–1572). For more on Hasidism, see particularly Martin Buber, *Hasidism and the Way of Man* (1948; rept. ed., New York, 1958–1960).

63. Beguin communities still exist in some Belgian towns. For the Brethren of the Free Spirit, the Beghards and the Beguines, see Robert E. Lerner, *The Heresy of the Free Spirit in the Later Middle Ages* (Berkeley, 1972).

64. C. Bigg, trans., *The Imitation of Christ* (London, 1898), bk. 4, chap. 42.

65. Gregory XI (pontificate 1370–1378) in a bull of 1377 condemned certain opinions of Wycliffe (also spelled "Wyclif"). William Courtenay, bishop of London, made efforts to persecute him and even secured the condemnation of certain of his theses by a council of theologians. See John Wycliffe, *De potestate Papae* [On the power of the pope] (1379), ed. Johann Loserth (London, 1907).

66. See John Wycliffe, *De veritate sacrae scripturae* [On the truth of the Holy Scriptures] (c. 1378), ed. Rudolf Buddensieg (London, 1905–7); neither the Waldenses, the Wycliffe group, nor Luther produced the first translations of the Bible into their respective languages, but theirs were the first translations made with the express aim of making the Bible accessible to the lay people.

67. See John Wycliffe, *De officio regis* [On the office of the king] (1378), ed. A. W. Pollard and C. Sayle (London, 1887).

68. The name "Lollards" (from medieval Dutch, lit., "mumblers") was a popular term to designate the Beghards and the Brethren of the Free Spirit. It was later derisively used by the adversaries of the Wycliffe group until the Lollards accepted the name themselves.

69. The 1967 *New Catholic Encyclopedia* (which bears the imprimatur of Patrick O'Boyle, archbishop of Washington) summed up the trial of Hus in the sentence: "He was condemned because he appeared before a tribunal that had already reached its verdict," s.v. "Hus, John."

70. The moderate wing of the Hussites was called both "Calixtines" and "Utraquists." These names were derived from the chalice (in Latin, *calix*), in which they passed the wine to the lay people, and from their insistence on communion in both kinds (*sub utraque species*). The radical wing of the Hussites was called "Taborites," a name derived from Tabor, a town the Hussites founded in 1420 and named after the biblical Mount Tabor in Palestine.

71. For Count Zinzendorf, see below, chapter VI, section 4. Prior to the establishment of the Herrnhut center, the Moravian Brethren found a prominent representative in the person of John Amos Comenius (Jan Amos Komensky, 1592–1670), a minister of the Brethren. Comenius was driven into exile by the battle of the White Mountain and became one of the greatest educational reformers. As bishop of the Moravian Brethren since 1632, he kept alive the free spirit of that community.

CHAPTER VI

1. The romantic story that Luther (1483–1546) nailed the Ninety-five Theses on the portal of the Schlosskirche at Wittenberg has no other source than a remark in a letter from Melanchthon written after Luther's death.

2. Immediately after having graduated as Master of Arts at the University of Erfurt in 1505, Luther joined the strictest congregation of the mendicant order of the Augustinian Hermits, the Observant Saxon congregation.

3. In an autobiographical note which Luther wrote in the preface to his *Works* (1545), he stated that when he began to understand Paul's doctrine of salvation by faith, he felt himself to have been reborn and to have entered through open gates into paradise itself. See *Encyclopaedia Britannica*, Macropedia, 1974, s.v. "Luther, Martin."

4. Prince Albrecht of Brandenburg, in violation of Canon Law, accumulated the archbishoprics of Mainz and Magdeburg and the administration of the Diocese of Halberstadt, for which he paid the Papal Curia 10,000 gold ducats, plus 14,000 gold ducats for tax arrears. To help him pay his debts, the Curia allowed Albrecht to receive half of the income from the sale of the St. Peter-indulgence in his dioceses. The banking house Fugger, to whom he was indebted, chose Tetzel as indulgence agent. See *New Catholic Encyclopedia*, 1967, s.v. "Luther, Martin."

5. Luther's lectures are known to us through transcripts of his students. This phrase appeared in his lectures on Paul's Letter to the Romans (1515–1516). See Martin Luther, *Luther's Lectures on Romans*, trans. Wilhelm Pauck (Philadelphia, 1962).

6. When Luther translated the New Testament into German, he retained this addition by stating: *allein durch den Glauben* ("solely through faith"). The Germans have remained so faithful to the Luther Bible that they still include this addition to Paul's words.

7. See a translation of the Ninety-five Theses in *Encyclopedia of the Lutheran Church* (Minneapolis, 1965), p. 2388 ff.

8. The 1476 bull of Pope Sixtus IV confined ecclesiastical intercession for the dead to a supplication. But there can be no doubt that the people to whom the Church appealed for donations were led to believe that the pope had the power to grant remission to souls in purgatory.

9. Martin Luther, *Preface to Romans* (1523).

10. Martin Luther, *Von der Freiheit eines Christenmenschen* [Of the freedom of a Christian man] (1520).

11. Martin Luther, *On the Bondage of the Will*, trans. J. I. Packer and O. R. Johnston (Westwood, New Jersey, 1957).

12. Martin Luther, *An den christlichen Adel deutscher Nation* [To the Christian nobility of the German nation] (1520).

13. Martin Luther, *Works*, vol. 10 (Philadelphia, 1958).

14. Luther, still under imperial ban, could not appear in person at the diet.

15. For a summary of the Augsburg Confession, see *Encyclopedia of the Lutheran Church*, 1965, s.v. "Augsburg Confession."

16. Several free Lutheran churches had developed in Germany and in some Scandinavian countries in the nineteenth century.

17. Swiss independence was achieved at the Peace of Basel in 1499, which ended the Swabian War between the Swiss cantons and Emperor Maximilian I (who reigned from 1486 to 1519).

18. The original edition of the *Institutes of the Christian Religion* underwent a number of modifications and amplifications during Calvin's lifetime. Its size had quadrupled in its final edition of 1559. See *Institutes of the Christian Religion*, trans. Ford Lewis Battles (Philadelphia, 1960).

19. In 1531 when the citizens of Geneva ousted the reigning bishop-prince, joined the Swiss Reformation, and established a republic (which they maintained until 1798), they became in fact part of the Swiss community although they did not formally join the Helvetic Confederation until 1814.

20. Huldrych Zwingli, *On the Lord's Supper* (1526).

21. Calvin, *Institutes*, 3. Quotations are from the 1960 translation. See note 18, above.

22. Calvin, *Institutes*, 1.

23. Max Weber, *The Protestant Ethics and the Spirit of Capitalism*, 7th ed. (New York, 1965). The original German treatise, entitled *Die protestantische Ethik und der Geist des Kapitalismus*, was published in 1904–1905. Weber has frequently been cited as having regarded capitalism as a product of the Calvinist spirit. However, while he stressed Calvinism's influence on the rise of capitalism, he denied that capitalism was a product of the Reformation. He stated: "We have no intention whatever of maintaining such a foolish and doctrinaire thesis as that . . . capitalism as an economic system is a creation of the Reformation. . . . We only wish to ascertain whether and to what extent religious forces have taken part in the qualitative formation and quantitative expansion of that spirit over the world (p. 91). Weber did not confine the "capitalist spirit" to Calvinism, but emphasized that Luther also regarded the fulfillment of worldly duties as the only way to live acceptably to God. See Weber, *Protestant Ethics*, p. 81.

24. Jean Calvin, *Psychopannychia* (1542), quoted in George Huntston Williams, *Radical Reformation* (Philadelphia, 1962), p. 583 n.

25. The Second Helvetic Confession was drafted by Heinrich Bullinger in 1562 and recognized by the Reformed Swiss churches in 1566.

26. The First Helvetic Confession ruled that the ministers of the church should warn, punish, or even expel evildoers from the church. The Second Helvetic Confession confirmed this disciplinary power. The Westminster Assembly affirmed the right of the church to call to account and censure men with erroneous opinions and practices or those who resist the ordinances of God (chapter 20 of the Westminster Confession of Faith; see note 27, below).

27. The Westminster Confession of Faith was adopted by the Westminster As-

sembly of Puritan Ministers in 1646 and approved by the Long Parliament in 1648.

28. The cause of Presbyterianism in Scotland was strongly promoted by the great Reformer, John Knox (c. 1514–1572). In 1559, after his return from Geneva where he had acted as minister in the Calvinist church, he succeeded in inducing the Scottish Parliament to adopt in 1560 the Scots Confession, which made Presbyterianism the established church in Scotland.

29. Even the Westminster Confession of Faith declared that "the church is the kingdom of the Lord Jesus Christ, the house and family of God, out of which there is no ordinary possibility of salvation" (chapter 25).

30. The term "Radical Reformation" appears in Williams, *Radical Reformation*, p. 583 n.

31. Ibid., p. 77. The Book of Daniel's vision was that of a kingdom of God, which would follow four kingdoms—the Babylonians, Medes, Persians, and Greeks (2:36–45). The vision of the Fifth Monarchy remained popular among millenarians, as the rise and the revolt of the Fifth Monarchy Men in Cromwell's England showed. They gained considerable power under Cromwell and were even strongly represented in the Nominated Parliament of 1653, but later turned against Cromwell and were crushed after unsuccessful armed uprisings in 1657 and 1661.

32. "They [the righteous preachers and teachers] . . . destroy all that which is against the Word of God, not by external force with iron and sword, but by the preaching of the Holy Word." Menno Simons, *Foundations of Christian Doctrine* (1539), in *The Complete Writings of Menno Simons*, trans. Leonard Verduin (Scottsdale, Pa., 1956), p. 172.

33. Calvin rejected psychopannychism in a neat definition of the new word: "Psychopannychism, by which the error of those is proved who believe that the souls after death sleep until the last judgment." See *Oxford English Dictionary*, 1933, s.v. "Psychopannychy."

34. The term "Anabaptism" (re-baptism) was not coined by the Anabaptists themselves, but by their Catholic and Protestant adversaries. The Anabaptists did not consider the baptism of believers as a re-baptism, but rather as the first baptism, since they refused to recognize the baptism of infants as valid.

35. *New Catholic Encyclopedia*, 1967, s.v. "Anabaptists."

36. Williams, *Radical Reformation*, pp. 182–84.

37. Ibid., p. 186.

38. Menno Simons, probably under the influence of Melchior Hofmann, believed in the spiritualist doctrine of the "celestial flesh" of Christ. However, this doctrine has completely disappeared from present day Mennonism. See *Mennonite Encyclopedia*, 1955–1959, s.v. "Incarnation of Christ."

39. The majority of Mennonites live in the United States, where they began to immigrate in the second half of the seventeenth century. Several Mennonite churches emerged in the United States. The Mennonite communities of the

Soviet Union originated from an immigration which began under Catherine the Great in the eighteenth century.

40. Williams, *Radical Reformation*, p. 433.

41. The German Peasants' Revolt of 1524–1525 received a powerful impetus from the Reformation. The Twelve Articles, adopted by the Peasants' Assembly, insisted on the preaching of the Gospels and the election of priests. Münzer contributed to the revolt by preaching his doctrines and by personally intervening through a clandestine military organization, the League of the Elect, whose millenary goal was "to wield the sword against the godless and cleanse the world of evil." See Guenter Lewy, *Religion and Revolution* (New York, 1942), p. 112.

42. The Unitarian communities were originally called "anti-Trinitarian," a name first used by their adversaries to mark their heretical character. The name "Unitarian" was not popular before the seventeenth century and was officially adopted by the Unitarians in 1638.

43. See Williams, *Radical Reformation*, p. 562.

44. Ferenc David began to advocate his anti-Trinitarian doctrines in 1568 when he was still a bishop of the Reformed Church. However, as he was opposed to any kind of worship of Christ, he was persecuted and died in prison.

45. Rakow is a town near Cracow which in Socinus's lifetime had become the spiritual center of Polish Unitarianism. The Racovian Catechism was preceded by a *Catechesis* of Rakow in 1574. Rakow's Unitarian institutions were destroyed by the Polish authorities in 1638.

46. Based on an English translation of the *Racovian Catechism* published in 1652. That edition gave as place of publication "Amsterledam," but was actually published in London. For details see Earl Morse Wilbur, *A History of Unitarianism in Transylvania, England, and America* (Cambridge, Mass., 1952), p. 201.

47. Quoted by Ernest Alexander Payne, *The Fellowship of Believers* (London, 1952).

48. Arminianism was first banned in the Netherlands, but later was tolerated. It survives there as a small organized community.

49. Roger Williams split off from the Calvinists, and was banned from the Massachusetts Bay Colony, over the issue of separation of the church from "the world," which in conformity with Baptism he considered fundamental. This Baptist tenet facilitated the spread of Baptism in Rhode Island. Williams himself, however, adhered to Baptism only for a short period.

50. Robert G. Torbet, *A History of the Baptists*, rev. ed. (Valley Forge, Penn., 1963). The membership figures for the Baptists and for other denominations mentioned in this chapter are taken from the *World Almanac and Book of Facts 1978* (New York).

51. George Fox derived the name "Quaker" from an episode in which a judge called him and his followers "quakers," "because we bid them tremble at the word of God." See *Encyclopaedia Britannica*, 1972, s.v. "Quakers."

52. William C. Braithwaite, *The Beginnings of Quakerism* (New York, 1942).

53. Quoted by Elbert Russell, *The History of Quakerism* (New York, 1942), p. 48.

54. Ibid.

55. The name "Methodists" was originally a nickname derived from the methodical studies to which John and Charles Wesley devoted themselves in the Holy Club, which they organized with a view to devoting themselves to a Christian life.

56. See above, chapter V, section 4.

57. In Martin Luther, *Preface to Paul's Letter to the Romans*.

58. John Wesley, *Journal*, abr. Nehemia Curnock (London, 1967), p. 51. Wesley did not consider his conversion to be a defection from the Church of England. He had been ordained as a minister and never left the Church of England.

59. Quoted by William John Townsend, *A New History of Methodism*, vol. 2 (London, 1909), p. 443 ff.

60. This and the following quotations from the fundamental work of Christian Science can be found in Mary Baker Eddy, *Science and Health with Key to the Scriptures* (Boston, 1934). The first edition of *Science and Health* appeared in 1875. Later editions showed numerous changes and additions, but those editions which followed the death of Mary Baker Eddy have remained unchanged.

61. For the number of churches, see *Encyclopedia Americana*, 1977, s.v. "Christian Scientists."

62. For source material on the history of English Unitarianism, see Wilbur, *History of Unitarianism*.

63. See above, chapter V, section 7.

64. The Book of Mormon tells the story of a family that emigrated from Jerusalem to America around 600 B.C. The family grew into two nations, one of which eventually turned Christian but later perished in a war between the two nations. Mormon, according to that story, was a prophet who witnessed the destruction of his people and was killed himself, but whose son Moroni saved the record his father had made of the history of his people, and buried it in 421 A.D. (See Robert R. Mullen, *The Mormons* [London, 1967], pp. 14–15). The puzzle of this strange chronicle's origin and its alleged early history of America has never been solved. A faint clue leads to a manuscript, written by a man named Solomon Spaulding, which contained a fanciful history of ancient America. Although the author found no publisher, his relatives and friends remembered that certain parts of the manuscript resembled the Book of Mormon. See William Alexander Linn, *The Story of the Mormons* (1902; rept. ed., New York, 1963), pp. 50–58.

65. Mullen, *Mormons*, p. 19.

66. Elmer T. Clark, *The Small Sects in America*, rev. ed. (New York, 1965), p. 37.

67. Booton Herndon, *The Seventh Day, the Story of the Seventh-Day Adventists* (New York, 1960), pp. 73–75.
68. For the millenarian beliefs of Jehovah's Witnesses, see William J. Whalen, *Armageddon around the Corner; a Report on Jehovah's Witnesses* (New York, 1962), pp. 89–94.
69. The major churches of the organized Holiness and Pentecostal bodies in the United States are: the Church of the Nazarene, the Churches of God, the Assemblies of God, the Church of God in Christ, and the Pentecostal Assemblies. Their combined membership was more than 3 million in 1977.
70. The Congregational Church was established in New England, except for Rhode Island, and the Church of England in New York, New Jersey, and the southern states.
71. John Milton, *A Treatise of Civil Power in Ecclesiastical Causes* (London, 1659).
72. In 1667 John Locke wrote the "Essay on Religious Toleration," and in the years 1689, 1690, and 1691, three *Letters for Toleration*.
73. However, the exclusion of religious dissidents from public offices, which had been established in the Test Act of 1673, was not abolished until 1828.
74. For religious currents in the era of Enlightenment see below, chapter IX, section 3.
75. The attempt of the French Revolution to carry out the separation of church and state (by the Convention of 1795) was short-lived. In 1801 Napoleon concluded a concordat with the pope. It was not until 1905, under the impact of the Dreyfus affair and a political swing to the left, that the separation of church and state was instituted in France. Belgium is another of the rare examples of an early separation of church and state. Its constitution, adopted in 1831, instituted the separation of church and state. However, the Catholic Church is so powerful in that country that the government subsidizes its schools.
76. The Episcopalians are the successor community of the Church of England in the American colonies. In 1789 they organized themselves in the United States as a separate Protestant Episcopalian Church. It remains one of the major churches in the United States, with a membership of nearly three million in 1977.
77. The Supreme Court undertook the decisive action in favor of complete separation of church and state in 1940.

CHAPTER VII

1. While the term "fundamentalism" has more or less fallen into disuse, some groups which call themselves Evangelicals adhere in substance to fundamentalist beliefs. They are to a large extent organized in the National Association of Evangelists, which in 1971 claimed a membership of about 3 million

in the United States. See *British Encyclopaedia*, Macropedia, 1974, s.v. "Fundamentalist and Evangelical Churches."

2. Recent events within American Lutheranism, however, have proved that the counterattack of fundamentalism against the critical spirit has not yet completely abated. In the Lutheran Church-Missouri Synod (whose 2,800,000 members comprise the second largest Lutheran community in the United States), the Concordia Seminary—the largest Lutheran seminary in America—was disrupted in 1974 when its president was suspended by church authorities for having interpreted Bible passages symbolically rather than literally. A strike of the teachers and students in his support ended with their secession and the establishment of a rival seminary, Seminex. After several church districts decided to ordinate graduates from Seminex, the 1975 convention of the church called for the closing of that break-away seminary. However, a substantial minority of the convention delegates disapproved of this decision and a number of churches have established a separate community.

3. The World Council of Churches is the international organization established by the Protestant and Eastern Orthodox churches in 1948, and can be considered as their official representative. However, the Unitarian-Universalists and all major millenarian churches (the Latter-Day Saints, Seventh-Day Adventists, Jehovah's Witnesses, and Pentecostal churches) have remained outside the World Council of Churches, according to a 1960 list of member churches, published by Paul Griswold Macy, *If It Be God: The Story of the World Council of Churches* (St. Louis, 1960), app. 4.

4. The conference report was unanimously adopted. Quoted by Hugh Martin, *Edinburgh 1937: The Story of the Second World Conference on Faith and Order* (London, 1938).

5. The report of the World Conference on Church and Society was published by the World Council of Churches in 1967.

6. Friedrich Schleiermacher, *Der christliche Glaube*, 1821. Published as *The Christian Faith* (Edinburgh, 1956), para. 97, p. 403; para. 100, p. 426.

7. Ibid., para. 90, p. 420.

8. Albrecht Ritschl, *Instruction in the Christian Religion*, trans. Alice M. Swing, in Albert T. Swing, *The Theology of Albrecht Ritschl* (New York, 1901), p. 264.

9. Ibid., pp. 223 and 195.

10. Ibid., pp. 174–76.

11. Ibid., pp. 203 and 263.

12. Ibid., pp. 212–15.

13. Hermann Kutter's position was summarized in the words: "The socialists are revolutionary because God is revolutionary. They must move forward because the kingdom of God must move forward." Quoted in an article in *NeueZürcher Zeitung* (August 21, 1965).

14. See *Encyclopedia Universalis*, Paris, 1968, s.v. "Mounier (Emmanuel)."
15. Josiah Strong, *The New Era or the Coming Kingdom* (New York, 1893), pp. 231–33.
16. Ibid., p. 242.
17. Walter Rauschenbusch, *A Theology for the Social Gospel* (New York, 1917), pp. 5, 142, and 178.
18. Ibid., pp. 142 and 3.
19. Catholic parties were formed in a number of European countries, the first in Germany, as *Zentrumspartei* (Center Party) in 1870. This party emerged after World War II as *Christlich-Demokratische Union* (Christian Democratic Union). In Austria the *Christlichsoziale Partei* (Christian Social Party) was organized in 1889. In Belgium and the Netherlands similar parties came into being at about the same time, while in Italy and France Catholic parties were formed in the wake of World War I. Catholic or Christian trade unions were a later product. In Germany and Austria they merged with the socialist-oriented trade unions after World War II.
20. Pope Leo XIII referred to Baron von Ketteler as his great predecessor and admitted that he had learned much from him. See *New Catholic Encyclopedia*, 1967, s.v. "Ketteler, Wilhelm Emanuel von."
21. The encyclical may have had in mind socialist tendencies in the Catholic camp, particularly the so-called Sillon (Furrow) movement in France, which had been initiated by Marc Sangnier (1873–1950), a radical pacifist and protagonist of Christian social democracy. The Sillon movement, which had a considerable following in France, had been condemned by Pope Pius X in 1910, but its successor movements played a great role in the 1944 formation of the French Christian Social Party (*Mouvement Republicain Populaire*).
22. In the Constitution of the Church in the World of Today, *Gaudium et Spes*, para. 26.
23. In the Constitution, *Lumen Gentium*, para. 13.
24. *Gaudium et Spes*, para. 39.
25. On Pierre Teilhard de Chardin, see section 7 of this chapter.
26. *Gaudium et Spes*, para. 25 and 42.
27. On Paul Johannes Tillich and Reinhold Niebuhr, see section 5 of this chapter.
28. Although Hermann Samuel Reimarus did not dare to publish his views, Gotthold Ephraim Lessing published the manuscript in fragmentary form after the death of Reimarus. On Lessing, see below, chapter IX, section 3.
29. The University of Tübingen has been outstanding for the quality of its theological faculty since its inception in 1477. In the Tübingen school of the nineteenth century were theologians who based their Bible criticism on Hegelian positions.
30. David Friedrich Strauss, *Das Leben Jesu kritisch bearbeitet* [The life of Jesus, critically examined] (1835–1836).
31. In his inaugural address at the Collège de France, Ernest Renan spoke of

Jesus as an incomparable man, whereupon he was promptly suspended from his post. He did not regain it until after the fall of the imperial regime.

32. Adolf von Harnack, *Lehrbuch der Dogmengeschichte* [The history of dogma] (1886–1890).

33. Adolf von Harnack, *Grundriss der Dogmengeschichte* [Outline of the history of dogma] (4th ed., 1909).

34. Ernst Troeltsch, *Der Historizismus und seine Überwindung* [Historicism and its downfall], in Hugh Ross Mackintosh, *Types of Modern Theology* (New York, 1937), p. 212.

35. Martin Dibelius, *Die Formgeschichte des Evangeliums* [Form criticism of the Gospel] (1919).

36. Rudolf Bultmann, *Die Geschichte der synoptischen Tradition* [History of the synoptic tradition] (Göttingen, 1921), and *Jesus* (1926).

37. Rudolf Bultmann, *Kerygma and Myth*, trans. Reginald H. Fuller (London, 1953), p. 35.

38. Albert Schweitzer, *The Quest for the Historical Jesus*, trans. W. Montgomery (London, 1910).

39. Ibid., p. 396.

40. Sören Aabye Kierkegaard, *Concluding Unscientific Postscript* (1846), in Mackintosh, *Types of Modern Theology*, p. 237.

41. Karl Barth's attack on the liberal theology was to a large extent expunged from the later editions of *Der Römerbrief*. The following quotations are from the English translation of the sixth German edition, *The Epistle to the Romans*, trans. Edwin C. Hoskins, 5th ed. (New York, 1966).

42. See particularly "Marxism and Christian Socialism," in Paul Johannes Tillich, *The Protestant Era*, trans. James Luther Adams (Chicago, 1948).

43. Ibid., p. 260.

44. Paul Johannes Tillich, *Systematic Theology*, 3 vols. (Chicago, 1951–1963). The following quotations are from the 1965 edition of volume 1, the 1963 edition of volume 2, and the 1963 edition of volume 3.

45. Reinhold Niebuhr, *The Nature and Destiny of Man* (New York, 1949), vol. 2, p. 211; and vol. 1, p. 16.

46. Ibid., vol. 2, p. 85.

47. Ibid., vol. 2, pp. 287–90; and vol. 2, p. 305.

48. See Bultmann, *Jesus*.

49. Ibid., pp. 36, 44.

50. Rudolf Bultmann, *Jesus und Paul*, in *Existence and Faith*, trans. Schubert M. Ogden, 4th ed. (Cleveland, 1965).

51. Published under the title "Man between the Times according to the New Testament," in Bultmann, *Existence and Faith*, pp. 253–55.

52. Ibid., p. 253.

53. Schubert M. Ogden, *Christ without Myth* (New York, 1961), p. 120.

54. Ibid., pp. 121, 143, and 153.

55. Harvey Cox, *The Secular City* (New York, 1965), pp. 21 and 63.

56. Ibid., pp. 111, 117, and 121.

57. The collection of the letters and essays which Dietrich Bonhoeffer wrote in prison, including the *Outline for a Book*, appeared in 1951 under the title *Widerstand und Ergebung*. An English edition appeared entitled *Letters and Papers from Prison* (New York, 1953). The quotations are from the third English edition (New York, 1967), pp. 209–10.

58. Paul Van Buren, *Secular Meaning of the Gospel*, pp. 121, 123, and 128.

59. Ibid., p. 179.

60. Ibid., p. 138.

61. Ibid., p. 67.

62. In an article by Paul Van Buren in *The New Yorker* (13 November 1965), quoted in Thomas W. Ogletree, *The Death of God Controversy* (Nashville, 1966).

63. Quoted from the article by Paul Van Buren in *The New Yorker* (13 November 1965). In a similar vein, Van Buren more recently wondered whether Christianity, which had "proclaimed a monistic view of the universe . . . as the only valid one, with a single and unique revelation of this truth, can live in a world from which the Absolute has been dissolved" (p. 42). He considered, however, the possibilities of the hypothesis of a limited God within a pluralistic universe. *Theological Exploration* (New York, 1968), pp. 42 and 125.

64. William Hamilton and J. J. Altizer, *Radical Theology and the Death of God* (Indianapolis, 1966), pp. 40 and 129.

65. Ibid., pp. 60, 169, 135, and 141.

66. *Populorum Progressio* is the title of a 1967 encyclical issued by Pope Paul VI which dealt with the problems of development in economically underdeveloped countries.

67. In the Constitution, *Lumen Gentium*, para. 5.

68. The New Catechism was published in 1966 by the Bishops of the Netherlands under the title *De Nieuwe Katechismus*, with the imprimatur of Cardinal Bernardus Afrink. An English edition was published under the title, *A New Catechism*, trans. Kelvyn Smith (New York, 1967). The New Catechism called the priestly celibate a custom of the Church of the West, which "need not always remain a law binding on all" (p. 360).

69. Ibid., p. 277.

70. Ibid., pp. 193, 355.

71. Ibid., pp. 453, 380.

72. *New Catholic Encyclopedia*, 1967, s.v. "Soul, Human, Immortality of, 4. Revelational Data"; "Judgment, Divine (in Theology)"; and "Resurrection of the Dead."

73. Pierre Teilhard de Chardin, *The Future of Man*, trans. Norman Denny (New York, 1964), p. 46. This book is a collection of papers and lectures which

during Teilhard's lifetime had either remained unpublished or had been published in periodicals.

74. Pierre Teilhard de Chardin, *The Phenomenon of Man*, trans. Bernard Wall (New York, 1964), p. 251.

75. Ibid., p. 259.

76. This essay was incorporated in Teilhard de Chardin, *Future of Man*.

77. Teilhard de Chardin, *Phenomenon of Man*, p. 257.

78. Ibid., p. 272; Teilhard de Chardin, *Future of Man*, p. 120; *Phenomenon of Man*, p. 308.

79. In some passages of *Phenomenon of Man*, and in other writings.

80. Teilhard de Chardin's credo was written in 1934 and published under the title *Comment je crois* [How I believe] in *Christianity and Evolution*, trans. Rene Hague (New York, 1971).

81. In an essay, *The New Spirit*, published in the French periodical *Psyché*; it appeared in English as part of Teilhard de Chardin, *Future of Man*.

82. Teilhard de Chardin, *Phenomenon of Man*, p. 287.

83. For the French text of this *Monitum*, see Philippe de Trinité, *Rome et Teilhard de Chardin* (Paris, 1964).

84. *New York Times*, January 15, 1971.

85. Hans Küng, *Why Priests?*, trans. John C. Cumming (Garden City, N.Y., 1972); Hans Küng, *Infallible? An Inquiry* (Garden City, N.Y., 1971). The dogma of the pope's infallibility "in discharge of his office as shepherd and teacher of all Christians, when defining a doctrine concerning faith or morals to be held by the whole Church" was adopted by the First Vatican Council in 1870.

86. Küng, *Why Priests?*, p. 19.

87. Ibid., pp. 67, 31.

88. See "Challenge to Vatican," *New York Times*, February 25, 1975. The article added that the Conference of German Bishops refrained from asking Hans Küng to recant. In a comprehensive work, *On Being a Christian*, trans. Edward Quinn (Garden City, 1976), Küng, while retaining the essence of Christian beliefs, but demythologizing such traditions as the Virgin birth of Jesus, maintained the views on priesthood and congregation delineated in *Why Priests?* All ministers—popes, bishops, and priests—should be elected by the clergy and the Catholic community. Küng added the right of women to be ordained.

89. For the policy of the Brazilian hierarchy, see Guenter Lewy, *Religion and Revolution* (New York, 1942), pp. 517–18, 528–30.

90. Ibid., pp. 530–32.

91. Edward Schillebeeckx, *God, Future of Man*, trans. N. D. Smith (New York, 1969), pp. 182, 185, 198

92. Johannes Baptist Metz, *Theology of the World*, trans. William Glenn-Doepel (London, 1969), pp. 113, 118–20.

93. René Laurentin, *Liberation, Development and Salvation*, trans. Charles Underhill Quinn (Maryknoll, N.Y., 1972), pp. 132, 210.

94. Jürgen Moltmann, *Theology of Hope*, trans. James W. Leitch (New York, 1967), pp. 158, 134, 329–30.

95. Jürgen Moltmann, *The Crucified God*, trans. R. A. Wilson and John Bowden (London, 1974), pp. 336–37.

CHAPTER VIII

1. The analogy with Unitarianism is striking. Like Unitarianism, the Koran asserted that Jesus, although not God-like, was Mary's son through Virgin birth (Koran 19:20–23). God gave him the gospel with its guidance and light (5:50), entrusted him with a divine mission, strengthened him through the Holy Spirit (2:81), and raised him up to Himself (4:156). The quotations from the Koran are numbered by *suras* (chapters), and followed by *ayat* (verses). All quotations are taken from *The Koran Interpreted*, trans. Arthur J. Arberry (New York, 1964).

2. Muhammad, the Arabic name of Mohammed, means "the Praised one." Since, however, the name Mohammed has acquired citizen rights in English, the English spelling will be retained. The same applies to such familiar words as Koran (Arabic, *Quran*) and Hegira (Arabic, *Higjra*). For other Arabic words the spelling follows that used in the *Encyclopaedia of Islam* (1924–1936; second ed., 1960–1971, Leiden, Netherlands, and London). As the second edition is incomplete, some quotations have been taken from the first edition.

3. The very word "Koran" means "recitation," implying that Mohammed recited what God had communicated to him.

4. The Koran sometimes addresses the supreme Devil by his Grecized Arabic name, Iblis (Greek, *diabolos*), sometimes by his Judeo-Christian name, Satan.

5. The pessimism implied in this passage (33:72) about the nature of man does not derive from any belief in original sin, which would be alien to the Koran, but seems to derive from the circumstances prevailing when this sura was written: at the end of a siege of Medina by non-Muslim hostile tribes, whose army was superior to that of the defenders. See the note on this sura in *The Koran*, trans. John Medow Rodwell (New York, 1963).

6. Sura 1, which introduces every Muslim prayer to the present time.

7. For this interpretation of Islamic universalism, see W. Montgomery Watt, *Islam and the Integration of Society* (Evanston, Ill., 1961), p. 219.

8. Significantly the Islamic calendar does not set the beginning of the Islamic era in the year of Mohammed's birth or of his first revelation (dates which are uncertain anyway), but in 622 A.D., the year of the Hegira, of Mohammed's emigration from Mecca to Medina, the place of his religious-secular reign.

9. Watt, *Islam and Integration*, p. 104 ff.
10. The word "caliph" has a religious connotation. It is derived from *khalifat-rasul-Allah*, meaning "successor of God's messenger," i.e., of Mohammed.
11. However, both the Fatimids and the Mogul emperors in India, beginning with Emperor Akbar (reign 1556–1605), claimed the title of caliph. After the conquest of Egypt in 1517, the Ottoman sultan also called himself caliph.
12. The word "sultan" signifies a secular ruler. It was first used as a regular title of the sovereign by the Seldjuks in the eleventh century.
13. The differences between the Sunnite and the Shi'ite Shari'a are not substantial. They stem mainly from the fact that the Shi'ites do not recognize all companions of the Prophet and place their Imams above Shari'a. See Watt, *Islam and Integration*, p. 208.
14. Whereas, in accordance with the rules of nomadic societies, the umma elected the first four caliphs, Mu'awiya nominated his son as his successor, thus introducing the heredity principle into the Muslim society.
15. *Encyclopaedia of Islam*, 1924, s.v. "Ta'ziya" (the name of the passion play).
16. For the Karmatians, see *Encyclopaedia of Islam*, 1927, s.v. "Karmatians."
17. In Syria the Alawis constitute a powerful political force. The present president of Syria, Hafi al-Assad (b. 1927), is an Alawi. The Shi'ite Alawis of the Middle East should not be confused with the still-reigning Alawi dynasty of Morocco. That dynasty, although claiming descent from 'Ali's son Hasan, is of the Sunnite faith. It gained ascendancy in Morocco in the seventeenth century.
18. *Encyclopaedia of Islam*, 1960, s.v. "Babis."
19. For Ibn Khaldun's statement, see *Encyclopaedia of Islam*, 1927, s.v. "al-Mahdi."
20. Almohads (in Arabic, *al-Muwahhidun*) means "Unitarians."
21. The name "Ansar" ("helpers") was derived from that of the followers of Mohammed in Medina. Mohammed Ahmad used the name for his followers. See Guenter Lewy, *Religion and Revolution* (New York, 1942), p. 180.
22. The quotations from Rabi'a are taken from *Encyclopaedia of Islam*, 1936, s.v. "Rabi'a al-Adawiya."
23. For al-'Halladj, see *Encyclopaedia of Islam*, 1971, s.v. "al-Halladj."
24. For Mu'tazilism, see section 5 of this chapter.
25. For al-Farabi and Avicenna, see *Encyclopedia of Philosophy*, s.v. "Islamic Philosophy"; for Avicenna, see ibid., s.v. "Avicenna."
26. Quoted by Arberry, *Koran Interpreted*, p. 96.
27. For Ibn al-'Arabi, see ibid., pp. 100–101, and *Encyclopaedia of Islam*, 1960, s.v. "Ibn al-'Arabi."
28. The Arabic word for "order" (*tarika*) indeed means "path."
29. *Encyclopaedia of Islam*, 1960, s.v. "'Abd al-Kadir al-Djilani."
30. The cult of the saints is partly a transformation of pre-Islamic beliefs and institutions. A striking instance is the cult of the Marabouts in the western

region of North Africa and the adjacent area south of the Sahara. The holy men of the pre-Islamic Berbers and the medicine men of African tribes south of the Sahara were transformed into Islamic saints. See Hamilton A. R. Gibb, *Mohammedanism* (New York, 1949), p. 157.

31. In Zanzibar the political ascendancy of the Ibadis was broken by the 1964 revolution of the Afro-Shirazi majority of that island country.

32. See Joachim Wach, *The Comparative Study of Religions* (New York, 1958). Wach defined Kalam as "the distinct articulation and demonstration of the rationality of the faith, in contrast to the unquestioning acceptance of the 'taklid' [authority]" (pp. 70–71).

33. The founder of one of the four schools of Islamic law. See section 2 of this chapter.

34. For Mu'tazilism and al-Ashari, see *Encyclopaedia Britannica*, Macropedia, 1974, s.v. "Islamic Theology and Philosophy, II. Theology."

35. A sharif is a real or alleged descendant of Mohammed. He is usually held in high esteem in Muslim countries.

36. The Muslim peoples of Central Asia, which fell under Russian domination, as well as the Muslim area of China have been subject to influences different from those exerted in all other Muslim countries.

37. For al-Afghani, see Charles C. Adams, *Islam and Modernism in Egypt* 1933; rept. ed., New York, 1968), pp. 4–17.

38. Ahmad Khan remained respectful of Islamic teaching, by prescribing compulsory Islamic teaching as a study object in his college. See Arif Hussain, *Pakistan* (London, 1966). The Islamic character of the University of Alighar was retained in modern India until 1974 when the government transformed it into a secular institution. See E. B. Fiske on India's Muslims, *New York Times*, September 17, 1974.

39. Quoted in Hamilton A. R. Gibb, *Modern Trends in Islam* (New York, 1947), pp. 78–81, from Mohammed Iqbal, *Six Lectures on the Reconstruction of Religious Thought in Islam* (1928).

40. Quoted by Javid Iqbal, *The Ideology of Pakistan and Its Implementation* (Lahore, 1959), p. 14, from Mohammed Iqbal, *Six Lectures*.

41. Ibid., p. 5.

42. The Muftis are *ulama* specialized in the study of canon law. They are entitled to issue *fatwas* ("opinions"), that is, interpretations of Shari'a.

43. Quoted by Malcolm Kerr, *Islamic Reform* (Berkeley, 1966), p. 110.

44. Quoted by Adams, *Islam and Modernism*, p. 129.

45. For the Muslim Brotherhood, see section 6 of this chapter.

46. See Clifford Geertz, *Islam Observed* (New Haven, 1968), pp. 69 and 72, about the moral authority which Mohammed 'Abduh still enjoys, also outside Egypt.

47. Among the Sufi orders, the Order of the "Whirling Dervishes" (*Mawlawiya*), which had been founded under the influence of the great Persian poet and mystic Djalal al-Din Rumi (1207–1273), was by far the most pow-

erful in Turkey. Other Dervish orders, of a more rebellious spirit and social composition than the Mawlawiya, were the Bektashi and the Rifai.

48. By way of illustration, the result of an examination of the official Turkish schoolbooks undertaken some time ago may be mentioned. It was found that "Islam is presented in these books as a, if not the, rational religion, perfectly compatible with science and modern civilization. Sufism . . . is almost completely ignored. Of the precepts of Islam the moral ones are given prominence; others are explained, or explained away by reason." See Uriel Heyd, *Revival of Islam in Modern Turkey* (Jerusalem, 1968).

49. In a similar vein, Wilfred E. Smith summarized the reformist action of the Turkish revolution as follows: "The Turks are a significant group of the modern interpretation of Islam. . . . The Turkish revolution liberated and recovered true Islam." *Islam in Modern History* (Princeton, 1957), p. 176. On the basis of a fundamentalist programme, the electoral successes which the National Salvation Party, founded in the early 1970s, has achieved and the role which it has been playing in Turkish policies seem to indicate a strengthening of the religious feelings in that country, but do not seem to mark an opposition to the structure of the Ataturk reforms.

50. Thus the secular universities of Cairo count far more students than the thousand-year-old venerated Al-Azhar. Even in that university, the Nasser regime introduced secular reforms in 1961. However, the right of the ulama of al-Azhar to issue fatwas has remained intact. They are still consulted in matters concerning the interpretation of Koran and Hadith by Muslims in all the world.

51. For the Muslim Brotherhood, see Ishaq Musa al-Hussaym, *The Moslem Brethren* (Beirut, 1956), and *Encyclopaedia of Islam*, 1971, s.v. "as-Ikhwan al-Muslimum."

52. The name *Ba'th* (Arabic for "resurrection") is meant to signify the resurrection of the Arab nation. For the text of the Constitution of the Syrian Ba'th Party, see Sylvia G. Haim, ed., *Arab Nationalism* (Berkeley, 1962), pp. 233–41.

53. Quoted from Edward H. F. Sheehan, "The Algerians Intend To Go It Alone, Raise Hell, Hold Out and Grow," *New York Times Magazine*, April 23, 1972.

54. Thus Gustave E. von Grunebaum summed up his analysis of modern Islam as follows: "Few culture areas have been subjected to so much and so violent change as that of Islam; none perhaps has so consistently refused to accept the ontological reality of change. The truth of Islam is not only one and indivisible, it is also immutable." *Modern Islam* (Berkeley, 1962), p. 209. Similarly, Wilfred C. Smith stated: "That there has been as yet virtually no explicit reconsideration of the central issues of the faith is attested both by Muslims themselves and by outside students." Smith, *Islam in Modern History*, p. 66 n.

CHAPTER IX

1. Thomas Aquinas *Summa Theologiae* I. qu. 83, art. 4.
2. Duns Scotus *Ordinatio* 1.17.1–2, in *New Catholic Encyclopedia*, 1967, s.v. "Will."
3. *Encyclopedia of Philosophy*, 1967, s.v. "William of Ockham."
4. Giovanni Pico della Mirandola, *On the Dignity of Man*, trans. Charles Glenn Wallis (Indianapolis, 1965), p. 5.
5. *New Catholic Encyclopedia*, 1967, s.v. "Erasmus, Desiderius."
6. See above, chapter VI, section 1.
7. Desiderius Erasmus, *De pueris statim ac liberaliter instituendis* [On a firm and appropriate education of boys], published under the title, *Desiderius Erasmus concerning the Aim and Method of Education*, trans. William H. Woodward (1904; rept. ed., New York, 1964).
8. *Encyclopedia of Philosophy*, 1967, s.v. "Cynics."
9. Thomas Aquinas *Summa Theologiae* II, 1st pt., QxCl, art. 2.
10. *Encyclopedia of Philosophy*, 1967, s.v. "Marsilius of Padua." Marsilius used his doctrine as a weapon in the fight between papal and civilian authority, a fight that continued through the Middle Ages. It was no coincidence that both Marsilius and William of Ockham, who also insisted on the independence of civil authority from papal supremacy, supported Emperor Louis IV (who reigned from 1314 to 1347) in his bitter fight against John XXII (pontificate 1316–1334). The pope condemned many theses contained in Marsilius's *Defensor pacis*. Both Marsilius and William of Ockham came to live at the court of Louis IV.
11. In 1584, the Scottish Parliament ordered the suppression of Buchanan's *De jure regni apud Scotos*. Although he and his followers were frequently called "monarchomachists" (foes of monarchism), they did not advocate the abolition of monarchical rule, only limitations on it.
12. *Politica methodice digesta* (1638), abr. in *The Politics of Johannes Althusius*, trans. Frederick S. Carney (London, 1965), p. 12.
13. Hugo Grotius, *The Law of War and Peace*, trans. Francis W. Kelsey (Indianapolis, 1925), pp. 38–40.
14. John Locke propounded these principles in paragraphs 57, 61, 95, and 221 of the second treatise. Locke, *Two Treatises of Government* (London, 1967). The Convention Parliament of the Glorious Revolution declared in the spirit of the doctrine of the social contract that King James II had "endeavoured to subvert the Constitution of the Kingdom by breaking the Original Contract between King and people." In George Macaulay Trevelyan, *The English Revolution, 1688–1689* (ed. of London, 1963), p. 146.
15. Diderot began to work on the *Encyclopédie* in 1745. The complete work was published from 1751 to 1780. Composed in the spirit of the Age of Enlightenment, it counted among its contributors such notables as

Montesquieu, Voltaire, Rousseau, Condillac, Helvetius, Holbach, Morellet, Quesnay, and Turgot.

16. Jean-Jacques Rousseau, *The Social Contract, Discourses*, trans. G. D. H. Cole (New York, 1955).

17. Marie Jean Antoine Nicolas Condorcet, *Esquisse d'un tableau historique des progrès de l'esprit humain* (1793). In the first English translation, *Outline of an Historical View of the Progress of the Human Mind* (Philadelphia, 1796), p. 260.

18. The complete title of Erasmus's c. 1516 treatise was *Querela Pacis undique gentium ejectae profligatae* [The complaint of peace which is everywhere despised and banished]. An English edition, which used the first translation by Thomas Paynell (1559), was published under the title, *The Complaint of Peace by Erasmus* (New York, 1946). The quotation is from pages 7 and 8 of that edition.

19. Hugo Grotius advocated the principle of freedom of the seas in an earlier treatise, *Mare Liberum* (1609). He wrote that treatise at the request of the Dutch East India Company in defense of the seizure of a Portuguese ship. Thus the proclamation of the freedom of the seas was originally a weapon in the struggle between the new colonial powers (Netherlands and England) and the older colonial powers (Portugal and Spain).

20. The proposal of a confederation of the Christian states of Europe antedated the "Project" of the Abbé de Saint-Pierre. It had been propounded as the *Grand Dessein* ("great design") by the Duc de Sully (Maximilien Bethune, Duc de Sully) (1560–1651) in his *Memoires* (1638).

21. *Völkerbund*, the name Kant used, has been retained by the German-speaking peoples as the designation of the historical League of Nations.

22. The translation is from Friedrich Schiller, *Anthology for Our Time* (New York, 1960), p. 42.

23. Julius Braunthal, *History of the International*, vol. 1 (New York, 1960), p. 42.

24. Immanuel Kant, *Perpetual Peace*, trans. M. Campbell Smith (New York, 1972).

25. The same view—that perpetual peace requires the progress of enlightenment in all nations—was propounded by Condorcet in his *Outline* (see below, section 3).

26. Francis Bacon, *Novum Organum*, bk. 1, sec. 84, in Carl Lotus Becker, *The Heavenly City of the Eighteenth Century Philosophers* (New Haven, 1932), p. 132. Becker also drew attention to a similar expression of trust in the modern age, offered by the French philosopher Blaise Pascal (1632–1662): "We have added the experience of the ages between us and them (the ancients) to what they knew." Pascal, *Pensees* 2.

27. Charles Perrault expounded his doctrine of progress in a 1687 poem dedicated to King Louis XIV, and in *Parallèle des anciens et des modernes* (1688–1692).

28. Francis Bacon, *In Praise of Knowledge,* in Max Horkheimer and Theodor Adorno, *Dialectic of Enlightenment* (New York, 1972); *New Atlantis* was published posthumously in 1627.

29. Quoted by John Arthur Passmore, *The Perfectibility of Man* (New York, 1971), p. 200.

30. Becker, *Heavenly City,* p. 57.

31. Charles Irenée Castel, Abbé de Saint-Pierre, *Observations on the Continual Progress of Universal Reason* (1737).

32. Quoted by John Bagnell Bury, *The Idea of Progress* (London, 1932), pp. 149–50.

33. Preceded by Chambers's *Cyclopedia* (1728), the *Encyclopaedia Britannica* appeared first in 1768–1771. The German *Brockhaus* was first published in 1796, preceded by *Lexikon* (1732).

34. Anne Robert Jacques Turgot, *Tableau philosophique des progrès successifs de l'esprit humain* [Philosophical tableau of the successive progress of the human spirit] (1750), and *Plan de deux discours sur l'histoire universelle* [Outline of two discourses on universal history] (1750).

35. Foremost among the atheists of the Age of Enlightenment were French philosophers Claude Adrien Helvetius (1717–1751) and Paul Henri Dietrich baron d'Holbach (1723–1789).

36. Francois-Marie Arquet Voltaire, *Sermon des cinquante,* in Peter Jack Gay, *Deism: An Anthology* (Princeton, 1968), p. 146.

37. The major works of English deism were: Edward Herbert of Cherbury, *De veritate* [On truth] (1624); John Toland, *Christianity Not Mysterious* (1696); and Matthew Tindal, *Christianity as Old as the Creation* (1730).

38. See Voltaire's statement, "The Christian sect is actually nothing more than the perversion of natural religion." In Voltaire, *Sermon des cinquante,* p. 157.

39. The 1794 decree on the "Worship of the Supreme Deity" stipulated that "the French people recognize the existence of the Supreme Being and the immortality of the soul. . . . The worship worthy of the Supreme Being is the practice of the duties of man." In Becker, *Heavenly City,* p. 157.

40. The leader of the Cambridge Platonists, Ralph Cudworth (1617–1688)—in a *Treatise Concerning Eternal and Immutable Morality* (published posthumously in 1731)—strongly insisted on the innate nature of the moral sense.

41. For Anthony Ashley Cooper Shaftesbury's doctrines, see his collection of essays, *Men, Manners, Opinions, Times* (1711).

42. Francis Hutcheson, *Inquiry Concerning Moral Good and Evil* (1726).

43. John A. Passmore, *Priestley's Writings on Philosophy, Science and Politics* (New York, 1965), Introduction, p. 28.

44. Jeremy Bentham, *Deontology, or the Science of Morality,* in Margaret Kennedy Knight, *Humanist Anthology* (London, 1961), p. 60.

45. See the arguments of Kenneth Joseph Arrow, *Social Choice and Individual Values* (New Haven, 1970), pp. 9–11, against the doctrine of the interpersonal measurability of utility.

46. In Leibniz's philosophy the monads are the substances which make up the universe; each monad is both material and spiritual by various degrees of conscience, and deploys various degrees of activity.

47. Gottfried Wilhelm Leibniz, *Essays on the Human Understanding* (1704). An English translation appeared in Leibniz, *Monadology and Other Philosophical Essays*, trans. Paul and Anne Martin Schrecker (Indianapolis, 1965).

48. Gotthold Ephraim Lessing, *Erziehung des Menschengeschlechts*. Translated by F. W. Robertson, under the title, *The Education of the Human Race* (New York, 1927). The quotations are from paragraphs 91, 92, and 85.

49. *Handle so, dass die Maxime deines Willens jederzeit zugleich als Prinzip einer allgemeinen Gesetzgebung dienen könne.* From Immanuel Kant, *Critique of Practical Reason* (1788).

50. See above, section 2.

51. See below, section 4.

52. The doctrine of a secret plan of Nature through which divine Providence works originated not only in the writings of Kant, but also in those of other authors of the same period. Thus Adam Smith (1723–1790) based his ideal of the free-market economy on the conviction that whereas in such an economic system everyone looks for his own gain, "he is . . . led by an invisible hand to promote an end which was no part of his intention," *Inquiry Into the Nature and Causes of the Wealth of Nations* (1776).

53. Johann Gottfried von Herder, *Auch eine Philosophie zur Geschichte der Menschheit* [Also a philosophy of the history of mankind] (1774).

54. An abridged English edition appeared under the title *Reflections on the Philosophy of the History of Mankind*, trans. T. Churchill (Chicago, 1969).

55. Johann Gottlieb Fichte, *The Characteristics of the Present Age* (1806), in *The Popular Works of J. G. Fichte*, trans. William Smith (London, 1889).

56. Ibid.; Fichte, *Vocation of Man*, vol. 1, p. 440; Fichte, *Characteristics of the Present Age*, vol. 2, pp. 9–10.

57. Ibid., vol. 2, pp. 2, 5, 159. Fichte elaborated his doctrine of an ideal state in which all men have equal privileges in the treatise *Der geschlossene Handelsstaat* [The closed commercial state] (1800). In modern terms, Fichte's *Handelsstaat* could be called a centrally planned economy, with a strict governmentally enforced division of crafts and professions, price controls, and a government monopoly of foreign trade.

58. Fichte, *Vocation of Man*, vol. 1, pp. 497, 502. In *Grundlage des Naturrechts* (1796–1797), Fichte even proposed a League of Nations, complete with an international court to which disputes between states must be submitted, and with ad hoc armies to curb aggression. See Helmuth Carol

Engelbrecht, *Johann Gottlieb Fichte* (1933; rept. ed., New York, 1968), pp. 69–70. *Grundlage des Naturrechts* was published under the title *The Science of Rights*, trans. A. E. Kroeger (Philadelphia, 1869).

59. Johann Gottlieb Fichte, *Reden an die deutsche Nation* (1807–1808). English edition: *Addresses to the German Nation*, trans. R. F. Jones and G. H. Turnbull (Chicago and London, 1922).

60. Friedrich Wilhelm Hegel, *Philosophy of History*, trans. J. Sibree (Chicago, 1956), p. 33.

61. "World-spirit" was only one of a plethora of names Hegel used to characterize his Supreme Being. Other names found in his writings were "The Pure Spirit," "The Absolute Being," "The Absolute Universal Being," "The Divine Spirit," "The Divine Being," or simply "God."

62. The quotations are from Hegel, *Philosophy of History*, pp. 55, 63.

63. Ibid., pp. 17–19.

64. Ibid., p. 39.

65. Friedrich Wilhelm Hegel, *Philosophy of Right*, trans. T. M. Knox (Oxford, 1967).

66. Ibid., p. 94.

67. Hegel, *Philosophy of History*, p. 445. A thorough analysis of Hegel's philosophy with respect to its hostility toward the "open society" can be found in Karl R. Popper, *The Open Society and Its Enemies*, vol. 2, 5th ed. (London, 1966).

68. *Die Philosophen haben die Welt nur verschieden interpretiert; es kommt darauf an, sie zu verändern.* This statement constituted the eleventh thesis in Karl Marx, *Thesen über Feuerbach* (1845), published posthumously in 1888. For a translation, see *Theses on Feuerbach*, in *Karl Marx: Economy, Class and Social Revolution*, ed. Z. A. Jordan (New York, 1971).

69. Morelly, *Code de la Nature ou le véritable esprit de ses lois, de tout temps négligé ou méconnu.* Montesquieu's *Esprit des lois*, to which the title alluded, had appeared seven years earlier.

70. Gabriel Bonnot de Mably, *Doutes proposés aux philosophes économistes sur l'ordre naturel et essentiel des sociétés* (1768).

71. Both the name Babeuf gave to his journal ("Tribune"), and the name he adopted for himself ("Gracchus," brothers and Roman tribunes who fought for radical social reform) were ways to present his revolutionary ideas as a continuation of ancient popular movements.

72. Claude Henri Saint-Simon's planning ideas were expounded in *Du système industriel* (1820–1823).

73. François Marie-Charles Fourier, *Théorie des quatre mouvements et des destinées générales* [Theory of the four movements and of general destinies] (1808). The four movements to which the title of the treatise referred were supposed to be the four ages of mankind, constructed in the manner of Condorcet. The fifth, utopian age, called "Guarantism," would bring about the perfect harmony of which Fourier dreamed. During Fourier's lifetime, an at-

tempt was made in France to establish a *phalanstère*. In the United States, 41 *phalanstères* were founded on similar principles, one of which was the famous Brook Farm in West Roxbury, Massachusetts (1841–1847); Nathaniel Hawthorne was a distinguished member of Brook Farm, which he described in *Blithedale Romance*.

74. Of the misery of the working class in England, Friedrich Engels presented a heartrending picture in *Die Lage der arbeitenden Klasse in England* (1895), *The Condition of the Working Class in England*, trans. W. O. Henderson and W. H. Chaloner (Stanford, 1968).

75. In French, the title of Pierre-Joseph Proudhon's treatise was *Qu'est-ce que la propriété?* and the answer, *La propriété c'est le vol*. This phrase had first been used in 1780 by Jacques Pierre Brissot de Warville (1754–1793), one of the first advocates of the abolition of slavery, whose life as a Girondist during the French Revolution ended on the guillotine.

76. Even the term "anarchy," in the sense of a stateless society, was first used in Proudhon's *What is Property?* He stated: "While I am a friend of order, I am an anarchist." Somewhat later, in the essay *Les confessions d'un révolutionnaire* (1849) he expressed the paradox: "The true form of government is anarchy."

77. Karl Marx's treatise appeared in French under the title *Le misère de la philosophie* (1847). The first German translation was published in 1885 by Friedrich Engels. Quotations are from *The Poverty of Philosophy* (New York, 1963).

78. Georges Sorel, *Introduction à l'économie moderne* (Paris, 1903); Karl Marx took this phrase (*le combat ou la mort, la lutte sanguine ou le néant*) from George Sand, *Jean Zyska* (1844), a novel about the Hussite leader Jan Žižka (c. 1376–1424). Madame George Sand (1804–1876) played an active part in the Socialist-Republican movement of the 1840s.

79. The Carbonari were originally an organization of Italian liberal nationalists who fought the reactionary monarchies of their country. The Carbonari movement spread to France during the fight of republican groups against the Bourbon dynasty.

80. Karl Marx, *Die ökonomisch-philosophischen Manuskripte aus dem Jahre 1844*. The following quotations are from *Writings of the Young Marx on Philosophy and Society*, trans. Lloyd D. Easton and Kurt H. Guddat (Garden City, N.Y., 1967).

81. *Private Property and Communism* also appeared in ibid.

82. Karl Marx, *Capital: A Critique of Political Economy*, trans. Samuel Moore and Edward Eveling (New York, 1967), p. 72; Karl Marx, *Das Kapital*, pt. 1, chap. 1, sect. 4, entitled "The Fetishism of Commodities and the Secret thereof," pp. 71–83.

83. In the preface to the second edition of *Das Kapital*, Marx expressed the difference between Hegel's and his own dialectical system as follows: "The mystification which dialectic suffers in Hegel's hands by no means prevents

him from being the first to present its general form of working in a comprehensive and conscious manner. With him it is standing on its head. It must be turned right side up again if you would discover the rational kernel within the mystical shell." Marx, *Das Kapital*, ed. Friedrich Engels (London, 1887), p. xvii.

84. Trans. R. Dixon (Moscow, 1956).

85. Marx, *Poverty of Philosophy*, p. 109.

86. The Communist League was the successor of the League of the Just, formed in Paris in 1838, and of the Worker's Educational Society, founded in London in 1840. At a congress in London in 1847, the name was changed to Communist League. A further congress, also convening in 1847, invited Marx and Engels to prepare a socialist programme; both had become well known for their political and literary activities in France, Belgium, and Germany. It was published in London in 1848 under the title *Das Kommunistische Manifest*. See Braunthal, *History of the International*, pp. 36–54. Quotations are from *The Communist Manifesto* (New York, 1968).

87. Karl Marx, *Zur Kritik der politischen Ökonomie* (1859). The quotation is from *Karl Marx: Economy, Class and Social Revolution* (London, 1971), pp. 197–98.

88. At a later period, in the *Critique of the Gotha Programme* (1875), Marx advocated "the revolutionary dictatorship of the proletariat," but with the same qualification as in *The Communist Manifesto*, that this form of government would characterize a "political transition period" corresponding to the period of the revolutionary transformation of the capitalist into the communist society. The two quotations are from a 1966 Moscow edition.

89. Braunthal, *History of the International*, p. 35.

90. Quoted from the preface to Karl Marx, *Contribution to a Critique of Political Economy*, trans. S. W. Ryazanskaya (London, 1971).

91. The Communist League was disbanded in 1852 on the initiative of Marx since the member organizations on the Continent had ceased to function.

92. For the text of the General Rules, see Braunthal, *History of the International*, pp. 357–60.

93. In France the defeat of the Commune in 1871 led to a ban on any socialist movement.

94. See above, note 90.

95. Friedrich Engels, *Herr Eugen Dühring's Revolution in Science* ("Anti-Dühring"), 1878 (New York, 1966), pp. 306–7. Karl Eugen Dühring (1833–1921) was a German philosopher who, while critical toward the capitalist society, was opposed to Marxism.

96. In *Materialism and Empirio-Criticism* (1909), Lenin contrasted historical materialism to the "empirio-criticism," of the German philosopher Richard Avenarius (1843–1896) and of his Russian follower Alexander A. Bogdanow (pseudonym for Malinowski, 1873–1928). Avenarius's doctrine constituted a positivist epistemology basing all knowledge of the world on

pure experience. See the translation by A. Fineberg (Moscow, 1947).

97. Vladimir Ilyich Lenin, *The State and Revolution, Selected Works* (1917) (Moscow, 1967), vol. 2, pp. 341–46.

98. In a "Report on the Party Programme" of March 1919, Lenin stated that "it was necessary to combat bureaucracy to the very last until it completely vanished, but this would only be possible if the whole population took part in the country's administration." In Roger Garaudy, *The Crisis in Communism: The Turning-Point of Socialism*, trans. Peter Ross and Betty Ross (New York, 1970), pp. 81–82.

99. See the address of Mihailo Marković of the University of Belgrade to a 1969 symposium held in Herceg Novy, Yugoslavia, in which he spoke of "the transformation of the revolutionary avant-garde into a privileged bureaucratic elite," and specifically called the Soviet system "a new type of post-capitalist bureaucratic society." In *Tolerance and Revolution* (Belgrade, 1970), pp. 90, 100. Marković was one of eight professors from the University of Belgrade who became the object of a fight between the government which tried to have them dismissed, and the university authorities who for a long time resisted this pressure. In the end, the "establishment" won and the professors were discharged.

100. See Irving Howe, ed., *The Basic Writings of Leon Trotsky* (London, 1964), p. 194, where he stated that "the conquest of power changes not only the relations of the proletariat to other classes, but also its inner structure. The wielding of power becomes the specialty of a definite social group." For Milovan Djilas's analysis of the Communist society, see particularly his *The New Class* (New York, 1957).

101. This famous phrase was used by Engels, in *Anti-Dühring*, p. 299.

102. Universal suffrage was achieved in 1867 for the North German League (*Norddeutscher Bund*) and in 1871 for the new German Reich. But in Prussia, which wielded the real power within the Reich, and in a few other member states suffrage was weighted toward the wealthy ("three-class electoral system"). Universal equal suffrage in these states had to wait until the end of the First World War.

103. Eduard Bernstein, *Die Voraussetzungen des Sozialismus und die Aufgaben der Sozialdemokratie* (1899), trans. Edith C. Harvey, under the title *Evolutionary Socialism* (New York, 1961).

104. After the demise of the First International, a Second International was formed in 1889. That organization comprised most socialist parties, mainly in Europe.

105. The Communist International (Comintern) was formed in 1919 under the leadership of the Soviet regime with the ultimate goal of world revolution. It was dissolved during the Second World War, in 1943, when the Soviet Union was interested in maintaining friendly relations with the Western powers. A successor organization, the Cominform, was active from 1947 to 1956.

106. After the Second International had been ruined by the outbreak of World

War I, and after the Labor and Socialist International, formed in 1923, foundered under the blows of the Hitler regime and World War II, the international socialist movement reconstituted itself in 1951 as the Socialist International.

107. The Radical-Socialist Party (Partie Republicain Radical et Radical-Socialiste) was formed in 1902 as a liberal group with strong anti-clerical sentiments. Until the Second World War, it was an important liberal element in French political life. After the war its influence declined, but has not entirely died.

108. The Socialist-Communist alliance underwent a severe crisis in the parliamentary elections of 1978. However, this setback did not signify a retreat by the Communists from their allegiance to democracy.

109. Antonio Gramsci, *The Modern Prince and Other Writings*, trans. Louis Marks (London, 1968), pp. 75, 160; Jean-Paul Sartre, *Critique de la raison dialectique* (Paris, 1960), esp. pp. 134, 142, 180.

110. Frederick Scott, *The Scientific Work of René Descartes* (London, 1952), pp. 170–181; Immanuel Kant, *Allgemeine Geschichte und Theorie des Himmels* [General history and theory of the universe] (1755), and Pierre Simon Laplace, *Exposition du système du monde* [Outline of the system of the universe] (1796).

111. Jean-Baptiste Lamarck, *Philosophie zoologique* (1809), and the Introduction to *Histoire naturelle des animaux sans vertèbres* [Natural history of non-vertebrate animals] (1815).

112. The curious episode of the triumph and downfall of Lamarckism in the Soviet Union, which was connected with the rise and fall of biologist Trophim Denisovich Lysenko (1898–1976), may have had its origin in Marx's and Engels's acceptance of Lamarckism. Lysenko, a staunch adherent of Lamarckism, was appointed head of Soviet biology in 1948. After the downfall of Khrushchev, who continued the Lamarckian line of Stalin, Lysenko lost his influence. He was dismissed as Director of the Institute of Genetics in 1965, and Lamarckism was virtually abandoned in the Soviet Union.

113. Herbert Spencer, *Progress: Its Law and Cause*, in *Essays: Scientific, Political, and Speculative*. Library edition (London, 1891), p. 35.

114. Herbert Spencer, *First Principles* (New York, 1957), pp. 511, 199–200, 529 ff.

115. A year before Darwin published the *Origin of Species*, he received a manuscript from Alfred Russel Wallace (1823–1913) which advanced the same theories as those Darwin was about to propound in public. Thereupon Darwin and Wallace jointly published *On the Tendency of Species to form Varieties; and on the Perpetuation of Varieties and Species by Natural Means of Selection* (1858).

116. Mendel reported his genetic findings to the *Naturforschender Verein* in Brno (Czechoslovakia) in 1865, but his discoveries remained unknown until 1900 when they were confirmed by some biologists.

117. In the penultimate paragraph of *Origin of Species*.
118. In the last paragraph of Darwin, *The Descent of Man*.
119. Julian Sorell Huxley, *Essays of a Humanist* (1936; rept. ed., New York, 1964), pp. 35–36; Julian Sorell Huxley, *Evolution, the Modern Synthesis*, (1942; rept. ed., New York, 1964), pp. 561–62, 564–66.
120. Karl R. Popper, *The Poverty of Historicism* (New York, 1963), pp. 106–9. Popper maintained that the law of biological evolution is not a universal law but a particular historical statement—even though certain universal laws of nature, such as laws of heredity and mutations, enter into the explanation. Being confined to the observation of one unique process, we cannot foresee its future development.
121. Popper stated that while no universally valid laws can be deduced from historical facts, "trends" can be found in human history; but as trends are also unique facts, they cannot be used as a basis for scientific predictions since the persistence of a trend "depends on the persistence of certain specific initial conditions." Ibid., p. 115 ff.

CHAPTER X

1. "All beings so far have created something beyond themselves." Friedrich Wilhelm Nietzsche, *Thus Spake Zarathustra*, in *The Portable Nietzsche*, trans. Walter Kaufmann (New York, 1954), p. 124.
2. Friedrich Wilhelm Nietzsche, *The Anti-Christ*, in ibid., p. 571. Like Nietzsche and probably under his influence, the French syndicalist-socialist Georges Sorel (1847–1922) called the idea of progress an illusion. He held that progress cannot be achieved by revolution, but only by continued direct action of the proletariat, including the general strike. *The Illusions of Progress*, trans. John Stanley and Charlotte Stanley (Berkeley, 1969).
3. Nietzsche, *Thus Spake Zarathustra*, pp. 129–30.
4. Friedrich Wilhelm Nietzsche, *Beyond Good and Evil*, trans. Walter Kaufmann (New York, 1966), p. 236. For Nietzsche's aristocratic, anti-democratic, anti-equalitarian philosophy, see especially pp. 72 ff, 111, 118, 153, 202.
5. For the quotations in this paragraph, see Nietzsche, *Thus Spake Zarathustra*, pp. 124, 129, 310, 374.
6. See above, chapter IX, notes 120 and 121.
7. Karl Raimund Popper, *The Open Society and Its Enemies* (New York, 1963), p. 3.
8. Ludwig Andreas Feuerbach, *Das Wesen des Christentums* (1841), in *The Essence of Christianity*, trans. George Eliot (New York, 1957), p. 14; Ludwig Andreas Feuerbach, *Vorlesungen über das Wesen der Religion*, quoted by Gustav Andreas Wetter, *Dialectical Materialism*, trans. Peter Heath (London, 1963), p. 12.

9. Marx's doctoral thesis was entitled *Differenz der demokritischen and epikureischen Naturphilosophie* [The difference between Democritus' and Epicureus' philosophy of nature] (1839–1841). For the quotation, see Henri François Lefebvre, *The Sociology of Marx*, trans. Norbert Guterman (New York, 1968), p. 19.

10. Karl Marx, *Critique of Hegel's Philosophy of Right*, trans. Annette O'Malley and Joseph O'Malley (Cambridge, England, 1970), Introduction, p. 131.

11. Sigmund Freud, *The Future of an Illusion*, trans. James Strachey (New York, 1969), pp. 24, 30, 50, 53.

12. See above, chapter VII, section 3.

13. Julian Sorell Huxley, *Religion without Revelation* (London, 1957), p. 114. Rudolf Otto understood by the term "numinous" the feeling—common to all religions—toward the sacred. The sacred is always considered a mystery, which appears to man under two aspects: attracting him (*mysterium fascinans*) and awe-inspiring (*mysterium tremendum*). Rudolf Otto, *The Idea of the Holy*, trans. John W. Harvey (London, 1923); John Dewey, *A Common Faith* (New Haven, 1934), p. 53.

14. For the text of the "Humanist Manifesto" of 1933, see Corliss Lamont, *The Philosophy of Humanism* (New York, 1965), Appendix. For the text of the "Humanist Manifesto II," see *The Humanist* (New York, Sept.–Oct. 1973).

15. Dewey, *Common Faith*, p. 46; Lamont, *Philosophy of Humanism*.

16. Bertrand Russell, *What I Believe* (London, 1925), p. 17.

17. John Dewey, *The Ethics of Democracy* (Ann Arbor, 1888), p. 23; Dewey, *Common Faith*, p. 25.

18. John Dewey, *Individualism Old and New* (New York, 1962), p. 53.

19. Dewey, *Ethics of Democracy*, pp. 22–23.

20. See the report on the symposium edited by Erich Fromm, *Socialist Humanism* (Garden City, N.Y., 1965).

21. The revolutionary motto *liberté, égalité, fraternité*, adopted by the National Convention in 1793, has remained the official motto of France, except for the periods from 1814 to 1848 (Bourbon and Orleans dynasties), from 1851 to 1875 (Napoleon III and the reaction against the Paris Commune), and from 1940 to 1944 (Pétain regime).

22. See Robert A. Dahl, *A Preface to Democratic Theory* (Chicago, 1956), pp. 70, 81.

23. Isaiah Berlin, *Four Essays on Liberty* (London, 1969).

24. Robert A. Dahl, *After the Revolution? Authority in a Good Society* (New Haven, 1970), p. 23.

25. John Rawls, *Theory of Justice* (Cambridge, Mass., 1971), pp. 3–4, 11.

26. In the United States the federal government has instituted and encouraged a policy of "affirmative action" in favor of disfavored minorities. The so-called "Bakke decision" of the United States Supreme Court (1978) sustained the principle of affirmative action, but ruled out the application of rigid quotas.

27. Roosevelt introduced the first New Deal measures before Keynes's *General Theory of Employment, Interest and Money* was published. It appears, however, that Keynes "had earlier outlined his ideas to Franklin Roosevelt and they were known to some of his advisers; they formed one intellectual ingredient in framing the Roosevelt policies for economic recovery." See *Encyclopaedia Britannica*, 1972, s.v. "John Maynard Keynes."

28. Terms of trade are determined by the relation of export prices to import prices of commodities traded between countries. Pre-industrial countries export mainly raw materials and foodstuffs. In inflationary periods prices for these commodities (except for fuel and a few other relatively rare materials) usually remain behind those of imported industrial commodities.

29. Rawls, *Theory of Justice*, pp. 73, 100, 105.

30. In a similar vein, Herbert J. Gans, *More Equality* (New York, 1973), proposed a system that would establish a floor and ceiling on incomes to enable each person to buy the goods and services considered essential for maintaining the American standard of living.

31. Rawls, *Theory of Justice*, pp. 275–77.

32. Max Horkheimer and Theodore W. Adorno, *Dialectic of Enlightenment*, trans. John Cunning (London, 1973), pp. 28 and 35.

33. Erich Fromm, *Man for Himself* (1947; rept. ed., New York, 1964), pp. 143–44, 158, 151.

34. Herbert Marcuse, *One Dimensional Man* (Boston, 1964), pp. 168–69, 32, 144.

35. Alain Touraine, *The Post-Industrial Society*, trans. Leonard F. X. Mayhew (New York, 1971), pp. 49–50, 63.

36. Robert Blauner, *Alienation and Freedom: The Factory Worker and His Industry* (Chicago, 1967), p. 15.

37. Erich Fromm, *Beyond the Chains of Illusion* (New York, 1962), p. 178; Marcuse, *One Dimensional Man*, p. 43.

38. Erich Fromm, ed., *Socialist Humanism* (Garden City, N.Y., 1965), pp. 308–9.

39. For more on the workers' council systems in several European countries, see Adolf Sturmthal, *Workers' Councils* (Cambridge, Mass., 1964).

40. U.S., Special Task Force of the Secretary of Health, Education, and Welfare, *Work in America* (Washington, D.C., 1972), p. 13.

41. Work reforms of this kind have been made by the Swedish automobile industry, of which the system introduced by Volvo is best known. The chief feature of this system is the replacement of the assembly line by small teams of workers who organize their own work. In Japan, "workers' circles, consisting of about a dozen workers engaged in a certain task, have been allowed to arrive at their own decisions on production methods and quality control. Several hundred thousands of such teams were operating in the early 1970s." *British Encyclopaedia*, Macropedia, 1974, s.v. "Work, Organization of."

42. Fromm, *Man for Himself*, pp. 218, 107. 129.

43. Fromm, *The Sane Society*, pp. 275, 298.

44. Russell, *What I Believe*, p. 20.

45. Fromm, *Man for Himself*, pp. 207–8.

46. Fromm, *The Sane Society*, p. 357.

47. Fromm, *Man for Himself*, pp. 207–8, and 101. In his recent book, *The Anatomy of Destructiveness* (New York, 1973), Fromm defended his view that man is not innately evil, against Konrad Lorenz's theory—expounded in *On Aggression* (New York, 1966)—that human aggressiveness is based on instinct.

48. Lamont, *Philosophy of Humanism*, pp. 258, 177.

49. Sigmund Freud, *Civilization and Its Discontents*, trans. W. D. Robson Scott, in *The Standard Edition of the Complete Psychological Works of Sigmund Freud*, vol. 21 (London, 1961).

50. Ibid., pp. 86 and 45.

51. Rawls, *Theory of Justice*, pp. 482, 476.

52. Fromm, *The Sane Society*, p. 360.

53. Marcuse, *One Dimensional Man*, pp. 256–57.

54. Titus Lucretius Carus, *De rerum natura*, published under the title, *The Way Things Are*, trans. Rolfe Humphries (Indianapolis, 1968), bk. 5, last lines.

55. Augustine *De Civitate Dei* 10.14.

56. Gottfried Wilhelm Leibniz, *The Monadology and Other Philosophical Writings* (1714), p. 376.

57. Russell, *What I Believe*, pp. 75, 76.

58. Ernst Bloch, *Das Prinzip Hoffnung* (Frankfurt, 1959), p. 1618.

59. Karl Raimund Popper, *The Open Society and Its Enemies*, vol. 1 (New York, 1963), pp. 157–58; vol. 2, p. 334 n. 4.

60. Karl Raimund Popper, *The Poverty of Historicism* (London, 1957), pp. 66–67.

61. Robert A. Dahl, *Polyarchy—Participation and Opposition* (New Haven, 1971), p. 45. Dahl defines the existing democratic systems, which are based on majority rule, as "polyarchies."

62. Rawls, *Theory of Justice*, p. 363.

63. Popper, *Open Society and Its Enemies*, vol. 1, p. 4.

64. The full title of the report, published under the auspices of the Massachusetts Institute of Technology, is *Limits to Growth, a Report of the Club of Rome's Project on the Predicament of Mankind* (New York, 1967). The quotation is from p. 23.

65. Robert Heilbroner, *An Inquiry into the Human Prospect* (New York, 1974), esp. pp. 22, 90, 110. In a more recent book, *Business Civilization in Decline* (New York, 1976), Heilbroner insists that "there seems to be no alternative to the extremes of organization, control and economic and political discipline over the activities of mankind" (p. 98), that "a high degree of political authority will be inescapable in the period of extreme exigency which we

can expect a hundred years hence" (p. 119), but that this need not imply a strictly authoritarian system: "The recognition of man as a unique and autonomous person" (p. 126) is entirely compatible with the exigencies of a society of constraints.

66. According to the United Nations Statistical Yearbook of 1976, in the period from 1960 to 1973, the GNP increased in democratic industrial countries by 87 percent, and by 63 percent per head of population; in the countries of the Soviet bloc, by 131 percent, and by 102 percent per capita; in the developing countries, by 103 percent, and by 46 percent per capita. In the following period, which was characterized by a depression in the democratic industrial sector, the GNP declined slightly in that sector but continued its rapid pace both in the Soviet bloc and in the developing countries.

67. The UNESCO Statistical Yearbook of 1976 showed for the period from 1960 to 1974 for the developed countries—all of Europe, the Soviet Union, the United States, Canada, Japan, Israel, Australia, New Zealand, South Africa—a 63 percent increase in the number of students on the high school level, and 160 percent increase on the academic level. Attendance by female students grew in the same period by 68 percent on the high school level, and by 221 percent on the academic level.

68. According to the UNESCO Statistical Yearbook of 1976, in the developing countries the number of pupils increased in the period from 1960 to 1974 by 97 percent on the elementary level, by 183 percent on the secondary level, and by 302 percent on the university level.

Glossary

Abbasids: a dynasty of caliphs (A.D. 759–1258)

Achaemenids: the first Persian dynasty (sixth century–330 B.C.)

Adoptionist: a Christian doctrine stating that Christ was God's son by adoption

Adventists: see Seventh-Day Adventists

Agape: in Christianity, man's love of God

Ahura Mazda: in Zoroastrianism, the sole God of the universe

Akkad: a northern region of ancient Babylonia

Amish: a Mennonite community

Amitabha: in Mahayana Buddhism, a saint who became a Buddha (Amida)

Ammonites: an ancient people east of the Jordan River, known from the thirteenth to the sixth century B.C.

Anabaptists: a sixteenth-century Protestant sect based on adult baptism

Anathema: in Catholicism, doctrines or persons declared heretic by ecclesiastical authorities

Animism: the belief that inanimate objects have conscious life

Antichrist: in Christianity, the eschatological antagonist of Christ

Apocalypse: a prophecy of the end of the world and the rise of a new one

Apocrypha: non-canonical Jewish and Christian scriptures

Arianism: a doctrine stating that Christ was not divine

Arminianists: Calvinists opposed to predestinarianism

Assumption: in Christianity, the Virgin's ascent to heaven

Atman: in Hinduism, man's soul

Avesta: the Zoroastrian scriptures

Ba'ath: Syrian and Iraqi parties with socialist and Arab nationalist goals

Bahaiism: a religion derived from a Shi'ite sect

Baptist: a Protestant denomination confining baptism to adults

Bhagavad Gita: a sacred Hindu song which established the belief in a savior God

Bhakti: in Hinduism, religious devotion

Bodhisattva: in Mahayana Buddhism, a saint who by renouncing release helps men attain it

Bogomils: a medieval Manichaean sect

Bohemian Brethren: a Protestant Reformist community (Moravian Brethren)

Book of the Dead: in ancient Egypt, collections of rites believed to ensure immortality

Brahman: in the Upanishads, the Supreme Being

Brahmanas: commentaries on Vedic scriptures

Brahmins: the highest caste in Hindu India

Caliph: in Islam, the supreme religious and secular leader

Cambridge Platonists: a seventeenth-century philosophical school based on the doctrine of an innate moral sense

Canon law: authoritatively recognized, mainly religious, laws and rules

Carbonari: a secret revolutionary movement, originating in Italy in the nineteenth century

Categorical imperative: an unconditional ethical rule apt to form the basis of a universal law (Kant)

Cathars: a medieval Manichaean sect

Charismatic: in Christianity, gifts granted by the Holy Spirit, such as the capacity of prophesying, healing, speaking in tongues

Charismatic communities: Christian communities stressing belief in charismatic gifts

Christian Scientists: a Christian denomination based on the teachings of Mary Baker Eddy (1821–1910)

Christology: doctrines of the nature of Christ

Codetermination: in German legislation, workers' participation in executive boards of companies

Commune: a revolutionary regime in Paris (1871)

Congregationalist: a Protestant denomination governed by local congregations

Consubstantial: a Christian doctrine that Christ and the Holy Spirit are of one substance with God (Nicene Creed)

Cynics: a Greek philosophical-ethical school based on a doctrine of obedience to the laws of nature as the sole source of happiness

Deism: in the seventeenth and eighteenth centuries, the belief in a Supreme Being governing the universe

Demiurge: in Gnosticism, an inferior god

Dervish orders: in Islam, ecstatic Sufic orders

Deuteronomy: the fifth book of the Old Testament

Dharma: in Buddhism, Buddha's doctrine

Dialectical: in Hegelian and Marxian systems, the doctrine that all historical processes evolve from thesis and antithesis to synthesis

Directoire: an oligarchic government ending the French Revolution (1795–1799)

Docetic: Christian doctrines that deny that Jesus had a natural body

Donatism: the Christian doctrine that divine grace depends on the worthiness of the officiating priest (fourth century A.D., in North Africa)

Druzes: a Shi'ite sect

Ecumenical: in Christianity, pertaining to, or aiming at, unity among Christian churches

Encyclical: a letter addressed by the pope to the entire Church

Encyclopédie: a French encyclopedia founded and edited by Diderot (1751–1780)

Enlightenment: a philosophical, political, and religious movement of the seventeenth and eighteenth centuries, based on doctrines of natural rights and of progress

Epistemology: philosophical investigations of the nature and validity of human knowledge

Eschatology: doctrines of the "last things," at the end of history

Eucharist: in Christianity, Christ's last supper (the communion meal)

Evangelicals: the name usually used for Christian movements and churches of fundamentalist leanings

Excommunication: in Christianity, exclusion from the community by ecclesiastical authorities

Existentialism: philosophical doctrine dealing with problems of human existence, and stressing man's responsibilities

Exodus: the second book of the Old Testament

Fatimid: an Isma'ili dynasty in North Africa and Asia (909–1169)

Friends, Society of: see Quakers

Fundamentalism: a belief in the inerrancy of the Sacred Scriptures (i.e., Bible, Koran)

Gathas: in Zoroastrianism, hymns of Avesta

Genesis: the first book of the Old Testament

Gilgamesh: King-hero in an Akkadian epic, who struggled for immortality

Girondins: a moderate revolutionary party of the French Revolution

Glorious Revolution: the English revolution of 1688–1689

Gnosticism: philosophical-religious doctrines, originating from the first century A.D., centering on the belief that man's soul is imprisoned in his body and yearns for union with God

Hadith: in Islam, authoritatively recognized original tradition

Harijans: in India, the name given by Gandhi to the untouchables

Hasidism: an Orthodox Jewish sect aiming at nearness to God

Hegira: flight of Mohammed from Mecca to Medina in A.D. 622

Hermetic: esoteric, mostly Gnostic doctrines

Hinayana: name given by Mahayana Buddhists to Theravada

Historical materialism: the doctrine put forth by Marx and Engels that all social, political, and cultural structures are based on economic relations

Hittites: an ancient Near Eastern people, flourishing in the fourteenth and thirteenth centuries B.C.

Hivites: a Canaanite tribe attested in the Old Testament

Holism: the doctrine that Nature produces wholes

Huguenots: the name by which the French Protestants were known from the sixteenth to the eighteenth century

Hussites: a Czech reformist movement that succeeded the execution of Jan Hus (c. 1372–1415)

Hutterites: a Mennonite community

Iconoclasm: hostility toward, or removal of, ritual images

Imam: in Islam, a religious leader, a leader of Mosque services. In the Shi'ite community, a divinely guided infallible leader

Imprimatur: in Catholicism, a license given by ecclesiastical authorities to publish a book

Index: in Catholicism, a list of writings banned by ecclesiastical authorities

Indulgences: in Catholicism, grants given by ecclesiastical authorities to relieve penances

International: the successive international socialist organizations

Isma'ilis: a Shi'ite sect

Jainism: an Indian religion, contemporaneous with Buddhism

Jehovah's Witnesses: a Protestant millenarian denomination

Justification: in Christianity, the act of being absolved from guilt and accepted by God

Ka'ba: a sacred building in the Grand Mosque of Mecca, center of the Muslim pilgrimage

Kabbalah: Jewish mystical doctrines (Cabala)

Karma: in Hinduism, Jainism, and Buddhism, retribution after death

Khatib: in Islam, a preacher in mosques

Latter-Day Saints: also called Mormons, a Protestant denomination based on the teachings of Joseph Smith (1805–1844)

Levites: religious dignitaries in ancient Israel

Leviticus: the third book of the Old Testament

Limbo: in Christianity, the post-mortem abode of unbaptized children

Logos: a term variously denoting cosmic order, Wisdom of God, and Son of God

Lollards: a religious movement based on the teachings of John Wycliffe (c. 1330–1384)

Maccabeans: leaders of the Jewish rebellion against the Seleucids

Mahayana: a form of Buddhism believing in salvation through Buddhas and Bodhisattvas

Mahdi: in Islam, an eschatological savior

Maitreya: in Buddhism, the future Buddha

Mandaeans: a Gnostic religion in the Near East

Manichaeism: a Gnostic religion derived from Zoroastrianism, founded by Mani (A.D. c. 216–c. 276)

Marabouts: Muslim saints in Africa

Mennonites: a Protestant sect based on the teachings of Menno Simons (1496–1561)

Messianism: the belief in a human or divine savior, the Messiah

Metanoia: repentance through a change in the direction of one's life

Methodist: a Protestant denomination based on the teachings of John Wesley (1703–1792)

Millenarianism: in Christianity, the belief in the imminent coming of Christ

Millennium: in Christianity, the thousand years of the reign of Christ

Moabites: an ancient people of present-day Jordan, known from the thirteenth to the fifth century B.C.

Moguls: a Muslim dynasty in India (1526–1857)

Molech: a Canaanite god, venerated occasionally in Israel (also Moloch)

Monads: according to the philosophy of Leibniz, the spiritual and material substances which form the universe

Monophysitism: the Christian doctrine that Christ is purely divine

Montanism: in Christianity, a millenarian sect active from the second to the sixth century A.D.

Moravian Brethren: a Protestant Reform community (Bohemian Brethren)

Mormons: see Latter-Day Saints

Mufti: in Islam, a scholar of canon law

Muslim Brotherhood: a political movement founded in Egypt in 1928 on the basis of the strict observance of Islam

Mu'tazilis: in Islam, a rationalist theological school

Mystery religions: in the Greek-Roman world, secret cults believing in the resurrection of their adherents

Natural selection: the Darwinian doctrine that those plants and animals best adapted to the environment survive

Neoplatonism: a philosophical system based on the doctrine of the world as a cycle of emanations from God

Nestorianism: a Christian doctrine that a divine and a human person are united in Christ

New Deal: the economic and social policy pursued by Franklin D. Roosevelt, inspired by the principles of the welfare state

New Kingdom: in ancient Egypt, the 18th through 20th dynasties (sixteenth–
eleventh century B.C.)
Nicene Creed: a doctrine of Christian faith, based on the belief in the consub-
stantiality of God and Christ, adopted by the Council of Nicaea (A.D. 325),
and amended by later councils
Nirvana: in Buddhism, the ultimate release from suffering
Novatians: a Christian sect, active from the third to the seventh century A.D.,
opposed to ecclesiastical leniency
Numbers: the fourth book of the Old Testament
Numinous: a feeling of reverence toward the sacred

Oligopoly: control of industrial and other markets by a small number of pro-
ducers or traders
Old Kingdom: in ancient Egypt, the 3rd through 8th dynasties (third millennium
B.C.)
Orphism: in ancient Greece, a religious group believing in the immortality of de-
serving souls

Paraclete: in Christianity, the Holy Spirit as comforter, as set forth in the Gospel
of John
Parousia: in Christianity, Christ's return for the last judgment
Paschal: pertaining to Passover and Easter
Patristic: in Christianity, pertaining to the early Church Fathers
Pelagianism: the Christian doctrine that man possesses the free will to accept or
reject divine grace (Pelagius, A.D. c. 354–c. 418)
Pentateuch: the Five Books of Moses
Pentecostal: in Christianity, pertaining to Whitsun (Pentecost)
Pentecostal communities: Christian communities stressing spiritual experiences
and gifts
Phalanstères: producers' cooperatives as proposed by Charles Fourier (1772–
1837)
Pharisees: in ancient Israel, a religious group of strict observance
Philistines: an ancient people residing in southern Palestine, known from the
twelfth to the sixth century B.C.
Physiocrats: an eighteenth-century school of French economists who regarded
land as the primary source of wealth
Pietism: a Christian movement—particularly within Lutheran Protestantism—
emphasizing emotional devotion
Pleroma: in Gnosticism, the fullness of the godhead
Polyarchy: government by many persons
Pontificate: in Christianity, the term in office of a prelate, usually of a pope
Popular Front: in France, an alliance of leftist parties in the 1930s
Predestinarianism: the doctrine that God has chosen those who will be saved and
those who will be condemned

Presbyterian: a Protestant denomination governed by ministers and elders

Proverbs: the Old Testament book of wisdom

Psychopannychism: the doctrine that the dead will sleep before being resurrected

Pythagoreanism: in ancient Greece, a religious movement believing in immortality of virtuous souls

Quakers: a Protestant denomination based on the teachings of George Fox (1624–1691), more formally known as the Society of Friends

Qumran community: an ancient Jewish sect whose existence was brought to light with the discovery of the Dead Sea Scrolls

Radical-Socialists: a French liberal party founded in 1901

Realized eschatology: the Christian doctrine that eschatological salvation is already realized through Christ's mission

Reformed Churches: Calvinist churches

Reification: the mental transformation of a person or a concept into a thing

Revivalism: in Christianity, missionary activities spreading religious fervor and renewal

Rochdale Pioneers: founders of the 1844 cooperative movement in Rochdale, England

Samsara: in Hinduism and Buddhism, "wheel of existence"

Sassanids: a Persian dynasty (A.D. 226–651)

Seleucids: a post-Alexandrian dynasty in the Near East (312–64 B.C.)

Senussis: a Muslim reform order, chiefly in Libya

Seventh-Day Adventists: a Protestant millenarian denomination

Shaik: in Islam, a venerable man, the head of a religious order

Shari'a: the Islamic canon law

Sharif: in Islam, a descendant of Mohammed

Shi'ites: a branch of the Muslim community which believes in divinely guided Imams

Shintoism: the national religion of Japan

Simony: in Christianity, the practice of buying ecclesiastical benefices and offices

Social contract: the doctrine that societies are based on a contract between the ruler and the people

Socinianism: a term for Unitarianism derived from Faustus Socinus (1539–1604)

Spartakusbund: the German communist movement of the First World War

Spiritualism: the Christian doctrine that faith is based on communication with Christ's spirit

Stoicism: a Greek philosophical-ethical system based on the doctrine of an orderly universe

Subordinationism: the Christian doctrine that Christ is subordinate to God

Sufism: Muslim mysticism

Sultan: in Islam, a secular ruler

Sumer: a southern region in ancient Babylonia

Sunnites: the major branch of the Muslim community, adhering to the Koran and Hadith

Supererogatory: going beyond what is required

Suras: the chapters of the Koran

Sutras: in Hinduism and Buddhism, doctrinal writings

Syndicalism: a movement aimed at establishing socialism by the workers' direct action

Synoptic: a term used for the Gospels of Mark, Matthew, and Luke

Taoism, classical: a Chinese pantheistic philosophy centered on the All

Taoism, religious: a Chinese religion centered on a belief in, and rituals for, immortality

Terms of trade: the relation between export and import prices of chiefly traded commodities

Theravada: the form of Buddhism closest to Buddha's teachings

Transubstantiation: the Christian doctrine that in the Eucharist, bread and wine are changed into Christ's body and blood

Treasure of merits: the Christian doctrine that the saints accumulated merits which ecclesiastical authorities can use for remitting sins

Trimurti: in Hinduism, the triad of Brahma, Vishnu, and Shiva

Trinitarianism: the Christian belief in the consubstantiality of God, Christ, and the Holy Spirit

Triune God: in Christianity, God conceived as consubstantial with Christ and the Holy Spirit

Ugarit: an ancient city in northern Syria, dating back to the seventh millennium B.C., and flourishing from the fifteenth to the twelfth century B.C.

'Ulama': a Muslim scholar

Umma: the religious-secular Muslim community

Unitarian: a Protestant denomination denying Trinitarianism

Universalism: the belief in the ultimate salvation of all men

Upanishads: collections of ancient Hindu teachings

Utilitarianism: an ethical doctrine centering on the happiness of the greatest number of men

Vedanta: in Hinduism, late-Upanishadic philosophical systems, mostly monistic

Vedas: the most ancient sacred scriptures of Hinduism

Venial: pardonable

Vulgate: the Latin version of the Bible, produced by St. Jerome (c. 347–c. 419)

Wahhabis: a Reformist Muslim movement in Arabia, founded by Muhammed Wahhab (1703–1792)

Waldenses: a Reformist Christian sect based on the teachings of Peter Valdes (twelfth century)

Yahweh: the Hebrew national god, later sole God of the universe

Yasna: in Zoroastrianism, parts of the Avesta

Yoga: in Hinduism, release from suffering through spiritual and physical concentration aiming at union with the All

Zen: a Buddhist school intent on awakening the Buddha-nature in man by meditation and inspiration

Zion: in the Old and New Testaments, synonymous with Jerusalem

Index

Library of Congress Cataloging in Publication Data
Braunthal, Alfred.
Salvation and the perfect society.
1. Salvation—Comparative studies.   2. Utopias.
3. Religions.   4. Humanism.   I. Title.
BL476.B7   291.2'2   79-4705
ISBN 0-87023-273-8